Intercultural Encounters

The Fundamentals
of Intercultural Communication

5th Edition

Donald W. Klopf

West Virginia University (Emeritus)
University of Hawaii (Emeritus)

Morton Publishing Company

925 W. Kenyon Avenue, Unit 12
Englewood, Colorado 80110
http://www.morton-pub.com

Book Team

Publisher:	Douglas N. Morton
Project Manager:	Dona Mendoza
Copy Editor:	Carolyn Acheson
Interior Design:	Bob Schram, Bookends
Cover Design:	Bob Schram, Bookends
Composition:	Ash Street Typecrafters, Inc.

To Beverly

Contents

104709

Preface

Readers of mystery novels by British authors are familiar with the term "early times." When the British constable is still piecing together the evidence of a heinous crime, it's "early times" in solving the mystery. The constable knows the crime has been committed and usually has a pile of evidence, but it just doesn't fit together yet — it's early times. The reader expects the solution to be forthcoming.

For communication departments across the nation and, for that matter, around the world, it's still early times in preparing students for effective communication in a diversified society. Educators have become aware that the United States is a mixture of all sorts of people. The census figures dramatically make the point. Educators are becoming aware that globalization is the trend of the future and that many nations, like the United States, are inhabited by a varied population.

Except for a token chapter or two in the communication fundamentals books, little has been done to ready students for the diversified world of communication they will enter upon graduation. Students are still being taught that what works for speakers or listeners who are "predominantly white and Anglo will be similarly effective for all speakers and audiences," to quote Pat Kearney and Tim Plax, authors of *Public Speaking in a Diverse Society*,[1] one of the few textbooks committed to a multicultural perspective — except, of course, for the increasing number of intercultural communication texts. But it is early times.

Even though most students will not travel abroad, do business in some strange and exotic place, or study overseas, they are going to encounter diversity — in their neighborhoods, at school, in the workplace, among their friends. They ought to be prepared to handle those intercultural encounters, and that is the aim of this book: to provide assistance so when they do interact with people who think, feel, and behave differently than they do, they will be prepared. Taking one course or reading one book won't prepare them to deal with every culture on the globe. They can be taught, however, to interact in a general sense with people who are culturally different from them whenever and wherever they meet.

Intercultural Encounters provides knowledge that will be valuable in interactions with diverse populations in general. If plans are being made to live in another culture for a long time, culture-specific training is advised. A person moving to Malaysia, for instance, should undertake training specifically directed to that country and its people. Nevertheless, *Intercultural Encounters* does offer overall guidelines for those who expect to live abroad.

Content and Organization

In covering the cultural-general content, the book follows the recommendations of expert practitioners, researchers, and teachers in intercultural communication. Like the previous four editions, this one is divided into four parts.

Part One, Communicating Across Cultures, in its three chapters, lays the foundation for understanding the process of multicultural communication. It presents a model of the communication process along with a model of the intercultural communication process. It introduces the concepts of communication and culture in conjunction with the realization that many microcultures are found within the larger culture, as smaller and slightly different units of the larger macroculture.

Part Two, Components of the Intercultural Communication Process, singles out the aspects that influence interactions between people from diverse cultures. This part covers factors that bear heavily on competent intercultural communication: perception, motivating forces, values, beliefs, attitudes. Factors that prevent effective interaction — cultural antipathy, deep-seated aversion or dislike — receive in-depth treatment. The social institutions that guide people's lives also receive attention, as does the process of relating interculturally.

Part Three, Transmitting Intercultural Messages, covers two vital topics: verbal and nonverbal behavior, the nuts and bolts of intercultural communication. We anticipate that trying to converse with people who speak a foreign language will present problems, but rarely do we expect difficulties to arise from the way we gesture or handle our physical behavior. Yet, many misunderstandings stem from inappropriate bodily movements.

The final part, Part Four, Achieving Competence in Intercultural Communication, is loaded with practical advice — how to adjust to a new culture, how to become sensitive to strangers in a different land, how to cope with problems of culture shock and readjustment. Differences in ethics, too, are considered.

Learning Aids

Certain features of the book highlight important principles that will hold the reader's attention.

- *How Different Cultures Behave.* Scattered throughout the book are special topics about some facet of a specific culture. This information illustrates a principle or theory noted in the text.

- *Expert Commentary.* Intercultural scholars share their views on special subjects: Maori power, Chinese compliments, and Fijian values, among others.

- *Know Yourself.* Readers judge some characteristic of their personal self so as to pinpoint a few of their strengths and weaknesses in communication situations.

- *Critical Incidents*. Problem situations related to a principle presented in a chapter appear occasionally for the reader to resolve. Each incident has options from which the reader chooses one, representing the reader's best judgment of the situation.

- *Think About This*. Each chapter ends with problems or questions related to the chapter's content. The answers to some are in the chapter; others require speculation on the reader's part.

In addition, several standard features are included to facilitate learning. Reviews conclude each chapter, highlighting the the major parts. Tables and figures offer graphic representations of important points and vital statistics. Examples help illustrate ideas.

Intercultural experts have repeatedly tested the university model of instruction and find it wanting. The model — a cognitive-centered, lecture-dominated, information-transfer pedagogy — does not do much to prepare students for actual encounters in intercultural communication. The experts believe that practical, hands-on training should accompany the body of knowledge contained in a textbook and classroom lectures. Awareness and sensitivity do not develop with someone talking at the student two or three times a week for an hour or more. The average student will profit more from activities that engage him or her in the skills used in real-life situations. Conscientiously used, the *Intercultural Encounters Workbook*, accompanying the textbook, supplies a variety of hands-on learning activities, all designed to enhance learning.

A Fundamentals Book

Communication as an academic subject is largely eclectic and multidisciplinary. Most scholars recognize that communication is central to all human experience and emphasize it above other disciplines. Others place a unique slant on it. Psychologists study individual behavior and view communication as a certain kind of behavior. Sociologists focus on society and the social process, perceiving communication as one of the social factors. Anthropologists are interested in culture, and communication is a part of their broader theme. This book draws heavily on the theories and practical knowledge of those disciplines just as they draw on the theories expounded by communicologists.

The position on *black* and *white* taken by many scholars writing on race designations is observed here. Both are written in lower case, black and white, opting for the reasoning those scholars offer. The terms are fraught with cultural baggage and capitalizing them unduly dignifies the terms. Elsewhere in the book, justification is provided for calling Americans "Americans," which need not be repeated here.

It's early times in diversifying the study of communication to account for the varied communicative practices Americans will encounter as they interact with their fellow Americans, many of varied cultural backgrounds. Time is fleeting, however, and the intercultural communication textbooks can fill the gap until the general communication texts become content-diversified.

COMMUNICATING ACROSS CULTURES

Diversity — The American Norm

In 2025, when the demographers' computers spit out the latest data about the complexion of the United States, the predominantly Anglo-Saxon visage of the nation's founders will have all but vanished. Instead, the emerging population statistics will show a conglomeration of races and ethnic groups. The nation's countenance will be Hawaii-like — a blending of diverse peoples — whites, Asians, Hispanics, and blacks.

Intermingled in the population's mass, the statisticians will find a grouping of 21 percent who will claim mixed ancestry, meaning some combination of white, Hispanic, black, and Asian. Golfer Tiger Woods exemplifies the mix, being black, white, American Indian, and Asian. Singer Mariah Carey also represents the mix (black, white, and Hispanic), as do actor Keanu Reeves (white, Chinese, and Hawaiian) and actor Lou Desmond Phillips (Filipino, Chinese, Hawaiian, Hispanic, American Indian, and white). Millions of others will embrace diverse ancestries.[1]

This union of races and ethnic groups already has brought change in the American way of life and will continue to do so in the years ahead. These fluctuations are not just physiognomical or skin-color differences. They concern the very nature of the country, its intermingling of people, cultures, languages, and behavior that constitute the national pool. On big-city streets, whites and blacks rub shoulders with Hispanics and Asians speaking English, Spanish, Tagalog, Chinese, Korean, and Vietnamese, among other languages. Educators estimate that 5 million school children whose native language is not English populate the nation's schools, causing pleas for bilingual education.[2]

The confluence of cultures is illustrated in the food Americans eat. An observer of the Hispanic influence notes that nachos have become a popular food snack, that beer drinkers take lime with their beer, and salsa is everywhere.[3] Americans eat so much Chinese food that many are becoming immune to the so-called Chinese restaurant syndrome — the ingestion of too much mono-sodium-glutamate spicy food. Sushi is a favorite of Japanese food lovers, but sashimi is slow in catching on. Thai restaurants are popular, as is Indian cuisine. Korean kimchee has its followers, even with burrito lovers who mix some of it with the filling. Continuing its prevalence, in the meantime, are the meat-and-potato variations of America's founders.

The cultural amalgamation makes its presence felt on the entertainment scene, too. A person can go to a hip-hop club in Los Angeles and dance to the all-black Wu-Tang Clan rapping about Shaolin fighters while a crowd of Tommy Hilfiger WASPs imbibe foreign brews.[4] The New York Yankees, like many other professional sports teams, field a mix of blacks, whites, Panamanians, Cubans, and Japanese. If a person desires relaxation, a Puerto Rican seaweed body wrap or a Shirodhara muscle treatment will do the job, as will a Hungarian thermal mineral bath with real Hungarian crystals.

A racial and ethnic mixture is not solely an American phenomenon. Diversity is commonplace worldwide, even in Japan, where many natives pride themselves on being members of a totally homogeneous country. Among its citizens, however, you can see Koreans, Chinese, Peruvians, Brazilians, Thai, and others, including the Ainu, the original Caucasian settlers of the archipelago, creating the impression that Japan is heterogeneous.[5]

Ever since Australia eliminated its European-only immigration rules, the nation has become a society of immigrants. People from 150 nations in Latin America, Africa, the Middle East, Asian countries, and former Russian states blend with the original Aussies. Sydney has an ever-growing Chinatown, and the country has grown into a multihued melting pot with 25 percent born overseas.[6]

The cultural invasion even has an impact on the stay-at-home Vietnamese, who live in one of the world's poorest nations. They enjoy foreign products, smoke American cigarettes, drink Latin American coffee, and gulp scoops of expensive American ice cream.[7] People, and their likes and dislikes, are spreading around the world in greater numbers and more rapidly than ever before.

With the reality of increasing intercultural contact of a physical sort, the mental distance that can divide cultural groups can become aggravated. Real or imagined controversies can multiply, necessitating a concentrated effort to understand people whose backgrounds and beliefs vastly differ.

Variations in cultural behavior can result in our perceptions of the customs of other people as peculiar or bizarre. Meat-eaters find blood-drinkers repulsive. Beef eaters are horrified to learn that eating dogs is common in many cultures. To the Hindus, who detest eating animal flesh, meat-eaters are cannibals. Eating raw fish is revolting to many people.

Shaking hands is a common greeting to us. But the culture of Japan espouses the bow, in India the traditional greeting is the *namste*, and in Thailand, the *wai* — none of which allows people to touch each other when greeting. Many cultures accept hand-holding by men as they walk together. In the United States, many people consider same-sex hand-holders to be homosexuals.

If we know the way other cultures perceive the world and understand the assumptions and values underlying their perceptions, we will gain access to the experiences of other human beings. With greater understanding and awareness, the desire to coexist peacefully with people unlike ourselves should become natural even though we have little in common.[8]

Knowledge of intercultural communication will help to solve communication problems before they arise. Knowing that gestures do not carry the same meaning from culture to culture, for example, we can avoid possible conflict situations. Knowing that an innocuous touch on someone's hand or arm can be misconstrued as a sexual advance, we might prevent a possible harassment charge. Many problems can be fore-stalled if we know the components of intercultural communication.[9]

With intercultural contact a worldwide reality, fruitful consequences can lead to new friendships and more satisfactory relationships. Conversely, unpleasant contact can bring on misunderstandings and unnecessary difficulty.

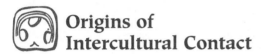

Origins of Intercultural Contact

Intercultural communication is as old as the history of human beings. Millennia ago, wandering herdsmen encountered people who were strangers to them. Mongol invaders, Christian Crusaders, and warriors from all locales communicated interculturally as they interacted with unknown people. The history of the Christian Church has been, in great part, an intercultural experience as the disciples of Jesus attempted to carry out his direction to preach the gospel throughout the world. Missionaries such as St. Augustine, St. Patrick, and St. Boniface spread the word of Christ through Asia Minor, Europe, and other civilized areas.[10]

American Pioneers

The ancestors of today's American Indians entered North America from Siberia, crossing a land bridge over the Bering Strait about 15,000 B.C. Their journey carried them throughout North and South America, with some settling down along the way and in the process forming many linguistic and cultural groups. Today, their descendants include members of hundreds of nations or tribes, each with its own cultural traditions.

The progenitors of other parts of the American population began arriving shortly after Columbus's discovery, many planting their family roots in the Caribbean islands. The first

permanent English colony was established in 1607 in Jamestown, Virginia. Following the English Protestant settlers came Germans, Swiss, Austrians, and Scotch-Irish. The English Puritans aboard the Mayflower landed at Plymouth Rock in 1620.

The first Africans came as slaves in 1619 and were put to work in the Jamestown area. By the start of the Civil War, when slavery was abolished, more than 4.5 million people of African origin had been brought to the United States.

During the 19th and early 20th centuries, the United States attracted immigrants from virtually every European and Middle Eastern nation, taking up residence in the Northeast, Midwest, and South. People of mixed Spanish and Indian ancestry found the Southwest and West appealing when those regions were still Spanish territories.[11]

Immigration Act of 1965

Most post-1965 immigrants to the United States have been economic migrants who crossed the Atlantic and Pacific Oceans mainly to seek a higher standard of living. The Immigration Act of 1965 received, with open arms, immigrants from all countries by abolishing discrimination based on national origin.

Prior to that time, for nearly 40 years, Asians had been barred. The 1965 Act did away with Asian exclusion and liberalized admittance requirements for all peoples. Nevertheless, Mexicans unable to enter legally under the 1965 Act and its subsequent revisions sneaked across the 1,500-mile border into the United States seeking employment.

A major effect of the 1965 Act was a shift in immigrant origins. Prior to 1965, Europeans constituted most of the immigrants. After 1965, immigration accelerated from Asia, South America, and the Caribbean islands — people who had been excluded under previous laws.

Before 1965, Europeans represented about 80 percent of the total number of immigrants.

By 1998 the number of Europeans had dropped to 13.7 percent, Asians had climbed to 33.3 percent, and Central and South American immigrants to 49.3 percent.[12] Figure 1.1 graphically depicts these percentages.

The 1965 Act, which began changing the face of the United States from East to West and North to South, continues to do so. With the influx of Asians and Latin Americans, the U.S. racial makeup has been altered, along with landscape and cityscape. Our preferences in food, clothing, and music have changed with the nation's perception of itself and its way of life. Diversity is the American norm, and intercultural communication represents the mode of interaction.

Reasons for Intercultural Growth

Contact between disparate peoples has increased for various reasons. Asians, Europeans, and Latin Americans probably would not have migrated to the United States in large numbers except for social, political, and economic changes throughout the world. Even then, intercultural communication would not have blossomed were it not for the technological advances that made frequent interaction possible.

Technological Advances

The last decades of the 20th century have produced more scientific and technological advances than the millions of years preceding it. Information networks relying on fiberoptic transmission lines and satellites orbiting high above the earth enable people just about everywhere to have instantaneous contact with one another. Satellites, radio, and television can broadcast their programs in an instant to anywhere in the world. As we proceed into the 21st century, we begin to move into a new age — which we can call the technological age, the knowledge age, or the computer age. Computers, programmed by humans, will accomplish a multitude of tasks.

With the expected proliferation of supersonic aircraft, the 21st century should see the movement of people and their products in a matter of hours, in contrast to the early 20th-century days and weeks when ships and jet planes were the mode. Prophets foresee our measuring travel time in minutes rather than hours when inexpensive, reliable, and dependable single-stage-to-orbit spaceships are developed.[13] Then we might wrap up a business deal in Berlin at lunch and begin negotiating another at a Honolulu dinner, while communicating in different languages and interacting in disparate cultures.

Although the future holds promises of supersonic airliners and ever more efficient technology, the present still allows us to communicate

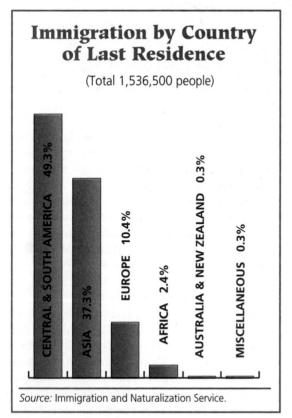

Immigration by Country of Last Residence

(Total 1,536,500 people)

CENTRAL & SOUTH AMERICA 49.3%
ASIA 37.3%
EUROPE 10.4%
AFRICA 2.4%
AUSTRALIA & NEW ZEALAND 0.3%
MISCELLANEOUS 0.3%

Source: Immigration and Naturalization Service.

FIGURE 1.1 Immigration to United States by Country of Last Residence, 1981–1990

quickly with people all over the world. Barely a city or village does not have telephones and almost all are in contact by radio. Buslines, railroads, highways, and airports link local, regional, and national levels of human organization. Mass mail systems, publishing syndicates, film industries, television networks, and newswire services are designed to make rapid and frequent interaction a reality.

If academicians could somehow convince students to tune in and complete the assigned learning and reading tasks, "distance education" might take the place of the college campus. With computer assisted instruction, educational television programming, and fax or e-mail exchanges with the instructor, the need to attend classes and listen to lectures could be eliminated. But most students require a learning community like a college campus to sustain their motivation to study and learn. Nevertheless, the technology is available to do away with classrooms and many other instructional facilities found on the typical college grounds.

Through the high-tech communication devices available today, we can contact people who are different from ourselves. Even though these people often speak languages dissimilar to ours, live anywhere in the world, have ethnic backgrounds unlike our own, and have little in common with us, the technology now on hand can help us overcome these difficulties so we can interact reasonably with them.

Social Advances

Intercultural communication has increased also because people throughout the world have demanded equal and inalienable rights. Their demands have reached receptive ears in most countries, and more and more people share the same rights and privileges that individuals in more dominant groups enjoy.

Heard with regularity in the United States are the voices of blacks, Latin Americans, American Indians, and Asians. Mingled with their voices are those of less powerful groups — the

As college campuses diversified in the 1980s, events pitting dominant student groups against nondominant groups led to protests and occasional violence. Punishment of perpetrators often restricted human rights, causing more harm than good.

elderly, the poor, and homosexuals who desire recognition as equals.

Civil rights and other legislation, along with major court decisions, have opened doors, making contact between people in nondominant and dominant positions unavoidable. Open housing, desegregated schools, and equal employment opportunities are the result. The legislation and consequent litigation, however, often lead to misunderstandings that turn out to be as serious as the original unequal treatment. School desegregation initially met with violent responses; equal opportunity resulted in reverse discrimination cases; and open housing led to neighborhood confrontations.

University campuses have attempted to correct inequities between ethnic groups. The codes and regulations created to overcome abusive communication events on university campuses led to problems just as serious, and personal mistreatment remains a major source of anxiety.

In the late 1980s, increasing enrollments of black, Hispanic, Asian, and American Indian students from the United States, plus a large increase in foreign-student populations, brought on a rash of scurrilous events on campuses throughout the nation. The schools reacted by developing sets of rules to prevent anticipated incidents, calling for punishment of the perpetrators.

The rules conceived at most schools tended to restrict individual rights granted by the First Amendment to the U.S. Constitution. In addition, they promoted punishment, yet failed to teach what is correct and proper behavior. The rules brought unequal treatment to the dominant group and, consequently, were considered as offensive as the events they were designed to stop. Personal mistreatment is still alive and well on today's campuses.[14]

Demands for equal rights are global in scope. Perhaps prompted by the United Nations' 1948 Universal Declaration of Human Rights, the General Assembly's Economic and Social Council and its agency, the U.N. Educational, Scientific and Cultural Organization, have helped nondominant peoples, especially in U.N. Member States.

Arab women, for example, fought to ease restrictions on their personal freedom, and now, in most Arab nations, they enjoy equal educational opportunities, employment opportunities, and certain legal rights. In Vietnam, the residents feel free to argue politics with friends and even talk to foreigners — behaviors that would have landed them in a police station a few years ago.

In Japan, residents of foreign countries often are refused shopping rights in certain stores and are turned away from public establishments such as bars, restaurants, and hot baths. Employment contracts treat them differently than Japanese, and frequently they are denied housing. In 1996, Japan signed on to the United Nations' Convention on the Elimination of All Forms of Racial Discrimination. Now, when discrimination cases are taken to court, judges usually rule in favor of those discriminated against.[15]

Social agitation sometimes opens doors to greater freedom. The consequences, however, are not always productive. Members of dominant and nondominant cultures have to learn about each other, which intensifies interest in intercultural communication.

Employment and Economics

Most immigrants come to the United States seeking employment. Some people come for money-making reasons, principally to sell their wares. Business people from Great Britain, Korea, Taiwan, Singapore, Mexico, Germany, Japan, France, and elsewhere come to sell automobiles, clothing, foodstuffs, electrical products, baseballs, and oil for much of the energy we consume.

The fruit grown in the United States tends to be seasonal, geared to the growing times of our generally temperate climate. Yet, we can buy fresh fruit throughout the year, grown in the Southern Hemisphere and shipped here. High labor costs cause us to buy cheaper but equally serviceable clothes from abroad. Instead of "Made in the USA" labels, many of our clothing purchases bear labels from Indonesia, China, Taiwan, Malaysia, Singapore, and Brazil, among others, where labor costs are less expensive. Although our farmers raise much of the chicken we eat, some comes from Europe, again because the price is more competitive.

Business people from around the world come not only to sell their products here but also to buy from us. They purchase land, businesses, and stock. Great Britain is the leading investor, then, Japan, the buyer of many American assets, now is selling them back at cheaper prices.

Americans distribute and sell their products abroad, too. U.S. companies have foreign branches that employ native workers. Foreign companies in America hire American workers. In their American manufacturing plants, Japanese car makers employ U.S. citizens almost exclusively. Trade, therefore, is not totally one-sided. Business allegiances are to products, not places, creating a "borderless economy."

The private sector has led globalization in the 20th century, withering the power of individual nations far more effectively than did the failed ideology of communism. The 21st century is expected to include the globalization of government as well. Predictions include international regulation of tax havens and capital flows with international safety nets to provide social security and unemployment insurance for those who change jobs and countries of residence.[16] Workers in multinational companies will find crosscultural training essential to operate successfully in the globalized work environments.

Tourists, Students, and the Military

Millions of tourists travel to the United States each year, and millions of Americans journey overseas to visit scenic and cultural spots. Likewise, many Americans enroll in foreign universities and many foreigners come to the United States to learn — in some cases invited specifically by American colleges.

Also, members of the armed services are stationed abroad, living, training, and working on foreign soil and in foreign ports. Japan and Korea alone host 48,000 American troops. Plying the surrounding waters is the U.S. Seventh Fleet, with its thousands of armed service personnel.[17] The mission of the armed services, vital to U.S. interests, requires effective interaction with foreign nationals, a requirement not always completed to the satisfaction of the local people. Abuses to the civilian populations in Okinawa, Tokyo, and Kosovo bear out the need for training armed forces personnel in the culture of the countries to which they are being sent.

What Would You Do?

You want to take a picture of a child in Hong Kong. Just as you are about to click the shutter, an old man rushes over and starts shouting at you.

a. You hesitate and decide not to photograph that child, but you look around for another subject.

b. You are aware that the old man doesn't want you to take the photo. You can't understand why, but you apologize and put away your camera.

c. You wait until you think the man can't see you, then snap the picture anyway.

Answer is on page 243.

Political Influences

Many immigrants have come to the United States to escape political persecution. War refugees were welcomed to the country following World War II, and many more migrated after the Korean conflict. In the late 1950s, 190,000 Hungarians fled the country during the revolt against a communist regime, most of whom came to the United States, where they were freely allowed. Deeply involved in the Vietnam conflict from the early 1960s until the fall of South Vietnam in April 1975, the United States took in some 18,000 Vietnamese, most of them wives of servicemen who fought in Vietnam. Since that country's fall, nearly 1 million people from Vietnam and other Indochinese countries have migrated to the United States.

During the 1961–1984 period, various refugee acts permitted additional people to immigrate from countries in political turmoil. Among them are Cuba, Laos, Russia, Kampuchea, Yugoslavia, China, Romania, Poland, and Czechoslovakia. During 1997, 40 countries saw roughly 14 million people take refuge elsewhere in the world. Most of those countries were at war or involved in internal conflicts. In 1996, 28 armed conflicts (1,000 or more battle-related deaths) occurred.

The United States accepts many of the people seeking refuge in politically stable areas. Since 1981, this has amounted to about 1½ million people.

The refugee traffic flowed in many directions, not exclusively to the United States. To escape political persecution and to find work, many people emigrated to European countries. About 12 million migrants fled to Europe during the 1970s. They left their lesser developed homelands to work on the farms and in the factories, doing work that native Europeans did not want to do. The European economy was booming, and the emigrants were welcomed with the expectation that they would return home once the boom subsided. When it did, however, the migrants remained. Their homelands did not want them back because, politically, they were seen as unreliable and, economically, no work existed for them. Their adopted lands did not want them either, because the countries to which they had emigrated no longer could afford them.

Before the new millennium is a few decades old, demographers predict, Europe will face a major challenge. To survive economically and socially, it may have to lower bars to immigration and change its ethnic and racial face through mass migration of labor. European countries (and Japan) will have more older people and fewer babies than ever before, foretelling severely shrunken labor forces and swollen ranks of pensioners. To keep their economies running, Europeans will be tempted to look to the politically persecuted and economically disadvantaged for workers. By 2025, Italy will need 9 million immigrants, Germany 14 million, and France 2 million. All told, the European Union will require 135 million immigrants. Yet most Europeans cling to a linguistic and racial basis for citizenship.[18]

If the predictions come true and millions migrate to Europe, Europe will be challenged to make these and other immigrants full citizens in every sense. Policies and programs to overcome hurdles to full citizenship will be demanded. Intercultural communication contact will burgeon, even more so than today.

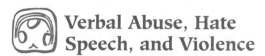

Verbal Abuse, Hate Speech, and Violence

Typical misunderstandings that result from intercultural experiences are illustrated by the

---

Some Types of Intercultural Contact

- *University students studying overseas*
- *Business people working overseas*
- *Diplomats and embassy workers assigned to foreign countries*
- *Language interpreters working with foreign people*
- *Technical assistance personnel working overseas for a government agency*
- *Workers in organized programs such as the Peace Corps*
- *Military personnel stationed overseas*
- *Researchers working in foreign cultures*
- *Tourists*
- *Ethnic group members interacting with members of other ethnic groups*
- *Emigrants moving from one country to another*
- *Ethnic groups forced to relocate from one section of a country to another*
- *Students participating in exchange programs that mix ethnic groups*

From *Cross-Cultural Encounters: Face-to-Face Interaction*, by R. W. Brislin (New York: Pergamon, 1981).

consternation of an American executive moving clumsily around Europe:

> *At a business dinner in Berlin, I opened the door to let my German associate enter the restaurant before me. As she entered, the manager scowled at me. I did something wrong, I guess. In Frankfurt, I was held up by traffic and arrived a few minutes late for a meeting with my German boss, Fritz. As I entered the meeting room, I apologized: "Fritz, I'm sorry I'm late." I could cut the tension with a knife. Meeting with potential customers at lunch, I continued discussions we had begun that morning, which we all were enthusiastic about. But they paid little attention to what I said. I goofed somehow.*

The executive traveling in Europe encountered some of the minor misunderstandings any of us could have faced when interacting with people from other cultures. These reactions are frustrating and anxiety-provoking. Fortunately, they usually do not bring on true conflict. They are merely a consequence of ignorance; we are unfamiliar with the cultures we meet.

The executive would have fared better had he known that in Germany the man opens the door and enters first, allowing the woman to follow. Stepping into unknown territory where danger may lurk, the man goes first, ready to deal with the unexpected. That is the polite way.

Germans are punctual and expect their guests to be on time regardless of the circumstances. Meetings start and end on time; appointments are not late. Then, too, care must be taken to address another by his or her proper rank unless the person is a close friend and the situation is a face-to-face encounter between the two. At a meeting, seniors are addressed formally, not as "Fritz" but rather by title or rank.

In France, discussions cease at mealtime if they are work-related. Mealtime is for socializing, for enjoying the food and the company of the others.

When confronting more serious, even life-threatening, situations, the travails of the executive seem trivial, trifling. Yet, for nondominant groups, misunderstandings could blossom into hate crimes or acts of bias, motivated by animosity toward the victims because of their race, religion, sexual orientation, or national origin.

Slavery and its attendant hate crimes rank as the greatest deprivation of civil liberties in U.S. history. Ranking a close second is the evacuation, incarceration. and resettlement of more than 100,000 Americans of Japanese ancestry during World War II.

Other hate-speech attacks mar the national record. Asian Indians suffer widespread prejudice and discrimination, which represent barriers to achieving equal opportunity. Korean businesses in black ghetto areas have been targets of hostile, even violent, reactions from customers.

Hate speech and violence directed to nondominant groups in nations other than the United States are just as prevalent. Filipinos hired to work in more affluent countries are subjected to abuse, especially in the Arab world. Filipino mail-order brides, married to men in other nations, often end up being physically exploited by their husbands. Gangs of racist thugs in Britain engage in "Paki bashing." France tries to prevent confrontations between natives and newcomers by stopping immigration. Neo-Nazis in Germany attack foreign workers and others seeking asylum from persecution in their homelands. Mutilation of the reproductive organs of females continues in many parts of the African continent. As we have noted, discrimination in Japan is subtle, but present nonetheless.

 ## Benefits and Harms

Intercultural contact is rewarding to most people, yet is a dangerous experience for some. Immigrants are likely to find more job opportunities than in the lands they left. Their children, however, are apt to learn attitudes in school that undermine their traditional practices at home. Business people garner overseas markets for their products. In the process, their gains often are offset by losses they incur as they adjust to differing work conditions and employment practices in the foreign lands. In the early stages of developing automobile manufacturing plants in the United States, for example, the Japanese were subjected to considerable ill feelings by their American workers who objected strenuously to Japanese management customs.

Military personnel provide protection for the host countries. At the same time, their presence can upset the natives. A source of friction centers on the off-duty activities of the occupying troops. American servicemen have caused antagonism by dating the local women, showering them with attention, especially food and entertainment the locals cannot afford.

Health hazards constitute another problem stemming from intercultural contact. Flu strains and AIDS have been transmitted worldwide through the movement of people from one culture to another. Jet airplanes speed up the process as infected persons carry their diseases around the world.

 ## Educational Enculturation

The family is the basic source of enculturation. In the family, we learn the values, beliefs, and attitudes that govern our lives. Schools play a secondary role in imparting cultural values. Teachers reinforce or more fully develop the informal instruction of parents, helping children fit into the dominant culture.

The mass migration of people in past decades has led to a tremendous diversification in the school population. Teachers are expected to impart knowledge but also to teach the appropriate values and behaviors to help the newcomers adjust to life in the new world. In the diversely

populated school, this expectation presents a challenge. Education is both culturally determined and culturally specific. It involves not only *what* the students learn but *how* they learn.

Some cultures rely on rote memorization as the way of learning. Others emphasize creativity. Americans stress experiential or participatory learning. Students participate in learning through demonstration and various exercises. Most of the world learns didactically — teachers tell the students what they need to know. Teaching techniques must consider how students from different cultures learn, and in a multicultural classroom the teacher likely has to adapt to the students' various learning methods.

Educators are beginning to confront the problems that mixed classrooms bring. Programs are being, or have been, developed to account for variations in educational instruction. Colleges

---

Diversity — Overemphasized?

A student exclaimed that he's "had it with all the cultural diversity stuff." History, English lit, and political science books tell about obscure people he's never heard about. "Why don't they just teach us what we need to know," he asks, "and cut out this diversity garbage?"

The changes are not motivated by an irrational desire to be politically correct. The changes are taking place because the United States is changing. The country is becoming increasingly culturally diverse. The student may not be planning to travel around the world; the world is traveling to the student. The student's boss, teacher, religious leader, best friend, or marriage partner may have grown up with different cultural traditions, and the texts are reflecting this change, not initiating it.

Source: *Interpersonal Communication: Relating to Others*, 2d ed. by S.A. Beebe, S.J. Beebe, and M. Redmond (Boston: Allyn and Bacon, 1999), 99–100.

and universities are focusing on courses that educate students about cultural differences. Gone are the days when teachers were admonished to obliterate all the distinguishing foreign characteristics and traits as obstructive and irritating elements.[19] Intercultural awareness within the educational environment enhances the quality of learning for all students. As our society becomes more diverse and as intercultural interaction increases globally, educators must consider the impact of culture on themselves and their profession. To be more effective with their students, educators probably have to expand their own stock of techniques and develop new competencies in intercultural communication.[20]

Communicating Competently

To be able to communicate competently with people from cultures foreign to ours, we first should be able to communicate skillfully within our own culture. From a repertoire of communication skills we have built up over our years of schooling, we should demonstrate the socially appropriate communicative behavior in our own culture.

The following 10 skills identify competent communicators:[21]

1. *Self-disclosure* — revealing oneself to others through speech.

2. *Empathy* — feeling *with* others in communicative situations.

3. *Social relaxation* — free of apprehension or anxiety in talking with others, even when criticized.

4. *Assertiveness* — standing up for our own rights in speaking situations without being aggressive or interfering with the rights of others.

5. *Interaction management* — appropriately handling ritualistic situations when speaking

with others, such as taking turns when speaking, negotiating topics of conversation, and starting and stopping conversations with assurance.

6. *Altercentrism* — taking interest in what others have to say, listening to them, and adapting to their conversations.

7. *Expressiveness* — verbally saying what is appropriate and nonverbally expressing personal feelings.

8. *Supportiveness* — reinforcing the remarks of other speakers by confirming their stand on issues.

9. *Immediacy* — being approachable and available to others.

10. *Environmental control* — being able to reach our own personal goals and to satisfy our own personal needs while managing possible conflict situations in a cooperative manner.

These general rules are explored in detail in chapters that follow, along with an additional set of skills that apply directly to intercultural communication situations.

Why Study Intercultural Communication?

Much of what has been written to this point provides defensible reasons. In addition, we study the motives suggested by early pioneers in the study of communication and culture to give us an inkling of their thoughts on what the study will mean to students universally.[22]

A.G. Smith surveyed the literature "way back when," and uncovered three principal causes. The most popular cause he found was that intercultural communication study enhances an individual's effectiveness as a communicator in multicultural situations. To Smith, this reason is a personal one — what he calls "street floor" or face-to-face, eyeball-to-eyeball, nose-to-nose communication, in which several people representing different cultures interact.

Smith's survey revealed a second popular reason for studying intercultural communication. This one relates to acquiring useful skills to use while at work, skills that help individuals become sensitive to the needs of their fellow workers from different cultures, to the desires of business representatives from foreign cultures, and to the wishes of potential customers from abroad. His second reason is a practical, job-related basis for intercultural study.

He detected a third reason, dealing with cosmopolitanism and the freedom from national limitations or prejudices. In enrolling in intercultural courses, students are taught to rise above their naive and simple provincialism and achieve a worldly and sophisticated outlook about their global environment.

Another pathfinder, P.E. Rohrlich, argued that intercultural communication is like a science in that it helps people understand the world around them. It is also like work in the humanities arena because it helps people understand themselves. The study is helpful to all people who depend upon human contact, and Rohrlich specifically names those in business, government, education, and those in learning or teaching language skills. Intercultural communication is a crucial link between the individual and the larger world, in Rohrlich's way of thinking. The subject is vital in promoting international understanding among all peoples, not as a means of solely furthering international policies.

The Korean communicologist Myung-seok Park offers slightly different reasoning. He contends that people should have access to the experiences of other human beings around the world. With an understanding of how other people live without necessarily acquiring their lifestyles or values, we should be better prepared to solve communication problems before they become unmanageable.

Landis and Bhagat concentrate on the benefits intercultural communication study will bring.

They maintain that the study will precipitate changes in people's cognitive, affective, and behavioral relationships with foreigners. This study will bring, emotionally, an increase in pleasure when interacting with non-natives while reducing personal anxieties about the interactions. Behaviorally, better interpersonal relations result, with less stress and more ease in interacting. Cognitively, people will react more positively to foreigners and will curtail the number of stereotypical images others hold about them.

Other scholars endorse these reasons for studying intercultural communication. Klopf and Ishii, however, are more pragmatic. To them, the most important reason for becoming interculturally educated relates to the multicultural world that is becoming a reality. The world is rapidly turning into a global village. If people want to live useful lives in it, they need the knowledge and training intercultural instruction provides.

 ## What We Should Learn — and Why

Achieving Multicultural Understanding (see Figure 1.2) serves as a paradigm of intercultural communication subject matter. It names the essential elements of intercultural study. Its components are derived from the investigations of a dozen cultural specialists.[23] They include the subject matter necessary to participate in positive and productive relationships with non-native people.

Awareness of self is the starting point of the paradigm, a "know yourself" component. Knowing the personal biases, values, and interests, all culture-bound, as well as being familiar with our own culture, should greatly enhance our sensitivity toward other cultures. Awareness of self is the first step in understanding others. Scattered throughout this book and the accompanying *Workbook* are a variety of self-awareness exercises.

Awareness of others is located at the other end of the paradigm's baseline, suggesting closure, a final component of the learning process. By the conclusion of the course, we should be enlightened about how people think, feel, and act in other cultures. The practices universal to most cultures are explained in the text, and features throughout this book offer culture-specific information.

Communication is a subject familiar to most of us. Here, it paves the way for an understanding of intercultural communication. For the incognizant, our review serves to introduce the subject.

Culture covers everything made by humans in our world. Its scope is broad. We look at it from the viewpoint of intercultural communication, a narrower interpretation.

Perception, like the terms *communication* and *culture*, is a basic concept, one vital to understanding our interactions with people of different cultures. Some authorities think of it as the *sine qua non*, an indispensable condition, of our study.

Personal orientation system examines the governing system that directs our behavior and controls our conduct in society. It consists of our *needs*, *values*, *beliefs*, and *attitudes*, each of which plays a role in our communication across cultures.

Social institutions, such as the family, school, religion, political system, and economic system, affect our growth and development and have an impact on how we communicate.

Relationships will develop as people contact individuals who are strange to them. In these contacts, glitches will arise. We sample relationships in different cultures to note where problems develop.

Language is the source of most intercultural problems. If we can't speak the language, we're going to have trouble. Our treatment is meant to sensitize us to the pitfalls of language.

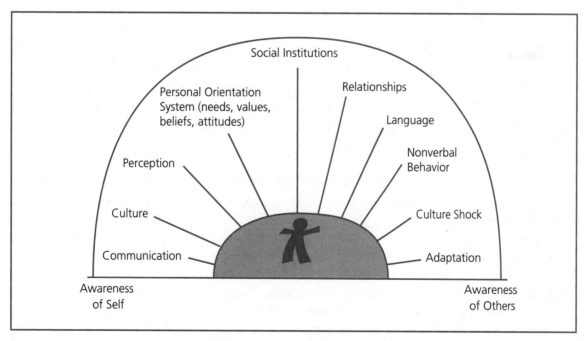

FIGURE 1.2 Achieving Multicultural Understanding

Nonverbal behavior, more so than language, can embroil us in difficulty quickly. An innocent gesture made in response to a simple question may be an unwitting insult, or worse. Nonverbal behavior is not pancultural, as we learn in this book.

Culture shock relates to the trauma most people experience as they enter a new culture or reenter their previous culture after a period of time away from it.

Adaptation refers to the changes needed when engaging in intercultural situations.

Chapter Review

Dramatic cultural and ethnic changes have taken place in the United States over time. The country now increasingly blends whites, blacks, Latinos, and Asians.

The increasing contact between cultures stems from technological advances, nondominant groups winning equal rights, people migrating for economic well-being, and politically persecuted people wanting greater freedom.

Increasing cultural contact also brings unfortunate consequences in the forms of verbal mistreatment and even criminal incidents.

The migration of people brings economic and political benefits. At the same time, traditional patterns of behavior often are undermined. When family authority weakens, anxiety develops.

Academicians and educational institutions are coming to grips with the challenges brought on by increased cultural contact. Programs to assimilate people more quickly and foster intercultural understanding are part of the response.

Benefits accrue to the student of intercultural communication. This study enhances effectiveness as a communicator in multicultural situations — on the job, in social situations, and in school. A student's cognitive, emotional, and behavioral relationships with strangers will change. The world is becoming multicultural, and intercultural instruction should prepare the student to live in it.

Elements of intercultural communication include the communication process, cultural influences, perception, the personal orientation system (needs, values, beliefs, attitudes), rules proscribed by social institutions (family, school, church, political system, economic system), interpersonal relationships, verbal and nonverbal language, culture shock, and adaptation.

This textbook aims to broaden knowledge concerning intercultural communication, blending the communication process and its respective components with the intercultural perspective.

Think About This...

1   After you have read "Diversity — Overemphasized?" on page 12, what is your opinion? In your judgment, does the student make a valid point? Do you agree with him? What are your feelings about immigration policies in the United States? Are we being too liberal? Not liberal enough?

2   Demographers predict several European nations, as well as Japan, will have to do something about their dwindling populations. Why? What is happening to cause the reduction? What can be done?

3   Abusive communication events persist on university campuses. Why? What should be done? What can be done?

4   Have you been overseas? If so, where? If not, do you plan to go overseas? If so, where? Why?

5   What do you expect from an intercultural communication course? Why did you enroll?

2 Culture Is Communication Is Culture

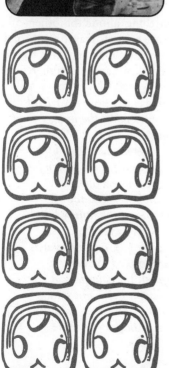

I n his 1959 book, *The Silent Language*, anthropologist Edward T. Hall advanced the notion that culture is communication and communication is culture.[1] By this, he meant that our culture determines the way we communicate. We learn the culture's language, rules, and norms, and we learn them at an early age. Our culture teaches us *how* to speak, *when* it is appropriate to speak, *what* to speak about, to *whom* to speak, and other facets of our oral communicative behavior. We learn to speak, therefore, following the dictates of our culture. Culture and communication become inseparable. The way people communicate reflects the way they live. It is their culture.

An American student and a Spanish student represent two different cultures. Because they do, their communication practices are likely to differ. They use different languages, follow different communication rules, and obey different sets of normative behavior. When American or Spanish students converse with people from dissimilar cultures, they will practice communication patterns that are different. When the properties of culture differ or change, the properties of communication also will differ or change. *Communication and culture are inseparable.*[2]

Hall's *The Silent Language* came out of his teaching at the Foreign Service Institute of the U.S. Department of State, a training program for prospective members of the nation's diplomatic corps. He taught trainees how to exchange information across cultures, to speak with people who were culturally dissimilar. U.S. foreign service personnel experienced considerable difficulty communicating with their foreign counterparts. The Institute training was designed to correct the faults.

Hall labeled what he was teaching *intercultural communication*, the first usage of that designation. Thus, he is credited with being the founder of this subject area in communication.[3]

The underlying lesson being taught to the prospective diplomats was that, to be effective in the cultures in which they expected to work, they needed to be knowledgeable about them. The fundamental lesson being professed in this book is just that: When seeking commonality in meaning with individuals from other cultures, we should be familiar with those cultures. To interact competently with a Spanish student, we should know about the Spanish culture and how it varies from the American culture. If the Spaniard wants to communicate with some success with us, he or she should understand the American culture. Cultural ignorance can make the difference between a fruitful or an unhappy experience for the communicators.

Cultural ignorance led to massive failures in U.S. programs to aid underdeveloped countries. In the 1950s and 1960s the nation provided technical assistance to Third World countries. The support included funds, technology, and technicians for a variety of programs: to teach adult literacy, improve health, build dams and steel mills, and increase agricultural yields. Though well intentioned, many programs failed. The planners did not consider local cultural factors in their designs.

The failures were documented in *The Ugly American,*[4] a best-selling book by William J. Lederer and Eugene Burdick. The book played a major role in alerting the nation to the inept, culturally insensitive Americans working in Third World countries, Americans who understood neither the language nor the culture of their hosts.

Lederer's "ugly American" message won converts. He spoke whenever and wherever he could about American ignorance of local cultural practices. For example, at a Waikiki Kiwanis speech, he fascinated, yet enraged the members with his accounts of bumbling U.S. project workers. He told how bridges were built over rivers that had run dry years ago, how wells were dug with high-energy pumps to draw water in countries that had no available power supply, how hospitals built of shoddy materials collapsed, how natives were taught to read although they could not afford reading materials, and much more — all disasters resulting from poor knowledge of local culture.

A University of Hawaii director of distance learning programs confirmed Lederer's conclusion. Courses were taught on a Pacific atoll for American scientists working on secret projects. To set up the project facilities, the atoll's natives were moved to a remote island in the atoll. Without seeking the natives' input, the government built houses and roads for them. The houses, made of concrete, had doors and screened windows, the latest plumbing fixtures, new furniture — all the newest conveniences. The natives saw the houses as jail cells, used the furniture for firewood, built their own thatched huts, and constructed a communal latrine, the place to socialize. Hall's instruction in intercultural communication had an auspicious beginning and filled a crucial need.

When billions of dollars are at stake, we ought to know something about the other culture. Even when we are tourists traveling abroad for a week or two, we should be sensitive to the local culture, recognizing we are guests there.

At a Majuro native craft shop, my friend asked the salesperson what the long, pointed, notched sticks were for. The salesperson said boys made these "love sticks" for their best girlfriend. When he desired a late-night rendezvous, he would poke the stick through the thatching on the side of the family hut to awaken the girl. Why the notches? The number tells the girl which boy was calling. My friend looked incredulous. Noting her disbelief, the salesperson rubbed her prominent belly and said, "It worked for me." My friend said little more, although she did buy several. Secondhand?

Third World development screwups, bureaucrats gone overboard, shoppers with foot-in-their-mouth disease illustrate what ignorance of local customs can bring about. Although a book of this nature cannot offer rules of communication for every culture or explain how one culture differs from another, we can provide information about the general nature of both communication and culture. This chapter offers a general description of the communication process and an explanation of culture, stressing the characteristics universal to all cultures. Knowing the universals, we should more readily recognize the distinctions between cultures.

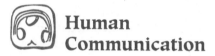

Human Communication

The world's cultures differ in many and various ways, yet they share the same process of transmitting meaning and feeling. Whether we are natives of Comoros, Lesotho, Maldives, or Palau, we engage in the same process of communicating. The results may be different and the practices we follow may be unalike. Nevertheless, the process is the same. The elements are identical in every act of speaking wherever it may occur.

Forms of Communication

Two forms of communication are *mediated* and *oral*. In the mediated form a device such as a telephone, a radio, television, smoke signals, or drum sounds comes between the message transmitter and the message receiver.

We are interested in oral communication, which in our usage includes the nonverbal messages that accompany or substitute for speech, as well as speech itself. Listening, as a simultaneous communicative behavior occurring with speech, is also a part of oral communication.

> ## Mediated Communication in 2000 A.D.
>
> *Thomas L. Friedman, who writes for the* New York Times, *relates an experience he had on a train ride from Cairo to Alexandria. He shared a car full of middle- and upper-class Egyptians. So many had cell phones, he wrote, that kept ringing with different piercing melodies during the 2-hour trip that he felt like getting up, taking out a baton, and conducting a cell-phone symphony. Yet, while all the phones were chirping inside the train, the passengers were passing along the Nile, where barefoot Egyptian villagers were tilling their fields with the same tools their ancestors had used in the days of the pharaoh. Friedman thought he could never imagine a wider technological gap within one country. Inside the train it was 2000 A.D.; outside it was 2000 B.C.*
>
> Source: *International Herald Tribune,* Jan. 29–30, 2000, 6.

Thus, oral communication is *the process by which individuals share information, meanings, and feelings through the exchange of verbal and nonverbal messages.* The definition becomes clearer with an understanding of *messages, communication process,* and *elements of communication.*

Messages

When we exchange verbal and nonverbal messages consciously, we normally do so for the purpose of affecting or altering the behavior of our listeners. We speak, therefore, with the intent to affect. Occasionally, we transmit messages unintentionally or accidentally.

Intentional Messages. In much of our communication, we deliberately attempt to convey information, meanings, and feelings. We consciously send messages to change others' behavior — messages that we might conceive instantly or plan carefully. These messages may be *utilitarian* (we want our listeners to do what we ask), *aesthetic* (we speak for enjoyment, pleasure, or entertainment), and *therapeutic* (a medical practitioner delivers a diagnosis of some sort of physical or mental illness).

Unintentional Messages. Unintentional messages are transmitted serendipitously or accidentally. We did not intend to stimulate meaning in the mind of other people, and we may not be aware that we even did so. Unintentional messages can have an adverse impact on intercultural communication.

> *My wife and I were honored to be guests in the home of my Japanese friend. Neither of us spoke the language, and our Japanese hosts were not experts in English. My wife tried using gestures, and whenever she wanted to communicate "me," she pointed to herself. Each time she did this, our hosts would point the way to the bathroom. We learned later that the Japanese interpret this gesture as, "I want to go to the bathroom."*

In this case, the wife stimulated meaning in her hosts unintentionally. She had no desire to go to the bathroom. She simply wanted them to know she was talking about herself when she pointed to herself. After she had done this a few times, the Japanese may have thought my wife had weak kidneys, drank too much, or was constantly primping.

The Communication Process

A multidimensional process, communication consists of a series of happenings that do not have a beginning, an end, or a fixed chain of events. It is dynamic, systematic, adaptive, continuous, transactional, and irreversible.

Communication is an act of proceeding, progressing, and advancing. Thus, it is *dynamic*,

ever-changing, not static. It is *systematic* in that the elements of oral communication work together interdependently to produce meaningful interaction. Each element affects every other element, and each affects the outcome of communication.

The process is *adaptive*, adjusting to and coping with change. Good communicators are flexible, adjusting to varying communication situations. Oral communication is a *continuous* activity with no fixed start or determinable end. Talk between people is based on their past experiences, and it has future implications, influencing their future talk together. Communication as a process, therefore, is ongoing, never-ending.

No specific communication encounter is exactly the same as any prior encounter. The day and time differ, and probably the circumstances and surroundings. Each speech act, then, is a *transactional* event, made up of a unique combination of people, circumstances, and messages, and unlike any previous act.

The communication process is *irreversible*. Once we say something, we cannot take it back. Whatever we say is said. Be it good or bad, we cannot erase it or reverse it. It becomes a part of the speaker's and listener's shared experience. When we say something we realize we shouldn't have said, we may try, to expunge it by denying we meant what we said or by claiming that we were misinterpreted. Attempts to blot out the oral record, however, do little except provide new information for the listener to consider. The attempts do not erase what was said. Oral communication moves forward like time itself. We cannot go back and eliminate from the listeners' thinking what was said.

The Elements of Communication

Process implies dynamic interaction, making an act of oral communication difficult to analyze because its parts are in constant motion and because it is a multidimensional human function. For example, various parts of the body are involved in making sound and making sense.

Communication, therefore, can be studied from a variety of perspectives. Speech therapists are mostly interested in a person's ability to make sounds. Linguists dissect the language used. Neurologists attend to the operation of the brain and nervous system. Psychologists review the impact of perception on the process. Specialists in intercultural communication focus on the elements that affect the interaction between people of different cultures. Our interest here is limited, then, to a portion of the communication process — albeit a major portion.

In our study of the elements, we treat them as separate entities, recognizing, of course, that each element is a part of a dynamic process with continuous interaction between the elements. We can understand better the role of each element in the process by analyzing each separately. We stop the dynamic interaction and make a blueprint or model of the part each plays in the process.

Figure 2.1 presents a model of oral communication between two people of the same culture.

A more definitive intercultural model can be found in Chapter 3. In the model in this chapter, the key elements are those representative of *interpersonal* communication, which is communication between two or more people.

The two communicators alternate as speaker and listener. Imagine that Person A initiates a conversation with Person B. Person A becomes the speaker and Person B the listener. When Person A finishes talking and Person B responds, the speaker and the listener roles are reversed. As the two keep talking, the roles continue to alternate.

When more people enter the conversation, the speaker and listener roles alternate among them. With three people, one speaks and two listen. With four, one speaks and three listen. The more people, the more listeners.

Communicators. The communicators are the speakers and the listeners. The speakers encode messages, which the listeners decode. Figure 2.1. also illustrates the functions of each.

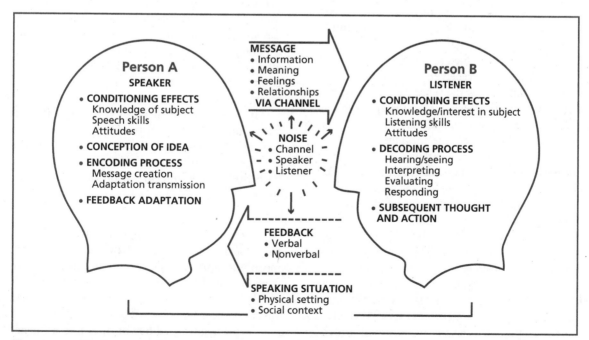

FIGURE 2.1 A Model of the Interpersonal Communication Process

The *speaker* (or source, or message sender) is the person speaking at a given moment. What he or she says and how it is said are conditioned by the person's speaking skills and knowledge of the subject. The message is affected also by the speaker's personal attitude toward himself or herself and toward the listener(s), and by the speaker's interest in the topic of conversation. With a confident and strong self-image and a positive feeling toward the listeners and the subject, the speaker will be more effective than without those attributes.

When he or she is ready to speak, the speaker conceives ideas about what to say. Then the encoding process comes into play. *Encoding* means to translate an already conceived idea into a message appropriate for sending to the listeners. It involves selecting the *symbols* that will make up the message. Symbols are either words or the nonverbal behaviors used to represent the idea being talked about.

The speaker's message is directed to a *listener* or message receiver, who *decodes* it. Decoding is conditioned by the listener's knowledge of the subject and interest in it, by the listener's ability to listen, and by the listener's attitude toward himself or herself. Decoding is akin to the technical process called *listening*.

The message receiver first must sense the message. Hearing is the sense used in most cases. But the nonverbal elements of the speaker's message may be seen, smelled, tasted, or felt. Then the receiver interprets the message to determine its meaning. When the receiver thinks he or she understands it, the message is evaluated. The receiver decides what the message means to him or her personally — whether he or she agrees or disagrees with what was said.

Once the message has been decoded, the listener prepares a response. This can be either overt and observable or heard by the speaker, or it can be covert and internal, not known to the speaker.

Decoding allows the listener to give meaning to the speaker's message. Culture largely determines the meaning the listener will attach to the speaker's words and actions.

Feedback. The listener responds in some manner to the speaker. The response is termed *feedback*. For our purposes, feedback is the listener's overt response to the speaker's message. The response can be verbal or nonverbal.

Noise. As the message moves from speaker to listener and as the feedback travels back to the speaker, hazards can crop up and interfere with the accurate understanding of what was sent. These hazards are called *noise* — any factor that interferes with the intended meaning of the message or feedback being transmitted.

Noise can be of two types: physical-setting noise or communicator-bound noise. Noise in the physical setting comes from obvious sources such as honking horns, low-flying helicopters, lawnmowers, leaf blowers, and traffic. Studying for an exam, we may hear people talking, radios blaring, dogs barking, or children playing. This makes concentration difficult for us.

Communicator-related noise is centered in the speaker and the listener. It can be traced to confused or murky thinking on the communicator's part, and is caused by poor knowledge of the subject, inadequate preparation, or inferior listening or speaking skills. Communicator noise also can come from physical ailments and psychological problems that prevent the accurate reception or delivery of messages.

In intercultural situations, noise can result from unfamiliarity with the language spoken or nonverbal codes used. Or it can result from a host of culturally related factors that interfere with the sensible interpretation of the messages being sent.

Messages. We know that a communicator's message is composed of the information, meanings, and feelings that he or she wishes to transmit to the listeners. It might be a simple "hello" or an hour-long speech delivered to a vast audience.

Two integral qualities of messages influence intercultural communication.

1. We cannot *not* communicate in the presence of another person. Our nonverbal behavior carries messages. Therefore, without uttering a word, we still communicate. All observable behavior can be considered a message. No word, manner, or gesture is neutral. Even when we try to act inconspicuous, we are communicating.

2. *Messages* define relationships. Through words or actions, a speaker can show who holds the higher status — the speaker or the listener. Two types of relationships affect intercultural communication: complementary and symmetrical. Both have a bearing on communicator success.

1. Complementary relationships are those between high-status and low-status persons. One person is superior, perhaps in rank, wealth, age, or ability. The other is subordinate, beholden to the person with higher status. The subordinate person defers to the superior person, and this deference appears in the messages both send. Verbally, the subordinate uses more honorifics ("sir," for example) when addressing the superior.

Asians are masters at submitting to superiors. The Japanese do so most overtly through use of the bow. The lowest, most polite, and respectful bow is called *saikeirei*, from the junior (kohai) to the senior (sempai), who guides the junior through his or her years of employment. Between people of the same rank, the lightest and most casual bow — the *eshaku* — is used. Bowing low and being polite in all negotiations, those wishing to succeed in Japanese society practice the *tei-shisei*, the low-posture bow, as those who can help them succeed control their destiny. The subordinate's behavior displays obeisance and the superior's, dominance.

2. Symmetrical relationships involve individuals of equal status. We are apt to be more self-disclosing and personal with those we consider our equals. The "sir" or "madam" we might use when addressing superiors gives way to a friendly "hi," followed by the person's first name. When greeting friends, the Japanese use the *eshaku*, the light and casual bow.

Channel. Once encoded, a message is transmitted via a channel, many of which are

In this example of a complementary relationship, the Japanese O L (office lady) greets the Japanese salaryman with a low bow, respecting his higher status. Both are properly clad — the O L in matching uniform of skirt, white blouse, and jacket, the man in his dark coat and gray trousers.

available. Messages can be sent via smoke signals, jungle drums, waving flags, sign language, flashing lights, telegraph keys, letters, and speaking, among other forms. Because our interest is oral communication, the channel that is important to us is the voice, and the nonverbal behavior that accompanies the vocal message.

Speaking Situation. The messages we send are conditioned by the speaking situation — the context or environment in which the act of speaking takes place. The situation directly affects how we communicate.

In a church we are peaceful and placid, respecting the sacredness of the place. Noise and loud behavior are not acceptable. At a football game, we can shout and scream at the players in keeping with the social context. In the classroom, we are reserved, dignified but alert, drinking in the teacher's words. When called upon to recite, we do so eagerly, wanting to share our knowledge. During a wedding our behavior is polite, as the context demands. At the reception following the wedding, we can talk freely, laugh, sing, and dance.

Time is another situational factor. If we have a lot of time, our talk is apt to be slower, more detailed, relaxed, and more satisfying. If pressed for time, we try to make our point quickly and be on our way. As students, we do not speak during class. The teacher speaks at that time. We rarely call people at night lest we disturb their sleep, unless an emergency is at hand. North Americans do not like to be kept waiting for an appointment. Latin Americans are expected to keep people waiting well past the appointed hour.

Our talk usually has a utilitarian purpose. We speak to accomplish something. *Purpose*, therefore, is a situational factor. We want to stimulate a specific meaning in the minds of our listeners. We speak to accomplish something, and we choose the situation that lends itself to meeting the purpose.

Photo by Debbie Whittig

The physical setting and the social context largely determine how a message is sent and received. In Japan, late March and early April bring families and friends to local parks for cherry blossom viewing and for picnicking. The viewers eat and chat while the children play. The situation conditions their talk. They banter, joke, and otherwise engage one another in socially appropriate talk to facilitate social interaction.

Culture: The Heart of Diversity

All communication bears cultural origins, conveys cultural meanings, and is interpreted through cultural frameworks. Yet many American communication textbooks assume a seemingly acultural perspective, meaning that culture does not figure dominantly in defining or describing the communication process. The prevailing, Anglophile, Eurowhite perspective that underlies most American theories of communication and prescriptions for effective communication is what students are expected to learn and emulate. When culture is mentioned, the impression created is that it is something belonging only to minorities, immigrants, and other special groups.[5]

Unlike good manners, culture is not something that certain individuals have and others do not. Culture is part of every person's life and in that sense provides direction in life. We all are influenced by similar aspects of culture. Nevertheless, the diversity in human behavior is attributable largely to the fact that the people of the world do not belong to the same culture. Wishing to communicate harmoniously across cultures, we are obligated to place ourselves into the cultural worlds the others inhabit. We must perceive the world as they see it.

That the people of the world behave differently becomes apparent even with a casual glance at what people do from one society to another. Disparities exist. When we compare typical American behavior with that of other people worldwide, the contrast is obvious. Average Americans welcome visitors to their homes.

The Yanomamo of Venezuela greet visitors with drawn bows, green mucus flowing from their nostrils with a wad of green leaves stuffed behind their lower lip. They shout at each other, strike each other with their fists, and club each other on the head. These men are fearful of being raided by members of another community when visitors arrive and they need to express their fierceness, their valued identity. The green leaves help them see visions and communicate with spirits from the lower world.[6]

Asian Indians are often physically repelled by American treatment of pets. Dogs actually live in the house with people, and cats, which to them are despicable, are underfoot everywhere. Filipinos would prefer that dogs be served as a dinner's main course, as would Koreans.

The Mae Enga of New Guinea may have the best of all worlds. They believe it is desirable for young men to postpone marriage as long as possible. When they do marry, men and women live in separate houses. The Nayar of India, however, prefer their brides to be young; 6-year-old brides are known. In the USA 80- and 90-year-old couples getting married is not uncommon.

The well-known proverb "Different strokes for different folks" characterizes cultures worldwide.

About Absolutes

After this course you will never be able to talk or think (if, indeed, you ever did) the way some American soldiers in Vietnam did. They used to laugh about the fact that you couldn't tell one "slope," or "dink," or "gook" from another. . . . If a friendly village was destroyed, it didn't matter — the inhabitants were all gooks.

But . . . there are no gooks or wogs. Or else we are all gooks and wogs. . . . There is unity to the human condition. People are different, to be sure, but nobody is better than anyone else. All people everywhere and at all times have tried, and continue to try, to make the best of their lives.

Source: *Anthropology: The Biocultural View*, by F. E. Johnston and Henry Shelby (Dubuque, IA: Wm. C. Brown, 1978, pp. 4–5.

Culture Defined

In his popular *The Innocents Abroad,* published in 1869, Mark Twain wrote of the people and places he visited on the first organized "pleasure party ever assembled for a transatlantic voyage." As he journeyed through Europe and the Holy Land, he recorded for posterity the strange sights and sounds he encountered, the people and their behavior that differed from place to place. Twain acclaimed in print what people who travel — missionaries, merchants, military personnel, tourists, and vagabonds — have observed for millennia, the behavior patterns that represent each place's culture and how they change with the passage of time.

Twain described the complexities of the cultures he visited, how the communication and intermingling of people with different origins, identities, and allegiances over time created groups that were unlike each other. From his descriptions, we discover a rationale for the contention that culture is ubiquitous, multidimensional, complex, and all-pervasive.[7] Culture is everywhere, varying in scope, consisting of related parts, and permeating everything. The concept of culture covers much ground and is difficult to precisely define, yet many scholars have attempted to do so.

Many definitions have been analyzed.[8] Each of the definitions points to something legitimate and important, and common strands can be found among the definitions. Essentially, cultures are composed of *symbolic systems* that provide webs of meaning. These are twofold.

1. The invisible, less tangible aspects of human behavior. These are made concrete only through their application in daily life. Among them are the values, attitudes, beliefs, norms of behavior, and other intangibles packed with symbolic meanings.

2. The tangibles, such as the clothes we wear, the cars we drive, the food we eat, and the books we read — all the things humans have made. These, too, depend upon abstract cultural meanings.

Another strand common to the definitions relates to the *longevity* of cultures. Although cultures undergo change and are constantly evolving, they tend to endure. The American culture exemplifies this second strand. It began in the Pilgrim days and slowly changed in the ensuing years until today, almost 400 years after arrival of the *Mayflower,* the culture remains.

A final thread running through the definitions is that cultures are *learned.* The lessons are explicit through formal instruction and implicit by imitating the behavior of others.

The definitions of culture cover a wide range of thought. The first is credited to Edward B. Tylor, an anthropologist, who in 1871 wrote words to the effect that culture is that complex whole which includes knowledge, belief, art, law, morals, custom, and any other habits acquired by humans who are members of society.[9] Kearney and Plax add to this definition by distinguishing between a society and its culture. A society, to them, is a number of people carrying on a common life, whereas culture is what these people collectively produce and practice. A culture is not a group of people. Rather, it is the things they use, the beliefs they share, and norms of behavior they follow.[10]

Broad Definition

Scholars characterize culture as consisting of the nonbiological parts of human life, that part of the environment made by humans. These nonbiological parts of human life include:

1. *Artifacts* — the things people make to enhance their lives, such as the food they eat, the clothes they wear, the houses in which they live, the tools and utensils they use, the transportation systems that convey them from place to place, the books, newspapers, and magazines they read, and the schools they attend, among a host of other objects that are a part of their daily life.

2. *Sociofacts* — the practices that people follow to regulate their lives, such as the written rules and regulations that govern their behavior in society, the unwritten codes of behavior controlling courtesy and comity toward others, the laws of the land.

3. *Mentifacts* — the cognitive and affective elements that influence human thinking, such as needs, values, beliefs, attitudes, and comparable cerebral processes.

A definition in this broad vein states that culture is a set of human-made objective and subjective elements. In the past, these elements have increased the possibility of survival for humans and brought about a satisfactory living arrangement for those who shared a common environment and communicated with each other through a common language.[11]

In this definition, the objective elements referred to are the artifacts or the external and overt material products that humans use. The subjective elements are the mentifacts and the sociofacts, the more internal, covert aspects of culture.

Culture: A Sampling of Definitions

"Culture is the man-made part of the environment." M. J. Herskovitz, *Cultural Anthropology* (New York: Knopf, 1955), 305.

"Culture is the total way of life of a people, composed of their learned and shared behavior patterns, values, norms, and material objects." E.M. Rogers and T.M. Steinfatt, *Intercultural Communication* (Prospect Heights, IL: Waveland, 1999), 79.

"Culture is the shared assumptions, values, and beliefs of a group of people which result in characteristic behaviors." C. Storti, *Figuring Foreigners Out: A Practical Guide* (Yarmouth, ME: Intercultural Press, 1999), 5.

"A complex frame of reference that consists of patterns of traditions, beliefs, values, norms, symbols, and meanings that are shared to varying degrees by interacting members of a community." S. Ting-Toomey, *Communicating Across Cultures* (New York: Guilford Press, 1999), 10.

"A learned set of shared interpretations about beliefs, values, and norms, which affect the behaviors of a relatively large group of people." M.W. Lustig and J. Koester, *Intercultural Competence: Interpersonal Communication Across Cultures* (New York: Longman, 1999), 30.

"Culture is a set of values, views of reality, and codes of behavior held in common by people who share a distinctive way of life." N.J. Smelser, *Sociology*, 4th ed. (Englewood Cliffs, NJ: Prentice Hall, 1991), 19.

"Culture is "the totality of transmitted behavior patterns, arts, beliefs, institutions, and all other products of human work and thought characteristic of a community or population". . . .*"A style of social and artistic expression peculiar to a society of class"*. . .*"Intellectual and artistic activity and the intellectual and social refinement resulting from that activity."* Reader's Digest Illustrated Encyclopedic Dictionary (Pleasantville, NY: Reader's Digest Association, 1989), 418.

Narrow Definition

Other definitions are not as broad, confining culture to the acquired knowledge that people use to interpret experience and generate behavior. Culture, in this sense, does not include the material things, people, behavior, and emotions. Rather, culture becomes a model for perceiving, interpreting, and relating to the world.[12]

A definition along those lines considers culture to be a set of rules for constructing, clarifying, and adapting to the world. Culture, therefore, is not made of things we can see and touch — the artifacts of life. Instead, culture is a set of rules for getting along in life. How we apply the rules leads to the artifacts. These rules are communicated to us by our parents and significant others. Once we master the rules, we can make the artifacts that environmental conditions require. [13]

Culture: A Blueprint

Whether we define culture in the broad sense or in the narrower one, our interpretation will satisfy the requirements for understanding intercultural communication. Important to this understanding is that culture provides the blueprint that determines the way we think, feel, and behave in society. Our blueprint, we should appreciate, is unlikely to be shared by other cultures. Although people of all cultures must fulfill certain biological and psychological needs to survive, how they actually meet these needs can vary greatly. The blueprints that other cultures follow to fill needs depend upon the resources available to them and the climatic conditions in which they live. The blueprint we follow, of course, is based on our environment.[14]

The consequence of obeying the rules of our culture is that we can predict how the members of our culture will behave in most situations. Unless we know the rules that other cultures practice, we will discover that it is almost impossible to tell how the members of other cultures will behave in similar situations. Whether we define culture broadly or in a narrower sense is not as essential to competent intercultural communication as is knowing the similar ties and differences between cultures.

The Characteristics of Culture

Before examining more closely the similarities and differences between cultures, we should know about the general characteristics of culture. Culture is pervasive, learned, shared, adaptable, explicit or implicit, changeable, and ethnocentric.

Pervasive Phenomenon

We should have noted from our definitions of culture that culture is pervasive. It permeates all of society and includes virtually everything that is not biological. Culture combines visible and invisible things around us. The visible things are the products of our cultural rules — the artifacts that surround us. They take the form of highways, buildings, computers, machines, pictures, and a myriad of other observable and touchable things. The invisible, the sociofacts and mentifacts, include the laws, rules, regulations, norms, customs, and an immense number of other written and unwritten directions that guide and govern our actions as members of society.

The term *culture* is often used in a more restricted sense, and we should be aware of this usage lest it confuse us. Many cultures differentiate between "high culture" and "low culture."[15] High culture alludes to cultural activities that are under the influence of the European upper class. Among those activities are ballet, opera, symphony, great literature, and fine art. They are peerless and timeless activities, appreciated by audiences in any culture and studied in universities the world over.

Low culture specifies activities of the non-elite who prefer game shows, music videos, stock car racing, sports events, rock, jazz, events that lack sophistication, unworthy of serious study.[16] We hear reference to "uncultured" individuals — bumpkins, louts, slobs — people who lack "culture." They do not have the refinement and gentility said to come from understanding and enjoying the finer things of life, the things that "high"-culture people like. The pervasive quality of culture, however, implies a far wider range of human experience than just the aesthetic.

With the rise of mass media (radio, television, large-scale printing, CDs, tapes), the division between high culture and low culture (or folk culture, as it was called in the 19th century) became blurred. A *mass culture* emerged that cut across class differences. Its products are standardized and communicated to vast audiences. Almost everyone, not just the elite, can share in the pleasures brought by fine art, literature, and music. The elite can enjoy, along with the "clods," television and radio.

Learned Behavior

The way we behave in our culture is learned — learned early in life from our parents and other adults who are important to us. Heredity does provide us with certain inherent human faculties. How we use these faculties stems from the rules of our culture. We are taught the right way, the culture's way, to use them.

Eating is a biological necessity. We have to eat to live. Our culture determines what we eat. We learn to consume beef if that is what our culture dictates, and we learn that eating dogs is offensive.

Sleep is another biological necessity. We have to sleep to live. Our culture determines how we will sleep — on the floor, in a bed, or in a hammock.

Protecting our person is a biological necessity. We have to shield our body from the elements. Our culture decides how we do this. We can wear kimonos, dresses, loincloths, burnoose, Mao or Nehru jackets, cheongsam, muumuus, or shintiyan — whatever our culture deems appropriate. We can live in teepees, houses, igloos, or fur skin huts to protect ourselves.

What we choose is what our culture teaches us to pick. Culture also gives meaning to some

of our physical reactions, and we are taught what these mean. A lump in the throat means sorrow; a tightening of the skin, fear; a sinking feeling in the stomach, fright; a certain movement of the mouth, a smile, signifying pleasure or something good — at least in our culture.

We learn what is right. If we deviate too much from the culture, we pay in some way. We pay through loss in comfort, status, peace of mind, safety, or in some other manner. We might have discovered this when we failed to act as our parents wished and a spanking helped us learn.

Shared Behavior

Shared cultural patterns bind us together as an identifiable group, enabling us to live harmoniously together. Although we disagree about some aspects of our culture, we agree about and accept most of it. We are not even aware of a lot of what we agree about. We do not realize that it is a part of our culture.

Adaptable Behavior

Our culture is an adaptation to our surroundings. Cultures develop to conform to certain environmental conditions and to the available natural and technological resources. The culture of city-dwellers differs from that of rural-area residents. Because inhabitants of cities have convenient transportation systems, stores, and supermarkets, handy medical facilities and schools, they have an easier time moving around. Lacking these conveniences, country-dwellers have to adjust their behavior to satisfy personal needs and be prepared to travel farther to make purchases, go to school, and visit doctors.

Often exposed to high winds, Guamanians adapt by building their houses of concrete, including the roofs, so their lodgings will not be blown away. Also exposed to high winds, Filipinos living in the country build their dwellings from inexpensive, easily replaced, local materials such as palm fronds, bamboo, and banana leaves. Alaskan natives adapt to their environment by building their dwellings from a material readily available to them — snow. Houses in

Wisconsin are constructed to withstand winter's frigid and snowy weather. In Hawaii, nearly all of the houses have thin walls and roofs and lots of windows — designed to keep out the rain and let the cool breezes blow through.

Explicit and Implicit Behaviors

Cultures are made up of overt, explicit ways of behaving, feeling, and acting. These are taught to us consciously. We eat with knives, forks, and spoons, and we know how to use them because someone took the trouble to instruct us in their use.

Cultures also are made up of implicit ways of behaving, feeling, and reacting. No one teaches us the implicit ways. They are unstated, covert ways of acting. We pick them up unconsciously, and we are apt to be totally unaware of what we are doing when we use them. Most of us do not think that wearing trousers and shirts or dresses, eating at a table, or sleeping in a bed is a culturally determined behavior. These are all habitual and customary, and we tend to perceive them as the only way to behave — if we think about them at all.

In intercultural situations, when we are most concerned about the appropriateness of our behavior, we are most likely to concentrate on the explicit behaviors and ignore the implicit ones. Yet, if we err, the miscues probably will be with the implicitly learned behaviors.

Consider dining out. When a group of North Americans eat together in a restaurant, they order the items they prefer. If someone else is paying for the meal, most will order in the price range equivalent to the host's order. In Japan, a foreigner who is asked "What will you have?" does not realize that his or her choice may have serious consequences for the others, especially if this is the senior person.

"I've noticed, when I'm in Japan," a friend comments, "that whatever I order, everyone else orders." In Japan, diners typically follow the lead of the senior person and order the same item, regardless of the cost and whether it is to their liking.

A similar situation exists in Korea. A colleague reports: "In Seoul, when dining out with friends, everyone orders what the senior person orders. I do, too. I can't read the menu anyway, so I go along with the rest. Unfortunately the senior is partial to dog. Home from Seoul, I want to bark!"

Nose-blowing is an implicitly learned behavior for many Americans. They take out their handkerchief and blow when they need to. "If I have a cold when I'm in Japan," an acquaintance remarks, "I blow my nose in my handkerchief when I have to. Everyone around me seems surprised and dismayed." The Japanese use tissue for nose-blowing, and usually when they are by themselves. The handkerchief is for wiping one's hands or face, but not for nose-cleaning. Blowing one's nose and then putting the handkerchief back into one's purse or pocket is seen as an unclean act. Around Japanese children, the sound of nose-blowing brings on outbursts of laughter.

Changeability

Cultures constantly undergo change. For a millennium in human history, the changes were slow and gradual. In the past century or two, the rate has accelerated, and today the pace is rapid. People's lifestyles are being altered and changed too quickly in some cases, and the reactions are not always positive. In farming societies, male children, who were expected to work the land when they grew up, left the farms for more lucrative jobs in nearby city factories, disrupting family life and often forcing the parents to give up the farms they had worked hard to develop.

"Parasite" single women are the focus of heated public debate in Japan, where the number of women in their late 20s who have not married has risen from 30 percent to 50 percent in the last few years. These single women are foregoing marriage to shop and travel, holding down jobs to pay for their leisure and luxury. They live at home and pay some rent to their parents — thus, the term "parasite" singles. A few years ago most women were married in their early 20s and their children helped Japan's population keep pace with its rapidly aging citizenry. To maintain its economic growth in the future, the country expects to hire workers from abroad to compensate for the dwindling number of births.[17]

In Thailand the *wat* was the heart of social as well as religious life. Today these monasteries play less of a social role and are visited rarely for religious observances. Accessibility is the problem. In rural areas the *wat* was a short walk away. With increased migration to the larger Thai cities in recent years, a wat visit entails long, hot drives through heavy traffic. Many homes now have a room set aside for prayer and meditation — daily rituals once performed at the village wat.

Like many Asian countries, the Thai enjoy Western foods. Hamburgers, hot dogs, pancakes, pizza, waffles, ice cream, jelly, bread, doughnuts, cakes, and chocolate are on the menus of most restaurants, augmenting the regular fare: steamed rice, clear soup, fried fish with ginger, a hot salad, and fresh fruit.

With the influx of refugees and immigrants, life in the United States is changing rapidly. While the Asians are adopting Western foods, Western countries are taking to tofu, kimchi, spicy concoctions from Thailand, sushi, unagi, and tempura.

In athletics, similar changes are taking place. Soccer and rugby are becoming more and more popular. Graceful exercises such as China's Luk Tung Kuen and Tai-Chi Chuan are attracting Americans who desire to be physically fit without lifting weights or engaging in strenuous exercises.

Why do cultures change? Cultural borrowing is becoming common as peoples intermingle worldwide. Disasters or crises force changes, and environmental conditions lead to lifestyle alterations.

Cultural Borrowing. Cultures borrow heavily from other cultures. American jazz is played in Paris nightclubs. American baseball is winning converts in countries around the globe. American football seems to have caught on in Europe, where at least one professional league is flourishing. Bikinis are worn on beaches throughout the world, and in Rio de Janeiro, comely young women are slipping off their bikini tops a la their sisters along the French Riviera. American use of deodorants is gaining ground worldwide, as are shaved heads among athletes. We borrow extensively from other cultures, and they in turn borrow from us.

Disasters and Crises. Natural disasters such as floods, earthquakes, hurricanes, and erupting volcanoes can alter people's behavior. The eruption of Mt. Pinatubo in the Philippines forced many people out of their homes onto safer ground — and a change in lifestyle. Forest fires in Western United States affect the lives of thousands who live in those areas. Heavy rains wash away homes built on earthen mountainsides, and winds blow away roofs and parts of houses, requiring changes in building codes to minimize future damage.

Crises such as wars create change. During World War II, many Japanese men were killed, causing a shortage of potential husbands for the women coming of age. They married members of the occupying forces, thereby changing century-old marriage practices.

The Vietnam war provides many examples of changes caused by armed conflict. After the Americans were overcome by the communists, Saigon became Ho Chi Minh City, and the bars, nightclubs, and brothels that had been frequented by the American troops were closed. Newspapers went out of business. Library materials were censored, and schools were forced to teach what the communists wanted.

Environmental Reasons. Population growth in many countries reduces the amount of arable land as cities encroach on farmlands. More people need food but there is less land to grow it on. To increase the yields on the smaller plots, new farming methods had to be devised.

New fertilizers were developed, and animals no longer grazed in pasture lands but instead were force-fed in pens to raise productivity.

Ethnocentric Behavior

Although ethnocentrism is described more fully in Chapter 6, ethnocentric behavior is noted here as a significant characteristic of culture. Because culture is highly influential in determining how we think, feel, and act, we use it as a means

---

Cultural Truisms

- *Human beings create culture.*
- *Thousands of years ago, in isolation, groups of people developed their own culture.*
- *Each group found a way to solve these 10 basic problems:*

  - *Food*
  - *Shelter*
  - *Social structure*
  - *Protection*
  - *Religion*

  - *Clothing*
  - *Family structure*
  - *Government*
  - *Arts/crafts*
  - *Knowledge/science*

- *Different groups developed different solutions to the 10 problems.*
- *No absolutely "right" ways were found, just ways right for each group.*
- *Each group created a culture of its own, not "better" or "worse" than those of the other groups — just different.*
- *Each group comes to believe its ways are best — they become ethnocentric.*
- *When children are born, they are encultur-ated — they are taught the group's ways.*
- *As long as each group remains isolated, no intercultural communication problems exist.*
- *Problems occur when persons from one group try to communicate with persons of another group.*

Source: *Developing Intercultural Awareness*, by L.R. Kohls, (Washington, DC: SIETAR, 1981).

---

for judging the world around us. Our culture becomes the center of everything, and our cultural traits are seen as natural, correct, and superior to those of other cultures. The ways in which people in other cultures think, feel, and act are perceived as odd, amusing, inferior, or immoral. We compare them to our culture, and ours comes out to be superior.

Ethnocentric behavior is a common characteristic of cultures, and in intercultural communication it can prevent us from understanding other cultures. We perceive others from our point of view, but we should see them from their point of view. By overcoming our ethnocentric view of the world, we can begin to respect other cultures and perhaps even function more effectively in them.[18]

 ## Cultural Contrasts

Weaver's conceptualization of eight groupings listing 62 contrasting descriptors is helpful in sorting out ways to characterize cultures.[19] Even then, Weaver asserts, he hasn't touched all of the possibilities.

All of these descriptors bear on communication, although some have more influence than others on the communication process. In the following chapters, we will review the ones significant in intercultural communication.

Hall likens culture to an iceberg, of which the tip or external culture is really the smallest part.[20] The largest part of culture is inside our heads and unconscious. Further, the internal culture is dominant over the external. To understand what motivates people to communicate, we must explore the internal culture.

 ## Cultural Universals

We usually are unaware of our culture until we leave it to interact with those who are culturally different. Aspects of our own culture then rise to cultural awareness. We begin to understand our own culture when we compare and contrast it with other cultures. Despite their many differences, all cultures have common features called cultural universals — general attributes that can help us locate potential areas of cultural variation.

A half-century ago George Murdock prepared a list of 73 common denominators of culture.[21] As far as he was concerned, these denominators, plus many more, are part of every culture known in history or ethnography. Reflecting on the items in this list, we should realize that every culture acts in some fashion to adorn the body, take care of its sick, and rear its children, although the methods may not be similar. Cultures depend partially upon the available resources and the environment in which the culture exists.

On the list we find games. All people play games, and the games they play vary between cultures. The members of most cultures amuse themselves with many contests, taking the forms of tournaments, regattas, meets, twosomes, foursomes, or singles. Games people play, among many others, are archery, bagatelle, bandy, battledore, boccie, charades, crambo, cricket, draughts, football, hide-and-seek, jai alai, Mah Jongg, merels, nine-pins, pelota, quoits, skittles, and even post office.

People of all cultures dance. How they dance varies. In a few individualistic cultures, the grind is popular, with each dancer soloing with arms and legs flaying and everything else jiggling in rhythm to the steady throb of a bass or bongo. Other cultures have discovered the sensuousness of dancing cheek-to-cheek. The hula or Tahitian attracts tourists to Hawaii and the South Seas. War dances are big in movies or films featuring African tribes. Among other dances are the barn dance, boogaloo, cakewalk,

Cultural Universals

age grading	athletic sports	bodily adornment	calendar
cleanliness training	community groups	cooking	cooperative labor
cosmology	courtship	dancing	decorative art
divination	division of labor	dream interpretation	education
eschatology	ethics	ethnobotany	etiquette
faith healing	family	feasting	firemaking
folklore	food taboos	funeral rites	games
gestures	gift giving	government	greetings
hair styles	hospitality	housing	hygiene
incest taboos	inheritance rules	joking	kin groups
kinship nomenclature	language	law	luck superstitions
magic	marriage	mealtimes	medicine
modesty	mourning	music	mythology
numerals	obstetrics	penal sanctions	personal names
population policy	postnatal care	pregnancy usages	property rites
puberty customs	religious ritual	residence rules	sexual restrictions
soul concepts	status differences	supernatural beings	surgery
tool making	trade	visiting	weaning
weather control			

Source: "The Common Denominator of Cultures," by G. Murdock, in *The Science of Man in World Crisis*, edited by R. Linton (New York: Columbia University Press, 1945).

Behavior: Universal, Cultural, Personal

Human behavior takes three forms: universal, cultural, and personal. *Universal behaviors* apply to everyone regardless of culture. *Cultural behaviors* are those representative of a specific culture. *Personal behaviors* are the private practices of individual — their own ways of behaving. Not all behaviors are cultural.

Consider eating. Eating is universal; everyone has to eat, and everyone eats food. What people eat is cultural; the Japanese eat sashimi, a culturally favorite food. A Japanese man, Nakamura san, eats sashimi while sipping sake, a personally favorite way of eating sashimi.

Each person is like everybody else in some ways (universal behaviors), like the people in a certain culture in other ways (cultural behaviors), and like no one else in still other ways (personal behaviors).

Are these behaviors universal, cultural, or personal? Identify each.

_____ Wearing a four-leaf clover

_____ Cooking

_____ Luck superstitions

_____ Bodily adornment

_____ Eating turkey on Thanksgiving

_____ Wearing a thong

_____ Liking Louis Armstrong music

_____ Cosmology

_____ Getting an annual vacation

_____ Reading intercultural textbooks

Answers on page 243.

Source: Based on *Figuring Foreigners Out*, by C. Storti, (Yarmouth, ME: Intercultural Press, 1999).

cha-cha, funky chicken, mambo, polka, rhumba, tango, and waltz — some with body contact, others with little touch.

All cultures communicate through language. Among the hundreds of languages are the lesser known Anatolic, Aymara, Berber, Caddoan, Celtic, Chad, Cushitic, Dard, Gur, Hokan, Jicaquean, Khoin, Kwa, Munda, and a host of others. A few people even use one of the 24 contrived languages such as Ido, Ro, and Solresol.

Murdock's list of universals is extensive, although it is not inclusive. Many other categories

An American Fertility Rite as Seen by a Non-Westerner

Americans choose the largest males in the society for the ritual of football. They are dressed in ritual costumes that emphasize parts of the anatomy defined as being sexually attractive. The shoulders are enlarged, and the genital area is fitted with special pads and cups to show off the warrior's sexual prowess.

Meanwhile, along the sidelines, there are special maidens called cheerleaders who are similarly costumed. Their hips are fitted with special skirts that make them look round and fit for bearing the warriors' children. Their breasts are partially exposed, which is said to be sexually attractive to the warriors. They wave giant paper testicles, which they call pom poms, and the leader of the cheerleaders twirls a stick of wood shaped like a penis, throwing it in the air and catching it.

Such is the most popular form of fertility rite by the Americans. It is unlike most fertility rites that we have witnessed in our travels, however, because it is held not once but repeatedly, and in the autumn rather than in the spring.

Source: *Anthropology: The Biocultural View,* by F.E. Johnson and H. Shelby, (Dubuque, IA: Wm. C. Brown, 1978), 22.

could be included. The list, nevertheless, allows us to consider the possible areas of similarities and differences between cultures. The universals provide direction for our study of the people with whom we wish to interact.

Culture is an abstract, complex, and pervasive structure of social elements that operates as an all-embracing way of life. It lays out a predictable world for us to follow as we go about our daily business.

Chapter Review

Culture is communication and communication is culture. Culture determines the way we communicate. At an early age we learn from our culture how to speak, when to speak, what to speak about, and to whom to speak.

Mediated communication is distinctive because some sort of device carries messages between the speaker and the listener.

Oral communication is the process by which people share information, meanings, and feelings through the exchange of verbal and nonverbal messages.

Intentional messages are utilitarian, aesthetic, or therapeutic. Unintentional messages are serendipitous or accidental.

The communication process is dynamic, systematic, adaptive, continuous, transactional, and irreversible.

The elements of communication are common to all human beings regardless of age, gender, status, rank, country, or culture.

The communicators are the speaker and the listeners. The speaker encodes messages, and the listeners decode them. Encoding means translating an already conceived idea into a message to send to listeners. Decoding means translating the message into comprehensible information, meanings, and feelings by the listeners.

Feedback is the overt verbal or nonverbal responses that listeners convey to the speaker.

Noise is any factor that interferes with the intended meaning of the message or of the feedback being transmitted.

Messages consist of the information, meanings, and feelings that speakers wish to send to their listeners. Messages can define relationships, either complementary or symmetrical.

The channel common to oral communication is the voice and the nonverbal behavior that accompanies it or substitutes for it.

(Continued)

Chapter Review continued

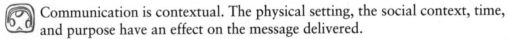

Communication is contextual. The physical setting, the social context, time, and purpose have an effect on the message delivered.

Broadly defined, culture refers to the nonbiological parts of human life — artifacts, mentifacts, and sociofacts. Narrowly defined, culture is a set of rules for getting along in life. We apply the rules to make things, devise the regulations that control society, and set the norms of our behavior.

Culture is pervasive, learned, shared, adaptable, explicit or implicit, changeable, and ethnocentric.

Cultures can be better understood by comparing and contrasting them with one another.

Think About This...

1 Hall claims that culture is communication and communication is culture. What does he mean?

2 "We cannot *not* communicate" is a significant truism. What does it mean?

3 Reading the typical American-authored communication textbook, we usually are exposed to Anglophile, Eurowhite techniques for communicating effectively. Are these techniques useful in communicating interculturally?

   With the increasing diversity of the USA, is this approach preparing students for improved communication in American society? Or are readers learning old-fashioned ways of communicating that are no longer meaningful in our diverse nation? If you think so, what should be done to prepare students for the realities of 21st-century communication?

4 Explain how America's culture developed using Kohl's formula (see page 34).

5 What are cultural universals? How do they differ from culture to culture?

Communicating Interculturally

Culture has a scope both broader and narrower than a single society. On the broader basis we recognize that the Western and Eastern cultures, each with defining customs, extend beyond the boundaries of a single nation. The West encompasses the developed countries of the former communist world plus Europe and North America. The East, geographically speaking, encompasses Asia and the surrounding islands. The Muslim culture observes no national limits; it spreads throughout much of the Middle East.

In the narrowest sense we can identify smaller cultural units within a larger culture — cultures within a culture. But even though they are smaller, they are significant variants and should not be perceived as being lesser. We call these smaller units *microcultures*. They are composed of people who have conscious membership in identifiable units of the larger cultural unit surrounding them. We term the larger unit the *macroculture*, or dominant culture.[1]

 ## Cultures Within Cultures

As a pluralistic country, the United States has many cultures. Most of the citizens share the macroculture, a universal or national culture called the *mainstream culture*.[2] The many microcultures within each macroculture have a distinct cultural pattern not common to the macroculture. The microcultures also have been termed *co-cultures*,[3] a label suggesting mutuality or interdependence, a condition not readily established. *Subculture,* another term frequently used for microculture, implies under, beneath, secondary, or inferior, but microcultures are not subordinate units. Therefore, the terminology *cultures within cultures* more accurately represent the smaller units we call microcultures.[4]

USA Macroculture

The dominant culture, or macroculture, in the United States is Anglo-Saxon, a designation loosely used to denote any of the people of, or the descendants of, the peoples of the British Isles and includes the Danes, Normans, Germanic tribes, and Jutes, among others. The USA macroculture, therefore, stems from political and social institutions influenced by Western European tradition.

These institutions — government, schools, banks, social welfare, business, laws — affect our lives greatly. They form the foundation for the dominant culture and provide the framework for the traits and values of much of the country's culture. Other aspects of the culture have been influenced by the many microcultures that comprise the population, but all share a core of universal cultural features.[5]

An overpowering value dominates the macroculture's core. That value is *individualism*, the notion that every individual is his or her own master. Each individual is in control of his or her own destiny and will advance in society only according to his or her own efforts. We see this core value exhibited in traits such as industriousness, ambition, competitiveness, self-reliance, independence, appreciation of the good life, and the belief that humans are separate and superior to nature.[6] We measure success and achievement by the acquisition of things: cars, boats, homes, and televisions, among many others.

Freedom is another vital value. Members of the dominant culture desire to be left alone by others, especially not having other people's lifestyles forced upon them. They want to be free of outside authority at work, in politics, and in family life. Chief Joseph of the Nez Percé tribe eloquently expressed this desire for freedom:

> Let me be a free man, free to travel, free
> to stop, free to work, free to trade
> where I choose, free to choose my own
> teachers, free to follow the religion of
> my fathers, free to talk, think, and act
> for myself — and I will obey every law
> or submit to the penalty.[7]

Many Americans share Chief Joseph's passion for freedom. We see signs of it in our impersonal relationships with people who are not friends or family, in our direct and confrontive communication style, and in our desire to be with people who have the same interests that we do.

Wanting to be free and individualistic, our personal affairs are based on "right and wrong" principles instead of shame, dishonor, or ridicule, as in some other cultures. Actions are judged as right or wrong, moral or immoral, rather than ranging along a continuum of degrees of right and wrong.[8]

To some extent, most members of the macroculture hold those core values of individualism and freedom, along with other Anglo-Saxon values, noted later. Some microcultures. however, especially those with Asian backgrounds, are apt to be more interdependent and collectivistic in outlook.

You will see references to "Americans" frequently in the pages that follow. This term refers here to citizens of the United States, particularly those who are members of the dominant Anglo-Saxon macroculture. Other groups in the Western hemisphere can rightly call themselves Americans, too, and they do. For our purposes, we are using the term pointedly to mean the dominant group in the United States.

 # American Microcultures

Members of microcultures share the political and social institutions of the macroculture. They can vote in local and national elections, attend public schools, obey all of the laws, buy things with U. S. currency, bank in the nation's banks, and move about the country as they wish. Yet they have distinctive cultural features of their

Who are Americans?

Who are the people that make up the melting pot that is the United States? We are a rich mix of Anglo-American, American Indians, African-descent people, Polish, Russian, Japanese, Chinese, Filipino, Vietnamese, and Arab influences, to name just a few. Indigenous people make up less than 1 percent of the total population. Most Americans are immigrants or have ancestors who were immigrants. At least 276 different ethnic groups, plus the 500 or more different American Indian groups, are represented.

The U. S. Bureau of the Census counts the number of people by racial categories. In 1999, 82.3 percent of the population was self-identified as white, 12.8 percent as black, less than 1 percent (0.9) as American Indian/Alaska Native, 4.0 percent as Asian and Pacific Islander, and 11.5 percent as Hispanic origin (Hispanics are often counted under more than one category). In 1999 the population totaled 272,878,000. The Asian/Pacific Islander group consisted of Chinese, Filipinos, Japanese, Asian Indians, and Koreans in the larger numbers.

The first settlers were Europeans, principally English, although the French, Dutch, and Spanish established early settlements. With the development of the United States, Europeans immigrated from Germany, Ireland, and Sweden, along with more from England, France, and Spain. The primary reasons for immigration were economic impoverishment and political repression in their homelands.

People of African descent came involuntarily. Thousands were kidnapped in their native lands by unscrupulous people and sold into bondage. Shipped to the United States, they provided labor for the expanding agricultural economy in the southern part of the United States.

With the annexation of northern sections of the Mexican territory, Mexicans and various American Indian people living within that area became citizens. Later, immigrants came from impoverished eastern and southern European countries including Poland, Russia, Hungary, Italy, and Greece. In the 19th century, Chinese, Japanese and Filipino workers were encouraged to enter the United States to provide much-needed labor for the western part of the nation. The large Asian population in Hawaii, for example, came about because of the need for pineapple and sugar cane fieldhands.

The country's population reflects remarkable ethnic diversity and non-white people outnumber whites in several American cities. Honolulu is a prime example. There, people often are referred to as Asian-Americans, Italian-Americans, German-Americans, or Black-Americans — linking their ethnic background to their American citizenship. Or people might be labeled by their skin color: white, brown, black, yellow, red.

The U. S. population includes Protestants of varied denominations, Catholics, Jews, Moslems, Buddhists, animists, and people without belief in a supreme being. At the extremes are the very rich and the very poor, with most people falling in between. The country supports Republicans, Democrats, independents, socialists, communists, libertarians, and followers of other political persuasions. It has doctors, lawyers, beggars, thieves, and persons employed in thousands of other occupations. Some people live in the cities and others in the country or rural areas.

Source: *Communicating with Americans*, by Donald W. Klopf and Myung-seok Park (Seoul, Korea: Han Shin Publishing, 1994). The population figures were updated to current figures in this version.

"American" Means...

Why do we call ourselves Americans when America is the name of a continent and not a country? Is it because we think we're the only ones who count? Or is it because we are the only nation in the world whose official name includes the word "America?" Every other nation in the continent, from Canada to Argentina, has a specific name that doesn't include the word.
— *B.E. Bobb, Emeritus Professor, Washington State University*

American — of, relating to, or characteristic of the United States or its inhabitants; a native or citizen of the United States.
— *Reader's Digest — Oxford Complete Wordfinder* (Pleasantville, NY: Reader's Digest Association, 1996)

homes, elderly patients are apt to be the recipients of "baby talk," like mother to infant. To be assured that children, adolescents, and elderly people understand college student speakers, the college students say more and explain more carefully when speaking to them than to young and middle-aged adults.[10]

The significant point is that membership in a microculture introduces unique forms of communicative behavior. Men speak differently than women; doctors use terminology distinctive to their profession, as do lawyers, bankers, and others. A Milwaukee resident speaks with a slightly different accent than a Bostonian. Membership in a microculture creates identifiable speech patterns.

Age

Each person who lives long enough will pass, without choice, from infancy, through childhood, then adolescence, adulthood, and, eventually, older adulthood. Throughout life, we feel, think, perceive, and behave in part according to

own. Most have certain commonalities or values that bind them together, and at the same time they observe the norms of the macroculture.

The eight microcultures are:[9]

age

gender/sex

ethnic or national origin

religion

class/occupation

geographic region

urban/suburban/rural location

exceptionality

Figure 3.1 illustrates these eight microcultures in relation to the macroculture that embraces them into a whole.

Each microculture presents its own unique set of communication idiosyncrasies. With age, many people undergo changes in identity that affect communication, message production, and perception. Older people are often discriminated against by younger individuals. In nursing

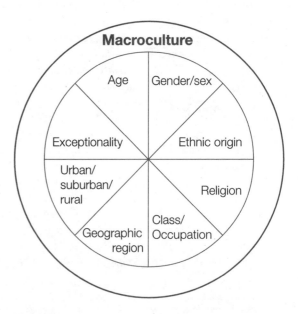

FIGURE 3.1 Dominant Macroculture and Subordinate Microcultures

the age group to which we belong. In his *Passionate Pilgrim*, Shakespeare scored several telling points about these stages:

> *Crabbed age and youth cannot live*
> *together: Youth is full of pleasance, age*
> *is full of care. . . . Age, I do abhor thee,*
> *youth, I do adore thee.*

With age, many people go through changes in identity. If a person's primary definition of a self-concept was a career and that person retires, that person's self-concept and self-esteem change, and changes in self-concept affect message production and perception.[11] When a mother who was completely involved in rearing her children sees them grow up and leave, her communication patterns change with her change in role and accompanying self-esteem. Shakespeare's "crabbed" age may take over as this mother seeks new outlets for her interaction needs.

Difficulties arise in communication between people of different ages. The so-called generation gap is more often a communication gap. Older people have different time perceptions than younger people, and differences in mobility. Older people are affected by health concerns such as hearing or vision impairment. And age also influences our perceptions. The older we get, the richer is our perspective for perceiving life and people. A 60 year-old has more wealth of experience than a 20-year-old to draw upon.[12]

> *During the Great Depression, I*
> *attended elementary school. My father*
> *had his own business and made enough*
> *to feed my brothers and me. He'd buy a*
> *case of soda for 60 cents — a dozen*
> *good-size bottles. Today my son thinks*
> *nothing of laying out 75 cents for one*
> *can of soda. I think that's outrageous.*
> *Our bases of comparison differ; I have*
> *a broader perspective than my son has*
> *on prices.*

As we get older, we express negative attitudes less frequently than we did when we were younger, unless the issue is extremely important.

If the issue is significant, the elders tend to have more heated, intense arguments with others than do younger people.[13]

Reference to age varies across cultures. In many Latin American as well as Arab societies, the aged are venerated and major family decisions are deferred to them. In European and American cultures, the opposite seems true. Youth is idolized and people are admired for remaining youthful. Liposuction removes excess fat on body parts to make men and women more youthful. Protruding bellies, sagging jowls, and flabby calves can be sculpted to make people look young again. In the United States, the elderly often are segregated from the youth by being placed in old-age homes or "golden-age" communities.[14]

Gender/Sex

Sex differences are biological differences between males and females: Only men can impregnate, and only women can menstruate, gestate, and lactate. Gender differences concern learned behavior associated culturally with being a man or a woman. Gender role definitions are flexible. A man can adopt female behavior and a woman, male behavior, as defined by a given culture.[15]

Whether we are a male or a female biologically elicits different responses at birth from our parents and society. Boy babies are described as big and strong and girls as cute and pretty. Hospital nametags often are coded blue or pink to designate the newborn's sex, and gifts arrive in blue or pink wrapping paper for the same reason. Clothes and toys differ for each sex. In short, babies receive different treatment depending upon their sex. Boys and girls begin life separated into distinct microcultures.[16]

Some communication scholars advance the idea that talk that takes place between men and women is intercultural communication. Actually, it more accurately can be called microcultural interaction. A boy and a girl growing up in the same house as members of the same macro culture still are growing up in a different world of words.[17]

As they mature, the communication behavior continues to contrast. Boys and girls speak differently. Boys use fewer words to describe colors, for example, and their vocabulary contains more male-related things. Girls typically have a larger vocabulary to describe the things that interest them. Girls tend to use more adjectives, such as "adorable," "darling," "charming," "sweet," and "lovely." Males like to tell jokes more than females do.[18] Other differences are described in Chapter 9.

Ethnic and National Origin

Ethnicity refers to a system of social classification. It has little relationship to skin color, genetically transmitted physical characteristics, or common descent. The system, instead, is based on various factors — nationality, religion, language, and ancestral heritage, among them. Those of Irish, British, Norwegian, or Spanish origin, for example, are called an ethnic group, not a race. Ethnicity encourages common bonds that affect communication patterns.[19]

Most Americans are recent immigrants or have ancestors who were immigrants. The United States is populated by about 276 different ethnic groups, including hundreds of American Indian groups, which in totality make up less than 1 percent of the total population. So just about all Americans can trace their ancestry to one or more nations that now or at some time existed in the world. Thus, people from all over the globe joined American Indians in populating America, and brought with them different cultural and communication experiences.[20]

Members of an ethnic group feel themselves tied together by a common history, values, and

Miscommunication can be anticipated if an American and an Ashanti warrior from Ghana interact. Physical appearance, language, religion, social attitudes, and self-concept will differ. Disagreements are to be expected.

behaviors. They tend to regard their own cultural traits as natural, correct, and superior to those of other ethnic groups. Other groups often are thought of as odd, amusing, inferior, or immoral. The ethnic group encourages group cohesiveness and helps sustain and enhance the ethnic identity of its members. It establishes the social networks and communicative patterns that optimize the group's position in society.

Because marriage across ethnic lines is common, children of these marriages may have a heritage of several ethnic groups. One university professor writes of her *hapa* background — *hapa* being a Hawaiian term that designates someone of Asian or Pacific Island origin mixed with European heritage.[21] Her biological parents represent Japanese, Mexican, Spanish, and Indian backgrounds. As a young girl, she was adopted by a family of Japanese, Lebanese, German, Greek, and Italian extraction. She enjoys her *hapa* status, she relates, because it allows her to speak with people of many cultures.[22] Like many other people, she holds membership in a number of ethnic microcultures.

By the year 2050, the representative face of America no longer will be mainly that of people of European heritage. Multiracial births are increasing, as is the immigration of people of color.[23] The dominant macroculture no longer will be Anglo-Saxon, although its political and social influences probably will remain strong. Given no new exclusionary legislation, by the year 2050, the population of U.S. whites will decrease to 60 percent, while Asians will increase to 16 percent, Hispanics will triple their numbers to 19.2 percent and blacks will increase their 12 percent only slightly.[24]

Most immigrants are assimilated completely into the macroculture and think of themselves only as Americans. One third-generation American of German heritage states the situation like this:

Both sets of my grandparents emigrated to America from Germany. I'm not sure why — the political situation in the early 20th century or economic condition, neither of which was good in Germany at the time. Their children — my parents, aunts and uncles — thought of themselves only as Americans. The German culture never entered into our life, although Milwaukee, where we lived, had lots of German cultural activities and clubs. My grandparents spoke English and lived as Americans, being individualistic and desiring to be free in all ways.

Other immigrants maintained cultural ties with the country from which their family emigrated. They view themselves as "hyphenated Americans": German-Americans, Korean-Americans, Polish-Americans, Japanese-Americans. Newcomers to the United States likely are still manifesting the culture and language of their nation of origin, yet trying to learn American ways.

In spite of the diverse traditions in the United States, the white Anglo-Saxon Protestant macroculture presently remains the norm, the standard, and the referent by which we define our social mainstream and identify our typical citizen. Yet, other cultural traditions are present — the ethnic microcultures represented by people from around the globe who live in this country.

Religion

Religion is clearly an important part of the lives of many people. Religion influences the way people think, perceive, and behave. Their communication reflects their religious perspective, not only in their language but their demeanor as well. For millions, religion constitutes an essential microculture and the forces of religious groups are far from dormant.

They can influence the curriculum in local school systems, what teachers are hired and fired, and what textbooks are used. They have an impact on who is elected to public office and legislation that is enacted. They can shut down objectionable businesses and determine the ethical practices followed. They can specify what clothing styles are acceptable and what television programs are unacceptable. Religion is discussed more fully in Chapter 7.

Class

To many Americans, the United States is a model of egalitarianism, a highly regarded and uniquely American value. In reality, true equality is elusive. Limitations on achievement often have less to do with willingness to work or the quality of work than socially defined positions based on unequal access to wealth, power and prestige, or class.[25]

Of the many systems of determining class, one stems from vocation and earnings. This system groups Americans into four social classes: underclass, working class, middle class, and upper class.[26] Class becomes an important microculture in the American macroculture.

1. The *underclass* consists of the passive poor (long-term welfare recipients), the hostile (street criminals who often are school dropouts and drug addicts), the hustlers (who live in an underground economy), and the traumatized (drunks, drifters, and homeless).

2. The *working class* engages in manual work for which remuneration varies widely depending upon the skill required. Members of this group include craft workers, transport equipment operatives, non-farm and farm laborers, and service workers. About 45 percent of the population make up this group.

3. The *middle class* consists of nonmanual or white-collar workers and professionals, managers, and administrators. They are slightly better off economically than the working class.

4. The *upper class* is composed of top-level administrators and professionals and the families and individuals who control great inherited wealth.

Americans exhibit and express less concern about class consciousness than their European counterparts do, yet a person's socioeconomic level has a dramatic impact on how that person lives and speaks. Although Americans do not identify themselves by class, they carry out most of their relationships within the same class. Their talk centers on the needs and interests typical of their class. Even though most Americans desire an opportunity for upward mobility, they tend to remain in the class to which they were born.

Geographic Region

Where we live has an impact on how we think, perceive, behave, and communicate. What we eat, how we dress, and what we do are among the social factors that vary from region to region in the United States. A resident of Hawaii likely will eat more rice and fish, dress more comfortably, and do more outdoor things than a resident of Minneapolis. The weather has a bearing, and so, too, does the ethnic makeup of each city. The speaking style varies also, in terms of delivery rate, warmth and openness, animation, eye contact, perceived abruptness, and so on. Examples of regional speech are given in Chapter 9. These regional variations can affect attitudes and behavior toward people who do not communicate in the same way.

Urban/Suburban/Rural Location

The behavioral norms of urban, suburban, and rural life are different from one another. The *urban* microculture is characterized by strong upward mobility and an emphasis on the symbols of success such as new cars, comfortable homes, and stylish clothes. We find also much crime and less personal territory in which to play and live. *Suburbanites* have more personal territory and less crime and seem to have a strong need for community integration. Church attendance is higher than in the cities. *Rural* microcultures stress personal knowledge, practicality, and simplicity. "Doing" skills are valued over "being," probably because fewer plumbers, carpenters, auto mechanics, doctors, and other technicians are within close proximity. Rural dwellers often are on their own when the time comes to make repairs to household and personal things.

Exceptionality

A significant segment of the U.S. population falls into the microculture of exceptionality. This microculture ranges from individuals with disabilities to those who are extremely gifted and talented. Among people with disabilities are those with disease, injury, or birth defects, and the specially gifted have high intelligence or other gifts, such as in art, music, and athletic ability. Mensa, an international organization restricts membership to an IQ in the top 2 percent of a country.

Members of the exceptional microculture are in it not by choice but because they are considered "different." They often are prevented from full participation in society because of the insensitivity, apathy, and prejudice of the majority, which by definition is not exceptional.

 ## Membership in More Than One Microculture

Most people belong to several microcultures, all of which influence their lives to some extent. Figure 3.2 depicts the degrees of difference. The man is a 19-year-old university student of working-class parentage whose ethnic background is Filipino. He lives in Los Angeles. A Catholic, religion plays a predominant role in his life and has a dominant impact on his thinking. He is inclined toward the priesthood. Although other microculture memberships carry meaning for him, they do so to a lesser extent.

The woman is 23 years old, Protestant, middle-class, and of German-American parentage.

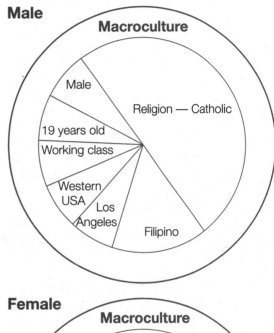

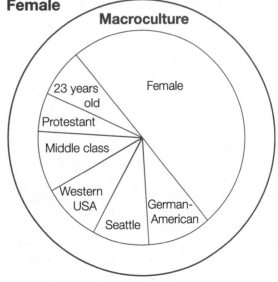

FIGURE 3.2 Relative Importance of Microcultures in the Lives of a Male and a Female

She lives in Seattle. The gender-sex microculture holds her interest, and she is active in women's rights groups. The other microcultures are less salient, but they all influence her life, helping to define and determine her identity.

Like the man and woman in the figure, each person belongs to a unique set of microcultures in a constantly changing environment. Each of us may participate in several different microcultures each day, week, and year. They provide us with an answer to the question, "Who am I?" We know that the 19-year-old in our illustration is a young Filipino man living in Los Angeles and attending university classes with the intention of becoming a Catholic priest. Examining his microcultural background — age, gender/sex, class, location, ethnicity, and religion — we can understand more fully his values, attitudes, and beliefs as they emerge in conversations. We become aware of his cultural identity.

Cultural identity is part of an individual's personality and a fundamental symbol of the person's existence. It is a coherent concept of self that depends upon stability of values along with a sense of wholeness and integration stemming from the culture in which the individual lives.

Multiculturalism

Multiculturalism is the recognition that several different cultures can exist in the same environment and benefit each other.[27] American educator Peter Adler humanizes multiculturalism, contending that the concept suggests people whose identifications and loyalties transcend the boundaries of nationalism and whose commitments are pinned to a larger vision of the global community.[28]

The Association of College Unions broadens the meaning of multiculturalism, reasoning that it is more than communication between people from diverse races and nationalities. Multiculturalism takes into account every conceivable human grouping that departs from the norm and develops a separate identity as well as a normative one. In this association's judgment, each person is of many cultures simultaneously. He or she has a sexual identity, a racial identity, a religious identity, a class identity, several geographic identities, and an age identity.[29]

The anthropologist William Goodenough corroborates the association's interpretation of multiculturalism. He argues that every person belongs to many cultures concurrently and underlines his argument by recognizing multiculturalism as the *normal human experience*. Everyone participates in more than one cultural group. To him, sex, age, religion, ethnicity, class, geographic region, and exceptionality represent cultural groups.[30]

The association warns that the human tendency to be relatively unconscious of other cultures is dysfunctional, resulting from ignorance and the failure to recognize their existence.[31] Fortunately, most students are aware of differences in communication patterns among the microcultures and are prepared to adapt their talk accordingly. If not, they can become more sensitive to the differences.

A heterosexual college teacher developed a friendship with a homosexual instructor and learned the language skills needed to communicate freely with the lesbian woman. She learned, for example, a communication move, sanitizing, in which a homosexual uses a noun or pronoun to reflect either gender neutrality or a heterosexual connotation.

Discussing what she did on a weekend, the lesbian might say to a co-worker, "My friend and I went dancing" or even, "My boyfriend and I went dancing," when in reality she had gone out with her lesbian girlfriend. She pretended, through her sanitizing, to be like people in mainstream society. The college teacher said she became more sensitive and enlightened through her friendship with the lesbian, thereby developing a proficiency in communicating with people of the lesbian's sexual microculture. The teacher came to be multicultural through her relationship.[32]

Interacting Across Cultures

While enjoying hot drinks in front of the fireplace of a Marburg, Germany home, the Finn Jaakko, the German Lothar, and the American Mariko discussed plans for a forthcoming convention in Frankfurt. The conversation was intercultural, the kind of talk that takes place whenever and wherever people belonging to different culture groups come into contact.

Intercultural communication is becoming common throughout the world as people travel for business and pleasure. Its growth stirs interest among communication scholars, and many approaches are suggested for researchers to study.[33] Although the terminology differs in the various definitions, the meaning essentially is that intercultural communication is *the interchange between persons of different cultures*. It occurs when a person (or persons) from one culture talks to a person (or persons) from another.[34]

When we interact with people who have different mindsets and ways of looking at and perceiving the world, we are communicating interculturally.[35] It need not take place solely at an international gathering. Walking along the main street in most cities, we will encounter people from other cultures with whom we may interact. Even the next door neighbor may provide that experience.

A Model of Intercultural Communication

We might think of intercultural communication as communication to which cultural distinctions are added. Adding the concept of culture to Figure 2.1 in Chapter 2, we have the depiction in Figure 3.3, the model of intercultural communication.

In this representation Person A encodes a message for Person B, based on A's cultural background. The shaded arrow carries that message. Person B receives the message and decodes it in keeping with B's cultural background. Thus, the message undergoes a transformation as it is decoded, indicated by the partial shading in the decoding process in Person B. What has happened is an alteration in the meaning of A's message because of the cultural differences between the speaker and the listener. The message now reflects what B *thinks* A meant. The partially shaded feedback signifies B's interpretation of A's meaning. Chances are great that A's meaning will not be the same as B's interpretation.

Just how much influence culture has on an intercultural exchange depends upon the similarity of cultures. The more the cultures are alike, the less influence the culture will have; the less they are alike, the more the cultural influence.

The Impact of Culture

Figure 3.4 portrays some effects of cultural differences. The first pairing depicts minimal differences as members of two microcultures talk. Elderly people have much in common with teenagers, both being members of the same macroculture and holding some of the same values, beliefs, and attitudes of that macroculture. An elderly person will have more and varied

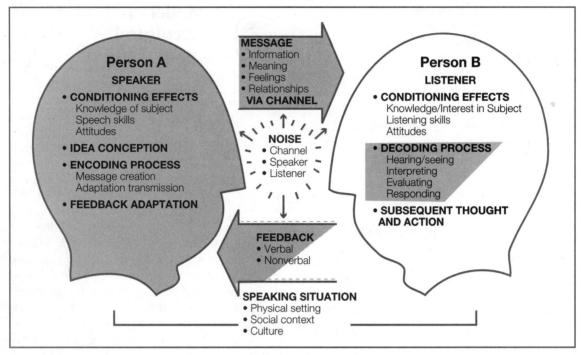

FIGURE 3.3   Model of Intercultural Speech Process

experiences than a teenager to draw on, so the experiential referents of the two will differ, causing some misunderstandings as they interact. The disparity is minor, however, so the overlap shown in the figure is great.

Pairing B shows a U.S. citizen speaking to a resident of Germany. The two communicators are similar in several ways. If the American is a white Anglo-Saxon, the American and German will have a close physical resemblance. The English language is partially derived from German and its ancestor languages. The roots of both American and German philosophies lie in Ancient Greece. Both share a Christian religious background.

The white Anglo-Saxon American and German will differ in several ways, though. The German family tends to be strongly patriarchal and authoritarian, whereas the American family tends toward egalitarianism. The socialization of German children is strict, rigid, and peremptory. American culture is much more permissive in childrearing. Germans hold manliness in high esteem. Although Americans worry that their children will become sissies, they channel their children's drive into socially approved activities, not the literal fisticuffs of the Germans.[36]

In Pairing C a member of the West is conferring with someone from the East. This pairing has little overlap, indicating that the differences are many. An Anglo-Saxon American conversing with a Japanese will differ in physical appearance, language, philosophy, religion, social attitudes, heritage, and concept of self. This makes the potential for miscommunication great. Disagreements can be expected.

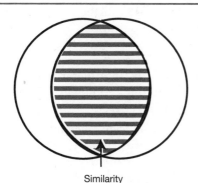

Similarity

A. Subculture communication between elder and teenager

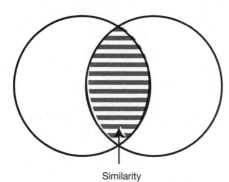

Similarity

B. Intercultural communication between American and German

Similarity

C. Intercultural communication between American and Japanese

FIGURE 3.4 Relative Impact of Culture on Communication

Understa...

*Communicators h...
before attempting...
cultures. Most people...
in their own daily affairs tr...
oblivious to the standards or pri...
behavior of their own culture. These
standards guide them in their own daily
activities, in their relations with others, in
their worldview, and in their attitudes
toward strangers.*

*To function well in a diverse society,
cultural awareness of self and of others is
a prerequisite to handling and managing
relationships with members of other cultures.
Knowledge of why people are the way they
are is essential to effective intercultural
communication.*

Source: *Intercultural Communication: Roots and
Routes*, by C. Calloway-Thomas, P.J. Cooper, and C.
Blake (Boston: Allyn and Bacon, 1999), p. 42.

 ## Assumptions About Intercultural Communication

Mindfulness is a vital constituent in the intercultural communication process.[37] We must be aware of our behavior and that of our fellow communicators when interacting across cultures. Instead of thinking and behaving in our habitual manner when speaking to others in our culture, we must keep in our consciousness the realization that when speaking interculturally, the situation is different; it is not ordinary. One of the first assumptions we must make when speaking with someone from another culture is that differences can be expected. And several additional assumptions underlie intercultural talk.

...nces to be Expected

...n people from different cultures interact, we ...uld expect variations in the way people ...ink, act, and speak. People from divergent cultures have dissimilar speech patterns, values, thought structures, and conduct in interpersonal relationships. These variations are what make intercultural talk challenging, exciting, and interesting. Taking into account these differences, we need to be mindful, realizing that intercultural communication will depart from normal, within-culture speech.

Relational Communication

A second assumption about intercultural communication is that intercultural talk is relational. The relationships we have with people from other cultures can determine how a message will

A Greek Puzzle

You are in Athens and need to change some dollars into drachmae. You enter a store and show a 20-dollar bill to the cashier. She jerks her head up and down as if (in your opinion) to say "okay." You hand her the 20. She looks puzzled and hands the money back.

_____a. You figure she doesn't like Americans, give her a dirty look, and leave.

_____b. You give her the 20-dollar bill again and add 50 cents for a tip.

_____c. You find an English-speaking Greek to help you out of your dilemma.

Answers on page 243.

be interpreted. Recall the two sets of relationships in communication — symmetrical and complementary. Knowing the relationship between communicators is essential in communicating effectively. In a hierarchical society like Japan, for example, knowing the status of a stranger is imperative.

On every occasion when Japanese businessmen are meeting for the first time, they immediately exchange business cards. The business card serves a number of useful functions. It provides a record of the person's name, job title, company name, address, telephone number, and fax number. It also clarifies the status relationship between the people meeting for the first time. The job title, company affiliation, and seniority in age actually dictate the language usage and the manner of speaking. For example, a younger sales person meeting an older purchasing manager speaks in very formal language and acts very politely.[38]

Communication Style

A third assumption relates to the influence of our personal speaking style. Each person has a distinct way of speaking, of uttering the words that make up his or her message. The way a person does this is the person's means or vehicle of communication. Included are speaking cues and tendencies such as posture, gestures, facial expression, voice inflection, sequence of ideas, and rhythm of the speech. These cues and tendencies constitute the communicator's style.[39]

A person's style becomes an instinctive part of his or her communicative behavior. Through it, close acquaintances can identify a person. Most of us can name acquaintances who represent disparate styles. Some have friendly, open, and attentive communication styles. Others are shy, uptight, and jittery. Through their style, some people appear confident, dominant, and relaxed. All sorts of styles are possible. In intercultural communication situations a person's style can affect the reactions of those with whom he or she talks. A confident, assertive U. S. woman interacting with most Asian men will have to "tone it down" if she does not want to inhibit the men of that culture. Asian women tend to be shy and nonassertive.[40]

> Two female representatives of an American educational association toured Asian cities seeking a site for an international convention. They met with their male hosts in Seoul, Tokyo, Kyoto, Osaka, and Sapporo with a list of conditions they wanted to be met. They aggressively sought what they were after, not realizing that they were antagonizing their Asian hosts, who react politely but negatively to dominant women. Any questions the males asked were responded to in a confrontative style, and issues most often ended up being debated. The American requests never were accepted. The American and Asian styles clashed.

In Germany, a smiling American stranger probably will be received poorly. Smiles are a sign of friendship. If the German does not know the smiling American, why should he or she smile back? Our personal style of communication should be adjusted to meet situational demands.

Reducing Uncertainty

A fourth assumption concerns how we act when meeting a stranger for the first time. In our first contact, we are apt to be uncertain. We do not know how the stranger feels about us, and vice versa. Both parties are likely to feel uncomfortable until the uncertainty is reduced.

When communicating with strangers in our own culture, we have learned ways of reducing the ambiguities that arise at a first meeting. We know what to say by way of greeting, and we have learned guidelines to follow as the conversation progresses. With strangers from another culture, reducing uncertainty takes on more meaning. We are not sure of the "ground rules" and have few models to help us through the first awkward moments. We work much harder to diminish vagueness with foreign strangers than with people of our own culture.

People from individualistic cultures such as the United States search for similarities between themselves and the foreign strangers. They are interested in the stranger's likes and dislikes to compare with their own, giving them a basis for further conversation. In contrast, people from collectivistic cultures such as those in Asia will search for group similarities, attempting to find out what groups the others belong to and what activities the groups engage in.[41]

Friendly Misunderstandings

A fifth assumption is that misunderstandings are common in intercultural communication. When persons from dissimilar cultures meet, their behavior and manners will reflect what their own culture deems appropriate. They observe the norms practiced in their own culture. Unfortunately, their norms may not exemplify the behaviors considered proper in the other culture. New Zealand Maoris may greet friends by rubbing noses. Greeting a foreign stranger in that manner could create a misunderstanding.

Intracultural Variations

The sixth assumption is that the normative behavior of a culture typifies the behavior of all the culture's members. What is central to a culture is typical of the culture's entire membership. Nothing is farther from the truth. What is central to any culture is variation.[42] Diversity characterizes a culture. Not everyone will conform to the norms. Some minority, a peripheral, secondary, or fringe group, will behave differently.

Related Concepts

The study of culture and communication interests scholars in a number of academic disciplines — anthropology, psychology, sociology, ethnology, to name a few. These professions use many terms to describe how communication and culture converge. Among them are *intracultural*, *cross-cultural*, *international*, *interracial*, and *interethnic*. To avoid confusion in their application, we review their meanings as they pertain to our focus here.

Intracultural Communication

Intra is a prefix meaning within, inside, or in. Intracultural communication, therefore, refers to communication within a culture, to communication between members of the same culture. Two Mexicans speaking together are engaged in intracultural communication.

Inter is a prefix meaning between. Intercultural communication occurs between members of different cultures. A Canadian speaking to a Mexican is communicating interculturally.

Cross-Cultural Communication

Although "cross-cultural" and "intercultural" are used synonymously, the two terms carry different meanings. "Cross-cultural" is proper when several phenomena are compared across cultures. Comparing communication apprehension in Australia and the United States is a cross-cultural study. A behavioral phenomenon, apprehension, is being compared across two different cultures. If the communication style of Malaysians and Vietnamese are compared, the study, likewise, is cross-cultural. It is a study of communication practices across several cultures.

International Communication

Narrower in scope, international communication concerns communication between official representatives of nations and is most likely political in nature. Taking place on governmental levels, talks between leaders of nations fall into this category. A U.S. President meeting with a British Prime Minister illustrates this type of talk, as do meetings between lesser ranking officials such as the U.S. Treasury Secretary meeting with Switzerland's Finance Minister.

Interethnic Communication

The talk between members of different ethnic groups is interethnic. An ethnic group consists of people with the same national and geographic origin. Group members or their ancestors were born and reared in the country of origin and share a common history, attitudes, values, and behaviors. A great deal of talk in the United States can be classed as interethnic.

The interethnic classification is not useful, however, as few Americans perceive their communication as following ethnic lines. Most Americans are assimilated in the American culture and do not consider ethnic origins in their communication practices.

Interracial Communication

Communication that crosses racial lines is interracial — race being defined as a group whose members share a certain set of inborn physical characteristics such as hair texture, skin color, and conspicuous physical features.[43] Talk between blacks and whites is often called interracial.

The usefulness of the term *race* to describe a group of people is limited. Race is a social construction, an attempt to assign meaning to physical differences. Race is biologically meaningless, because biological variations blend from one racial category to another. [44]

Chapter Review

A macroculture is a universal or national culture. In the United States the macroculture is Anglo-Saxon, originating in the political and social units of Western European tradition.

Microcultures exist within the framework of the macroculture. They share the political and social institutions of the macroculture, but in addition they have their own distinctive features.

Eight general classes of microcultures include age, sex/gender, ethnic or national origin, religion, class, geographic region, urban/suburban/rural location, and exceptionality.

Most Americans are members of several microcultures, and these heavily influence their thinking, perceptions, and behavior. In turn, these affect their communicative ability.

Some people master the knowledge and develop the ability to communicate effectively with people of several cultures that are not their own. These people can be considered multicultural.

In the minds of some experts, we all are multicultural. We participate in more than one microculture, and because we do so, we become proficient communicators in each of the microcultures.

Intercultural communication is the communication between people of different cultures. It occurs when individuals from one culture talk to individuals from another or several other cultures.

The intercultural communication process incorporates the characteristics of the interpersonal communication process with an emphasis on culture.

In an intercultural communication situation, the more the cultures are alike, the less impact culture will have. The more they differ, the greater will be the impact of culture.

The cultural emphasis assumes that:

1. Differences in communication practices are to be expected.

2. Relational communication will be a major factor in the communicative interaction.

3. A person's speaking style may have to be adapted to the circumstances of the intercultural encounter.

(Continued)

Chapter Review continued

4. Reducing uncertainty will be a major factor in an intercultural transaction.

5. Misunderstandings are common in intercultural communication.

6. A culture's speaking norms are not necessarily observed by all members of a culture. Variations from the norm should be expected.

 Terms related to intercultural communication carrying different meanings include:

1. Intracultural communication — communication between members of the same culture.

2. Cross-cultural communication — the study of communication phenomena across several cultures.

3. International communication — communication between official representatives of nations, usually political in nature.

4. Interethnic communication — communication between several members of different ethnic groups.

5. Interracial communication — communication between several members of two or more races.

Think About This...

1 Distinguish between microculture, co-culture, culture within a culture, and subculture.

2 What qualities are associated with the microcultures of the elderly, ethnicity, religion, location?

3 The United States is supposed to be classless. Do we or don't we have classes? If so, how are they identified? Who makes them up?

4 Intercultural communication is said to take place between people of different cultures. If so, wouldn't talk between a teenager and an older person be intercultural? Between a man and woman? If so, why? If not, why not?

5 Differentiate intercultural, cross-cultural, international, interethnic, and interracial communication.

PART TWO

COMPONENTS OF THE INTERCULTURAL COMMUNICATION PROCESS

4 Perceptual Influences on Intercultural Communication

T he sensory world incorporates an almost infinite number of discrete impulses in ever-changing patterns. Vision alone confronts the human eye with 7,500,000 distinguishable colors. When we add the other dimensions of seeing, such as the perception of form, lightness, and space, our visual world becomes an array of bewildering stimulation. Hearing can provide roughly 340,000 discrete tones. Add to these smell, taste, kinesthesis, touch, pain, and other sensations, and we have a wealth of perceptual sensation beyond our understanding.

Unfortunately, perceptual stimulation does not necessarily predict how we will react to what we perceive, and what we perceive may not be a true picture of the external world. We perceive only what we expect to sense. Our expectations endow what we sense with meaning, making extensions of ourselves the objects, persons, and actions we perceive.

The meanings we attach to our sensations of the external world are learned. We learn the meanings from various sources, among them our parents, relatives, friends, teachers, and acquaintances. One lesson we learn — categorization — helps us to reduce the overwhelming complexity of the sensory world into manageable proportions. We place what we perceive into categories or classes. We learn, for example, to deal with the 7,500,000 colors by assigning them to categories, such as red, blue, green, brown, yellow, and so on.

Our culture determined the categories into which we put the colors. Likewise, our culture defined the other categories to which we assign the things we perceive, and we learn to respond to them as our culture dictates. What we perceive is culture-bound.

Photo by Debbie Whittig

What we say about what we sense, therefore, is culturally based. Our communication reflects our cultural heritage. Because that is so, intercultural theorists argue that one way to understand intercultural communication is to know a culture's influence on perception. Put another way, the key to understanding intercultural communication is perception and its cultural base. Each culture looks at the sensory world somewhat differently, and therein lie the clues to effective communication with people from other cultures. People *see* the world differently.

 # Perception Defined

Perception is one of the oldest subjects of speculation and research in the study of life, and it has a correspondingly long history of theory and fact. The concept has a plethora of definitions, most of which are similar in meaning. For our use, perception is *the process by which people select, organize, and interpret sensory stimulation into a meaningful and coherent picture of the world.*[1]

From the definition, we construe that perception is the process by which we become aware of objects and events in the external world through our senses. We attach meaning to the things we sense. The senses usually are thought of as seeing, hearing, feeling, tasting, and smelling. These senses fit one of three classes:

1. *The major distance senses* — seeing and hearing.
2. *The skin senses* — touch, warmth, cold, pain, and the closely related chemical senses of taste and smell.
3. *The deep senses* — position and motion of muscles and joints (kinesthesis), the senses of equilibrium, and the senses of the internal organs.[2]

Under the typical conditions of everyday life, several senses, or *receptors,* as they frequently are termed, are simultaneously activated by a stimulus. We not only see the stimulus object but also hear and maybe even smell it at the same time. Watching a cook at work, we see him take pieces of chicken out of the batter and toss them on the grill, and co-instantaneously we hear them sizzle and smell the aroma from cooking.

Even though only one receptor is involved — sight, for example — there is more to the process of sensing. Seeing the stimulus sets off a complicated pattern of neural events that recall former stimulation. The sight of chicken frying may remind us of the sizzle and smell even though we cannot hear or smell it cooking. We recollect the sound and odor in spite of their absence.

 # The Perception Process

An almost endless number of distinct impulses in constantly changing patterns comprise the sensory world. But the specific, objective, and physical data in the external environment usually do not correspond with our perceptions. The data interact with certain cultural predispositions and states we already hold, forming our perceptions. The nature of our perceptions, as a consequence, depends upon the physical stimuli from the environment and upon our learned reactions. This sets in motion the perceptual process, which our definition says involves three steps: selection, organization, and interpretation.

Selection

The process begins when the observer selects what aspects of the environment will be perceived. Of all the possible stimuli capable of being perceived, only a small portion becomes part of the actual act of perceiving, and that portion is not a random sample. As observers, we engage in *selective exposure*; we look at some things, ignore others, and turn away from still others. Of those to which we expose ourselves, only a few reach awareness; *selective awareness* operates.

Think for a moment about what you are doing right now. You are aware you are reading. Other objects, however, intrude upon your field of vision, above, below, and to the sides of the book, and you are not aware of them — at least not until now, when they were just called to your attention. Now perhaps you have become aware of them, even though they were there all the while you were reading. The other senses also may have been registering noises, smells, and pressures on the skin as you read. Selective awareness prevented them from ever reaching your attention.

Why we select what we select depends upon three factors: differential intensity, past experiences, and motivation.

1. *Differential intensity or quality.* An *italicized* word or the use of **boldfaced type** in this book are examples. In a quiet environment a loud explosion will capture our attention. The instructor can get our attention if she stops speaking suddenly and silence descends on the room. We look up wondering what happened.

2. *Past experience.* We perceive what is familiar to us, what we like or dislike, and what is novel. Even identical twins born into and reared in the same family will not have identical perceptions of the world. Their experiences will be dissimilar.[3] Perhaps one had chicken pox and the other did not. Perhaps one developed a fondness for cooked cereal and the other preferred his from a box. Perhaps a dog bit one and not the other. Whatever the specifics, there is no question that they will share similar experiences. But the twins also will have dissimilar experiences. Therefore, they will grow up not being identical. Because that is so, they will not view the world similarly.

3. *Motivation.* We perceive the things we need and want, and the stronger the need, the more we will ignore the irrelevant. If we are extremely hungry and thirsty, we will seek food and drink and tend to disregard everything else around us. We are motivated to act because of our need to satisfy our desire for food and drink. Needs activate our behavior. We describe needs more fully later in this chapter.

Organization

The second stage in the perception process, organization, refers to the human need to place what we perceive into a whole to which the thing perceived seems to belong. To accomplish this, we regard each stimulus in the context of the other stimuli we have selected. We try to form meaningful patterns out of what we select, and we do so in various ways, three of which we consider next: figure and ground, grouping, and closure.

Figure and Ground

In the figure and ground organizational pattern, the figure stands out from the ground. It is well-defined, in a definite location, solid, and in front of the ground. The ground appears shapeless, indefinite, and continuous behind the figure. What we focus on in our environment stands out from the rest.

The intercultural implications of figure on ground are illustrated by a World War II account of blacks in Europe. American black soldiers sometimes complained that American white soldiers had spread anti-black propaganda to the natives. They believed this because in Europe people stared at them and regarded them strangely. The truth was that few White Europeans had seen blacks before and, hence, observed them carefully. To the Europeans, the blacks were figures who stood out from the white soldiers (the ground) who looked so much like Europeans.

Grouping

We group the stimuli we perceive automatically according to proximity, similarity, and continuity. We put together stimuli that are near each other, that are alike, and that form an unbroken, continuous whole. We do the same with other elements that we believe to be comparable or belong to the same category.

This natural, human tendency sometimes can lead to misunderstandings. When we group, we often fail to discriminate. We recognize only the similarities and overlook important differences. This failure is called *indiscrimination;* our categories harden.

Closure

We organize what we perceive into wholes — called closure. If a stimulus pattern is incomplete, we tend to unconsciously fill in the missing elements. We turn a partial circle into a full circle, continue a broken line as a full line, and form two unjoined right angles into a box.

When we listen to a person talk, we might become an "out loud closer." If the person pauses longer than what seems appropriate, we supply the rest of the sentence, closing out the person's statement for him or her. If our closure is inaccurate, the person probably will correct us, supplying the words he or she had planned to utter. Someone from another culture, however, may not correct an incorrect closure, perhaps deeming it to be impolite. A misunderstanding could result.

Figure/ground, grouping, and closure apply more frequently to complex phenomena. Our simple examples merely illustrate their functioning. For example, we may structure the world into two parts — free and totalitarian — ignoring many other differences between nations and governments. We see those who live near each other or who associate frequently with each other as sharing common beliefs and attitudes. We group people who look alike, exhibit similar mannerisms, or wear comparable clothing, and assume they are more kindred than the likeness assures. Misperceptions result, with communication problems as byproducts.

Interpretation

The third step in the perception process, interpretation, calls for us to attach meaning to what we perceive. When we interpret, we evaluate subjectively what we sense, basing our interpretations on our past experience, our needs and values, and our beliefs about the way things are or should be. Our physical and emotional states bear upon our interpretations, as do our expectations. Our interpretations are not founded solely on the things we sense.

With all of these influences coming to bear upon our interpretations, two individuals, sensing the same stimulus, rarely, if ever, will give it the same meaning. Although both will be exposed to the same stimulus, their interpretations will be quite different.

Recognizing that within our own culture people will view the same stimulus differently, we should not be surprised, when conversing with someone from another culture, that perceptual differences will be the rule rather than the exception. For example, when asked how to distribute a bonus most fairly, people in India probably will perceive the neediest workers as most deserving, whereas Americans want to reward the hardest workers. Koreans and Americans differ in their perceptions of the family. Americans perceive the nuclear family (mother, father, children) as most important, while Koreans stress the extended family (nuclear family plus other relatives). Australians perceive the world as divided into two parts — the rich, capitalistic countries with a European heritage and the rest of the world. New Guinea natives perceive all countries as part of one undivided world.

People perceive as they are taught, and they are taught to perceive in the way that helps them function most effectively in their environment. We can expect culture to have a strong impact on perception. When communicating interculturally, we should anticipate differences — among them disconfirmed expectations, predispositions to behave, and attribution.

Disconfirmed Expectations

We anticipate that something will happen in a certain way because that is the way it happened to us before, or that is the way it happened to people we know, or that is the way it happened in accounts we read. If our expectation is not met in the way we anticipated, our expectation is disconfirmed. The usual result is frustration, upsetting us.

Businesspersons, teachers, military personnel, students, and tourists planning to visit, study, or work in a foreign country do so with expectations about what they are going to do and see. When they arrive, conditions often are not what they had anticipated, and they encounter difficulties. Housing may be unsatisfactory, working conditions might not be as expected, and cultural differences could be pronounced. The expectations are disconfirmed; culture shock sets in.

Predispositions to Behave

Needs, values, beliefs, and attitudes predispose us to behave in certain ways. These behaviors circumscribe how we perceive people. They help us decide what is good or bad, right or wrong, important or unimportant in what we perceive. They weigh heavily on the meanings we assign to the stimuli we sense. In this chapter we deal with needs, and in Chapter 5 with values, beliefs, and attitudes.

Attribution

The process of seeking explanations for the behavior we observe is termed *attribution*. We try to make sense out of others' behavior and, in doing so, we attribute causes to their behavior. Even though we may not really know why a person behaved as he or she did, we nevertheless assign a cause, because this is a natural way of behaving for us. Most of the time, we guess. We are not sure of the facts, so we speculate or imagine about the causes. This could bring us problems.

By understanding another's culture, we can make more accurate attributions about the

Nancy is Attacked

Nancy moved from California to Iran with her husband, an official with an oil company that maintained Iranian offices. Because the area where they had lived was hot and humid, Nancy wore her California-style attire, appearing in cool summer shorts at the local market and shops, and often was seen chatting with local acquaintances in her casual clothes. As Nancy walked to the market one day, a seedy-looking person grabbed her and made lewd and suggestive comments to her. Nancy shook herself free and called the police, upset and shaken.

To what can you attribute the attack?

_____ 1. Nancy smiled and made friendly gestures at the man.

_____ 2. Nancy dressed improperly while walking alone to the market.

_____ 3. Nancy saw the man as a bum and told him off.

_____ 4. Nancy had no business walking alone.

Answers on page 243.

person's behavior. An example is arranged marriages, a practice many Americans disdain.[4] Americans perceive it as antiquated, and believe people who marry should first fall in love. From the perspective of the cultures in which arranged marriages is a custom, however, it makes sense. Parents understand, far better than most young people do, their children and the demands placed upon married adults. Parents, therefore, are best qualified to choose the mate who will be most compatible with their child. Once wed, the couple will learn to love one another; they will grow into love. Understanding the motivations behind the behavior of those from other

Arranged marriages are common in some cultures. In others love prevails, as in Milan, Italy, where this man on bended knee proposes marriage to his intended bride.

cultures improves intercultural understanding and relations.

Other Perceptual Factors

Additional factors bear upon the interpretation stage of perception.

1. *Primacy* (first impression) and *recency* (most recent impression) of a person give us an idea of what the person is like. Then we use whatever information we pick up in our subsequent meetings to confirm our first impressions.

2. *Self-fulfilling prophecies* come about when we make a projection about a person or event and then go about making it come true.

3. *Perceptual accentuation* means that we expect to see what we want to see, magnifying or accentuating that which will satisfy our needs and wants.

4. *Consistency* requires us to maintain balance in our beliefs and attitudes. We expect our friend to like our other friends and dislike our enemies. We expect a person we like to like us, and a person we dislike to dislike us.

5. *Stereotyping* is a tendency most people have to overgeneralize about groups of people, usually false and most likely based on half-truths. A form of attitude, stereotyping is discussed in Chapter 6.

 Perceptual Differences

Two observers may respond very differently to the same perceptual events even though they confront their sense organs equally. The differences may arise for numerous reasons. For one, the two observers do not have the same history of perceptual learning. Differences might arise also because the two did not pay attention to the event in the same way. Among other reasons for differences to surface are physiological and psychological limitations.

Physiological Limitations

We do not perceive all we sense, nor do we necessarily perceive accurately what does come to our attention. Faulty perceptions may be caused by *illusions*, whereby a person accurately detects a stimulus but decodes it improperly. The moon seems larger when it is near the horizon than when it is overhead. The eye detects it accurately, but our interpretation is in error.

Faulty perceptions are caused also by *neurological inhibitions*. When the body's neural networks become overloaded, inhibitions occur, reducing the overload. This results in faulty perceptions. The neural networks act like fuses in an electrical system. When too much current comes in, the fuses blow.

Then, too, the networks sometimes adapt. Under continuous stimulation, they respond less and less to, a given stimulus. Sanitation workers who work around odoriferous materials 8 hours a day become immune to the smell. Their olfactory receptors adapt to the redolent refuse.

Faulty perceptions can come also with characteristics *innate* to ourself. The structure of our ears, for example, determines our ability to discriminate between vocal and nonvocal tones, an innate quality. We hear only the tones our ear structure permits us to hear.

Psychological Limitations

Of greater importance than physiological limitations in hindering perception are the psychological limitations of experience, emotion, and selection.

Experience

Most perception is based on *past experience.* As we have already learned, we tend to interpret the new on the basis of what we learned before. An object we sense today will have a history of meaning to it if we have had associations with similar objects in the past. Even if we did sense the same object in the same manner as another person, our prior experience with the object likely will cause us to perceive the object differently than the other person will perceive it.

Emotion

Our *emotional state* colors our perception of an object at the time we encounter it. In the 17th century, the Comte de Bussy-Rabutin perceived love as blind, discoloring the lover's perception toward the object of love. Love is the triumph of imagination over intelligence, whereas fear casts out intelligence, allowing imagination to triumph and leading to erroneous perceptions.

Selection

Selective perception, discussed previously, causes us to zero-in on certain of the stimuli bombarding us and disregarding the others. Our perceptions will be limited to the objects we are predisposed to select.

 # Motivators

Motivation is a predominant factor in the way we behave. We are predisposed to behave in ways that bear on how we perceive people, their behaviors, and ideas, as well as the things that surround us.

Our needs, values, beliefs, and attitudes comprise our predispositions to behave. They serve to orient our communicative behavior, activating and directing that behavior and helping determine our relationship to the ideas being discussed and the people discussing them. These predispositions are learned within the framework of a specific culture. They are culturally imposed and vary from culture to culture.

In this chapter and Chapter 5 we focus on values, beliefs, and attitudes as they relate to intercultural communication. The remainder of this chapter addresses needs, the motivators of action, or the influences that account for the initiation, direction, intensity, and persistence of behavior.[5]

Definition of Needs

The term *needs,* as used here, refers to the striving conditions or motivating forces that energize us to reach the goals we seek. Among these are drives, wants, desires, reasons, causes, and urges. Satisfaction of needs is the aim of motivation.

Needs are defined formally and described as *physical and psychological feelings that give rise to tensions.* To overcome the tensions, we are motivated to act.[6] This definition implies that a physical or psychological force causes stresses within us and those stresses cause us to move in some manner to relieve the stress.

Satisfaction of needs is tied to interpersonal communication. People communicate because people need to talk to someone for their psychological well-being just as eating and drinking are vital to a person's physical well-being. People communicate also because communication is the medium through which many needs are satisfied.

And communication does more than satisfy the speaker's needs; it helps satisfy the needs of the other individuals in the communication transaction as well. Interpersonal needs and interpersonal communication are fundamentally interdependent. The ability to recognize other people's needs explains much of human behavior.[7]

These ideas can be expanded to intercultural communication. Understanding the extent to which needs are satisfied in differing cultures should help explain the "why" of intercultural interactions.[8]

Types of Needs

Needs fall into two major classes.

1. *Primary* or physiological or biological needs for oxygen, food, water, rest, waste elimination, exercise, and sexual activity.

2. *Secondary* needs — learned or acquired needs resulting from our social development and representative of the culture in which we grow up.

Dozens of secondary needs have been identified. One list suggests that seven needs serve as motivating factors: the needs for security, trust, group inclusion, anxiety diffusion, sharing a common world, symbolic/material gratification, and self-sustainment.[9]

Maslow's Hierarchy

At any given time, many needs may motivate us to act. What determines which ones will lead to actions? Abraham Maslow proposed a theory addressing this question.[10] He conceived of five major classes of needs influencing human behavior. These classes are arranged in a hierarchy, or pyramid, in which the most basic or primary form the foundation, followed in order by the secondary needs. The classes — physiological, safety/security, love, esteem, and self-actualization — are illustrated in Figure 4.1. The lowest-level needs in the hierarchy must be at least partially satisfied before people can be motivated to satisfy higher-level needs.

1. *Physiological needs.* First in terms of priority are the biological needs — oxygen, food, water, rest, exercise, sex, and excretion. These are related to self-preservation. If they are not satisfied, none of the other needs will surface.

2. *Safety/Security needs.* Most people want a safe environment, free from personal harm, violence, and disease. A sense of security prompts us to lock our doors, buy life insurance, and even take jobs that offer protection against indiscriminate firing.

3. *Love needs.* We need to feel wanted by others and accepted by them. Sharing our love with others is important, and we satisfy this need most often through our family and friends. We also need the acceptance of our classmates, fellow workers, and others with whom we associate. If we are denied their attention, we are apt to alter our behavior to earn their acceptance.

4. *Esteem needs.* Extremely important in the American culture, we seek to be strong, adequate, and confident in the face of the world around us, and free and independent. We have a desire to gain the respect of other people. We want recognition and attention from them to feel important or appreciated. Our esteem needs rise to the fore when the more basic needs, related to our physical well-being, safety, and love, are met.

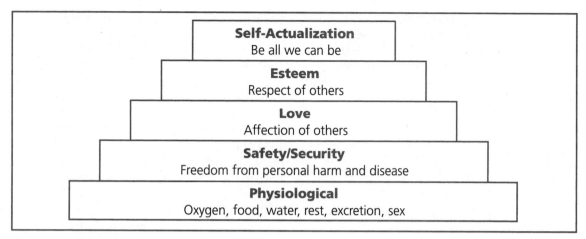

FIGURE 4.1 Maslow's Hierarchy of Needs

5. *Self-actualization needs.* Our desire to reach the height of our personal abilities becomes increasingly important as our other needs are satisfied — unless we are doing already what we believe we are best fitted to do. As Maslow puts it, a musician must make music, a poet must compose poetry, a physician has to heal, if they are to be ultimately at peace with themselves. The armed forces recruiting slogan is, "Be all you can be" — the government's way of saying "become self-fulfilled."

Maslow's theory became extremely popular because it seems logical and is optimistic about human nature. Although scientific research has not supported it, the theory has many adherents and students usually encounter it in their courses of study.

One of the theory's problems is that it is just as possible to organize our needs in a horizontal fashion as in a vertical one. We can have simultaneous needs for basic physical comfort, safety, love, and esteem. Even hungry people can be motivated to be loved and secure at the same time. Too, we can satisfy our physiological needs and be happy without being motivated to

fulfill any of the other needs. History is replete with people who would rather starve than be humiliated (a self-esteem need).

Critics of Maslow's theory conclude that we are on safer ground by believing that each of us develops an individual hierarchy of needs in the course of our development from childhood to old age. For some, the need for success will rule. For others, power is what spurs them on. Immortality, money, duty, equality, or liberty may motivate others. Most of us, however, combine many motives in a way that suits our personalities and experiences.[11]

Maslow's Theory Across Cultures

Needs vary in degree and mode of expression across cultures — especially the needs that are culturally acquired. Geert Hofstede offers support for this contention on the basis of extensive research involving more than 60,000 respondents from an international business with employees in roughly 70 countries.

The Hofstede findings seem to confirm some of Maslow's contentions. The Maslow priorities apparently fit business persons in the United

States, Great Britain, and Britain's former dominions and colonies. The business people in these cultures seem to be motivated by personal, individual success in the form of wealth, recognition, and self-actualization. For the rest of the cultures he studied, though, Hofstede found little support for Maslow's hierarchy.

Respondents in Hofstede's research from another grouping of countries (Greece, Japan, the German-speaking countries, Italy, Mexico, Colombia, Argentina, and Venezuela) indicated that personal, individual security is the prime motivating factor, as found in wealth and hard work. For another grouping (France, Spain, Portugal, Yugoslavia, Chile, Brazil, Turkey, Iran, Pakistan, Israel, Taiwan, and Thailand), security and belonging are the main motivators. People in that grouping place less importance on individual wealth than on group solidarity.

Another Hofstede grouping (Sweden, Norway, Finland, the Netherlands, Denmark, and Singapore) is moved by success and belonging — success being measured collectively by the quality of living and a pleasant human environment. Thus, Hofstede's research paints a motivational map of the world that is a far cry from the universal order of needs that Maslow's hierarchy represents.[12]

Schutz's Interpersonal Theory

William Schutz postulated that every individual has three categories of interpersonal needs that can be satisfied only through interaction with other people. These needs — for inclusion, control, and affection — are secondary needs, psychological in nature, and they do not form a hierarchy as Maslow's do.

1. *Inclusion* is the need to establish and maintain a satisfactory relationship with other people. It shows itself as the desire to be recognized, attract attention, and interest others, and can be either positive or negative. The bright student may receive recognition because of high grades; the classroom hellion may misbehave to receive attention, too, but in a negative fashion.

2. *Control* comes from influence, power, leadership, and authority on the positive side. From the negative side, control shows itself

---

Know Yourself . . .

These 10 need statements represent physiological and security needs to help you determine their importance in your life. For each statement you strongly agree with, place a "2" in the blank. Place a "1" in any blank you feel neutral toward. Place a "0" in the blanks with which you strongly disagree. Each statement should be prefaced with, "I would like . . ."

_____ 1. More and better meals.

_____ 2. To be sure of security in my old age.

_____ 3. A more certain future.

_____ 4. More rest.

_____ 5. Better health.

_____ 6. A safe way out of my present situation.

_____ 7. A better physical shape.

_____ 8. To gain/lose weight.

_____ 9. To plan better for my future.

_____ 10. To be more certain of my comfort in old age.

To score, add the items as follows:

Physiological needs: 1, 4, 5, 7, 8

Security needs: 2, 3, 6, 9, 10

If the score for a need is 9 or higher, the need is strong.

in resistance to authority, rebellion, submission, and following along with the group.

3. *Affection* is the need to establish and maintain love and affection in relational situations with another person. Negatively, it refers to hate or hostility toward another. [13]

Schutz's Theory Across Cultures

Schutz developed a scale — the Fundamental Interpersonal Relations Orientation–Behavior scale, or FIRO-B — to measure a person's interpersonal needs. It was used to compare the interpersonal needs of students in Australia, China, Japan, Korea, Micronesia, Taiwan, and the United States. The results indicated differences between the groups, none of which were significant.

The Japanese, the results showed, need to be controlled, whereas the Koreans want to control. The Chinese and Americans desire affection, and the Americans in the study had stronger inclusion needs than did respondents from the other cultures. Of the groups studied, the needs of the Australians and Micronesians were satisfied the most.

Literature about the cultures provides explanations for the findings about the Japanese, Korean, Chinese, and Americans. The Japanese are taught to be selfless and group-centered, learning at an early age the rules and rituals for life-long family membership. Strong bonds of loyalty to the family are forged in that training. As a consequence, the Japanese rarely seek group affiliation, except for that thrust upon them in school and at work. Their interpersonal needs are well taken care of, and the unmet need to be controlled suggests that they seek to be controlled by others, having been reared that way.

Americans are educated differently. For them, the family functions primarily to protect the children while preparing them to assume constantly expanding roles in society as they grow older. Independence is encouraged, and the children are readied to leave the home as they

 Know Yourself . . .

These 15 statements representing love, esteem and self-actualization needs, will help you determine their importance in your life. For each statement you strongly agree with, place a "2" in the blank. Place a "1" in the blank representing a statement you feel neutral toward. Place a "0" in the blank accompanying a statement with which you strongly disagree. Each statement should be prefaced with, "I would like . . ."

_____ 1. More friends.

_____ 2. To improve my knowledge.

_____ 3. More people to talk to.

_____ 4. To attain my fullest potential.

_____ 5. To reach more of my personal goals.

_____ 6. To meet more people.

_____ 7. The company of more people.

_____ 8. To develop my mind more than I have.

_____ 9. More people as mentors.

_____ 10. More skills in certain areas.

_____ 11. More recognition for the things I do.

_____ 12. To know more people.

_____ 13. To be able to converse more ably.

_____ 14. To be associated with more school leaders.

_____ 15. More interest from others.

To score, add the items as follows:

Love needs: 1, 3, 6, 7, 12

Esteem needs: 9, 11, 13, 14, 15

Self-actualization needs: 2, 4, 5, 8, 10

If the score for a need is 9 or higher, the need is strong.

grow older. This upbringing does not create an all-consuming motive to belong to one or two groups as in the Japanese culture. Instead, Americans are on the lookout to join new groups. Their inclusion needs are stronger than those of the Japanese. Americans are motivated to join groups and seek new ones to which they can belong.

The Chinese, like the Japanese, have a rich group life. Their family and neighborhood groups afford them opportunities to satisfy the inclusion need. Apparently these affiliations do not provide as much affection as they need, because they have stronger affection needs than students from the other countries.

Koreans want to control, and this need may result from years of being controlled by foreign powers. Koreans are more apt to be more aggressive, talkative, and interactive than students from the other cultures, and exert leadership when necessary.

The FIRO-B research shows that needs vary across cultures. What may motivate the people in one culture may not motivate those in another. [14]

Chapter Review

Our senses take in an almost endless number of distinct impulses in constantly changing patterns. Out of these impulses we perceive what we are taught to sense based on the influences of our culture.

Perception is the process by which people select, organize, and interpret sensory stimulation into a meaningful and coherent picture of the world.

First we select, and what we select depends upon differential intensity, past experience and training, and motivation.

We then organize what we select, in many ways, including figure and ground, grouping, and closure.

Finally, we interpret. We do this by attributing meaning to what we select and organize. Our interpretations are influenced by our expectations (which can be confirmed or disconfirmed), predispositions to behave, giving causes to the behavior we sense, primacy/recency, self-fulfilling prophecies, perceptual accentuations, consistency, and stereotyping.

Our perceptions differ from those of others because of physiological limitations such as the effect of illusions, neurological inhibitions, and innate characteristics of our physical being. They also differ because of differences in past experiences, learning and training, emotional state at the time of perception, and our predispositions to behave.

(Continued)

Chapter Review continued

Throughout the process, culture plays a determining role in what we sense and how we interpret it. Our culture is the important factor in our perception, as it is with people all over the globe. As cultures differ, so will perceptions.

Our predispositions to behave make up our personal orientation system, consisting of needs, values, beliefs, and attitudes.

Needs are motivators of action — motivation being the inner striving that energizes, activates, and moves people toward the goals we seek.

Sources of motivation are biological needs, mental processes, emotional factors, and social influences.

Needs, the physical and psychological feelings that give rise to tensions, and hence motivate us in such a way as to over come the tensions, offer a means of analyzing motivation across cultures.

Physiological, or primary, needs are for food, drink, rest, sex, exercise, and excretion. Psychological, or secondary, needs are many and vary from person to person. They are acquired through learning, which differs from culture to culture.

Maslow's hierarchy of needs asserts that human beings are influenced by five need categories: physiological, safety, love, esteem, and self-actualization, moving from the most basic physiological needs to self-actualization needs. When the lower needs are satisfied, the next in the hierarchy comes into play.

Hofstede's research across cultures does not support the universal order of needs that Maslow's hierarchy represents. People in different cultures are motivated in different ways. Self-actualization is not the ultimate goal in every culture, as it is alleged to be in the United States. Security and belonging may be more important measures of need satisfaction in some other cultures.

Schutz contends that three interpersonal needs — inclusion, control, and affection — motivate people. Crosscultural study using his FIRO-B scale reveals that the three needs vary in strength from one culture to another.

Think About This...

1 Explain the perception process. Why is it an important aspect of intercultural communication?

2 Explain disconfirmed expectations, attribution, predispositions to behave, and physiological differences, and indicate how culture affects each.

3 How do needs influence our behavior?

4 The Maslow theory does not have universal acceptance. Why not?

5 Explain the differences between the Maslow and Schutz need theories and Hofstede's crosscultural study of needs.

5 The Influence of Culture on Behavioral Predispositions

Interrnational lawyer and business consultant Mu Dan Ping asks, "How can people from different cultures interact effectively to achieve mutual goals?" Successful interaction with others, she believes, depends upon how we interpret their behavior, and it depends also on how well others perceive and interpret our own behavior. We observe behavior through our personal "lens," she claims — our perception process.

The lens we use to interpret the various behaviors we see is influenced by our own cultural environment. Our lens may be one that cannot focus on the cultural environments of those with whom we communicate. Their lens, in turn, may not be focused clearly on our culture, and misunderstandings result. Understanding how people are predisposed to behave assists in our intercultural experiences.[1]

In this chapter we continue our exploration of people's behavior inclinations by examining the elements in addition to needs in our personal orientation system — values, beliefs and attitudes. They provide clues as to why and how people communicate as we do.

 ## Values: Cultural Guides

A person's existing value system has a significant bearing on a person's religious and social beliefs, on his or her kinship patterns, and on the person's identity, offering guidelines as to the person's behavior.[2] Values are "the currently held normative expectations underlying individual and social conduct."[3] Or values are universalistic statements about what we think is desirable or attractive.[4]

Values serve as standards or criteria to guide not only our actions but also our judgments, choices, attitudes, evaluations, arguments, exhortations, and attributions of causality. The values of any culture dictate what is a desirable or an undesirable state of affairs.[5] Values define appropriate behavior in a culture. Because cultures are not static entities but, rather, are changeable, values change, too, and they differ from time to time in differing circumstances.

Although values are the desired behaviors of a culture's members, they may not represent the actual behaviors of the entire membership. Individual differences occur. Nevertheless, values do offer guidance in understanding the ways in which people interact.

Like all knowledge, values are mental conceptions. They are not observable in themselves. What we see is the behaviors a value brings forth. For example, a newspaper reported that a young man found a wallet containing $100. The man returned the wallet with the money to its owner. The man's *act* of honesty was observed. The value underlying the act could only be inferred. From the newspaper report, we would deduce that the value of honesty guided the man's action.

Like the young man, each of us has our own set of values, originating within the larger principles or laws that govern our society. Those principles specify what should be done in that society. They tell us what is proper or improper.

Values are viewed from varying perspectives across cultures. Even though most cultures value honesty in their people, its application can differ in salience, direction, and degree among the culture's members.

Salience

The perceived importance of a value (*salience*) is classified as primary, secondary, tertiary, or valueless.[6] Values are not always preeminent; they could be less than primary in a person's behavior or, for that matter, among the people in some other culture.

For example, most Americans consider democracy as a primary value. It is worth guarding at all costs, and wars have been fought to

preserve it. Elsewhere in the world, it does not hold the the same predominance. People in African and Asian cultures perceive democracy as of secondary importance — nice to have but not worth fighting over.

Direction

Values among people and across cultures differ in *direction* — positive, negative, or neutral (having no value). For many Americans, sexual equality is positive and inequality is negative. For most Koreans, the opposite is true.

Kerekere — A Fijian Value

In this remote Fijian mountain community, Lomai Village natives greeted us upon our arrival with a kava ceremony. As we imbibed, they listed the do's and don'ts of the Fijian lifestyle: no bare arms, no backpacks slung over the shoulders, no whistling, and long dresses required. But they forgave us ahead of time for the breaches in Fijian customs we might make.

Kerekere impressed us the most. A South Seas custom, it instructs, "What's yours is mine and what's mine is yours." If I have two papayas and you have none, I would be expected to give you my extra one. While in Lomai Village for 2 weeks to build houses for Habitat for Humanity, we obeyed the kerekere custom and left behind several hundreds of dollars' of tools, sleeping bags, and medical supplies. When we returned home, we raised money for two chainsaws and other items. In return, they blessed us and requested a four-wheel drive.

—Ramona Klinger,
Professor, North Idaho College

Degree

Values also differ in *degree*, the intensity or strength of a value. Most Americans consider honesty as important, but they may fudge on degree. Preparing their income tax, they intentionally may not report an item or two of income.

 ## Cultural Value Orientations

Our identities are being challenged constantly in diverse cultural situations. When interacting with peers from different countries or immigrant groups, we encounter unspoken differences from nonverbal to language differences, most of which are underscored by intercultural differences in values.

Cultural value orientations give order and direction to the dissimilarities we meet in intercultural interaction. Cultural value orientations form the lenses through which we can view our own actions and those of others. They establish the background criteria for how to communicate appropriately with others.[7]

Now we will review dominant American values, Schwartz's value range, and Hofstede's work-related value dimensions, in addition to Kluckhohn and Strodtbeck's classical value orientations.

Values Dominant in America

We need to be familiar with our own value orientation for two reasons:

1. We carry our culture with us wherever we go, and it affects our communicative behavior with whomever we meet. Therefore, we should be acquainted not only with the cultural patterns of those with whom we communicate but with our own as well.

2. When we examine our own cultural patterns, we discover information about ourselves that we otherwise may overlook.[8]

Our introduction to the dominant American values centers on those characteristic of the American macroculture, the prevailing Anglo-Saxon national culture.[9]

Individualism

To understand individualism is to begin to understand Americans. This value is probably the most important in Americans' lives. From early childhood, Americans are taught that they are separate individuals who are responsible for their own stations in life and are in command of their own destinies. They are independent and responsible people, worthy of respect, and they do not see themselves as members of close-knit, interdependent family, clan, or nation. Americans focus on the individual rather than on the group.

By the time American children graduate from high school, the expectation is that they are about ready to move out of the parents' house and make their own way in the world, ideally being able to fend for themselves. If they are unable to do so, they could be thought of as immature or too closely "tied to mother's apron strings" — a deplorable state for most Americans.

Allowances are made for those attending college or receiving special training of some sort. With the training completed, Americans are supposed to be self-reliant and function on their own. If they do live with their parents, most will contribute to household expenses or pay for their room and board. They will be paying their own way and thereby demonstrating their independence.

Freedom

Closely associated with individualism, freedom permeates the American culture and is imbedded in the U.S. Constitution as an inalienable right. Americans value the right to exercise choice in all things, to move from place to place free from restraints, to be immune from arbitrary exercise of authority, and to enjoy all of the privileges of citizenship. They do not want to be beholden to anyone for any reason. They believe in the freedom of enterprise permitting private industry to operate with minimal regulation. They expect full liberty — to decide as they see fit.

Associated with the notion of freedom is *privacy*, the condition of being alone when they so desire, secluded from contact with others — from the sight, presence, or intrusion of others. In the household, father and mother desire their own private space, and if space is available, the children have separate bedrooms and places for their own possessions.

Equality

A prominent theme throughout U.S. history, the nation's Declaration of Independence boldly states that "all men are created equal." Most American children grow up believing that all humans are created equal, and running through American social relationships is the theme of equality. Presumably interpersonal relations take place on a horizontal level, conducted between assumed equals.

In work situations involving superior-subordinate positions, rank is not supposed to enter in, authority is not to be exercised, and communication is expected to take place as between equals. Even in the military with its authoritarian policies, equality is advocated. Only in extreme circumstances does the good officer exert authority to get action taken. Discussion is encouraged.

Although equality is the prevailing value, not all groups are treated equally. Blacks, females, and the elderly are among those who are discriminated against at times. Strong hierarchies appear in some businesses and industries, political institutions, and federal agencies. But laws have been passed to ensure equality for all.

Democracy

Closely allied with equality, freedom, and individualism is the American value of democracy. Majority rule is emphasized at all levels of government, as is equal representation. Government is by, of, and for the people. The people are considered the source of political authority. A condition of respect for the individual is the rule in the community.

In Honolulu neighborhood boards are elected by small groups of citizens to transmit their needs to the city's governing bodies, also elected by the people. In other American cities, similar citizens' groups function to provide direct input into city government. Volunteer groups of citizens monitor government agencies to see to it that the wishes of the people are fulfilled. The League of Women Voters operates in most communities to keep watch over politicians and ensure that they practice democracy.

Humanitarianism

Americans are concerned with the well being of humankind and believe that humans have a moral obligation to work for the improved welfare of humanity. The government of the United States and private citizens contribute millions of dollars to improve the lives of less fortunate people throughout the world. Within the United States efforts are made to rehabilitate people with physical ailments, as well as those with social problems such as jail inmates. Americans support an array of activities that work for the improvement of their fellow humans. Most of this support is on a volunteer basis, with Americans helping the less fortunate through community service clubs, parent-teacher organizations, church groups, and similar volunteer associations.

Communities are beautified through campaigns to clean and fix up local neighborhoods. Money is raised for worthy causes. Help is forthcoming in times of natural disasters. The "adopt-a-highway" program is an example of volunteers devoting several hours a week to cleaning sections of public roads, removing rubbish and other debris that accumulates and makes the highways unsightly.

Self-improvement is a way of life for most Americans. They believe they can improve their personal lot in life by enrolling in various educational and training programs. Programs in weight-loss training, physical conditioning, job skill improvement, and many other personal improvement areas are available to those who are interested. "How-to-do-it" books are available to those interested in enhancing their life in some manner. Workshops, seminars, classes of all sorts, and regularly scheduled learning programs are accessible in local schools, colleges, and universities for those wishing to better themselves.

Progress

Americans stress the future. They pay attention to the past and present only to the extent that what has happened will provide impetus to change the future. They are receptive to change, always with the goal of advancing toward a more desirable way of life. They have faith in the perfectibility of the ordinary individual and admire those who achieve — they are achievement-motivated.

Activism

In the fast-paced society of the United States, action is prized. Strenuous competition, ceaseless activity, energy expenditure, vigorous and lively participation are hallmarks of American life. Americans like action. They believe they should be doing something just about all of the time. Work is purposeful, rational action that dominates typical Americans' lives. Socially, Americans would rather be doing almost anything — playing games, engaging in athletics — other than sitting around philosophizing about people and events over which they have little control.

While visiting an Australian family, an American was perturbed with his hosts, who enjoyed spending mealtimes and evenings discussing aesthetics, existentialism, abortion, paternalism, euthanasia, and other topics philosophical in nature. The visitor wanted to be accomplishing something worthwhile — spending his time doing, not talking.

Achievement

Americans respect the high achiever and self-made person. This value is closely allied with activism. They like people who succeed, and they turn away from those who fail. Defeated candidates for public office are quickly forgotten; they are losers, not to be remembered.

University professors succeed by doing research and publishing the results. Those who do not, regardless of their other qualities, are passed over for promotion to higher position. Seniority, or being around longer than someone else, does not count. Productivity is the mark of success.

Practicality

A value tied to activism and achievement is practicality. Americans are governed by what is possible and attainable. Rather than theorizing, speculating, or idealizing, they want to get things done in as expedient a manner as possible. They emphasize efficiency, producing with a minimum of waste, expense, or unnecessary effort. Competency — being well qualified with adequate skills and ability — is stressed.

In the communication field in the United States, speaking competency is a high priority. Secondary school and university classes place importance on graduating competent communicators, ones with the skills and training to succeed as speakers.

Time

Time is money to Americans. They realize that only so much time is available in life, and they want to use it wisely. An American business magazine offers suggestions on how business travelers can use their traveling time more productively. Smart travelers spend their time constructively on trains, buses, or airplanes. They work. They bring their calculators, tape recorders with earphones, and laptop computers and work in their seat as they move from place to place. Wasted time between flights or trains can be spent exercising rather than sitting and waiting for the plane or train. the magazine admonishes.

The fast-food industry provides speedy meals for people with limited time to eat. Frozen meals can be popped into the oven and served in a matter of minutes, eliminating food preparation and cooking time.

Americans are open, frank, and direct in their interactions with others. They like to get to the point quickly and not "beat around the bush," as the adage states.

In contrast many Asian businessmen prefer to take their time when conducting business, wanting to be come acquainted first with those they expect to deal with. Americans are not like that, desiring to complete the business as quickly as possible. They are likely to be direct and assertive in this sort of communicative situation.

Informality

In keeping with equality as an important value, Americans tend to be informal in their

---

Dominant Values

The following statements reflect 10 of the American value types explained in this chapter. Select one of the three options given for each statement and, by doing so, you indicate your preference for each value.

Value	Agree	Neutral	Disagree
1. I am the most important person in my life. (individuality)	___	___	___
2. I have the right to pick what is best for me. (freedom)	___	___	___
3. I think all people should be treated equally. (equality)	___	___	___
4. I believe government should be of the people, by the people, and for the people. (democracy)	___	___	___
5. I believe I have an obligation to help others. (humanitarianism)	___	___	___
6. I have faith in the future, and I believe in progress. (progress)	___	___	___
7. I prize action, competition, vigorous activity. (activism)	___	___	___
8. I am motivated to succeed in life. (achievement)	___	___	___
9. I govern my behavior by what is practical and possible. (practicality)	___	___	___
10. Time is like money; it is not to be wasted. (time)	___	___	___

relations with people. In speech, dress, and posture, Americans are likely to be casual and relaxed. They call each other by their given names, appear nonchalant, avoid ceremony, and dress casually. They slouch in chairs, lean on walls or furniture, and use slang as they talk.

Their approach is informal and equalitarian with a friendly demeanor. The friendliness, however, tends to be superficial. They will say "hello" to nearly everyone and engage many in "small talk." Rarely do typical Americans develop lasting relationships with people with whom they are merely friendly.

Morality

Americans are apt to judge people's behavior in terms of what is right or wrong, good or bad, proper or improper, ethical or unethical. The Ten Commandments of the Christian Bible serve as a guide to the goodness and correctness of people's behavior. They may not always abide by Biblical teachings, yet these precepts govern them, and they are taught from early childhood to recognize right from wrong.

Universal Value Orientations

From an extensive research project involving 49 countries, Shalom Schwartz isolated 10 value patterns that can serve the interests of individualistic, collectivistic and mixed cultures.[10] These universal patterns follow, along with specific examples of the values.

1. *Achievement* — characterized by personal success through demonstrated competence [socially recognized, successful, capable]

2. *Benevolence* — characterized by preservation and enhancement of the welfare of people with whom they are frequently in contact [helpful, loyal, responsible]

3. *Conformity* — restraint of actions, inclinations, and impulses that could harm others [obedient, polite, self-disciplined]

4. *Hedonism* — personal pleasure or sensuous gratification [seeking pleasure or enjoyment]

5. *Power* — social status and prestige, control, dominance over people [seeking authority, wealth, power]

6. *Security* — safety, harmony, and stability of society [seeking family security, national security, social order]

7. *Self-direction* — independence of thought and action, selecting own goals [creative, free, independent]

8. *Stimulation* — excitement, novelty, and challenge in life [having an exciting life, daring]

9. *Tradition* — respect, commitment, and acceptance of the customs and ideas that our culture imposes on us [respect for tradition, humble, devout, moderate]

10. *Universalism* — understanding, appreciating, tolerating, and protecting the welfare of all people and nature [seeking equality, social justice, peace in the world]

Hofstede's Value Dimensions

During the 1980s, Geert Hofstede, then a Dutch university professor of management, surveyed more than 100,000 workers in 40 countries on four value dimensions that he found to have a significant impact on behavior in all cultures. The workers surveyed were middle managers in a multinational business organization. Hence, his findings are work-related. The 40 countries did not include Arab and African nations except for South Africa, because the business organization did not have branches in those areas.

The study was conducted 20 years ago. Therefore, the pertinence of his findings may be questionable today. Samovar, Porter, and Stefani, however, contend that Hofstede studied values resistant to change and relevant in the contemporary world.[11] The values studied are grouped into four dimensions: individualism/collectivism, avoidance of uncertainty, power distance, and masculinity/femininity.

Individualism and Collectivism

Communication behavior distinctions across cultures can be accounted for largely by individualism/collectivism. Broadly speaking, the Western cultures fall into the individualistic category and the Asian and Latin American countries into the collectivistic. But in every culture, some people have individualistic or collectivistic tendencies. Table 5.1 shows the ranking of 40 countries on the values of individualism versus collectivism. The differences between the two types of culture become apparent when their characteristics are delineated in terms of self-construal, group perceptions, and status perceptions.

Differences in Self-Construal. The principal distinction focuses on the concept of self-construal — our perception and evaluation of ourselves as human beings. In the individualistic cultures, the self is independent, an entity autonomous from groups. The self-concept is an integral part of the American culture. We assume that every person is not only a biological entity but also a unique psychological being who is a singular member of the American society. The self is deeply ingrained in our culture, and its value is seldom questioned. Our dominant self, visible in the form of individualism, pervades our relationships and is part of all of

TABLE 5.1   Ranking of 40 Countries on Individualism and Collectivism

Country	Ranking*	Country	Ranking*
USA	1	India	21
Australia	2	Japan	22
Great Britain	3	Argentina	23
Canada	4	Iran	24
Netherlands	5	Brazil	25
New Zealand	6	Turkey	26
Italy	7	Greece	27
Belgium	8	Philippines	28
Denmark	9	Mexico	29
Sweden	10	Portugal	30
France	11	Yugoslavia	31
Ireland	12	Hong Kong	32
Norway	13	Chile	33
Switzerland	14	Singapore	34
Germany	15	Thailand	35
South Africa	16	Taiwan	36
Finland	17	Peru	37
Austria	18	Pakistan	38
Israel	19	Colombia	39
Spain	20	Venezuela	40

*A high score means the country can be classified as collective, a lower score is associated with a culture that promotes individualism.

Source: Adapted from *Culture's Consequences: International Differences in Work-Related Values* by Geert Hofstede (Beverly Hills, CA: Sage, 1984).

our activities. It is as though we have a wall around our self that differentiates our self from that of other people. We are distinct from others.

People in the USA typically are interested in their self-image, self-esteem, self-reliance, self-awareness, self-actualization, and self-determination. The self is a unifying concept, providing a direction in thinking, a perspective for activity, a source of motivation, and a focus for decision making. We can be persuaded to do something if our self-interests are at stake.

In the collectivistic cultures, the self assumes a converse quality. The emphasis on self-concept, as illustrated by the behavior of the individualistic person and typical of many Western cultures, is not apparent. In the collectivistic cultures people may not think their own selves are much different from those of other people in their culture. In India, for example, the tendency is not to erect a wall between oneself and others. Another person's self is not independent from one's own self.

Collectivists perceive themselves as being a part of a group, whether extended family, clan, or organization. An individual's personal goals overlap those of the group, and if they do not, the group's goals take precedence over the personal ones. The "I"/"me" value of the individualistic cultures is replaced by the "we" and "us."

The Chinese self-concept, for example, has deep roots in the social structure of the society. Identities of individuals are inclined to form around the lineal family, including ancestors and future offspring. The Chinese self-concept implies that anything that has to be done, is done, or will be done by family members is an action of the self.[12]

The group, not the individual member's self, is the vital entity in non-Western cultures. The group's fate is more important than the individual's fate. The group's image, esteem, and achievement are primary. The individual is subservient to the group. Improving the individual's self-concept is not essential as it is in the West. The counseling, workshops, and courses designed to improve Western self-concept are not offered in the collectivistic cultures.

Differences in Group Perceptions. In individualistic cultures the members tend to join and belong to many groups, establishing a wide range of social relationships. Their attachment to these groups is apt to be weak, however, and their own personal goals take precedence over group aims. Many types of groups are open to membership. In the United States, an estimated 4 to 5 billion groups enroll members. Included among them are neighborhood, athletic, church, recreational, political, professional, and school groups. Members join mostly for the personal satisfaction they get from their membership.

Group life in the individualistic cultures is likely to reveal communication behavior that is assertive and confrontative. Group members perceive confrontations as advantageous. Disagreements help clear the air, and winning a verbal battle is a measure of personal worth. Completing a task successfully is highly prized. If a member loses too many fights in one group, he or she can find other groups in which to test his or her skill.

Members of collectivistic cultures are less likely to join many groups. They restrict their membership to a group or two, usually the family and the work or school group. Their attachments to the groups to which they belong are strong, however, and the group's goals are their goals.

The types of groups in collectivistic cultures are similar to those in individualistic cultures but do not have the large number of members. Their communication practices encourage harmony and cooperation among members, and they value group success more than individual accomplishments.

Differences in Status Perceptions. Individualistic cultures tend to reject status differences. Although these differences obviously are present, they prefer equalitarianism. Authority figures confer frequently with their underlings

Individualism Versus Collectivism

The statements below represent either individualism or collectivism. For each item, place an I in the blank if you think it is consistent with individualism or a C if you think it is consistent with collectivism.

_____ 1. The university presents an annual teacher-of-the year award.

_____ 2. Friendships are for life, people have only a friend or two.

_____ 3. It is acceptable to be the life of the party.

_____ 4. Signed contracts aren't really necessary in a business deal.

_____ 5. Group harmony is essential.

_____ 6. Marriages are often arranged.

_____ 7. To succeed, a person must be productive and get results.

_____ 8. Decisions are made by consensus.

_____ 9. One protects oneself.

_____ 10. Promotion is based on productivity.

Answers on page 244.

and try to avoid ordering or telling. Democracy is fostered. In fact, federal governmental regulations, especially in America, require equality in virtually all areas of life.

In collectivistic cultures status differences represent the status quo, being accepted with little question. Paternalism is expected. Age or seniority, not ability or knowledge, is often the basis for promotion. The person holding an important position is kowtowed to; discussion with underlings is discouraged. A colleague reports:

When interacting with the director of an educational center my Korean friend donates millions to, he defers to the director's judgment, accepting the director's word as indisputable. Most of the time my friend is right; the director is wrong. But my friend acquiesces. I tell my friend, you're older, a millionaire, better educated. You're crazy for agreeing with him all of the time. Stand up for your rights. He wouldn't think of disagreeing.

At home, in collectivistic cultures, the eldest male rules, and each family member has a carefully defined role.

Avoidance of Uncertainty

As a characteristic of a culture, avoidance of uncertainty indicates the extent to which people within a culture become nervous in situations that they perceive as unstructured, unclear, or unpredictable. The stronger the uncertainty avoidance, the greater is the feeling of threat and the inclination toward avoidance. Members of the culture try to avoid uncertainty situations by adopting clear procedures, strict codes of behavior, formal rules, an intolerance for deviant ideas, and a belief in absolute truth.

Cultures ranking highest in uncertainty avoidance are Greece, Portugal, Belgium, Japan, Yugoslavia, Peru, France, Chile, Spain, and Argentina. Table 5.2 shows the rankings of 40 cultures in the value of avoiding uncertainty, from Hofstede's study.

The weaker the uncertainty avoidance, the more readily members of the culture accept the uncertainty inherent in life. They are relatively tolerant, contemplative, less aggressive, accepting of personal risk, and unemotional. Cultures weakest in uncertainty avoidance are Singapore, Denmark, Sweden, Hong Kong, Ireland, Great Britain, India, Philippines, USA, and Canada.[13]

Samovar, Porter, and Stefani pondered the affects of uncertainty avoidance on intercultural communication situations. A meeting involving representatives from both the weak and the strong groups would invite frustration. Members

TABLE 5.2   Ranking of 40 Countries on Uncertainty Avoidance

Country	Ranking*	Country	Ranking*
Greece	1	Germany	21
Portugal	2	Thailand	22
Belgium	3	Iran	23
Japan	4	Finland	24
Yugoslavia	5	Switzerland	25
Peru	6	Netherlands	26
France	7	Australia	27
Chile	8	Norway	28
Spain	9	South Africa	29
Argentina	10	New Zealand	30
Turkey	11	Canada	31
Mexico	12	USA	32
Israel	13	Philippines	33
Colombia	14	India	34
Venezuela	15	Great Britain	35
Brazil	16	Ireland	36
Italy	17	Hong Kong	37
Pakistan	18	Sweden	38
Austria	19	Denmark	39
Taiwan	20	Singapore	40

*A low score means the country can be classified as one that does not like uncertainty; a high score is associated with cultures that do not feel uncomfortable with uncertainty.

Source: Adapted from *Culture's Consequences: International Differences in Work-Related Values* by Geert Hofstede (Beverly Hills, CA: Sage, 1984).

of the strong group would want to move slowly and desire a great deal of detail and planning. The level of formality would differ — the strong being formal, and the weak, informal. The weak group could care less about having a highly structured meeting and would willingly take risks.[14]

Masculinity and Femininity

As a characteristic of a culture, masculinity is the opposite of femininity. The nomenclature has nothing to do with biological qualities. Masculine cultures expect men to be assertive, ambitious, and competitive, to strive for material success, and to respect whatever is big, strong, and fast. They expect women to serve and care for the nonmaterial quality of life, for children, and for the weak.

Feminine cultures, in contrast, perceive social roles as overlapping for men and women alike. Neither men nor women need to be ambitious or competitive. Both sexes may opt for any sort of life not built on material success and may respect whatever is weak, small, and slow.

In both types of culture, the dominant values in political and work organizations are those of men. In masculine cultures the political/organizational values stress material success and assertiveness. In feminine cultures they stress other types of quality of life, service, and benevolence, and are people-centered. In feminine cultures the members work to live, not live to work as in the masculine cultures.[15]

As shown in Table 5.3, among the most masculine cultures are Japan, Austria, Venezuela, Italy, Switzerland, and Mexico. The most feminine cultures include Sweden, Norway, Netherlands, Denmark, Yugoslavia, and Finland. The USA ranks approximately in the middle.

Power Distance

The fourth Hofstede dimension, power distance, defines the extent to which the less powerful person accepts inequality in power and considers it normal. Power is the potential to determine or direct the behavior of other people.[16]

High-power-distance cultures are rigidly stratified. The bosses make up the elite, and the workers are the powerless, who are expected to follow orders. Privileges are reserved for the power-holders, and the powerless accept the disparity between themselves and the powerful. Communication between the two groups is

TABLE 5.3 Ranking of 40 Countries on Masculinity and Femininity

Country	Ranking*	Country	Ranking*
Japan	1	Canada	21
Austria	2	Pakistan	22
Venezuela	3	Brazil	23
Italy	4	Singapore	24
Switzerland	5	Israel	25
Mexico	6	Turkey	26
Ireland	7	Taiwan	27
Great Britain	8	Iran	28
Germany	9	France	29
Philippines	10	Spain	30
Colombia	11	Peru	31
South Africa	12	Thailand	32
USA	13	Portugal	33
Australia	14	Chile	34
New Zealand	15	Finland	35
Greece	16	Yugoslavia	36
Hong Kong	17	Denmark	37
Argentina	18	Netherlands	38
India	19	Norway	39
Belgium	20	Sweden	40

*A high score means the country can be classified as one that favors feminine traits; a lower score is associated with cultures that prefer masculine traits.

Source: Adapted from *Culture's Consequences: International Differences in Work-Related Values* by Geert Hofstede (Beverly Hills, CA: Sage, 1984).

limited or nonexistent. When they do talk, the powerless normally agree with the powerful, and they prefer authoritarian leadership.

Low-power-distance cultures support equality for all people, with latent harmony between the powerful and powerless. They value independence and do not seek obedience. Decisions are based on the input of all involved, and communication between everyone is encouraged.

Hofstede reported salient data regarding power distance in 39 countries (see Table 5.4). The 10 countries that had the largest power distance (the most inequality between the boss and his employees) were the Philippines, Mexico, Venezuela, Yugoslavia, India, Singapore, Brazil, Hong Kong, France, and Colombia. The company workers in those countries reported much inequality between themselves and their bosses. The bosses were perceived as extremely powerful and maintained little contact with the workers.

In France, the power distance was attributed to the implied rule that bosses and workers rarely converse; it is neither expected nor encouraged. The other nine countries are linked to tropical or subtropical climates. Human intervention with nature is not perceived as a need to survive

and grow. Less technology and less education are apparent, and there is a weak middle class. The national wealth is held by a small elite and political power and resides with the military or an oligarchy. Heavily populated, these countries have a history of occupation, colonization, and imperialistic rule.

With the exception of France, values are similar. These countries value child obedience, and the children value conformity. Authoritarian attitudes are a social norm. Company managers make autocratic decisions and operate paternalistically. Workers like close supervision and display a weak work ethic. They do not disagree with their bosses and do not trust each other.

The 10 countries with the least power distance were Austria, Israel, Denmark, New Zealand, Ireland, Sweden, Norway, Finland, Switzerland, and Great Britain. The workers reported slight inequality between themselves and their bosses, the bosses being less distant.

This group of countries is quite different from the first 10. The climate is moderate to cold and the people depend more upon human intervention with nature. They need technology and emphasize industry over agriculture. Education

Representing a high-power-distance country, this Singaporean probably will accept societal norms favoring inequality and dependency in the workplace. Fearing to disagree with authority, he will conform, doing his job as he is told. If something goes wrong on the job, he, not higher authority or the system, will be blamed. His educational background will be limited, and he will have little opportunity to change jobs or move about the country.

TABLE 5.4   Ranking of 40 Countries on Power Distance

Country	Ranking*	Country	Ranking*
Philippines	1	Pakistan	21
Mexico	2	Japan	22
Venezuela	3	Italy	23
India	4	South Africa	24
Yugoslavia	5	Argentina	25
Singapore	6	USA	26
Brazil	7	Canada	27
Hong Kong	8	Netherlands	28
France	9	Australia	29
Colombia	10	Germany	30
Turkey	11	Great Britain	31
Belgium	12	Switzerland	32
Peru	13	Finland	33
Thailand	14	Norway	34
Chile	15	Sweden	35
Portugal	16	Ireland	36
Greece	17	New Zealand	37
Iran	18	Denmark	38
Taiwan	19	Israel	39
Spain	20	Austria	40

*A low score means the country can be classified as one that prefers a large power distance; a high score is associated with cultures that prefer a small power distance.

Source: Adapted from *Culture's Consequences: International Differences in Work-Related Values* by Geert Hofstede (Beverly Hills, CA: Sage, 1984).

is vital, and these countries have a strong middle class. Political power is based on a representation of the people's wishes. Independence characterizes their past, along with federalism and a less centralized government.

Parents place less value on their children's obedience, and the children feel strongly about being independent. People like to work and have a strong work ethic. Employees disagree with their bosses when need be, and the bosses tend to be considerate of their needs.[17]

Vietnam offers an excellent illustration of a high-power culture. A middle-level sector officer relates how the system functions. He became

aware of a situation that required immediate action — action he was not authorized to take. An American visitor, trying to help him with the situation, suggested that the worker pick up the telephone on his desk and call the province chief so the chief could decide what to do. The officer replied that the telephone was not placed on his desk so he could call the province chief. It was put there so the chief could call him. Thus, modern methods of communication were clogged by traditional values. Modern military and civilian institutions presupposed a rapid, steady, and reliable flow of information. But the implicit cultural rule in Vietnam was that subordinates do not initiate interaction with their superiors. The flow of information is from top to bottom, downward rather than upward or horizontal.[18]

Kluckhohn and Strodtbeck Value Orientations

The ideas of Florence Kluckhohn and Fred Strodtbeck have been extremely influential in guiding the work of intercultural communication scholars, and they form the foundation for understanding cultural patterns.[19] Kluckhohn and Strodtbeck's work has provided a way to map and contrast broad cultural differences and function as a way to analyze cultural differences.[20]

Authors cited in *Hispanic Psychology* commenting on the Kluckhohn and Strodtbeck value orientation found the orientations too broad to generate measures of cultural identity and too difficult to translate to decisions in everyday-life. They also believed that Latino/Latina and other cultures were treated negatively in comparison to the Americans.[21] Yet, the Kluckhohn-Strodtbeck orientations underlie most intercultural communication analyses of values.

Kluckhohn and Strodtbeck maintain that all human cultures face five universally shared problems stemming from relationships with their fellow human beings, time, activities, and nature. The five problems are:[22]

1. What is a human's relation to nature? (man-nature orientation)

2. What is the modality of human activity? (activity orientation)

3. What is the temporal focus of human life? (time orientation)

4. What is the character of innate human nature? (human nature orientation)

5. What is the relationship of the individual to others? (relational orientation).

Using the matrix in Figure 5.1, we find a range of solutions to the five questions. The matrix suggests that each culture has a preferred way of responding to each question from among the three alternatives presented. Using the Harris and Moran simplified answers to the questions, we obtain a better understanding of our own value orientations, as well as the orientations of people from different cultures.[23]

1. *What is a human's relation to nature?* Most Americans believe that human beings are the masters of nature. Humans in harmony with nature orientation can be seen in Japanese, Chinese, and many American Indian tribes. The societies placing a high belief in fate, like the Philippines, accept the inevitable and the subjugation of humans to nature.

2. *What is the modality of human activity?* The spontaneous expression of impulses and desires is exemplified in Brazil at Mardi Gras time. Activities that stress development of the entire person can be seen in Eastern cultures and Western groups that emphasize development of the whole person. Activity directed toward accomplishing something is familiar to most Westerners.

3. *What is the temporal focus of human life?* The past, present, and future directions are present in all cultures, but how they are ordered distinguishes one culture from another. Most working class and middle class Americans are future-oriented. Lower classes in many cultures focus on the "now" more than the past or future. The Chinese orientation is in the past.

4. *What is the character of innate human nature?* In the United States most agree that the influence of Puritan ancestors is strong, and many believe that human nature is basically evil but perfectible. Control and discipline are required to achieve goodness. Other Americans believe that humans are a mixture of good and evil. No culture seems to be committed to the concept that human nature is immutably good.

Cultural Orientations	Cultural Groups		
	1	2	3
What is a human's relation to nature?	Humans are subject to nature	Humans are in harmony with nature	Humans are master of nature
What is the modality of human activity?	A spontaneous expression in desires	Activity emphasizing holism	Activity motivated to achievement
What is the temporal focus of human life?	To the past	To the present	To the future
What is the character of innate human nature?	Evil	Mixture of good and evil	Good
What is the relationship of the individual to others?	Lineal — group goals primary	Collateral — group goals are primary	Individual — personal goals important

Matrix modified from *Variations in Value Orientations*, by F. Kluckhohn and F. Strodtbeck (Chicago: Row, Petersom, 1961), 11.

FIGURE 5.1 Cultural Influences on Life Issues

5. *What is the relationship of the individual to others?* Most Americans are individualistically oriented, which means that the individual's welfare is most important. The collectivistic cultures exemplify the collateral group, with the group's goals superseding the welfare of individual members. The English aristocracy illustrates the lineal group orientation in which the welfare of the group is important and the social class continues through time.[24]

 **Beliefs**

Among the ancient Hawaiians, superstitions flourished. These unfounded beliefs directed the lives of the Hawaiians, just as unproven beliefs did for other primitive peoples. For the Hawaiians the appearance of a rainbow was a portent, and the message it carried depended upon where it appeared, when, and its size. A rainbow directly in front of a person could mean, "Go back. There is danger ahead." Or a rainbow appearing just as a baby is being born could mean this is an especially blessed baby. Often, a rainbow's appearance was believed to be a portent that somebody close and loved was going to die.

The Hawaiians believed that a pit is a portent of death. The ancients were cautioned, "If a dog digs a hole near the house, fill the hole immediately." A dog howling was a universal death portent — the dog howled because it saw the spirit of a dead or dying person.

The green leaves of a tropical member of the lily family, the *ti*, were believed to protect against harm and invoke the protection of the gods. In the old days, before visiting a holy place, Hawaiian women would stuff green ti leaves into their bras. Then they would feel safe.

This belief did not die with the passing of time. "Before an athletic contest," said a high school coach, "the cheerleaders run around the stadium waving ti leaves to ward off evil spirits." Visiting college coaches believe their losses are attributable to poor play. Hawaiian coaches know better. They place ti leaves all around the field of play. "We've got so many ti plants growing around our house," one homeowner explained, "we must have the safest place in the state." Even hula dancers use ti leaves, making their hula skirts out of split ti leaves. When their hips shake, everyone in sight feels protected.

These superstitions are beliefs, and we can make thousands and thousands of belief statements about our self and the world around us. These are probability statements of evaluation or judgment, statements of confidence in the existence or truth of something. Like the primitive people who inferred much about their world and voiced these inferences through their superstitions, we continue to do so today. Much of our thinking about why we exist, where we came from, and how we got here is based on belief — some of which is true, but much of which is probability. These ontological issues of why, where, and how form beliefs systems in most cultures. These systems are called the culture's *worldview*.

If we perceive some relationship between two things or between some thing and a characteristic of it, we are said to hold a belief. For example, we might suppose that ti leaves ward off evil, holes are signs of death, and rainbows are portents of the future. If we think this way, we are expressing our beliefs about the things around us. We are making judgments about what is true or probable. We are stating our beliefs.

Beliefs cluster together in a hierarchical system of relative importance.[25] At the center are the well-established beliefs that are relatively unchangeable. They are most important to us and form the core of our self. Examples are: I believe in God. I believe that proper diet and exercise will keep me fit. I believe that the Republicans do the best job of running the country.

At the periphery of the system lie the unimportant, changeable beliefs. Examples are: I believe it will rain tomorrow. I believe I will get an "A" on next week's exam. I believe I will go shopping tomorrow.

Beliefs may be about the past, present, or future, as in these examples: I believe it was cold yesterday. I believe it is very hot today. I believe it will rain tomorrow. Beliefs may be conceptual ($2 \times 2 = 4$), descriptions of the real world (Denver is located on the plains), or causal inferences (I believe he likes her because she is a redhead). Beliefs may be about objects in the environment (I believe that car is a Toyota), about people (I believe she is Latina), or about ourselves (I believe in equality).

Beliefs are a significant aspect of our study of intercultural communication. Beliefs are at the core of people's thoughts and actions. They are learned and, hence, subject to cultural interpretation and cultural diversity. They affect our conscious and unconscious minds, as well as the manner in which we communicate.[26]

Reasoning and Beliefs

In developing our beliefs, we reason. We perceive a stimulus and draw conclusions from our perception. We read this book and make conclusions about its content. We miss class and infer that we will not be penalized. We reason: Because something happened, we believe something else will occur.

Reasoning or thinking sometimes differs from culture to culture. People in Asia do not share the Aristotelian mode of reasoning prevalent in the Western world. What is reasonable, logical, and self-evident to an American may be unreasonable, illogical, and not self-evident to an Asian.[27]

The thinking in English is linear. Those who speak Semitic languages seem to use various kinds of parallels in their thinking, whereas the thinking of Chinese and Koreans is marked by indirection and turning in a widening gyre. Figure 5.2 presents a graphic representation of these ideas. [28]

Singer cautions that we must be careful not to believe that all Chinese and Koreans think by a process of indirection, that all English speakers think in a linear fashion, and that all Semitic speakers think in a parallel manner, even though most probably do, most of the time.[29]

Worldview

Worldview is a set of interrelated assumptions and beliefs about the nature of reality, the organization of the universe, the purposes of human life, God, and other philosophical matters that are concerned with the concept of being.[30] Worldview concerns a culture's orientations toward ontological matters or the nature of being and serves to explain how and why things got to be as they are and why they continue that way. It helps to support people during crises and aids them in adjusting to environmental conditions.

A culture's worldview includes both implicit and explicit assumptions underlying the values, norms, and behaviors of its people. The effects of a culture's worldview are usually quite subtle, spreading over a culture and permeating every aspect of it. Worldview is a powerful, although tenuous, determinant in intercultural communication. Deeply buried in every person's mind, most people take their worldview for granted. Because it operates in such a latent fashion, communicators are apt to believe that people from other cultures see the world as they do.[31]

Underscoring the religious differences in worldview is the realization that the worldview of a Catholic is different from that of a Moslem, Hindu, Jew, or Taoist. American Indians view a person's place in nature much differently than Euro-Americans do. An American Indian sees the person as one with nature. The Euro-American places the human at the center of the universe, supreme and apart from nature. In the Euro-American worldview the universe belongs to the human; it is a place to carry out human desires and wishes.

The worldview of the traditional cultures throughout Asia (India, Tibet, Japan, China, Korea, and Southeast Asia) has been influenced heavily by the religious and philosophical systems of Buddhism, Hinduism, Taoism, and Zen. The

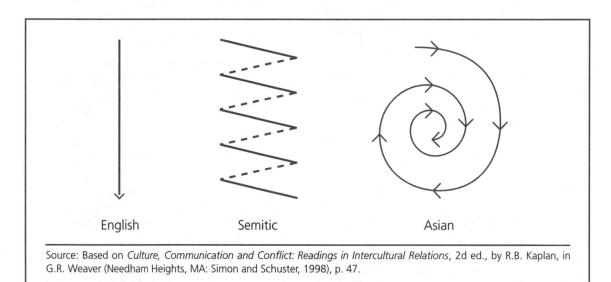

English   Semitic   Asian

Source: Based on *Culture, Communication and Conflict: Readings in Intercultural Relations*, 2d ed., by R.B. Kaplan, in G.R. Weaver (Needham Heights, MA: Simon and Schuster, 1998), p. 47.

FIGURE 5.2   Thought Processes of Three Language Groups

Know Yourself . . .

Some people blame fate for their misfortune. Others believe they are responsible. Who do you blame — fate or yourself?

In the following, select one of the two alternatives.

_____ 1. a. Many personal troubles are caused by bad luck.
   b. People's troubles are caused by their mistakes.

_____ 2. a. Without the right breaks, we can't succeed in life.
   b. Capable people who fail to succeed haven't taken advantage of their opportunities.

_____ 3. a. What will happen will happen.
   b. Taking a definite course of action works better for me.

_____ 4. a. If I'm well prepared, I know that the outcome of a test whatever it is, is fair.
   b. Often, quiz items are so unrelated to coursework that studying is useless.

_____ 5. a. The government is run by a few people in power, and I can do little about it.
   b. As an average citizen, I can have an influence in the workings of government.

If you believe you are responsible for your own success in life, you will have chosen "b" for 1, 2, 3, and 5, and "a" for 4.

Western European nations have followed Greek and Judeo-Christian customs. Asian or Eastern cultures stress direct, immediate, and aesthetic components in a human's experiences of the world. The West encourages a rational, analytic, and indirect outlook of the world, as seen in reasoning and speaking. These differences are reflected in people's conceptions of the self, of others, and of the group over the individual.[32]

Attitudes

An attitude is a covert affective (or feeling) response to a stimulus.[33] In a more comprehensible fashion, attitudes are emotional responses to objects, ideas, and people.[34] Like beliefs, attitudes are general, internalized dispositions to behave in particular ways, being evaluative reactions to our environment. Attitudes are our likes and dislikes.[35]

Attitudes, like beliefs, are covert. They are not directly observable. We cannot know a person's attitudes or beliefs directly. We can observe, however, what the person does or says and from our observations, we can infer the person's attitudes or beliefs.

Attitudes and beliefs indicate behavioral tendencies, or intentions to respond to events, ideas, and people in certain ways. For example, if a student knows (belief) what a communication course is and likes (attitude) the course, the student is likely to take (behavioral intention) the course. Many attitudes and beliefs are stored in our attitude-belief system. Just because we believe does not mean we will act on our belief. We may like communication courses but because we like them does not necessarily mean we will register for them. Other likes and dislikes are competing for our time and energy, and these may be stronger than our like for communication courses. Thus, attitudes and beliefs indicate intentions that may or may not lead to action.[36]

Know Yourself . . .

Some people have an Eastern outlook on life; others have a Western worldview. What is yours? Check it by responding to each of the items with a "1" if it never relates to you, "2" if it rarely does, "3" if it sometimes does, "4" if it often does, and "5" if it usually does.

_____ 1. People should strive to return to nature.

_____ 2. I believe in a personal soul that will continue after death.

_____ 3. I hate to kill anything, even insects.

_____ 4. I get little pleasure from material things.

_____ 5. We should accept our role in life as it is given to us by our parents' status in society.

_____ 6. Meditation is the best form of enlightenment.

_____ 7. The use of artificial organs is going too far.

_____ 8. I feel real kinship with most plants and animals.

_____ 9. We should try to harmonize with nature rather than try to conquer it.

_____ 10. A meaningful life depends more upon learning to cooperate than to compete.

Add the points for the 10 items (10–50). Scores of 40–50 suggest an Eastern outlook on life or worldview.

Based on "Questionnaire to Measure Eastern and Western Thought," by A.R. Gilgen and J.H. Cho in _Psychological Reports, 44,_ 1979.

Attitude Formation

We are not born with attitudes. They begin to form soon after we are old enough to comprehend the world around us. Factors that influence these important behavioral dispositions are socialization, experience, and personality.[37]

Socialization

Perhaps the most obvious reason we form attitudes is that we were taught to feel favorably or unfavorably toward the objects around us. As we grow up, our parents and significant others in our life try to make sure we have the "right" attitude.

Experience

Generally we like the things that fulfill our needs and we dislike those that inhibit our getting or doing the things we want. When we were hungry babies, our mothers fed us certain kinds of food to satisfy our hunger. Experience taught us that foods filled our needs and we developed a favorable attitude toward them. Familiarity with objects and people lead to positive effects. We come to like our pets, our room, our car, just by being around them often and actually living with them. Objects or events that are repeatedly paired with positive experiences are evaluated more positively than those associated with negative experiences.

Personality

A major player in the development of our attitudes is our personality. People with authoritarian personalities are prone to hold prejudices, particularly against minority groups, and often are political conservatives with a preference for a structured social hierarchy in which everyone knows his or her place. The authoritarian personality carries strong moral attitudes about sex and is inclined to fatalism. Then, too, some personalities hold negative attitudes toward others not because of bad experiences with those others but instead as a way of making them feel good by comparison.

Characteristics of Attitudes

Attitudes have four characteristics: direction, degree, endurance, and responsiveness.

Direction

Attitudes are favorable or unfavorable, for or against. We may think favorably about intercultural communication and unfavorably about school in general, or vice versa. We may think favorably about the Israelis and unfavorably about the Arabs. We may have a favorable attitude toward ice cream and an unfavorable attitude toward cake.

Degree

Attitudes can be strong, moderate, mild, or weak, and other variations in between. We may have a strong, favorable attitude toward intercultural communication and a strong, unfavorable attitude toward school. We may strongly favor blondes and mildly dislike redheads. We may weakly favor baseball and moderately dislike all other sports.

Endurance

Attitudes are relatively enduring. They can and do change, however, depending often upon the degree with which they are held. They can change because of *shifting reference groups.*

> *A confirmed racist, Dave's attitude toward minorities slowly shifted to a more favorable one. The members of his work group changed. The older conservative members retired or left the group and were replaced by younger, more liberal men, some of whom represented minorities. The change in Dave's reference group produced alteration in his attitudes toward minorities.*

Sometimes attitudes change in response to *altered reinforcement contingencies.* American auto workers with negative attitudes toward Japanese cars might become more positive if they were to start working for a new company with cars built by the Japanese.

Attitudes often change because other people intentionally use *persuasive communication* to try to change them. From our persuasion communication courses, we know that the success of persuasion depends upon credible communicators, message content, and the listener's susceptibility to persuasion.

Responsiveness

Attitudes are responses to something — people, objects, ideas. We hold attitudes about ourselves, other people, policies, procedures, things, and almost anything in our perceptual field. Like beliefs, we hold thousands of attitudes.

Cultural Antipathy

Attitude and belief systems are at the heart of most communicated antipathies directed at cultural groups. A host of these are identifiable. In Chapter 6 we examine most of those deep-seated aversions.

Chapter Review

Values are the evaluative aspect of our personal orientation system, guiding and directing our behavior. They tell us what is right and wrong, good and bad, providing standards to judge our behavior.

Knowing the values of those with whom we interact is necessary to be effective communicators.

Values can be dissimilar in salience, direction, and degree.

The dominant values in U.S. culture are individualism, freedom, equality, democracy, humanitarianism, self-improvement, progress, activism, achievement, practicality, time, informality, and morality.

Schwartz isolated 10 value patterns that are universally applicable: achievement, benevolence, conformity, hedonism, power, security, self-direction, stimulation, tradition, and universalism.

Hofstede analyzed work-related values and found four cross-culturally useful dimensions: individualism/collectivism, avoidance of uncertainty, masculinity/femininity, and power distance.

Kluckhohn and Strodtbeck contend that all cultures face five universally shared problems: humans' relationship to nature, the modality of human activity, the temporal focus of human life, the relationship of humans to each other, and the innate character of human nature.

Beliefs — judgments about what is true or probable — are potent forces in our personal orientation system.

Beliefs cluster in hierarchical fashion. The most important beliefs form the core or center of our belief system. Beliefs of lesser importance are changed more readily.

Our beliefs originate within the framework of our culture and are learned early in life.

In developing our beliefs, we reason. Cultures reason differently. What is reasonable, logical, and self-evident to Americans may be unreasonable, illogical, and not self-evident to members of another culture.

(Continued)

Chapter Review continued

Worldview is a set of beliefs and assumptions about the culture's orientations toward ontological matters such as the nature of reality, organization of the universe, purposes of life, God, and the nature of being.

Worldview differs among cultures. Religious differences illustrate this point as that of Catholics varies from those of Moslems, Hindus, Jews, and Taoists, among others.

Attitudes are emotional responses to objects, ideas, and people. They are generalized, internal dispositions to behave in terms of our likes and dislikes.

We form attitudes through socialization, experience, and personality.

Attitudes are characterized by direction, degree, endurance, and responsiveness.

Think About This...

1 What values govern your behavior? What superstitious beliefs do you hold? What are some of your likes and dislikes?

2 How do values, beliefs, and attitudes influence intercultural communication?

3 What do the Schwartz, Hofstede, and Kluckhohn-Strodtbeck value orientations have in common? How do they differ?

4 What are your beliefs with respect to nature, to activity, to time, to innate human nature, and to other people? Use the Kluckhohn-Strodtbeck scheme to help answer the question.

5 What is your overall worldview? Do you believe in the existence of a Supreme Being? It is God? How did humans come into being? What is the future of humankind?

6 Cultural Antipathy

In areas of the United States, "dot busting" is alive and well. "Dot" refers to the mark on a Hindu woman's forehead, which symbolizes Lord Shiva's third eye, protecting her, and also indicates the woman's marital status. Members of the Asian Indian American community are randomly harassed in parts of the eastern United States with high concentrations of Indians. Not only are the women subjected to ethnic slurs and violence, but among the other forms of harassment undergone by Asian Indian Americans are physical threats and beating of Indian university students and professionals, painting of swastikas and bombing threats on Indian temples, taunting and degrading of Indian children by American pupils and teachers, the beating of an Indian physician by a police commissioner's son, and the chemical burning of the eyes and face and knife stabbing of an Indian man while his wife and child watched.[1]

Asian Indians are not the only group that has suffered from cultural antipathy. Almost all immigrant groups have received similar treatment, along with the aged, homosexuals, women, and American Indians. Cultural antipathy encompasses a family of cognitive, affective, and behavioral aversions to other people, among them prejudice, racism, discrimination, ageism, heterosexism, classism, stereotyping, and sexism — all spread worldwide.

These types of antipathy are basically beliefs or attitudes, predisposing people to behave with strong dislike for others. Underlying much of the antipathy is ethnocentrism, a way of thinking we will consider first.

 ## Ethnocentrism

Ask Caribs whence they came, and the Caribs will reply, "We alone are people." The Indian tribe's name, Kiowa, means "real or principal people." A Laplander is a "man" or a "human being." The highest

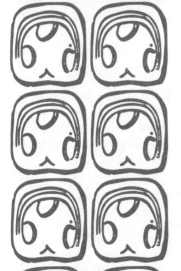

praise a Greenlander has for a European visiting the island is that the European, by studying virtue and good manners from the Greenlanders, soon will be as good as the Greenlanders. As a rule, nature peoples call themselves "men." All other people are something else but not men.

Jewish people divide all humans into the Jews themselves and Gentiles, the Jews being the "chosen people." Greeks and Romans call outsiders "barbarians." Arabs consider themselves as the noblest nation and all others barbarians. Russian books and newspapers talk about its "civilizing mission," as do the books and journals of France, Germany, and the United States. Each nation regards itself as the leader of civilization, the best, the freest, and the wisest. All others are inferior.

These cases exemplify ethnocentrism at the beginning of the 20th century, and many are still applicable today. Ethnocentrism has not changed or dissipated much in the intervening years. It remains a barrier to intercultural communication.[2]

Ethnocentrism is the inability to believe that other cultures offer viable alternatives for organizing reality. The term consists of two Greek words — *ethnos*, meaning nation, and *kentron*, meaning center. Combined, the two words take on the meaning, "Our nation is the center of the world." In his classic *Folkways*, William Graham Sumner defines ethnocentrism as *the technical name for this view of things in which one's own group is the center of everything, and all others are scaled and rated with reference to it.*[3]

Culture helps determine the way we think, feel, and act, and in doing so it becomes the lens through which we judge the world. Functioning in this manner, it unconsciously blinds us to other ways of thinking, feeling, and acting. Our own culture is automatically inborn, native, and natural. In our thinking, it is the only way to function in the world. What makes sense to us should make sense to the rest of the world.

Viewing the world through our cultural lens, we compare other cultures with ours and they are evaluated by our cultural standards. To view another culture as separate from our own is difficult, if not impossible. We should judge people on their cultural background and experience rather than judging them by our standards.

Perceiving our own culture as the natural way to think, act, and behave is beneficial. We ought to take pride in what our culture represents. At the same time, being too arrogant, we may assume feelings of superiority over many other cultures and fail to respect them, which makes learning to function in more than one cultural group difficult.

Cultural Relativism

Cultural relativism advocates the ability to understand other cultures in their own terms, not in terms of our cultural beliefs. Every culture does things differently. What works for one group is right and correct from its point of view, even though it may be different from our own. Then, too, within our nation's boundaries are people from a multitude of cultures. When one of these cultural groups is largely ignorant of another, misunderstandings arise. Cultural relativism would have us learn more about other cultures — after we learn more about our own.[4]

In-Groups and Out-Groups

In 1906 William Graham Sumner introduced the in-group/out-group concept, one basic to and helping to explain ethnocentrism. In-groups are the ones with which we identify; out-groups are the ones to which we do not belong.[5]

In-groups are the ones we are born into and the ones we join as we grow older. They are essential to us because they supply many of our basic needs. They provide us with a ready-made *Weltanschauung* (German for worldview), a philosophy that helps us evaluate what goes on around us. It helps us select an acceptable religion, marriage partners, and proper employment, and helps in other aspects of life. The norms of our in-groups rule our life, and as loyal and reliable members, we defend them if the need arises.

Out-groups, in contrast, are perceived as different, and its members are strange, possibly inferior, and certainly not as good as we are. Some of us are taught to avoid specific out-groups. They are different, perhaps in skin color, religion, social status, ethnicity, parentage, or some behavior.

Our in-group's members behave correctly. An out-group's members behave incorrectly. What is good for our in-group, therefore, is good for everybody. Because our in-group's norms, roles, and values obviously are proper, we must behave as the rest of the in-group behaves, and take pride in what the in-group does.

In-groups provide us with identity. Out-groups provide people to blame for our troubles. The Jews are a historical example of an out-group used as scapegoats by the Nazis during the rise of the Third Reich.

Ethnocentric Statements

The following statements indicate the sort of attitudes that can be labeled ethnocentric:

- *Most other cultures are backward compared to my culture.*
- *My culture should be the role model for other cultures.*
- *I have little respect for the values of other cultures.*
- *People in my culture have just about the best lifestyle anywhere.*
- *I do not trust people who are different.*
- *I dislike interacting with people from different cultures.*

Source: *Ethnocentrism Trait Measurement: Intercultural Communication Research Instruments,* by J.W. Neuliep & J.C. McCroskey, paper presented at International and Intercultural Communication Conference, Miami, 1998.

The Cure

Replacing ethnocentrism, the belief that my way is the best way, is *cultural contingency.* This approach recognizes that there are many ways to reach a final goal and all may be equally valid. The best choice depends upon the cultural mix of the people involved. My way is just one possibility. Undoubtedly other, equally good ways are available. The one we choose should be the one that is most satisfactory to all those taking part.[6]

 ## Stereotyping

According to professional basketball coach Doc Rivers, stereotypes are alive and well in the National Basketball Association. Black athletes are described in team scouting reports as "athletically gifted," "explosive," and "have great instincts." White athletes, in comparison, are "determined," "take-charge guys," "floor generals" with a "work ethic," and having a "thorough understanding of their games.[7]

Stereotypes are not restricted to professional sports. Studies of textbooks and books that children read (comics included), which are primary sources of information for students, reveal stereotypical portraits of minorities based on dated images.[8] For example, the Dutch often appear wearing wooden shoes, the Chinese in pigtails, Africans living in the bush, and Eskimos in igloos. In Western societies, blacks frequently are associated with carelessness, crime, and drug abuse. Often they are depicted as servants, slaves, helpers, or assistants to whites. They have been portrayed as stupid, lazy, cannibalistic, naked, and generally backward.

Geography and history textbooks used in the schools studied in the 1980s brought a Western or European perspective to student readers. Westerners "discovered" America. They civilized the "barbarians" and helped the impoverished, hungry, and underdeveloped. Overlooked in recounting Western exploits is the violence, the slavery, and the extortion or profiteering. The Western conquerors are presented either positively or minimally in a neutral fashion. The conclusion that young readers reach is that the Westerners did "good things" for the savages. In these books, non-Westerners tend to be delineated in a stereotypical manner, often leaving the reader with a negative impression of these people.

The term *stereotyping* was coined by Walter Lippman, a New York newspaper columnist,

Stereotype of the "Silent Finn"

Aino Sallinen

Aino Sallinen

Newspapers, magazines, television programs, and the literature portray the typical Finn as silent, timid, and taciturn. Referring to bilingualism in Finland, Bertolt Brecht has commented that the Finns keep silent in two languages.

Culturally, Finland, a land of mystic twilight representing pre-Siberian traditions, is characterized as tight-lipped. Finnish folklore expresses the mistrust of talkative people. Loquaciousness is considered foolish.

A variation of the "silent Finn" stereotype implies that when a Finn does talk, the resulting performance is slow, laborious, disfluent, poorly articulated, stiff, and inexpressive. Finnish reticence is attributed broadly from low self-esteem, national character, racial origin, the Nordic climate, and lack of oral skills, to tension elicited in interactive encounters.

To verify the "silent Finn" stereotype, I undertook a series of studies, empirical in nature, on reticence among Finnish communicators. Generally, the stereotype was not confirmed. Discrepancy between the stereotype and the study results was considerable.

Reticence followed a normal curve of distribution. I found that socioeconomic levels, education, genus, environment, and speech instruction influenced Finnish reticence. Cultural norms contributed also to the low self-image of many Finns.

Quiet communicative behavior is frequently interpreted as indicative of apprehensive communicators. That interpretation is not meaningful across cultures. In Finland, for example, culture stresses the importance of the message receiver, with politeness being a factor on the speaker's part. Confidence, strength, and wisdom are qualities speakers should exude, not argumentativeness, snubbing, or humiliating behavior directed at listeners. Yet, in public speaking situations, as in other cultures, my studies revealed stage fright among the Finns. In interpersonal interaction, typical Finns seek harmony and consensus.

The "silent Finn" stereotype is being challenged these days by the rapid internationalization of the Finnish-speaking methodologies. The willingness of Finns to adopt modern communication technology suggests a desire to adapt to 21st-century communication demands. A sign of adaptation is the realization that the Finns hold the world record for number of mobile phones per capita.

Dr. Sallinen is president of the University of Jyvaskyla, Jyvaskyla, Finland. That university granted the doctorate in speech communication to Dr. Sallinen in 1986.

public relations expert, and author. He originally described the term in 1922 as a picture inside one's head that helped to manage the complexity of one's environment by simplifying the social world. Lippman derived the name from the printing industry, wherein a stereotype is a type of printing plate from which the same image is obtained again and again. Today the term has taken on a broader meaning, suggesting a widely held image of a group or its members that observers consider unjustified.

Another definition of a stereotype is *a cognitive structure containing the perceiver's knowledge, belief, and expectancies about some human social group.*[9] By examining the definition's principal parts, we obtain a broader understanding of it.

1. *Cognitive structure:* The stereotype resides in the head of the individual perceiver and is not necessarily shared by members of a group. Each individual's experience and interpretation of experience are unique; therefore, each individual's social stereotypes might be different.

The content of a stereotype, however, might be widely shared among members of a group, and, in those cases, the perceiver of a stereotype also may share the stereotype with the group.

2. *Knowledge, beliefs, and expectancies:* All-encompassing, this part of the definition broadens the scope of stereotypes by including not only beliefs about general characteristics of the stereotyped group or person but also knowledge of physical features, attitudes, roles, typical preferences, knowledge gained from personal experience and interactions with the stereotyped subject, and knowledge and beliefs gained secondhand from the media or from others.

3. *Some human social group:* Also an all-encompassing term, this part means two or more people who are seen as sharing some common characteristic socially meaningful to themselves and others, thereby not limiting "groups" to racial, national, or gender categories.[10]

Stereotyping greatly influences interpersonal communication and has a similar impact on intracultural communication. Note these descriptions of people belonging to American microcultures:

- *the aged* — elder statesperson, senior citizen, golden ager, wise, grouchy, demented, negative qualities outweighing the positive
- *homosexuals* — sexually abnormal, perverted, maladjusted, prey on young children, gender deviants with gay men perceived as more feminine, more emotional, more submissive, weaker than heterosexual men, and lesbians perceived as more dominant, direct, forceful, strong, liberated, and nonconforming than heterosexual women
- *welfare recipients* — dishonest, dependent, lazy, uninterested in education, promiscuous.[11]

In any case, everybody stereotypes. By doing so, we have a way of organizing experiences, helping us to make sense of the differences among individuals and groups, and thereby helping us predict how people will behave.

Stereotypes of Americans

- *By visitor from India: Americans are in a perpetual hurry, never allowing themselves the leisure to enjoy life.*
- *By visitor from Kenya: Americans are distant and highly individualistic.*
- *By visitor from Indonesia: Americans have to talk about everything, and analyze. Even the little things have to be Why? Why? Why?*
- *By visitor from Iran: They're like primitive tribes sending their old and infirm to die alone, in a nursing home.*
- *By visitor from Afghanistan: In America, everyone tries to lose weight. In my country, we try to gain it.*

American Stereotypes of Russians — Changing Over Time

During World War II	Cold War Years	Post Cold War	Recently
hardworking	cruel	serious	disciplined
brave	hardworking	hardworking	hardworking
radical	domineering	firm	obedient
ordinary	backward	intelligent	serious
progressive	progressive	thrifty	strong

Based on "Russia and the West," by Walter G. Stephan & Marina Abalakina-Paap, in *Handbook of Intercultural Training,* 2d ed., edited by D. Landis & R. S. Bhagat (Thousand Oaks, CA: Sage, 1996), p. 370.

Therefore, stereotyping is a necessity for thinking and communicating. We cannot respond individually to the millions of isolated elements we perceive every day, so we are forced to group them into categories. Then we respond to the categories.

Walking the city's streets, we stereotype the people approaching us. Those whom we categorize as dangerous, we avoid. Those who look friendly, we will not turn from, and perhaps will greet. At a crowded party, we decide who seems likely to share our interests and seek them out, acting on our stereotype of who is attractive to us. When we meet someone who, to us, represents a certain group, we see the person as a member of the group and apply to that person all of the qualities we associate with the group.

Distortions of Reality

Stereotypes assist us in making the world more understandable. They can distort reality, however, in three ways.

1. *Accentuate differences*. Stereotypes can intensify dissimilarities between groups. They emphasize the way groups differ, not the common features, making stereotyped groups seem odd, unfamiliar, or even dangerous. They are not like us. Stereotyping professors as intelligent, virile, handsome, and honest accentuates the differences between them and us. They certainly are not like us! But we know that professors are individuals and not all fit the stereotype. Many are unattractive, weak, and known to occasionally fib — just like us.

2. *Underestimate differences*. Stereotypes underestimate differences within groups. We know that the groups to which we belong are made up of all kinds of people. Stereotypes, however, give the impression that all members of stereotyped groups are the same. One rude taxi driver means that all taxi drivers are rude. One discourteous store clerk means that all store clerks are discourteous. Our experience with groups of cab drivers and store clerks, however, tells us that they are not all the same. They have individual qualities that set each apart, one from the other, even though they are members of the same group.

3. *Selective perception*. Another cause of distortion is our tendency to see in a person or group of people only those qualities that conform to the stereotype we have of them. If we believe taxi drivers are rude, when we ride with one, we expect him or her to be rude. If the driver is not, we are apt to perceive him or her as an anomaly, a deviation from our norm.

Transmitting Stereotypes

Stereotypes are transmitted verbally and nonverbally. Verbally, they are transmitted through vocabulary (Jap, kike, nigger, sex-specific words), mass communication (textbooks, magazines, news reports, books), and interpersonal communication (parent-child, student-teacher interactions). Nonverbally, stereotypes are transmitted through observation (children watching their parents avoid contact with certain groups), bodily movements (giving someone "the finger"), and facial expressions (sneering at a person from a disliked group).

It seems unlikely, however, that the specific content of a stereotype can be transmitted without some sort of linguistic label. A child can observe a parent avoiding a homeless person and sense that the homeless person belongs to an out-group. Without the linguistic labels, the child will not know how to refer to that person. Children whose parents or teachers are more prejudiced will learn the stereotypic beliefs about groups faster and to a greater extent than children whose parents and teachers are not as prejudiced.

Crosscultural Phenomenon

Stereotyping is common to all cultures, although the less contact stereotypers have with the group being stereotyped, the less strongly held the stereotypes seem to be.

Supporting the notion that stereotyping is a crosscultural phenomenon is this stereotype of the Japanese by the Chinese:

> A Japanese man is an irrational, brutal, temperamental, and war-loving person, who lives with his hypocritical wife in a miserably small house in a hierarchical, submission-oriented and feudalistic society, communicating with his fellow men in an inadequate language, while cooperating with the government and big business in the economic, but soon to be military, invasion of other Asian

> countries, all the while being unconsciously under the influence of the dominantly superior Chinese culture and civilization.[12]

A Japanese communication specialist uncovered this stereotype while conducting a research project in the People's Republic of China. In his analysis of the stereotype, this researcher makes a vital point about stereotypes: Stereotypers, through overgeneralization and oversimplification, can elevate their own people's pride and satisfy their superiority complex. The researcher

---

Stereotypes About Hawaii's Residents

Here are examples of stereotypes held about various ethnic groups living in Hawaii:

Caucasian: *Successful, independent, self-confident, loud, insensitive, bossy, outspoken, prestige- and power-oriented, boastful, conceited*

Chinese: *Think in reverse, launderers, restaurant operators, shrewd, frugal, hardworking, "the Jews of the Orient," cold, stoic, unemotional*

Japanese: *Personally clean, orderly, stoic, group-oriented, hierarchical, clannish, stubborn, reluctant to state opinion, unoriginal, emotionless, hardworking*

Korean: *Hot-tempered, quick-fisted, persnickety, loud, aggressive, proud, stubborn, hardworking, tenacious, factionalistic*

Filipino: *Sensitive, friendly, courteous, hottempered, family-oriented, helpful, supportive, hardworking, hierarchical*

Source: *People and Cultures of Hawaii*, by J. F. McDermott, Jr., W-S. Tseng & T.W. Maretzki (Honolulu: University Press of Hawaii, 1980).

touches on the self-evaluative benefits of differentiating one's own group from other groups.

These differentiations are driven by the stereotyper's desire for positive self-evaluation, part of which comes from his or her membership in social groups. To the extent that we have favorable evaluations of our own groups or can at least disparage other groups, we will obtain some benefit of consequence to our own self-esteem.

The Japanese communication specialist goes on to note that effective intercultural communication partially depends upon knowing what stereotypical images, positive or negative, exist, and suspending judgments about them until the communicators understand each other better. When people like a group, their stereotypes are likely to be positive, and negative if they dislike the group.

 Prejudice

In the archetypal volume, *The Nature of Prejudice,* author Gordon Allport noted how humans have gained mastery over energy, matter, and inanimate nature and now are learning to control illnesses and even premature death. Yet, he laments, we seem to have remained in the Stone Age in our handling of human relations.[13] The example introducing this chapter and others to follow should serve to remind us that Allport's pessimism is warranted. Prejudice and racial hatred continue to permeate the world. They are rooted in our verbal and nonverbal behavior, and reflected in our communicative interactions with others.

Although prejudice is not a new social issue, it is one that is highly salient in modern society. Diversity issues have blossomed as the demographic character of the United States evolves from one numerically dominated by European Americans, and as resources no longer seem plentiful. Rather than encouraging tolerance or even embracing differences, the diversity issues

seem to have intensified prejudice. Classism, racism, sexism, ageism, discrimination, and other distinctions seem to have become even more polarized and negatively emotionalized.[14]

Prejudice is a serious problem in contemporary society, and news reports support that contention. Hate groups are increasing, with gay men the number-one target and blacks and Jews second and third, respectively.[15] The report of the U.S. Commission on Civil Rights enumerates the growing rate of attacks on Asian Americans. Even among people who profess a Christian religious identity, prejudice appears prevalent.[16]

The Nature of Prejudice

Like other attitudes, prejudice is generally conceptualized as having a *cognitive* component (in the form of irrationally based beliefs about a target group), an *affective* component (in the form of dislike), and a *behavioral* predisposition (in the form of avoidance of the target group). Thus, prejudice is a negative attitude directed to a group as a whole or toward an individual who is a member of that group.[17]

Allport provides the most widely accepted conceptualization of prejudice. Historically, the term stems from the Latin noun *praejudicium,* meaning a precedent or judgment based on previous decisions or experiences. Prejudice can be either positive or negative, or both. Allport's definition is bipolar: *Prejudice is an antipathy based on faulty and inflexible generalization, either felt or expressed, directed toward a group, or toward an individual because he*[sic] *is a member of that group.*[18]

The definition includes three components deserving explanation.[19]

1. Although prejudice can be either positive or negative, the term has taken on a primarily negative connotation, and we consider it in that way.

2. Prejudice is based on faulty or unsubstantiated data. It has no basis in fact. The prejudiced person certainly will claim a plethora

of facts to support his or her claim, but those facts usually are strained and typically are based on limited personal experience, recounted memories mixed with hearsay, and overgeneralizations.

3. Prejudice is rooted in inflexible generalizations. These are not necessarily expressed or acted upon, but mostly are internal beliefs and attitudes.

Diffusion of Prejudice

Some prejudices, such as a disagreeable or perplexing meeting with a person from another ethnic group, come from experience. Many prejudices are passed along from parents to children. "My father used to tell me," one student reported, "we don't talk to people like that, mostly vagrants or drunks, or people who are not of our religion or race." Many come from images the media convey.

Teun A. van Dijk, a University of Amsterdam professor, analyzed prejudice in thought and talk in the Netherlands and the United States. He discovered how prejudice is diffused through personal communication and other channels of expression.[20]

Negative prejudices against homeless people are prevalent.

Personal Communication

Informal, interpersonal interaction is at the core of transmission of prejudice in society. The face-to-face channel is the most significant one. Parents and teachers speaking to children pass on their prejudices, as do friends talking with friends.

News Media

Newspapers, magazines, radio, television, and the Internet score high as sources of ethnic beliefs and opinions. Major themes of media reports are crime, police action, racial hostilities, housing, employment, immigration, and cultural differences.

Educational Materials

Many prejudices can be traced to children's books and textbooks. History, geography, and social science textbooks have included content indicating varying degrees of ethnocentrism, stereotypes, and prejudice. The home country is portrayed more favorably than Third World and black countries. The white perspective prevails and systematically underrepresents American Indians, blacks, and Hispanics. Colonial history is described in terms of adventure, exploration, heroic feats, and the spread of "civilization," while downplaying exploitation, slavery, and brutality.

Sociopolitical Elite

The sociopolitical elite are members of national, state, and local governments, legislative bodies, educational institutions, courts, police, welfare agencies, and health institutions, among others. These groups formulate and justify policies that tend to favor some ethnic groups over others. The danger lies in giving preference to the white majority, where most of the votes or power lies.

Common Themes of Prejudice

In his book *Communicating Racism*, Teun van Dijk analyzed prejudiced discourse, after examining hundreds of samples of talk between people from various groups in different cultures. From his study he found the principal themes in prejudiced discourse. He discovered that people do not have a different set of prejudices for each out-group they talk about but, instead, follow the same general themes regardless of the group.[21] The following themes represent their reasons for believing as they do about the out-groups they dislike:

1. *General.* The talk reflects a general attitude of dislike: I don't like them (the out-group); my friends don't like them; my family doesn't like them.

2. *Origin and appearance.* Statements that fit this category include: We shouldn't have invited them. Send them back where they came from. Immigration policies should be stricter. They look different. They wear funny clothes.

3. *Socioeconomic goals and status.* Among the statements typical of this theme are: They take our jobs. They abuse our social system. They are a financial threat.

4. *Sociocultural differences.* Typical statements are: They have a different lifestyle and should adapt to ours. They have too many children. They need to learn to speak our language. They're dirty. Their children cause problems at school.

5. *Personal characteristics.* Statements like these are heard in prejudiced discourse: They're aggressive (violent). They increase the crime rate. They're lazy. They're noisy.

When we boil down the statements representing these five themes, we recognize some of the causes for in-group prejudices against out-group members. In-group members are prejudiced against out-group members because they are perceived as an economic threat to the in-group. The out-group members are culturally different and socially deviant from in-group norms. Out-group members are a threat economically, culturally, and socially.

Understanding Prejudice

In his multidisciplinary view of prejudice, Baldwin looks at four perspectives or groups of theories advanced to explain prejudice: evolutionary theories, group-level theories, individual-level theories, and message-based theories.[22]

Evolutionary Perspectives

One set of explanations suggests that prejudice is innate, or at least has a biological basis — the evolutionary approach. This approach may take one of two directions. One is that character dispositions, intelligence, and other traits are biologically specific to race or gender. Another suggests that prejudice is explained through heredity; physiology (genetics or structure of the brain) influences behavior in some way, causing people to fear difference.

Group-Level Approaches

One group-level approach emphasizes political or economic competition caused by a dominant group trying to exploit a minority group to gain a material advantage — for example, Anglo-Americans being prejudiced against Mexican-Americans who compete against each other for a limited number of jobs. In another variation, a controlling group does not allow a group without political clout to assimilate or maintain its own culture.

Individual-Level Approaches

Individual-level of explanations center on the individual and his/her relationships with social groups. These could be cognitive — how people experience and categorize reality. Stereotypical thinking is an example. Or the explanations could be developmental, with ethnocentrism an example of prejudice developing against a group.

Message-Based Approaches

Message-based approaches explain the creation of prejudice through rhetorical devices such as propaganda, a system to encourage intergroup enmity through explicit means such as posters, or leaflets, or implicit means such as misinformation, disinformation, and lies in the media.

Acting Out Prejudice

Although many people are prejudiced, only a small percentage act on their prejudice.[23] Prejudice can take various forms, ranging from mild and covert to harsh and overt. One model presents expressions of prejudice on a five-level continuum, from least to most intense. These levels are antilocution, avoidance, discrimination, physical attack, and extermination.

Antilocution

Antilocution is characterized by prejudicial talk among friends, neighbors, fellow workers, and other like-minded people. Antilocution appears in verbal abuse and hate speech.

Verbal Abuse. *Verbal abuse* is a mild form of antilocution in which abusers cast negative aspersions on out-group members. Ethnic joke-telling, name-calling, and derisive talk are stronger forms.

Some ethnic joke-tellers consider their stories to be merely another form of humor, and the derogatory or racial intent of the humor is not the reason for relating the stories. In Hawaii, for instance, telling ethnic jokes can be a friendly means of bridging existing cultural gaps and helping make the members of all cultures feel part of the total society. The jokes are accepted more readily, however, when a Portuguese person tells jokes about the Portuguese, a Samoan tells jokes about Samoans, or a Tongan tells jokes about Tongans. Nevertheless, ethnic jokes are a disengaging way of ridiculing out-groups while enhancing the joke teller's in-group.

Native American Humor

In the Native American world, humor functions to guide social situations when various tribal communities interact. Pueblos tease Sioux that their hamburgers bark when they bite into them. (Sioux Indians traditionally ate dogs.) Chippewas tease Pueblos that their outdoor ovens would make good bomb shelters.

Native Americans share jokes to create a bond and a solid feeling of unity and purpose — for example, "Custer wore Arrow shirts." "It's a good thing Columbus wasn't looking for Turkey or else we would be called Turkeys instead of Indians." "For the evening look, glue high heels to a pair of moccasins." "A Native American operating on Indian time is an individual who is either early or not so early, but never late."

Source: "Native American Culture and Communication Through Humor," by C. Shutiva, in *Our Voices*, 3d ed., edited by M. Houston & V. Chen (Los Angeles: Roxbury, 2000), pp. 113–117.

Name-calling, another type of verbal abuse, is used to taunt out-group members. Names such as Polack, Chink, Hun, Dago, Whitey, squaw, stud, commie, pinko, yo-yo, kotonk, pig, and Buddha-head, when tossed around in the heat of an argument, could lead to violence.

Talk that ridicules or mocks an out-group and its members is derisive, demeaning, and indicative of prejudice. "I can't tell one Asian from another" is humiliating, as is a white calling a black "boy."

Hate Speech. For our purposes, *hate speech* is defined as *oral communication that expresses strong dislike, animosity, or loathing toward a person or an out-group.*[24] It is a cleverly contrived scheme for gaining an end. Rather than win over an audience through superior reasoning, hate speech aims to move an audience by creating a symbolic code for violence. Hate speech seeks to inflame the emotions of followers, to denigrate the designated out-group, to inflict permanent and irreparable harm to opponents, and finally to conquer.

Hate speech hurts the out-group it targets, emotionally if not physically. It also legitimizes and encourages attitudes of hatred, possibly even to the point of promoting hate crimes against minority groups. For example, some people consider pornography a form of hate speech against women, and well-designed studies show that people exposed to much pornography develop more negative attitudes toward women and more acceptance of violence against women.[25]

Epithets like those mentioned in name-calling, which are meant to demean or denigrate on the basis of race, ethnicity, religion, gender, sexual orientation, age, appearance, and handicap, constitute hate speech. Thus, words such as nigger, spic, wop, gook, kike, dot, bitch, faggot, dyke, blue-hair, geezer, fatso, and crip can be construed as hate speech. In comparison to name-calling, in which such words may be tossed into the heat of argument unintentionally because of insensitivity or ignorance, these words become hate speech when they are intended to denigrate or demean.

On college and university campuses, hate speech is alive and well. Remarks that attack individuals on the basis of race, gender, handicap, or sexual orientation continue to be reported on many campuses. In response, hundreds of schools have established codes to regulate this form of speech.[26] When tested in courts of law, however, many of these codes have fared poorly. One ruling pointed out that a university may not suppress expression simply because it finds that expression offensive. The First Amendment secures the fundamental right of free, uncensored expression, even on matters that some may find trivial, vulgar, or profane.[27] Hate speech continues as a form of prejudice protected in the United States, at least by the Constitution.

Elsewhere in the world the trend has been to protect individuals and groups from expressions of hatred. A dozen countries have statutes or constitutional provisions prohibiting forms of hate speech. The International Covenant of Civil and Political Rights, Article 20(2), prohibits the advocacy of national, racial, or religious hatred. In ratifying this treaty, the U.S. Senate stipulated that it would not be bound by this provision. Instead, it would adhere to the U.S. Constitution.[28]

Avoidance

Avoidance is the mode when individuals make a conscious effort to stay away from groups they are prejudiced against. Individuals who avoid will tolerate inconvenience for the sake of avoidance. To avoid shopping in a neighborhood store run by people they do not like avoiders will shop elsewhere even though the local store is more convenient, has lower prices, and carries a more complete line of grocery products. The inconvenience is self-directed, and the individual takes no harmful action against those he or she avoids.

Discrimination

Discrimination means taking active steps to exclude or deny members of another group entrance or participation in a desired activity. Discrimination practices lead to segregation in education, employment, politics, social privileges, and recreational activities.[29]

In employment, for example, many barriers prevent equal participation in the labor market. These barriers often are erected against foreign-born people who seek employment commensurate with their education. The advancement of ethnic minorities and women's status have been thwarted by artificial barriers such as "glass ceilings" and jobs that have limited opportunity for advancement.

Discrimination is widely practiced in education. For example, in violation of federal civil rights laws, limited-English-proficient students are denied participation in public education programs because of their poor English language skills. Minority students give up trying to learn because of cultural and linguistic gaps. Textbooks and lesson plans are geared to mainstream American students and are inappropriate for immigrant students.[30]

Discrimination is directed toward microcultures. The elderly, women, poor, homosexuals, and racial minorities, are frequent targets.

Ageism. Discrimination based on chronological age, ageism, continues to be largely unchecked in the United States. Older people have more limited access to health care and productive employment in particular. Yet, older people represent the only stigmatized group that, barring premature death, every American will join. They are more heterogeneous than any other age group, along just about every dimension. The elderly include the wisest members of society as well as the most demented, but the stereotypes about them are more negative than positive, beliefs are more negative, and evaluations are more negative than for younger people. Ageism is well documented.[31]

In work settings, mandatory retirement is an ageist policy. Mandatory retirement ignores a person's actual job performance — a better basis than age for retirement decisions. In medical care the implication is that the older person's life is not worth saving because the person is close to death anyway. Younger people often speak to older ones as if they were babies. They speak slowly and use simple language to help their elders understand. Elderly women are less likely to have retirement benefits and their received benefits are generally less than men's. Poverty in later life is a risk for people who work in low-status jobs. Ageism is a human problem affecting everyone. Combating ageism hurts no one and helps everyone.[32]

Sexism. Sexism can be defined as the oppression or inhibition of women through a vast network of everyday practices, attitudes, assumptions, behaviors, and institutional rules. It is structural and systemic, resulting in the privileging of men. Sexism is an omnipotent part of life, and it achieves its separation powers from men through exclusion, avoidance, or distancing.[33]

Gender differences that subordinate women are justified on religious, biological, and social science bases. Those who use religion to support a sexist viewpoint refer to the natural order of things as accounted for in holy texts or the teachings of prophets and priests.

Biological justifications assert essential and immutable differences among humans on the basis of their primary and secondary sex characteristics, both physical and genetic, as well as "commonsense" knowledge that men are stronger and women weaker, more emotional, and more nurturing. Social scientific literature suggests that women's being more nurturing best serves the social order by women's performing relationship maintenance tasks in the home and workplace as caregivers, wives, nurses, and kindergarten teachers.[34]

Sexism is communicated by language, in interaction (the bifurcation of individuals into "male" and "female" categories), and systems of representation (white women as homemakers or sex objects, black women as maids or wanton sex animals, American Indian women as princesses or squaws, Asian women as "dragon ladies" or exotic or submissive sexual objects, and Latinas as suffering mother figures or cantina girls.)[35]

Discrimination is illustrated by wages, with women often being paid less than men for equal work or by workplace and societal opportunity, in which women have difficulty obtaining certain positions and membership in certain clubs and organizations. Employment discrimination against Asian American women is well-documented by the federal government. Immigrant Asian American women frequently work with few other women and thus have no informal support network of co-workers to turn to for advice and counsel, and are vulnerable to discriminatory practices as well as sexual advances.[36]

Classism. In Chapter 3 we noted the four social class categories: lower or underclass, working class, middle class, and upper class. These four categories also are applicable to discrimination. Discriminatory behavior is experienced particularly by the underclass or poor people. Poor people typically are excluded from social institutions such as hospitals and well-equipped schools, welfare recipients and the homeless from equal employment opportunities, not receiving loans from banks, in violation of fair lending laws, unequal health care and mental health treatment, and help in the legal system.[37]

Dreama Moon describes a white, middle-class woman portraying working-class women as sitting around in a bar watching television, drinking, laughing, and loudly carrying on. Middle-class women patronize cocktail lounges, maybe with television, but are quieter and tuned to the news, not sporting events, and drinking something other than beer, probably wine, while discussing things. Upper-class women might be in their drawing rooms, sipping Port and talking about something intellectual, art, or literature. The white woman's description moves up the class hierarchy in her description.[38]

Relations between working and middle classes usually are one-way dialogues. From above come commands, diagnoses, instructions, judgments. Ideas seldom flow upward, because there are no channels for the upward flow of thought from class to class. More important than personal communication, the dominant classes are able to act on the unfavorable judgments by implementing policies against nondominant groups.[39]

Heterosexism. Heterosexism is defined as an *ideological system that denies, denigrates, and stigmatizes any nonheterosexual form of behavior, relationship, or community*.[40] Heterosexism appears in social customs and institutions as discriminatory behaviors against gay men and lesbians.

Discriminatory behavior takes many forms, ranging from jokes to putdowns and to murder. In between are exclusion from social institutions, distancing between homosexuals and other people, harassment, insults, intimidation, and physical attacks. According to a study of lesbians and gay men, homosexuals are vandalized, spat upon, chased, followed, or pelted with objects. When seeking police help, they frequently are victimized by those helping to investigate their case.[41]

Racism. Racism consists of three independent but positively related constructs — prejudice, stereotypical beliefs about minorities, and overt discriminatory behaviors toward minorities. Three levels of racism are:[42]

1. *Institutional racism.* At this level a subordinate racial group is denied equal participation in stable, organized, and systematized associations or procedures.

2. *Collective racism.* This level refers to less formal group and social norms that reinforce collective acts, such as opposition to blacks moving into white neighborhoods.

3. *Individual racism* (interpersonal racism). This level is defined as *a set of attitudes held by a particular person that members of a minority group are culturally or physically inferior to the dominant group and therefore can be exploited or discriminated against.*

Racism classifies people on the basis of their external physical traits — skin color, eye shape, hair, facial features. Racism is a social construction, an attempt to give social meaning to physical differences when racism is biologically meaningless. Biological variations blend from one racial category to another.[43] The concern is that, through subtle socializing influences, people come to accept the stereotypes of people as a social fact based solely on skin color, facial features, and hair texture — none of which has a genetic relationship to intelligence or personality.

Genetically, No Race

At the genetic level, race does not exist, writes Dawn Stover, science editor for Popular Science *magazine. Studies of human DNA have found that individuals within any given "racial" group have more genetic variability than individuals between two such groups.*

Although human coloration tends to vary with latitude, skin color is not a reliable indicator of biological kinship. Sub-Saharan Africans are more similar to Europeans genetically than to Melanesians, despite the fact that Melanesians and sub-Saharan Africans share dark skin and curly hair. Yet the U.S. Census Bureau continues to divide Americans into distinct racial groups, making race a potent cultural and political issue, though not a biological one.

Source: *International Herald Tribune*, April 20, 2000.

Physical Attack

A fourth way of acting out our prejudices is the physical attack, as seen in fistfights, gang fights, vandalism, pogroms, riots, and lynchings.

How do the physical attacks start? To remove the brakes that stop verbal aggression from becoming an attack, certain conditions are required. In his classic, *The Nature of Prejudice*, Allport describes the progression in a physical encounter that becomes violent.[44]

Members of an in-group hold prejudicial attitudes toward members of an out-group. The in-group is having problems and blames the out-group for them. The in-group's perception of the out-group turns negative, first as verbal abuse, and in time name-calling and derisive talk enter the picture.

If the progression continues, with the in-group constantly feeling put upon by the out-group, tension develops. The out-group then is ostracized in some manner, perhaps being barred from interacting with in-group members, excluded from mutual functions, school, or community activities. Out-group members may be banished from the local playground, the neighborhood bar, or favorite hangouts.

A strain or stress befalls the in-group, the cause of which is blamed on the out-group. Soon the in-group tires of the stresses and strains and organizes to fight the out-group. An event of some sort kindles flames of hatred, and violence breaks out. A shooting of a black immigrant by white policemen in New York led to a court trial of the policemen involved, who were exonerated. Riots broke out.

Physical attacks typically happen in places where an in-group and out-group are thrown into close contact — as examples, local parks, beaches, schoolgrounds, boundaries of residential districts. Hot weather favors violence. People become irritable, and the heat brings them out-of-doors. Young people are the primary participants.[45]

Extermination

The final phase in acting-out prejudice, extermination, involves the systematic and planned destruction of a group of people. Lynchings, pogroms, and massacres are not common today, at least in the United States. But in the first years of the 20th century, about 4,000 lynchings were carried out in this country; 80 percent of the victims were black. Elsewhere in the world, the practice of extermination continues, with eastern Europe as an example.

Bigotry and bias are alive and well, writes Mary Robinson, United Nations high commissioner for human rights. Racism and xenophobia are on the rise, with genocide in Rwanda and "ethnic cleansing" in the former Yugoslavia. Indigenous peoples have been marginalized and pushed into more inhospitable parts of their territories. Migrant workers are exploited. The right to seek asylum is almost impossible because of "nonadmission" policies by most industrialized countries. The Roma community is the object of discrimination.[46]

Hate speech is increasing and now disseminated on the Internet at little financial cost. Sent through U.S.-based sites, the disseminators are protected by the First Amendment of the U. S. Constitution. The first article of the Universal Declaration of Human Rights — "Everyone is born free and equal in dignity and rights" — has not become a reality, Robinson asserts.[47]

Chapter Review

Cultural antipathy encompasses a family of cognitive, affective, and behavioral aversions to other people — among them, ethnocentrism, stereotypes, prejudice, discrimination, ageism, heterosexism, classism, sexism, and racism — all worldwide in scope.

Ethnocentrism is the view in which one's own group is the center of everything and all others are scaled and rated with reference to it.

In the cultural relativism approach, we understand other cultures in their terms, not in terms of our culture's beliefs.

Stereotypes are fixed impressions of a group of people through which we perceive specific individuals. Stereotypes distort reality by accentuating differences, underestimating differences, and perceiving selectively.

Stereotypes are transmitted verbally through language, mass communication, and interpersonal communication, as well as in nonverbal ways.

Stereotyping is an intercultural phenomenon.

Prejudice is a negative feeling based upon faulty and inflexible generalizations. It may be overt or covert and is directed toward an individual or a group of people.

Prejudice is disseminated through interpersonal communication, news media, educational materials, and the sociopolitical elite.

Prejudice has been explained through four perspectives: evolutionary, group-level, individual-level, and message-based approaches.

Prejudice is acted out through antilocution, avoidance, discrimination, physical attack, and extermination.

Antilocution takes the form of verbal abuse and hate speech.

(Continued)

Chapter Review continued

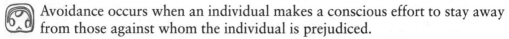 Avoidance occurs when an individual makes a conscious effort to stay away from those against whom the individual is prejudiced.

Discrimination occurs when individuals are denied or excluded from participating in a desired activity. Groups discriminated against include the aged, women, poor, homosexuals, and racial minorities.

Ageism is discrimination based on chronological age.

Sexism is the oppression or inhibition of women from a vast network of activities and institutions.

Classism is the exclusion of certain classes of people from activities and institutions, predominantly the poor.

Heterosexism opposes nonheterosexual forms of behavior, relationships, and community.

Racism is a set of attitudes holding that certain minority groups are inferior and should be discriminated against.

Physical attack involves acting out prejudice in a violent form.

Extermination means to eliminate individuals or groups of people in a systematic, planned manner.

Think About This . . .

1 Explain ethnocentrism, cultural relativism, stereotyping, and cultural contingency.

2 How is prejudice diffused? Give examples from your own experience.

3 How do people act out prejudice? Explain each way described in this chapter.

4 Explain each of the "isms."

5 The chapter reports that antipathy is alive and well. What is meant by that statement?

7 Cultural Foundations: Social Institutions

To cope with the nitty-gritty of daily life, humans have invented and developed an array of social institutions. The pervasiveness of these institutions is implied by a look at how typical people spend their time in the cultures of the world. On weekdays in most cultures, adults work and children go to school. On Sundays, a holiday for many people, church beckons for those with a religious inclination. For others, a day of rest and relaxation is in order, with visits to relatives or friends a possibility.

Throughout the week, voluntary associations that function in some cultures occupy people's nonwork time. Clubs, athletic groups, community organizations, and church and school groups take up much of the free time. In all these instances, people are behaving in ways influenced and even regulated by social institutions established for that purpose.

Our focus in this chapter is on the major social institutions responsible for our growth and development as human beings, those that greatly influence our lives, and those in which we spend much of our time. The family, educational institutions, religion, political institutions, and economic systems impact on our daily living in some form or other. All have an effect on how and why we communicate with people from other cultures.

 ## The Family

The family and the institution of marriage exist in every known human society, a conclusion reached after sampling 250 diverse societies and

Photo by Sam Pegues

115

finding not a single exception.[1] As the agency of procreation, birth, and care of the young, the family is an indispensable organization to humans. It is the group to which an individual belongs for a long time, usually for life, and it is one from which a member cannot easily withdraw.

Families, however, appear in so many different forms that it is difficult to say exactly what a family is. In the general sense, a family is defined as *two or more persons who are linked by marriage or descent and who engage in common activities*. The smallest family is a *nuclear* family — a married couple and their children. Not all families fit this model. A family can take many forms. It might be a single-parent household or a married couple sharing their home with a relative who is living with them temporarily. It could be a large group of parents, children, and in-laws who live together on a permanent basis. When relatives outside the nuclear family share the same household, this family group is known as an *extended family*.

Even this definition of the family varies from society to society. The wives of the Nayar of India live with their mothers instead of the husbands. In this warrior subcaste, the mother's brother replaces the father. Young Nayar girls marry after they reach menarche, but they live apart from their husbands and are allowed to take on lovers. In the Israeli kibbutz, children are reared separately from their parents and visit them on weekends. Harem life continues in a few places, and in others marriages are arranged between young children. Matrifocal households are found throughout Latin America and parts of Africa, wherein the family unit is made up of a mother and her children.

The Incest Taboo

The common denominator in all cultures is the *incest taboo*, an unwritten rule that creates two classes of opposite-sex members. There are those with whom we may have sexual relations and there are those with whom we may not. Although the taboo takes varied forms, a universal practice is observed: no sexual relations within the nuclear family. Nuclear incest is tabooed everywhere. Theories abound as to why nuclear incest is forbidden, and no firm reason accounts for its origin. But it has a vital result: Because nuclear incest is taboo, for procreation purposes sons and daughters must marry out of the nuclear family. Alliances are formed with other nuclear families, usually not of the same relation, and this creates new families. Instead of being tied socially and emotionally to only a few members of one group, everyone becomes part of a larger social structure. Marriage thus creates a network of affiliations that help bind a culture's social structure together.

Family Structure

Because families regulate sexual behavior, the fact that *monogamy* (marriage between one man and one woman) is the most common form of marriage should not be surprising. Some cultures, however, have a shortage of eligible mates and *polygamy* (marriage to more than one partner) is allowed.

Polygamy can take different forms.

1. *Polygyny* (marriage between one man and two or more women). This is the most common form, with roughly 75 percent of the mostly tribal cultures practicing it. More than one wife indicates wealth, bringing prestige to the husband. The more wives, the more children are produced, and they provide additional labor. Of course, they cost more to support.

2. *Polyandry* (marriage of one woman to two or more men). This form usually occurs under the severest of economic conditions, and then usually with brothers sharing one wife.

The mate-selection process differs among cultures. In North America, Europe, and parts of Asia, marriage depends upon mutual acceptance of the husband and bride-to-be. Romantic love plays the principal role, and it typically develops after a period of dating. *Exogamy* (marriage outside a certain group) is the practice in this process of mate choice. But *endogamy* (marriage restricted to members of a certain class or ethnic group) finds favor in caste societies or homogenous cultures wanting to perpetuate their kind.

In some cultures, marriages are arranged between family heads, and the couple involved is not consulted. Marriage, in that case, is the joining of two families and not the union of two people.

Every culture maintains control over the selection process. Nuclear family members cannot marry, and in many cases, extended family members are forbidden to marry. Usually a minimum age limit is set, and a legal sanction of some sort is required. This approval comes either in the form of a marriage license or official approval from the governing body. Caste cultures prohibit intercaste marriages.

Patriarchal families represent the universal practice. The men dominate, usually under the husband's leadership or that of the oldest man, and the presiding man ordinarily exerts great influence over the lives of family members. In advanced industrial cultures, however, patriarchal arrangements tend to break down. In the United States, the men, for instance, no longer control the purse strings and, therefore, the power to make decisions for the family. Women who work now have as much power as the men in managing the household.

A few cultures, Ghana and Zaire, for instance, illustrate the *matriarchal* family, in which the wife or mother assumes the dominant role and the other females have some say. An increasing number of "solo mums," as they are known in New Zealand, run the house. They are unmarried or divorced women. In the United States, if not in other cultures, a divorced woman and children may join another woman who also is a lesbian, and together rear the children. And more and more cultures are recognizing common-law marriages between man and woman, especially when children are born.

The Hindu Family

In the Hindu family, the women are the principal conduit through which love of family and society is passed on to the children. They are the core family strength and serve as a model for their children of respect, tolerance, sharing, giving, and helping.

No dating is allowed and the girls are carefully protected. Most women are married through a full or partial parental arrangement. Marriage is a means of cementing families and ensuring family continuity. Hence, parents play a role in mate selection. Hindus believe that one comes to love the man or woman one marries. In contrast, Westerners maintain the romantic belief that one marries the man or woman one loves.

Source: "The Experience of Contrasting Subjective Cultures," by J. C. Naidoo in *Social Psychology and Cultural Context*, edited by J. Adamopoulos & Y. Kashima (Thousand Oaks, CA: Sage, 1999), p. 135.

Cultures differ in where newly married couples are expected to live. In *neolocal residence,* typical of the United States, the newlyweds set up a residence away from their parents. A *patrilocal residence* is the norm, wherein the bride leaves her family to live with her husband near or with his parents. The *matrilocal residence* is one in which the husband lives in or near the bride's parents.

Systems for tracing descent and handing down property are of three types.

1. *Patrilineal descent,* with kinship traced through the male line.

2. *Matrilineal descent,* wherein kinship is traced through the female line.

3. *Bilateral descent,* in which kinship is traced equally through both sets of biological relatives, as in the United States.

Table 7.1 shows the number of cultures having the various family structures.

Family Functions

The family performs innumerable functions for its members. The incest taboo, requiring sexual partners to come from outside the family, regulates sexual relations. The family provides legitimacy for the children. Every child must have a social father, giving the child inherited social status.

TABLE 7.1 Variations in Family Structure Across Cultures

Structural Type	Number of Cultures*
Family Type	
Nuclear	47
Extended Family	92
Marriage Type	
Monogamy	40
Polygyny	145
Polyandry	2
Marriage Partner	
Exogamy	70
Endogamy	33
Type of Residence	
Matrilocal	24
Patrilocal	101
Neolocal	13
Line of Descent	
Matrilineal	23
Patrilocal	61
Bilateral	2

*Number of cultures" differences result from lack of data in some categories.

Source: Based on *Sociology*, 5th ed., by N. J. Smelser (Englewood Cliffs, NJ: Prentice Hall, 1991).

The family also provides its members with intimacy and social support, assuming the responsibility for feeding, clothing, and healing. It serves as an agency for motivation and training. Because of this function, the family is considered an important cultural influence.

In industrial societies, other institutions have assumed responsibility for many tasks that traditionally have been family obligations. Social welfare agencies are called upon to help the poor and hospitals and nursing homes look after the sick and aged. Schools perform much of the training and are expected to teach the culture's values while forming character.

 Education

Almost two centuries ago, representatives of the Six Indian Nations sent a message to the Commissioner of Virginia, who had offered to enroll tribal youth in Virginia schools. The representatives declined the offer, pointing out what the members of their culture must know, knowledge the Virginia schools apparently did not teach.

> *Several of our young people were formerly brought up in the colleges of the northern provinces. They were instructed in all your sciences. But when they came back to us, they were bad runners, ignorant of every means of living in the woods, unable to bear either cold or hunger, knew neither how to build a cabin nor take a deer, and spoke our language imperfectly. They were therefore not fit for hunters, warriors, or counselors.*[2]

The Indian representatives were grateful for the invitation and invited the Commissioner to send them a dozen sons of Virginia instead. They would educate the Virginians, they said, in all they knew and make men of them in the process.

A culture's educational system has the responsibility for maintaining a culture and passing it on. In many cultures the schools carry this obligation. In others, the responsibility is shared among the people in other ways, but it entails providing the instruction necessary to live in the culture. Representatives of the Six Indian Nations knew what their children had to learn to survive, and apparently those subjects were not taught in the northern-province schools.

Whatever the educational process involves in a given culture, it represents an important social organization. Teachers provide the culture's link to the past and serve to continue the cultural heritage for the future. They help maintain a culture by relating to the students what happened in the past, what was and is important, and what members of the culture must know. The educational system transmits more than facts. Along with the family, the system exposes students to the culture's values and beliefs while helping them form attitudes. The culture determines what is taught.[3]

The Learning Environment

A child's entry into the world signifies the start of the educational process. The child learns the requirements of a specific family, cultural group, and the society at large. The learning is both informal and formal.

Informal Learning

Before the child reaches school age, significant learning takes place as the child goes through the daily routine of living. Informal learning results from teaching efforts of the family, peers, and the media. Without an explicit curriculum, the child learns through observation and imitation, mimicking what he or she sees and hears. When the child reaches school age, formal classroom learning supplements the informal process, which continues throughout life.

In many preliterate cultures — those without a written language — the informal learning is the only process available. The family assumes responsibility for what the child learns, and carries out instruction informally without benefit of schools, learning materials, and trained teachers. Family members supply instruction in the area of their expertise. The best cook may teach cooking, the best hunter hunting, and the best fisher fishing — teaching by doing. Learning takes place in the cooking area, the field, or lakes and streams — wherever the lessons are best learned in an apprenticeship-by-experience method.[4] This is *in-context learning*, learning in a real-life setting. The child learns by being involved, a hands-on learning process. This is common in hunting and gathering economies.

Among Hawaiians, informal learning of this nature is practiced in a *cofigurative* manner. Peers do the teaching, or siblings perform the instruction under the guidance of the child's parents.

Formal Learning

In the formal learning environment, schools are where people learn. Here, the instruction is *out-of-context*. Students learn in an environment different from that in which the learning is applied. What they learn in school, they use out of school at a later time and in a different place.

For example, we learn about intercultural communication in the classroom setting, from the professor's lectures, the textbook, and class exercises. Guided practice in a real-life setting is nonexistent. No foreigners are available in the classroom with whom to practice techniques picked up in the lectures and readings. In school, we learn the theory, and someday we may apply it in an intercultural setting.

Formal learning tends to be highly verbal, with lecture, questioning, and discussion developed around a highly organized curriculum. Teachers impart the knowledge impersonally, stressing memorization of specific facts, as teacher and students move through the subject matter in a logical, linear approach. Schools are highly scheduled and are task- and rule-oriented, rewarding *field-independent* learners — students who can work independently without direct intervention by the teacher. In contrast, *field-sensitive learners* need guidance and demonstration from the teacher and, upon receiving it, they are highly motivated. In-context learners fit this classification.

In the school system, *postfigurative* instruction is the mode. An older, subject-matter expert teaches younger, less experienced, and less knowledgeable students. Occasionally, however, we see *prefigurative* learning. In this type, the students are older than the instructor, and probably much more knowledgeable except in the subject matter area.

Japanese Students — Smarter, or What?

Japanese students outdo American students in school math and science. Why? The Japanese are inherently smarter than the Americans? No, there is no proof to support that contention. Do the Japanese have fewer students per classroom? No, American classes are smaller. Is the Japanese teacher's status higher than American teachers? Yes, the Japanese teacher is one of the most respected persons in the country. Do Japanese students spend more time in school? Yes, they average 240 days per year, compared to Americans' 178.

Do the Japanese spend more time on homework? Yes. For example, fifth graders study for 368 minutes per week, compared to Americans' 256 minutes. Do Japanese mothers help with homework? Yes, they help an average of 24 minutes per night, compared to American mothers' 14 minutes. Until children go to school, Japanese mothers devote themselves to rearing children in verbal and nonverbal ways.

Source: "The Best 'Jewish Mother' in the World," by P. Garfinkel, in *Culture, Communication and Conflict*, 2d ed., edited by G. R. Weaver (Needham, MA: Simon and Schuster, 1998), pp. 315–318.

In the Western world, for example, older business and professional people go back to school to learn new technological and scientific information, and they gain this information from teachers younger than they.[5]

"My medical doctor is forever taking classes," says one university professor. "He's seventy, and constantly attends classes to get the latest medical information in his special field, internal medicine. That's good; I'm all for it. What's not so hot is the fact the drug companies pay his travel expenses, and when he gets back, he unloads their pills on us."

Learning Styles

Differences in learning styles have been identified across cultures. The learning characteristics of culturally different elementary-school children were compared in the United States. Blacks preferred quiet, warmth, bright light, mobility, routine and patterns, frequent feedback from authority figures, and action-oriented instructional experiences. They wanted afternoon or evening class times. Chinese Americans desired sound, bright light, mornings, variety, and peer learning. Greek-Americans chose learning alone, mobility, variety, and auditory instructions. Mexican-Americans selected low light, structure, tactile and visual instruction, learning alone, and feedback from an authority figure.[6]

Other classroom preferences indicate extensive variations from culture to culture. Some cultures permit lots of talking and questions. Others, Vietnamese classes among them, prohibit talking. The Israeli kibutz is noisy, with spontaneous interaction. In Mexico the teacher tightly controls and directs all oral interaction. Chinese classrooms are quiet, reflecting a Buddhist tradition that knowledge, truth, and wisdom come to those whose silence allows the spirit to enter. Japanese students busily take notes while the teacher lectures.

Saudi Arabian students listen and take notes. In Algeria the students are highly critical of what is taught and are prepared to question and debate anything the teacher says. Quranic students have to chant aloud verses from the Quran and recite other teachings from memory. Frequent touching is the norm in Italian classrooms, and the children greet the teacher with a kiss on both cheeks. In the United States, depending upon the grade level, a teacher who touches excessively could be in serious trouble. In Jamaica looking at the teacher is a sign of disrespect, but in the United States students show respect by looking at the teacher.[7]

Asian and American Student Performance: A Comparison

To verify Asian learning styles, John Briggs analyzed student learning in Confucian-heritage cultures — China, Hong Kong, Taiwan, Singapore, Korea, Japan, and others.[8] Western observers, Briggs reported, believe Asian students learn by memorization with little attention to tasks that demand a high level of intellectual effort. The data prove those observers wrong. Asian students perform at an exceptionally high cognitive level and do far better than typical Western students.

Asians tend to be *deep-approach* learners, wishing to maximize their understanding of subject matter by focusing on underlying meanings, and thereby gaining a firm knowledge base as well as a strong conceptual framework. In comparison to deep-approach learning is *surface-approach* learning, in which students invest little time and effort, avoiding failure by cutting corners and memorizing the essentials. In another style, the *achieving approach,* the goal is high grades, achieved through well-organized time and efficient work habits.

Compared to Western students, who attribute success to ability and failure to its lack, Asian students attribute success to effort and failure to its lack. Asian students collaborate in groups as they study and give learning assignments as much time as necessary. Westerners collaborate little and are not as willing to spend a lot of time to master a subject.

In spite of large classes, cold classrooms, and other extremely poor environmental conditions, Asians seem to be able to focus on the important task of learning, ignoring superficial conditions. Briggs concluded that Asian students are not rote learners exclusively even though, when necessary, they will invest in repetitive efforts. They perform ably at highly cognitive academic tasks.

Cultural Choice

Nothing about the educational process is absolute. Every aspect results from cultural choice, conscious or unconscious, about whom to educate, how, in what subjects, for what purposes, and in what manner. Fifty years ago American schools encouraged a militant ethnocentrism. School children were taught that the world outside of the United states was a veritable jungle, China a land of inscrutable ways and mysterious opium dens, Africa a "dark continent" inhabited by cannibals and wild animals, and Europe a backward place, its only export a decadent culture.

Students going abroad to study bring to the foreign classroom naively ethnocentric attitudes and expectations, as do teachers going overseas to instruct in the foreign setting. They err when they judge the new learning situation against the way they learned at home. Styles, standards, and expectations differ widely. A culture's practices reflect cultural values rather than the superiority of any one method. The culture chooses what best fits its people's needs.

Internationalizing the Curriculum

The past two decades have brought tremendous diversification in American schools and in the schools of many other nations. Roughly one-third of the school population consists of cultural or ethnic minorities. Great Britain, France, the Netherlands, Australia, Canada, and Israel show similar increases in minority enrollments.

Although the student populations are diversifying, the instructional staff is not. By the century's end, the teaching force was increasingly female and white, indicating a paucity of cultural and ethnic faculty. In addition, most teachers have little experience with students representing cultural backgrounds different from theirs. This problem is not confined to the United States.

Educators encourage internationalizing the curriculum. School curricula and programs should be designed to meet five dimensions of a global perspective:[9]

1. The recognition that our view of the world is not universally shared

2. An understanding of prevailing world conditions and development needs

3. A recognition of the diversity of ideas and practices found in the cultures around the globe

4. An understanding of the principal traits and mechanisms of a world system in change

5. An introduction of the problems of choice confronting individuals and nations as the global system expands.

Adding international or intercultural courses to already overcrowded curricula is not the ideal way to meet these five elements of a global perspective. But adding a cultural component to existing courses is possible, as is bringing cultural flavor to textbooks used in the nation's schools.

 Religion

Rituals characterize religions. These required practices connect with the sacred, the spiritual, and the holy. They are patterns of behavior expressing a relationship with the consecrated. A funeral is a ritual. For the monks at the Sera monastery near Lhasa in Tibet, it is a ceremonial feeding of the eagles. For Thai monks, the local monastery places the body on a pyre, which is communally set afire, first by the monks, then by the family, and finally by friends, with the hope that the corpse will be reborn into a higher existence.

Christians and Muslims bury their dead, in effect feeding them to the worms. The Parsis feed their dead, bodies intact, to vultures in the Towers of Silence. The Tibetan ritual calls for bodies to be chopped up and mixed with barley meal. Easter Islanders wrap the corpse in a straw mat and place it on a heap of stones or on a wooden platform until it has decomposed. Sometimes the wrapped corpse is concealed in caves or in a cleft of a rock. After decomposition, the skeleton is removed to an *ahu*, or stone vault.

Rituals are one of the basic elements of a religion, a seldom recognized complexity in intercultural communication. Religion is a deep and pervasive determinant in establishing cultural patterns. Even the most secularized cultures reveal the influence of religion. Those that reject religious faith and order nevertheless are predisposed to obey the religious heritage that affects their culture. Most people, church-goers and atheists alike, adhere to the commandment "Thou shalt not kill," a tenet with a religious base that virtually all cultures follow. To ignore the religious dimension of intercultural communication will only complicate our ability to communicate with people in other cultures.

The Nature of Religion

Sociologists perceive religion as an institution of shared beliefs and practices created by human beings as a response to forces that they cannot understand rationally and that they believe give ultimate meaning to their lives.[10] Anthropologists define religion as cultural knowledge of the supernatural that people use to cope with the ultimate problems of human existence.[11] We like the definition that identifies religion *as a unified system of beliefs and practices relative to sacred things, which unite into one single moral community called a Church all those who adhere to them.*[12]

The *sacred things* are the things set aside and forbidden. They represent the central feature of religion. They are extrahuman and mysterious, and thus command awe and respect. What is sacred and what is profane (the ordinary and understandable) depend upon how the believers define them. To Catholics, a cross is a sacred image and Mecca just another city. To Moslems, a cross is a couple of pieces of wood but Mecca is a sacred place.

The *beliefs and practices* indicated in the definition are connected with the *sacred,* and are spiritual and holy, as opposed to the *profane,* the worldly and secular. In the Christian religion, bread and wine have symbolic significance in Christ's martyrdom. At the profane level, they provide food and drink.

The definition features a *unified system* that unites people in a Church. The people who are part of the Church share its religious beliefs and practices. We may hold a private faith, but it is not a religion unless others hold it as well. Jesus could not have founded a new religion if he had not persuaded his followers to accept his beliefs about the nature of ultimate reality. Religion, therefore, is a community of believers who share norms and values that delineate human behavior in the world.

However defined, religion, along with the family, is probably one of the oldest of all human institutions. Every known culture has had religious beliefs and conducted some sort of religious activity. Strong evidence implies that religion was part of Neanderthal existence late in the Pleistocene Age, almost a million years ago. Religions came about apparently because humans always have felt the need to explain the mysteries of human life. Questions that have troubled humans for time eternal include: Why are we here? Why do we suffer? What happens when we die?

Religions, whether primitive or modern, Eastern or Western, are searches for the meaning of life. All try to understand and harmonize with a spiritual reality whatever it is called — The Way, Allah, or God.[13]

Primitive Religions

The term *primitive religion* refers to the belief systems of a nonliterate tribe or group. Primitive religions are broken into two major classes: preanimism and animism.[14]

Preanimism

The primitive religions of Preanimism believe the world around them is in flux. A force or fluid spirit moves about, and this force may envelop itself in an object, giving the object a potency it otherwise would not have. The object will evoke awe, admiration, and perhaps fear. To the Japanese, this force is *kami.* Hawaiians call it *mana,* creating a presence affecting various events. Believers practice rituals to ensure its presence. Before engaging in battle, the Cheyenne prayed, fasted, and refrained from sexual intercourse to ensure that the force would be strong, increasing their chances of victory. "May the force be with you" is a Star Wars way of hoping a person will have great powers.

Animism

The Animism belief system holds that the social and physical world is inhabited by spirits, who may or may not be spirits of the dead. They are erratic and impulsive and must be indulged lest they strike out from the spirit world and do harm to the living. They are placated through rituals.

The African Kung tribe, for instance, leaves part of its kill after a hunt to mollify the spirits. In some other tribes, the names of the dead are never mentioned for fear of awakening them and causing harm.

Modern Religions

The modern or advanced religions are held by literate cultural groups or cultural groups with a learned subgroup of religious leaders. Three types are classed as advanced: Monotheism, Polytheism, and Abstract.

Monotheism

The religious belief system Monotheism recognizes one god, although that "god" may be different from religion to religion. Christianity, Judaism, and Islam acknowledge one god, but their conceptions of this supreme being vary.

Polytheism

Polytheistic religions recognize a number of gods or goddesses, with each god controlling some facet of nature. In Hawaii the *akuas* were impersonal gods — powerful and distant deities who combined supernatural qualities with many human frailties. They could be vengeful, helpful, destructive, wise, or capricious, in direct contrast to the Christian God and the devil, good and evil. The four major Hawaiian gods were *Kane*, creator of man, symbol of life, god of fresh water and sunlight; *Lono*, god of agriculture, clouds, and weather; *Ku*, god of war and chiefs; and *Kanaloa*, the ocean god.

Abstract

Abstract religions assert that a force totally exceeds humans and nature. This force is timeless, eternal, and can be understood only if people reach an exceptional state that is true enlightenment. Buddhism, several Hinduism forms, and mysticism are examples of abstract religions.

The Functions of Religion

A religious belief system provides people with shared views of the world. The individual members receive from their religion a set of answers for questions regarding life and their place in it. The social support that comes with belonging to a religion is helpful in times of personal tragedy. Illness, death, natural disasters, personal failures such as bankruptcy, divorce, and similar misfortunes can be explained by the religious belief system. Those who share in the religion can

supply personal, social, and ideological support in times of crisis.

Anxieties caused by the crises can be ameliorated when viewed as part of a "divine plan." The crises become understandable because meaning is assigned to them. In this way, religion helps make the mysterious and unknown familiar and understandable.

Religions offer explanations for life and death. Because all humans die, solace can be gained from one's religion. Some religions believe the deceased is embarking on a trip to "paradise," where he or she will be free of pain and suffering. Other religions believe the dead are in a better state and their survivors will rejoin them someday. For ancient Hawaiians, belief in eternal reunion with one's ancestors in Po (afterlife) must have been reassuring to family-conscious Hawaiians. In a few religions, the belief is that the deceased will return to life, perhaps even in a nonhuman form.[15]

For many people, religious identity is important. It fulfills a needs to belong. They are part of something and something bigger than themselves, which others recognize. "I'm a Protestant," one person boasted. "I rarely go to church, but I know it will be there when I need it. I went for our babies' baptisms, for their confirmations, for their weddings, and their children's baptisms. I attend the funerals of my friends and relatives. It's part of my heritage and gives me comfort when I'm in need."

Far Eastern and Western Religions[16]

A manageable way to consider the world religions is in a two-division grouping: The Far Eastern and Western divisions help us comprehend the diverse faiths of humankind and their impact on culture and intercultural communication.

These two groupings, Far Eastern and Western, influence about 90 percent of the world's population,[17] although there are notable exceptions to the two divisions. Shamanism, with its strong appeal in Korea and elsewhere, and

Animism, powerful among Africans and American Indians, are two such exclusions.

Far Eastern Religions

The countries of Eastern Asia (Korea, China, Japan, India) embrace religious traditions that perceive the ultimate good in *harmonization*. Hinduism, Buddhism, Shintoism, Confucianism, and Taoism see harmony as The Way.

Although these religions differ, the foundations of each are similar. Deity is in every place and every form, and in a single place or form. Everything is benign; nothing is worth worrying about. True believers respond to important issues with a smile. Being pleasant helps keep things in perspective because nothing is going to mean much in the long run anyway.

Ethically, there is no absolute right. Everything is relative to the situation. Then, too, life is circular. Reincarnation occurs after death; upon death, one's essence is put into another physical form. This goes on and on, without end. The sphere of what is desirable is in everything in the world, not just in special places or acts called sacred. What is important is the here and now.

Hinduism. With almost 800 million followers, the major religion of India, Hinduism, has no founder. Likely the world's oldest religion, it dates back to prehistoric times. It has no single creed or doctrine. It is a syncretic religion incorporating a variety of influences. The sacred texts are the *Vedas*, of which the Upanishads are commentaries on them. Brahman is the principle and source of the universe. Life is determined by the law of karma. Earthly life is transient and a burden. The goal of existence is liberation from the cycle of rebirth and death to enter the indescribable state of *moksha*, or liberation.

Buddhism. Founded in the fourth or fifth century B.C. in northern India, Buddhism has 325,275,000 followers. Siddhartha Gautama, the founder, was the son of a warrior prince who left a pampered life at age 29 to wander as an ascetic, seeking religious insight. Meditating under the bodhi tree, he reached enlightenment and taught his followers about his new spiritual understanding, at the core of which are the Four Noble Truths:

1. All living beings suffer.
2. The origin of suffering is desire for material possessions, power, and so on.
3. Desire can be overcome.
4. The path that leads to release from desire is called the Noble Eightfold Path: right views, right intention, right speech, right action, right livelihood, right effort, right concentration, and right ecstasy.

Gautama traveled to preach the *dharma* (sacred truth) and was recognized as Buddha (enlightened one).

Confucianism. Confucius (K'ung Fu-tzu), born in northern China, lived from 551 to 479 B.C. A brilliant teacher, he viewed education as a means of self-transformation, not merely as a way to accumulate knowledge. His teachings are contained in the *Analects,* a collection of sayings as remembered by his students. They emphasize moral conduct and right relationships among humans, with cultivation of virtue as a central tenet. Important virtues are *jen,* a benevolent and humanitarian attitude, and *li,* maintaining proper relationships and rituals that enhance the life of the individual, family, and state. Roughly 5 million people are members.

Shinto. Shinto comprises the religious ideas and practices indigenous to Japan and has about 3 million followers. Ancient Shinto focused on the worship of *kami,* a host of supernatural beings that could be known through forms (objects of nature, remarkable people, abstract concepts such as justice) but were ultimately mysterious. With no formal dogma and no holy writ, collections of Japanese religious thought and practice are highly regarded. Shinto became the official state religion, and State

Shinto, the national cult, emphasized the divinity of the emperor.

Taoism. A major religion in China with an unknown number of members, but likely in the millions, Taoism is based on ancient philosophical works, primarily the Tao Te Ching. Believed to be the work of Lao-tzu Tao, "the Way" is the ultimate reality of the universe. Longevity and immorality were sought by regulating body energies through breathing exercises, meditation, use of medicinal plants, talismans, and magical formulas. Some Chinese belong to several religions simultaneously and therefore can be Taoist, Buddhist, and Confucianist, among others.

Western Religions

The religions making up this division perceive the ultimate good as *transformation*. Members of the Jewish, Christian, and Islamic faiths believe that divine grace is the desired end, whether in this life or the next.

As in the Far Eastern division, differences among these three groups are apparent. Yet they, too, have a common foundation:. They are *monotheistic*. There is one God. He is out there, and everything else is here, with a great gulf in between.

The world is split in two: the way it was intended to be versus the way it is. There is the good and desirable, and there is sin. What is absolutely desirable is what constitutes ethics, what is right

In the Western religions everything is headed somewhere — to the Kingdom of God or to heaven — to an end. At the end of individual life will be an accounting or payoff, either life after death or resurrection of the individual's body. At the end of human life will be an apocalypse, a disclosure.

Some things are sacred, belonging to God and religion. Some things are special, to be treated with awe and reverence. What is important is felicity — happiness or bliss — beyond this life.

Judaism. The oldest of the monotheistic faiths, Judaism affirms the existence of one God, Yahweh, who entered into a covenant with the descendants of Abraham, God's chosen people. Judaism's holy writings reveal how God has been present with them throughout their history. These writings are known as the Torah, the five books of Moses, or the Hebrew Scriptures (to Christians, the Old Testament), and the compilation of oral tradition called the Talmud. Abraham founded Judaism around the 20th century B.C. About 13,866,000 people are members.

Christianity. Founded by the followers of Jesus Christ, Christianity also is a monotheistic faith with almost 2 billion followers, roughly evenly divided between the Protestant and Catholic churches. A Jew, Jesus was born about 7 B.C. and assumed public life as a teacher when he was 30 years old in Galilee. He proclaimed the kingdom of God, which required a change of heart and repentance of sins, love of God and neighbor, and concern for justice. Jesus was executed on a cross in Jerusalem because he was considered a political threat to the Roman Empire. After his death his followers accepted him as the Christ, the Messiah. The apostle Paul spread the faith in his missionary travels.

Islam. Another monotheistic faith, Islam was founded in Arabia by Muhammad between 610 and 632 A.D. Worldwide, Muslims number about 1 billion, with an estimated 5.5 million in North America. Islam means "surrender to the will of Allah," the all-powerful, who determines humanity's fate. Good deeds are rewarded in paradise and evil deeds in hell. The primary duties, or Five Pillars, are profession of faith; prayer, to be performed five times a day; almsgiving to the poor and to the mosque; fasting during daylight hours in the month of Ramadan; and a pilgrimage to Mecca once in a lifetime.

This brief description of Far Eastern and Western religions is a simplified summary of the differences in world religions. Many differences are present among the religions in each division.

Nevertheless, one or the other of these two divisions dominates the lives of those growing up in their sphere of influence. In that sense, they provide initial stereotypes through which we can bridge gaps between ourselves and people in other cultures.

Worldview

Recall, in our discussion of beliefs, our emphasis on *worldview*, that core of relatively stable and permanent beliefs imbuing all cultures. Worldview has religious implications, and it deals with a culture's orientation toward ontological matters, helping explain the why and wherefor of human existence.

The differences between the Eastern and Western worldviews are associated with the Far Eastern and Western religious divisions, thereby increasing our conception of religion. Religion and worldview permeate every facet of culture. Both affect attitudes, values, beliefs, and many other components of culture. Both, therefore, are potent forces in intercultural communication.

 # Political Institutions

In politics there is a fertile field for pointed critiques. To one, pundit, politics is the science of who gets what, when, and why. To another, the goal of politics is to extract resources from the taxpayer with minimum offense and to distribute the proceeds among numerous claimants in such a way as to maximize support at the polls.

Another sees politics as the only profession for which no preparation is necessary. Government is said to be nothing but an entity that collects the money and determines how to spend it.

The pundits moralize about the political system, but it is a necessity, and every culture has such *a process of making and carrying out public policy according to cultural categories and rules.*[18] To combat smallpox in their Sudan homeland, the Nuer must decide whether to

hold a religious ceremony, thereby making a political decision. The Polynesian chief who chooses to allow labor recruiters on his island makes a political decision. The inhabitants of a Japanese fishing village who discover that their fishing grounds are polluted and seek government help are initiating a political action.

The structures for making political decisions, the issues that affect the public, and the rules for making and enforcing decisions vary enormously from one culture to another. The political structure might be a dictatorship, military government, socialist republic, democracy, monarchy, communist state, or ones that change between coups. Some tribal cultures are ruled by chiefs and councils. Some Arab countries have a ruling family with a king as headman. Some, such as Japan and Great Britain, have royal families that have no ruling power. Whatever their form, political systems originate because of self-appointment, inherited rights, vote of the people, consensus, or political takeover.

Types of Political Systems

Britain's prime minister during World War II, Winston Churchill, proved to be a pundit with his acrimonious remarks about politics. His most memorable statement, "Democracy is the worst system devised by the wit of man, except for all the others," recognized the advantages and disadvantages of the democratic system. It is one of three systems that are used to govern nations: authoritarianism, totalitarianism, and democracy.

Authoritarianism

Authoritarian governments are ruled by a strongman or a small elite. Some are dictatorships ruled by a person who seizes power illegitimately. Most are oligarchies led by an elite of aristocrats, bureaucrats, or military people who also seize power illegally.

The strongman or elite rule principally through strong-arm tactics — forbidding freedom of the press, prohibiting opposition parties, and ruthlessly suppressing dissent among the people. They most likely assume power through a coup d'etat and have no legitimate political claim to hold office. The military juntas that rule in Latin American countries are examples of oligarchies, as are the one-party states in communist Europe. North Korea is one country that is is ruled by a dictator. Authoritarian rule tends to be short-lived, as their government usually is corrupt.

Totalitarianism

In totalitarian states, the government controls all social institutions. The state controls every aspect of life — the family, religion, education, and employment. A single party, run by a self-appointed leader, holds the power over the people, with an elaborate bureaucracy to enforce total domination over people's minds and bodies. Suppression of individual liberties is pronounced, with any deviation considered subversive because it weakens the goals of the State. Conformity of attitude and behavior is enforced through propaganda and terror.

Nazi Germany is the best example of a regime in total control of all human activities. China under Mao and Russia under Stalin also illustrate totalitarianism.

Democracy

In democracies the consent of the governed determines how the country will be run. Legally qualified citizens can vote, run for office, and engage in other political activities. Legal authority gives power to the persons elected to govern. Members of the governing bodies — legislatures, city councils, boards of education, and others — are picked in free elections. Their power is restricted by laws protecting the rights of the people, including the right to assemble, free speech, and equal protection under the law.

Democracies are rare, appearing largely in industrial countries in Western Europe and North America, as well as Japan. A literate, urban population and a stable middle class seem to be necessary for a democracy. Prolonged internal conflicts cause democracies to fail, and intolerance of dissenting political opinions tend to weaken them. In the United States, we are seeing the decline of political parties and the erosion of governmental authority with special-interest groups rising to the fore.

Power

Although these three political systems are important in their own right, what is more essential to intercultural communication is how people, groups, and nations go about getting what they want from other people, groups, and

Mao Tse Tung of China is an example of a totalitarian leader.

nations. The concern is who gets what, when, and how.

The concepts of power and influence underlie political systems. Political institutions actively engage in the process of shaping, distributing, and exercising power. Power exists as an operative factor at every level of every interpersonal, intergroup, regional, national, and international relationship.

Power is defined as *the ability to determine the behavior of others, even against their will*. It comes from influence, coercion, or authority.

Influence

Influence, the power to persuade, can come from personal appeal, prestige, wealth, numbers, or effective organization. Ronald Reagan's personal charm gave him influence over the Congress and the people during his years as President. The prestige of the presidency wields tremendous political power through its potential ability to persuade millions of voters. The wealth of the Rockefeller family gives its members considerable influence with most voters. The People's Republic of China, with its billions of people, carries more weight than Taiwan in international relations. The National Rifle Association, through its well-developed organization, has been able to persuade legislators to oppose gun controls.

Coercion

Coercion is the power that comes from superior force or from the power to punish for noncompliance. Calling out the troops to maintain or restore order is a form of power that heads of government have, but they want to use that form of power only as a last resort and as part of their legitimate right to govern. Legitimacy results from the wishes of the people. They have to give their consent; otherwise the government heads would be acting without sanction.

Authority

A form of legitimate power because it has the approval of the nation's majority, authority as practiced in the United States is restricted to rules and regulations established by legislative bodies. For example, the Internal Revenue Service has legitimate authority by statute to collect income taxes.

Whatever form it takes, power is constant in political institutions. Political parties and types of government are here today and gone tomorrow. What remains constant is who gets what, when, and how.

The government in the Philippines illustrates the point. The semi-military dictatorship of Ferdinand Marcos gave way to the democratic regime of Corazon Aquino and the presidents who followed her, yet the power factor changed very little. Most of the Marcos powerbrokers switched to Aquino's side, and very little changed with the change in leadership.

 # Economic Systems

Just as every culture is unique, so are its economic systems. The Japanese economic system is different from the economic system in Thailand. Comparable variations are distinguishable in European and North American styles of capitalism. France and Germany emphasize industrial guidance and national policy.

Two economic philosophies predominate in the world — an Asian and an Anglo-American model. Those models undergo periodic change with the advent of the internationalization of business and technological advancement. Nevertheless, insights have been gained into the Asian and Anglo-American models, in terms of purpose, power, surprise, and national borders.[19]

Purpose of an Economy

The purpose of economic life differs between the two systems. The Anglo-American style advocates an economy as a basic means of raising the people's standard of living. It is a materialistic aim. The Asian system sees the economy as a means of increasing the collective national strength. The Asian nations view independence and self-sufficiency as goals, making them free from assistance from outsiders for survival. For the Asians, the goal is political — likely caused by years of oppression by outside governments.

The Anglo-American economic purpose is characterized in one word — "more."[20] If the people have more choice, more leisure, more wealth, more chances to pursue happiness, society will be successful. Anything the market permits will be good for the people.

The goal of the Asian system is to develop the productive base of the nation, either through the industries within the nation or through its industries located elsewhere in the world. Anything good for the producer is a good economic policy.

A number of examples illustrate the point that the Asian system favors the producer. Rice provides one example. Japan and Korea protect their rice markets and do not allow its purchase from overseas even though the consumer's price would be considerably lower were it not protected. Korea stirred up internal violence when it opened its markets to overseas purchases because of crop failures.

A second example deals with the anti-consumer, high-priced retail system, rigged to help the producer. Japan has the most successful of these systems, doubling the cost of most purchases for the average Japanese. Clothes cost twice as much in Tokyo as New York, food three times as much, gasoline two and one-half times as much. "Thank goodness for Japan's rigged prices," a Honolulu merchant exclaims. "Japanese visitors to the Islands stock up, not only on clothes and accessories but foodstuffs as well. They get higher quality, name-brand items for half the price.

In Asian countries, the parts of life that encourage consumption are made difficult. The parts that encourage savings are made easy.

Power to Set Policies

In the American sense, power corrupts. To avoid the concentration of power in setting economic policies, the Anglo-American system has checks and balances to prevent that power from falling into the hands of a few. In the Asian system, concentrated power is a fact of life. Many Asian societies have a center of power — a military strongman in Thailand, Indonesia, and often Korea; a statesman-leader in Singapore; a tyrant in North Korea and Burma; a political boss in Malaysia and Taiwan.

Surprise in Economic Life

The Anglo-American economic system encourages surprise and unpredictability in the marketplace. The Asian system does not. The Anglo-American market fluctuates with the choices of its people. Americans, for example, can choose from a variety of products competing with each other, and the competition can be cut-throat, with winners and losers. The Asian system allows no surprises. Cartels often are formed to control prices so there are no winners and losers; every company makes out. The Korean government, in fact, divides up the work of national development among its major companies. One group of companies run the shipyards, another group something else.

National Borders Versus Borderless

The Anglo-American economic system avoids the concept of national interest; economically, the world should be borderless. In the Anglo-American model paying higher prices for home-grown products makes no sense when they can be purchased cheaper elsewhere. Why buy poor-quality, higher-priced, home-built cars when better and cheaper cars are available elsewhere? In the Asian model it is natural to be xenophobic; people should buy from the home country only. The world consists of us and them, and we had better look out after us.

Anglo-American theory teaches Westerners that economics is a positive-sum game from which all can emerge winners. The Asian system instructs its citizens that economic competition is a form of war. To be strong is much better than to be weak; to give orders is much better than to take them.

Other Distinctions

In addition to the four Asian and Anglo-American patterns described, other differences are noticeable in the economic systems of the world's cultures. Monetary units constitute an obvious difference. Crossing a national border, we confront this difference as soon as we decide to buy something. Do we pay in dollars, pounds, shekels, lira, yen, won, pesos, or cruzeiro, among other possibilities? In New Guinea, sweet potatoes would be appropriate as the means of exchange — at least among the highlanders of Papua.

Farmers in many cultures swap work. One farmer helps another and the second reciprocates, with no money exchanged. Doctors, dentists, and lawyers are among the professional people who exchange professional services. Some render their services for foodstuffs or assistance from auto mechanics, plumbers, electricians, and other service workers, all without an exchange of money.

Property ownership and utilization are a part of economic systems, and land ownership is a goal of many people throughout the world. In China, a culture prizing land, a piece of land can be passed from generation to generation. Many Americans perceive their land as a business asset to be used for financial gain.

The economic success of immigrants to the United States has led to confrontations. White fishermen in California and Texas have clashed with Vietnamese immigrant competitors. Blacks in New York, Washington, and Pittsburgh have demonstrated against Korean immigrants in the grocery business. Wage rates around the nation are said to have been lowered because immigrants are willing to work cheaper than local citizens. Many immigrants see little benefit to union membership, which upsets union leaders.

Many agricultural cultures lose their young people to industry, damaging family life in the process. The young people leave home to earn more money than they did working on family farms.

Countries with a small industrial base have few jobs available for their citizens, and they leave the country to find work elsewhere. The oil-producing Middle East countries attract Filipinos, Malaysians, Indians, Jordanians, and Pakistanis to work the oil fields.

Chapter Review

The major social institutions influencing intercultural communication are the family, educational system, religion, political system, and economic system.

The family can be defined as two or more persons linked by marriage or descent who engage in common activities. Although the family takes many forms in the world, the principal ones remain the nuclear and extended family systems.

(Continued)

Chapter Review continued

The incest taboo is universal, causing sons and daughters to marry outside of the family and thereby creating new families and a network of affiliations.

Monogamy is the principal form of marriage. Polygamy (polygyny or polyandry) is practiced in cultures that have a disparity of eligible mates.

The patriarchal family structure is most common, although the matriarchal structure is the norm in a few cultures. Newlyweds may live in a neolocal form of residence away from the parents. Some maintain a patrilocal residence with bride and groom living with or near the groom's parents. Others maintain a matrilocal residence, with or near the bride's parents. The line of descent may be patrilineal, through the male line, or matrilineal, through the female line. In the USA, the kinship is traced through both.

The educational system of a culture is responsible for continuing the cultural heritage by teaching the cultural history, values, beliefs, and attitudes.

In preliterate cultures, learning is informal and in-context. In literate cultures, it is formal and out-of-context.

Teaching methods and learning styles differ from culture to culture. The culture chooses what best fits the people's needs.

Confucian-heritage cultures emphasize a *deep-approach* learning style that fosters a firm learning base and strong conceptual framework. They attribute their success or failure to the effort they put forth to learn.

Religion is a unified system of beliefs and practices relative to sacred things, which unite into one single moral community called a Church, all those who accept its teachings.

Religions answer questions concerned with existence: Why are we here? Why do we suffer? What happens when we die?

Primitive religions fall into one of two classes: Preanimism or Animism.

Advanced or modern religions are monotheistic, polytheistic, or abstract.

Far Eastern religions stress harmony. God is in everything. Life goes on after death through reincarnation. What is important is the here-and-now. Variations

(Continued)

Chapter Review continued

in these themes are slight among the principal groups: Hinduism, Buddhism, Confucianism, Shintoism, and Taoism.

Western religions believe in transformation, making oneself in the image of God, of which there is but one. Good and evil vie, with the Kingdom of God awaiting the good. The major Western religions are Judaism, Christianity, and Islam.

Every culture has a political system that makes public policy and carries it out according to cultural categories and rules.

Three major political systems are authoritarian, totalitarian, and democratic. All three rely on power, which is the ability to determine the behavior of others, even against their will.

Power comes from influence, coercion, and authority. While politicians come and go, power is constant. Whoever has power rules.

Although every culture has its own economic system, two predominant ones are the Asian and the Anglo-American systems. They differ in purpose, who determines economic policies, predictability, and nationalistic bent.

Think About This. . .

Consider the influences of social institutions in your life. These questions concern personal matters, and the answers need not be divulged to anyone.

1 Begin with your family name. What is it? Where did it originate? What does it mean?

2 Think about your family. Is it nuclear, extended, or does it take some other form? What is your married status? If married, is it endogamous or exogamous? Did you choose your mate? What about your parents' background?

3 Think about your ethnic background. What is it? Are you a member of the macroculture or an ethnic microculture?

4 Think about your prior education. Was it in-context or out-of-context? Where did you go to school?

5 Think about your religion. To what religion do you belong, if any? Are you active in it? Does your worldview best fit the Eastern or the Western perspective? Why?

6 Think about your political beliefs. Are you a member of a political party? Do you vote? If so, do you vote a party line? In your ancestors' native land (if not the USA), what sort of political system operated?

7 What sort of work do you do, if any? Your father? Your mother? Your mate?

8 Cultural Diversity in Interpersonal Relationships

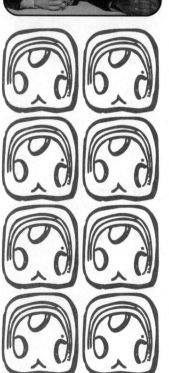

Intercultural interpersonal relationships are inevitable in the United States and throughout the world as people move from place to place for whatever reasons — political, social, or economic. With those contacts will come close personal interactions and relationships that differ at their core. The cultural gap introduces glitches.

Blonde Diane met Gerry — a Japanese-American young man born and reared in Hawaii — at a University of Minnesota dorm. She told her mother, who was less than thrilled with the encounter. Diane's mother thought the meeting was "nice." "Keep him as a good friend," she encouraged, not sure about the interaction of people from different ethnic backgrounds. But Diane and Gerry formed a relationship anyway — one still going strong after 16 years of marriage and a few adjustments along the way. Diane curbed her southern European desire to dominate conversations and hug and kiss in public. Gerry, quiet and reserved like many Japanese-Americans, learned to express his feelings more easily.[1] Interpersonal relationships carry different meanings across cultures with differing expectations and obligations.

In Greece, developing friendships and good relationships with locals means that the outsider must not be disturbed by a great deal of debate or take it personally when Greeks disagree with what the stranger says. Greeks are encouraged to discover truth through dialogue and believe lively conversation makes for good company.[2] In Germany, developing friendships takes a long time, as Germans require a lot of attention, interest, and a lifetime of commitment. Because they are private people, typical Germans do not respond kindly to personal questions from acquaintances. Honest and blunt, they speak their mind in situations in which Americans would be more tactful.[3]

135

To avoid misunderstandings, we must bear in mind what interpersonal relationships entail. This chapter focuses on the characteristics of relationships and the factors affecting them, as we sample interpersonal relationships in various cultures, noting differences one from the other. Throughout our study, we would do well to follow the advice of Kenny, a Hawaiian-Chinese, Hawaii-born Californian married to a Pennsylvanian: "Realize that your culture isn't better, just different." Mutual respect for cultural backgrounds and family traditions is essential when relating interculturally.

The Concept of Relationship

To establish a common conception of the term *relationship* and gain an understanding of *interpersonal relationship,* we should recognize that relationship is the *state of being mutually or reciprocally* interested, as in social or business matters. The several parties involved in the relationship must realize that they are parts of the relationship and have entered into it for reasons of companionship or practical gain.[4]

The relationship does not have to be intimate. Few relationships turn into extremely personal and private ones. Among our closest friends, we include our spouse or spouse-to-be and a few others — likely not more than five. We may have five to 10 other good friends, and a larger social network of acquaintances including some family members. We probably can name another hundred people, whom we greet by name but who have little influence in our life. Another half dozen familiar strangers possibly include the mail carrier, paper carrier, people with whom we may stop and chat a few minutes when we see them.

Relationships have varying degrees of closeness and are formed for a variety of reasons. We form some relationships, however, because we

desire to be with the people involved. Most relationships result as an outgrowth of a joint task or activity. We collaborate with a fellow student on a class project or work with several people in our occupation. We might have a health problem and enter into a mutually reciprocal state with the doctor and staff. A relationship can be for other than companionship.

As the relationship evolves, our expectations govern its growth. For example, we would not expect the relationship with our physician to become intimate. We want the doctor to cure our illness and nothing more. Yet, that relationship could be a stable and enduring one, albeit limited to the care of our health.

How much satisfaction we receive from the relationship varies with its context and intimacy. With the doctor, we expect painstaking and thorough care. How well our health improves will determine the extent of our satisfaction. With a close friend, we expect our desire for companionship to be fulfilled. If it is, we are satisfied.[5]

In intercultural situations, our expectations likely will differ from those of the people with whom we communicate. Because people from other cultures might expect more or they may expect less than we do, communication problems could result. Arabs expect more from a relationship than North Americans do, so interaction between Arabs and North Americans could lead to misunderstandings because their expectations are not met.

Reducing Uncertainty

The Japanese expert Kazuo Nishiyama tells how difficult it is to initiate contacts, especially business contacts, with the Japanese. Most Japanese people are not friendly with strangers and prefer not to interact with foreigners. Business people choose to do business with people they have known personally for many years. The Japanese hesitate to enter into any new relationship without some sort of introduction from a reliable friend, and they take much time developing a relationship. Typical Japanese people rarely strike up conversations with individuals they encounter for the first time, in contrast to most Americans, who freely engage a new acquaintance in conversation.[6]

Meeting someone for the first time involves some uncertainty within one's own culture. We are not sure what to expect as we start a conversation with someone we have not met previously, so we are apt to experiment if we find the stranger attractive to us. Usually we know what to do — how to open the conversation, what to talk about, how to end it. When meeting someone from a different culture, we are more prone to be uncertain about what to do. We are uncertain about what rules to follow — what we can say and how we can say it. Because the situation is ambiguous, reducing uncertainty and overcoming the ambiguity are challenging.

Reducing uncertainty becomes crucial in starting a relationship with people from other cultures. A three-step process is involved: precontact, initial contact, and closure.[7]

> ## Relationships Around the World: Thailand
>
> *Thais have two kind of friends: "eating friends" and "friends to the death." Eating friends eat with you when you can feast with them and disappear quickly when your money runs out. The other kind of friends are friends through thick and thin, sticking with you through the good times and the bad. But Thais are reluctant to impose on their friends, at least for routine favors. They are taught not to ask but to give to those who do ask.*
>
> *Although they try to be self-sufficient and not impose on others, they will kindly help at all times. If several Thais argue — which is rare because of the emphasis on group harmony — Thais take the disagreement seriously and may even become enemies.*
>
> Source: *A Common Core: Thais and North Americans*, by John Fieg (Chicago: Intercultural Press, 1989).

Precontact

Reducing uncertainty first entails forming impressions. When coming into contact with a stranger, we move from unfocused scanning of the environment to focused scanning. We first perceive the people and objects around us in a general sense. What we see is a blur until something catches our eye. We zero-in on that something, bringing it into focus. When we come into contact with a group of people, we scan them in an unfocused manner until someone captures our attention. The individual may be introduced to us, pointed out to us, or seem attractive to us. We become aware of the person's presence and begin to eyeball him or her, gathering what details we can. When the other person does the same, we are engaged in reciprocal scanning.

Initial Contact and Impression

Next we initiate a conversation, usually by introducing ourself and making small talk. The initial impression we obtain from the other person helps us decide whether to continue the conversation. We make judgments about the person, deciding whether we like or dislike him or her. Through our conversation, we try to discover how much the person is like us as we look for similarities in background and interest.

The Japanese ask many personal questions, attempting to assess the person's personality, professional knowledge and skills, and personal background. They feel they should know the person well enough to anticipate reactions and to plan their strategies while trying to establish rapport. The Japanese ask questions such as, "Where did you go to school? Where were you

To strike up a relationship, smile. What physical feature makes people attractive? The smile wins without question as the most desirable characteristic of a person's physical appearance.

born? Do you play golf? Have you been to Japan before? Do you like Japanese food? Do you speak Japanese? What year were you born?"[8]

Closure

Finally we arrive at a decision regarding the stranger. We pigeonhole the person mentally, classifying him or her as someone we like or dislike, and decide whether we want to continue the relationship and develop it more fully. Our goal in reducing the ambiguity is to be able to increase the predictability of the other person's communicative behavior. When we know more about the person, we can become more informal and talkative, revealing more of ourself. If we fail to reduce the uncertainty, communication will cease and the relationship will not develop.

Low-context and high-context cultures behave differently in the ambiguous situations involving communicators who meet for the first time. *Low-context* cultures are those that utilize an elaborate communication code in which listeners need to be told practically everything. Whatever information being communicated must

be explained in detail; nothing can be taken for granted. The heterogeneous cultures of the Western and Middle Eastern world fit this mode. The United States, for example, is a low-context culture in which a conversation goes into excessive detail.

In *high-context* cultures, typified by the homogenous Asian world, the listeners presumably know much about the subject and do not require excessive background information. They use a restrictive verbal code. The bulk of meaning of a message is either internalized in the listener with no need to express it or it is in the physical context and understood by the communicators. The coded, explicit, and spoken part of the message carries little meaning.

In low-context cultures uncertainty can be reduced by asking questions, talking things over, and self-disclosing. Members of high-context cultures do not reduce uncertainty verbally in the early phases of coming together, as in the case of the Japanese. More meetings are in order, and closer attention is given to the nonverbal meanings the speaker generates. Relationships develop more quickly in low-context cultures because of the emphasis on talk that

Relationships Around the World: Australia

The importance of a relationship to the Australians is revealed in the term "mateship," reflecting an attitude of "we are in this together; let's do the best we can." Australians believe that people are responsible for their neighbors, and they are extremely loyal to friends. As a friendship develops, they make a deeper and deeper commitment to it and don't switch relationships regularly as many Americans do.

Source: *A Fair Go for All: Australian/American Interaction*, by George W. Renwick (Yarmouth, ME: Intercultural Press, 1991).

reduces uncertainty. In high-context cultures, more time is required to begin a relationship.

When attempting to interact interculturally, we are tempted to rely on stereotypes, judging the individuals we meet on the basis of the preconceived judgment we hold of the cultural group they represent. If the stereotypes are negative, we probably will not make many lasting friends. A wiser course of action would be to withhold our judgments until we have gathered as much information as we can about these people.

 ## Factors Affecting Relationships

Interpersonal intercultural communication assumes that two or more people representing different cultures are in direct verbal and nonverbal communication. Many factors affect that kind of talk. In our examination, we group them into four general topical areas: social structure, presentational behavior, adaptive behavior, and relational behavior.

Social Structure

When several people interact, their talk brings individual differences to the surface. Some say more than others. Some are more active than others. Some elicit more respect from their fellow communicators. The differences result in inequalities along many dimensions. The disparity may be in an individual's outlook on self, the roles he or she plays, and the rank or status he or she holds, to name just a few. These distinctions are the basis for forming a culture's social structure, a concept we define as an *integrated pattern of relationships among the culture's members*. Five facets of structure help us gain a better understanding of intercultural relationships: the self, roles, status, power, and stratification.

The Self

The self-concept is significant in the Western world and plays a lesser part in most non-Western cultures, in which the group is the primary social entity. Americans carry with them a sense of who they are, what they should be, and what they want to be. Americans' behavior is determined in large part by the perception of self as being the identity, personality, or individualism of a given person as distinct from all other people.[9] It is the individual's answer to the question, "Who am I?"

Unlike the people of many other cultures, Americans are interested in their self-image, self-esteem, self-help, self-awareness, self-actualization, self-determination. The self is a unifying concept. It provides a perspective in thinking: What should *I* do? It gives direction for activity: Why should *I* do it? It provides a source of motivation: Will doing this be good for *me*? It is a locus for decision-making: How should *I* do it?[10]

North Americans react with bewilderment when confronted with people who do not carry the same image of self. The idea that the self is not paramount is contrary to the belief system of many Americans. As a result, when Americans interact with members of cultures not

Chinese Relationships

Rita Mei-Ching Ng

Rita Mei-Ching Ng

Confucian values underlie Chinese society. Their impact is apparent in the smooth and harmonious relationships that delineate the Chinese conception of self. Despite the political, social, and economic upheavals that have brought dramatic changes in the life of the average Chinese person, the people are linked in a web of interrelatedness, the consequence of the Confucian belief that humans are interdependent. A Chinese person who is not sensitive or responsive to the needs of others is considered self-centered, a quality leading to a closed world.

The American assumption that humans are independent, self-oriented individuals contrasts with the Confucian ethic of interpersonal accommodation. Chinese people are not expected to ask, "What are my rights?" or openly assert their feelings and thereby invite possible confrontation with and criticism from others in the social network, a network that from birth defines and organizes their existence.

Fundamental to the Chinese are three concepts: *ren qing, mian zi,* and *guan xi.* Ren qing (human feeling) is a derivative of reciprocity. When someone is sympathetic to another person's feelings or when a person is ready to help another in great need, that person is practicing ren qing. Even though the act of ren qing may involve only an exchange of feelings, the recipient is expected to pay back the debt of gratitude. A Chinese saying governs the situation: "If you receive a drop of beneficence from other people you should return them a fountain of beneficence." Ren qing not only involves expressions of good will but reciprocal obligations as well.

Failure to reciprocate entails a loss of mian zi (face) in the presence of others. In a culture where social evaluations are highly valued, it becomes crucial for Chinese to maintain face and to do facework in the presence of others. Simply stated, "face" means credibility, respect for others, and good reputation, and "facework" means to preserve one's reputation and esteem and avoid humiliation. When persuading others or attempting to gain compliance, a person's ability to present a favorable image to the others becomes important.

Guan xi or guanxi has no precise English equivalent, but it connotes relationship, connection, obligation, and dependency in English. Guan xi often is spoken of as something linking two people who in some way have developed a relationship of mutual dependence. Using guan xi refers to efforts to establish connections with others. Gifts may be given or a feast may be arranged for the express purpose of cultivating and maintaining relationships with others. The receiver of the gift is obligated to give later on, usually something the giver needs but cannot obtain on his or her own.

Ren qing, mian zi, and guan xi are forms of Chinese behavior that help create and maintain relationships in Chinese society. They are essential for smooth and harmonious interactions among the Chinese.

Rita Mei-Ching Ng is an assistant professor, Ohio University-Zanesville. Formerly she was on the faculty of Hong Kong Baptist University. Her doctorate is from Indiana University. She has published extensively in intercultural communication, persuasion, and management.

Self-Esteem Among Arabs

Foremost in an Arab's view of the self is self esteem. In communication with Arabs, it is important to pay tribute to their self-esteem and to avoid offending it. Arabs are touchy and the self-esteem is easily bruised. Typical Arabs find that being objective about their behavior is difficult, and they do not accept graciously someone's criticism of their behavior. Fault-finding should be masked to protect the self.

Source: *Understanding Arabs: A Guide for Westerners,* by N. O. Nydell (Yarmouth, ME: Intercultural Press, 1997).

bound to the self-concept, cultural gaps can develop.

Throughout Asia and in other countries as well, to varying degrees, the self is not a person's primary concern. The predominant value is congeniality in social interactions based on relationships among individuals rather than on the self. The point of reference is not the self but, rather, the network of obligations among members of the group. In most Asian cultures, behavior is directed first at maintaining affiliations in groups and upholding congenial social relationships. Personally rewarding goals, enhancing the self, are of secondary importance.

In Korea, for example, human relationships center on the thoughts of someone else. A Korean feels the presence of another person. In contrast, Westerners do not count-on someone else to do something for them. They prefer to be independent, to do it themselves.

In most Western cultures, each person is respected as an individual. In Korea, all human relationships are deeply affected by the consideration of others. A Korean seems to be more concerned about how others regard him or her than how the individual regards himself or herself.

Americans value themselves as the center, attaching priority to things that are closest to the self. They identify themselves as unique individuals, different from other people, including family members. Americans refer to themselves with a proud "I," whereas Koreans, like many Asians, either omit the "I" or refer to themselves as humble beings. Korean society is a totality in which "we" supersedes "I."

China offers another of many examples of how the East and West differ on the matter of self. The Chinese, more so than the Koreans, emphasize the group, somewhat at the expense of the individual. They are inclined to function best in groups, quite content to conform to the group's norms in dress, conduct, lifestyle, and thought. Maintaining "face" before members of the group concerns the Chinese most.

Roles

A role is a *set of behaviors associated with a position a person holds at a certain time.* These behaviors may be *ascribed* to the position, meaning that the culture assigned them to the position. The role of "mother" is a case in point.

Relationships Around the World: Brazil

Brazilians think of a friend as someone like a brother or sister. A person can share things with them and be honest with them. Brazilians accept the person as he or she is. They form friendships easily but differentiate levels of friendship.

A colega is a fellow or colleague, a "little friend," of which the typical Brazilian has many. A real friend, however, is an amigo, *someone who can be counted on, like family. Amigos usually have lifelong relationships, are welcome in each others' homes, and know all about each other.*

Source: *Behaving Brazilian: A Comparison of Brazilian and North American Social Behavior,* by Phyllis A. Harrison (Cambridge, MA: Newbury House, 1983).

Ages ago the culture assigned child-rearing duties and responsibilities to the mother.

Role behaviors also may be *achieved*. A lawyer, for example, undertakes an extensive training program for the right to practice. The lawyer obtains the behaviors assigned to the lawyer role through hard work.

Most of us hold certain behavioral expectations of those in specific roles. We expect the lawyer to defend us in court, the professor to teach us and do research, the police officer to protect us, and the mother to provide nurturance. These behaviors are culture-bound, determined by the culture at large. As such, individuals are socialized into the roles they play and are socialized in the ways of interacting with others in their roles. These behavior patterns or roles become internalized and are integrated into each person's personality.

The behaviors associated with the roles people play differ from culture to culture. For example, in Kenya, an American woman who headed a large development project decided her secretary was overworked and the American assigned one of the secretary's tasks — preparing and serving tea for the staff — to a chauffeur who had plenty of free time. The office employees protested because they saw serving tea as a woman's job. A woman would have to be hired, and one was employed with the sole job of preparing and serving tea. In Kenya, role assignments between men and women are strictly defined. Jobs for men and jobs for women are not interchanged.[11]

Mexican fathers and American fathers have different roles. The Mexican father demands obedience and love from his children. That role is reversed for most American fathers, who give love and do not expect total subservience.

Relationships Around the World: France

Relationship styles of the French are specialized, but they tend to be organized in patterns of long duration, often with the expectation that family relationships will extend over several generations. French people are like Russians in that they are not competitive in their relationships as Americans are. They are not trying to out-do one another, to get ahead, or to beat the other in some way.

French people may argue, and if they do, their friendship is put in abeyance but not broken. The individuals concerned are not on speaking terms but expect a reconciliation and stand ready to give mutual aid in some grave circumstance. Under similar circumstances, Americans would quietly drift apart and Russians would seek immediate resolution through a stormy scene.

Source: *American Cultural Patterns: A Cross-Cultural Perspective*, by E. C. Stewart (Washington, DC: Society for Intercultural Education, 1991).

Status

Status relates to a person's position in a hierarchy of some sort. It is defined as *the standing or ranking of a person in the hierarchy of a group's structure*. Status is a power-oriented dimension. People in the top position, such as the president of a business, a teacher in the classroom, and a dean of a college, wield the most power and hold the higher status. These people are in the superordinate position. Ordinary members of the group, such as employees in a business, students in a classroom, and faculty members in a college, are in subordinate positions and have little power. As subordinates, they have lower status.

In all cultures, the status difference is a significant communication factor. In a relationship, the high-status person tends to control the communication. He or she tells the others what to do and has the freedom to initiate and terminate conversations. The high-status person tends to speak louder than the low-status person and can interrupt low-status persons at will. The high-status person touches more and controls the distance between himself or herself and the low-status person.

Status is relative to the situation. The teacher is in charge of the classroom and is the high-status person in that situation. In the dean's office, however, the dean is in charge and the teacher assumes the low-status position. At home, the dean might be subjected to the attempts of his wife to rule and thus becomes a henpecked husband, a low-status person. Different situations call for different hierarchical relationships.

Australians and Americans are similar in many respects. Both groups live in nations of immigrants. For the most part, they speak the same language, follow the Christian religion, and believe in social and political democracy. They differ mainly in acknowledgement of status. Americans derive status from their company position and their professional title, whereas Australians are intolerant of the class distinctions they encounter and resist being categorized themselves, particularly if their status is lower than the status of those with whom they interact. Their strong egalitarian feelings make typical Australians approachable, regardless of how high their status, and employers and employees more readily mix socially than American bosses and workers do.

Status is ephemeral, transitory, lasting only as long as the holder maintains the power attached to the position he or she holds. Saigon during the American occupation in the Vietnam war illustrates the point. High-status Vietnamese doctors, dentists, lawyers, accountants, army officers, and other persons serving in the city's hierarchy suffered severe losses in economic well-being, and hence in social status and influence. The Vietnamese who owned bars, hotels, shops, or fleets of taxis grew rich by tapping the wealth of the American GIs. The status-conscious urban middle class experienced the massive American presence as a disaster. Bar girls made more money than their physician fathers or college-graduate relatives. The traditional order of life in Vietnam suffered reversals as the high-status leaders earned less than an enterprising harlot who had the means to purchase the finest food and clothing.

Power

In Chapter 5 we explored power distance, the degree of inequality in power between powerful and less powerful people in an international corporation with offices across cultures. Now we examine power in terms of interpersonal relationships. Power in this sense means the ability of a person to control or influence another — to get another to do what the person wants.

All communicative relationships involve power. We try to establish and maintain a satisfying amount of influence over others — sometimes by dominating, ruling, or leading, and sometimes to resist the control and domination of others. We try to dominate by winning arguments, by making suggestions that others will adopt, by controlling conversations, and sometimes by rebelling against the desires of other people.

Some relationships have a predetermined imbalance of power — for example, the teacher-student, doctor-patient, lawyer-client relationships. *Complementary relationships* are those that involve high- and low-status individuals. One person occupies the superior position and the other, the subordinate. The lower-status person defers to the person in the superior position.

Symmetrical relationships involve people of equal status. Yet, depending upon the situation, the power will shift continually from one to the other. Information is a source of power. People who possess special information or knowledge that both need at a given moment will be empowered to act. Recognizing the impact of power in intercultural communication situations is necessary for effective interaction.

The classic framework for defining bases of power consists of five power sources that we use to influence others: legitimate power, referent power, expert power, reward power, and coercive power.[12]

Shifts in Power
for Polynesians in New Zealand

Meredith G. Caisley

Meredith G. Caisley

Auckland not only is the largest city in New Zealand but also is the largest Polynesian center in the world. Many of its residents come from the neighboring islands of Western Samoa. Tonga, and Fiji for their education and employment.

Just one of the many cultural changes that these people face is the issue of legitimate power. New Zealand boasts a policy of equal opportunity across ethnic groups, gender differences, and social classes. Also, because industry in New Zealand is promoting a change from hierarchical structure to flat structure, it is ranked as having a small power distance between management and workers.

To fit our young people for this environment, the education system promotes the rights of individual students. All of them are encouraged to show independence and initiative. Students are praised for holding opinions and expressing them strongly.

The Polynesian culture is quite the opposite, with children trained in total obedience to their parents, students in blind obedience to their teachers, and females completely subordinated to males. This is particularly noticeable in the classroom when students sit in a passive state not prepared to participate in any way for fear of derision or punishment. Students will not establish eye contact with a teacher and do their very best to avoid any form of contact. As soon as a New Zealand teacher makes an approach, Polynesian students recoil as if expecting some negative outcome. Much patience and time are required to win their confidence and befriend them because of the barrier of status. Obviously, the students have the bitter experience of coercive power in their home education system.

When Polynesian children are sent to New Zealand for high school education and subsequent employment, cultural confusion arises. This is particularly so with young women who have accepted the dependent status and then have such high demands placed on them in Auckland.

Once Polynesians have been appointed to a position of responsibility in industry in New Zealand, employers expect them to take a proactive stance in the team. They should be assertive and confident to form and voice their opinions. Employers find that, given encouragement, Polynesians are well able to do this and make major contributions to the firm. Women particularly are valued for their insight and sensitivity, interacting well with colleagues and clients alike.

Some Polynesian women have accepted the challenge of corporate life and are extremely successful in large-city legal, financial, and medical environments in New Zealand. Then they encounter the reverse problem when they return to their homeland and face the traditional power bases in their familial groups. These women no longer accept that males automatically hold authoritative positions. Thus, cultural conflict arises at family gatherings where women often are banned from speaking or from holding opinions of their own.

Meredith G. Caisley is a teacher of oral communication in her own consultancy. She lectures in business communication at Auckland University of Technology and Massey University. She also is an examiner and a trustee of the New Zealand Speech Board.

1. *Legitimate power* comes from the respect we hold for a position that another person possesses. Teachers, police officers, mayors, company presidents, and congressional members all have power because of the position they hold relative to other people. In Russia, high-level bureaucrats wield great power. When a bureaucrat tells citizens what to do, they respond to this enactment of legitimate power by doing what the bureaucrat asks.

2. *Referent power* comes from the personal attraction we have for another person — the charisma that person has. People with personal charm, beauty, fame, status, or other personal qualities we like are able to influence us. We alter our behavior to meet their demands or desires because we find them attractive and likeable. Many people found the movie star John Wayne to be a person of charisma, and they watched his movies because of his attractive aura and talent.

3. *Expert power* stems from a person's knowledge and experience. We convey power to those who know more than we do or possess a skill we do not have but desire. To us, our teacher is an expert, having knowledge we have not yet mastered. Our auto mechanic holds expert power in our eyes if he or she can repair our car.

4. *Reward power* is based on another person's ability to satisfy our needs. That person controls resources and uses them to recompense those who support him or her. The resources may be money, a promotion, pay raise, better job, affection, membership in a group, or desired gifts. The teacher has reward power, as does our boss at work.

5. *Coercive power* entails the application of sanctions or punishment to influence others. The teacher can impose penalties if we fail to do our homework on time or are late for class, giving the teacher coercive power. Our parents had the power to "ground" us for failing to complete a household chore, come home on time, and do our schoolwork. Our partner may withhold physical affection if we fail to comply with a given request. Representative of coercive power are blaming, inflicting punishment, imposing fines, taking legal action, and ignoring.

Social Stratification

Humans tend to characterize people by social class, ranking or categorizing them in relationship to others. We see some people getting ahead in the world. We see others moving down the ladder. When we characterize people as moving up or down, or as being higher or lower than others socially, we are stratifying.

Although the criteria are not the same across cultures and they change periodically, we usually rank people by authority, power, property ownership, income, lifestyle, occupation, educational background, altruistic activity, kinship connections, and work with volunteer associations. High-ranking people are likely to be wealthy individuals, the politically powerful, business moguls, members of ruling families, and religious dignitaries, among others.

The qualities one culture considers important may not be considered important in another. Kinship is significant in Great Britain. In the United States, relatives are less important in terms of stratification. Education is more highly valued in Germany, Sweden, and Japan than most other countries. In Japan, professors are ranked highly; in America they barely make the list.

Caste. One form of social stratification is the caste system. The caste into which a person is born is the one in which he or she remains. Each caste has certain duties, status, and rights. Detailed rules help caste members determine to whom they can talk, about what, and how. This system is waning in most countries where it has been practiced.

In India, the highest caste, the *Brahmins*, consists of the priests or seers who teach or preach. The *Kashtryas*, protectors of life and treasure, follow, as the administrators and ruling class. Next are the *Vaisyas*, the cultivators, traders, business people, and herders. The Sudras are the artisans — carpenters, blacksmiths, and laborers. Finally, the *Harijas* (Children of God, as Ghandi named them) are the untouchables, outcasts, or castless ones, who do the least desirable work — scavenging, slaughtering animals, sweeping the streets.

Bureaucracies. Another form of social stratification is the bureaucracy, representing a

hierarchy between the average citizen and the government. Government employees have the right to approve or disapprove, to provide or not provide information about essential items such as a driver's license, a motor vehicle license, income tax information, and a multitude of similar documents and data.

Stratification Differences. The East and West differ in social stratification. Eastern cultures, generally speaking, observe a system of

Stratification Differences: The Eastern World

Takehide Kawashima

Eastern stratification has advantages. The hierarchical system, based on Confucian beliefs, is common to most Eastern cultures. It supplies the individual with guidelines on how to behave. Communication rules give the individual direction regarding whom to talk to, when, and how. The talk is structured according to status; hence, it becomes predictable. Accepted forms of address, language, and manner exist for virtually every social situation, and they prescribe methods of structuring social situations.

Following the social rules, a student, for instance, knows what is proper when speaking to a professor. By following the rules, the student will have little problem saying what is appropriate, although a caution is in order: In the last few years, this way of thinking has eroded and the absolute formality is becoming a thing of the past.

Throughout the Eastern world, generally speaking, differences in age, gender, status, and rank are maximized in communication situations. The order of preference is elder over younger, male over female, in business settings college graduate over non-college worker, first-rate college over second-rate college, most years of service over the least years. Merit always gives way to age, gender, education, and years of service. At home, everyone in the family has a position, but the elders have more power and the male rules over the female.

Maintaining harmonious relationships with family members, close friends and colleagues, and other primary group members is essential in the Eastern world. Stratification requires strict communication patterns. Otherwise, discourtesies could occur and problems result. Among friends and acquaintances, the communication can be informal. As the relationship becomes more distant in terms of age, gender, status, and rank, the style becomes more formal.

In the traditional East, a carefully determined hierarchy prevails for respective status groups. Social interaction tends to be vertical, with little heed to equality. Times are changing, though, and bits and pieces of the old system are disappearing.

Takehide Kawashima is a professor at Nihon University, Tokyo, Japan. The author or co-author of speech communication textbooks, he has been co-editor of a speech textbook series. He is a founder of the Communication Association of Japan, Communication Association of the Pacific, Pacific and Asian Communication Association, organizations he served in official capacities.

hierarchical relationships. Most Western countries profess equality to some extent, although subtle stratification appears in terms of economic differentiation, ethnic background, age, and gender.

Presentational Communicative Behavior

How do people present themselves to others in relational situations? Are they dominant —

Stratification Differences: The Western World

The East and the West differ in their outlook on social stratification. Eastern cultures, generally speaking, closely observe a system of hierarchical relationships. In the West, most countries advocate equality to some degree, although stratification appears, subtly perhaps, in terms of economic differentiation, ethnic background, age, and gender. To understand how cultures are unlike on the stratification issue, the East and the West are compared, using the United States to represent the West.

Most American children grow up believing that all humans are created equal. Running through American social relationships is this theme of equality. Interpersonal relations take place on a horizontal level, conducted between assumed equals. Nonetheless, the United States has upper, middle, and lower classes. Be that as it may, Americans stand for equality.

That sense of equality carries over into most social situations, even in personal confrontation situations involving superordinate and subordinate positions. If an employer has a personal disagreement with an employee, rank is not expected to enter in, authority is not to be exercised, and the talk is supposed to take place on an equal level. Work-related disagreements may call for a less than equal attitude, but even then, care is taken to maintain an atmosphere of equality, depending on the situation. Even within the authoritarian mode of the military, equality is advocated. From the enlisted person's perspective, the mark of a good officer is that he or she does not rely on the right of command except under extreme circumstances. Discussion is more likely to be in order.

Though equality remains a pervasive cultural norm, it is not always extended to certain groups -- for instance, blacks, females, and elderly people. In large business and industrial organizations, in politics, and in federal agencies strong hierarchical emphases also appear. In each instance, however, federal law or common sense is beginning to reduce the inequities. Laws are helping to reduce the inequalities shown toward the elderly, racial minorities, and females.

Because typical Americans function better interpersonally on a level of equality, confusion often sets in when they are in other cultures. Attempts to treat everyone as equals can lead to misunderstanding. Americans visiting in countries where servants wait on their every need feel uncomfortable, if the feelings of a frequent traveler abroad are representative. Speaking of Korea in particular, he reported that his friends' servants and chauffeurs rebuffed his attempts to treat them as equals. Knowing their place and being quite content with their lot, the servants resented his gestures of equality.

strong, loud, assertive? Are they dramatic — given to exaggeration? Are they attentive — listening with empathy?

Culture, along with personality and communicative skills, is a factor in how people present themselves and affects how others perceive them. Along with individuals, cultures also are distinguished by their presentational communicative behavior. A predominant stereotype of the Greeks, for example, is that of a contrapuntal virtuosity, incisive, combative, loud group of people. Every conversation seems to be an argument, and gentleness seems to play no part in the dialogue.[13] The Chinese are reserved, contained, implicit, and indirect.[14] Australians have developed the art of deadpan understatement. To them, utterance is better not done at all. When it is done, it is better if it is slow, flat, and expressionless to acknowledge that the subject is hardly worth talking about.[15]

Although these are stereotypical accounts, they do illustrate how cultures are identified through their communicative behavior. They also suggest that cultural differences exist in the way people from a culture present themselves.

Next we will analyze cultural similarities and differences in the presentational areas of communication apprehension, predispositions to verbal behavior, communicative style, and self-disclosure.

Communication Apprehension

Variously described as stage fright, reticence, speaking anxiety, and shyness, communication apprehension is a *person's level of anxiety associated with either real or anticipated talk with one or more persons.*[16] Communication apprehension can be a stumbling block in achieving fruitful relationships.

Any rewarding relationships people can expect from speaking will be surpassed for the apprehensives by fear, so they do not talk unless they are obligated to do so. When the apprehensives speak, they appear shy, nonassertive, nervous, embarrassed, or uncomfortable. They react negatively to speaking situations and are not

perceived positively in school, on the job, or in social interactions.[17]

Communication apprehension comparisons across cultures showed the following: Of nine countries sampled, the Korean population had the lowest apprehension. Roughly 2 percent of the sample indicated high apprehensiveness in speaking situations. The Taiwanese sample had a slightly but not significantly higher level — about 5 percent. The Philippines followed, with 13 percent. Approximately 25 percent of the Micronesian, Australian, American, and Chinese samples perceived themselves as high apprehensives. Switzerland had 30 percent in the high category, and Japan — with more than one-third of the population sampled indicating high apprehensiveness — had the highest percentage. The Koreans and the Taiwanese feel the most comfortable speaking in interpersonal relationships, and the Japanese the least.[18]

Predispositions Toward Verbal Behavior

Most people have impressions of their own verbal aptitude, which others generally confirm. If a person views his or her speaking in a conversation as slow and deliberate, for example, others tend to agree.

People's impressions come from five features of their verbal behavior:[19]

1. Domination of communication situations.

2. Assumption of responsibility for initiating and maintaining talk with others.

3. Length and frequency of the communication.

4. Reluctance to talk with others.

5. Apprehensiveness when communicating.

Comparison of the predispositions across four cultures indicated that, of the four populations sampled, the Korean population was the most predisposed to dominate and the least predisposed to initiate and and maintain conversations. The Koreans also perceived themselves to be less reluctant to talk and less apprehensive

Know Yourself . . .

How willing are you to talk with different kinds of people — friends, acquaintances, strangers? Presuming you have completely free choice, indicate what percent of the time you would choose to communicate.

0 = never   100 = always

_____ 1. Present a talk to a group of strangers.

_____ 2. Talk with an acquaintance while standing in line.

_____ 3. Talk in a large meeting with friends.

_____ 4. Talk in a small group of strangers.

_____ 5. Talk with a friend while standing in line.

_____ 6. Talk in a large meeting of acquaintances.

_____ 7. Talk with a stranger while standing in line.

_____ 8. Present a talk to a group of friends.

_____ 9. Talk to a small group of acquaintances.

_____ 10. Talk in a large meeting of strangers.

_____ 11. Talk in a small group of friends.

_____ 12. Present a talk to a group of acquaintances.

To compute your score, follow these instructions:

Willing to talk to strangers: Add scores for items 1, 4, 7, 10, then divide by 4: Willing = 63+

Willing to talk with acquaintances: Add scores for items 2, 6, 9, 12, then divide by 4. Willing = 92+

Willing to talk with friends: Add scores for items 3, 5, 8, 11, then divide by 4: Willing = 99+

To compute your total willingness to talk score, add the subscores for the three, and then divide by 3. Willing = 84+

Adapted from "Willingness to Communicate Scale," by J. C. McCroskey and V.P. Richmond, in _Personality and Interpersonal Communication_ (Newbury Park, CA: Sage Publications, 1987), pp. 129–156.

than the American, Australian, and Japanese participants in the comparison. The four groups were similar in length and frequency of their conversations, and the Americans and Australians were similar to each other on the five features. The Japanese sample showed the highest apprehensiveness.[20]

Communication Style

Two basic speech behaviors act simultaneously to influence interpersonal interaction. One behavior, what is said, refers to the *content* of the message. The other, how it is said, refers to the way the message is presented or the *style* of communication.

Style is composed of 10 traits: impression-leaving, contentious, open, dramatic, dominant, precise, relaxed, friendly, attentive, and animated. The degree to which a speaker possesses these traits contributes to the person's image as a communicator, his or her style of communicating.

In comparing style across seven cultures, a summary of the comparisons suggests something of the typical communication style of the culture's members. Of the seven sampled, the Micronesian respondents had the strongest communicator image, perceiving themselves as friendly, dramatic, and impression-leaving communicators. The Koreans believe they are effective communicators also, being dominant, attentive, and relaxed — qualities implying competence. The Filipinos hold a good communicator image of themselves with a style characterized as friendly, relaxed, open, animated, and impression-leaving. The contentious Chinese are not overly dramatic, dominant, attentive, or relaxed but are quarrelsome. The Australians perceive themselves as good communicators and more animated than the others. The Americans are middle-grounders, not exceptional in comparison to the others, in any of the 10 traits. The Japanese, although open, do not feel as orally capable as the others and perceive themselves as shy, apprehensive, and reluctant to verbalize.

Self-Disclosure

Revealing intimate information about oneself, self-disclosure, plays a significant role in developing close relationships. Self-closure concerns messages about the self that listeners are

Chinese Humility in Praise-Giving

Mary Fong

Mary Fong

To establish and maintain rapport in interpersonal relationships, complimenting another person is a common practice, although the methods vary across cultural groups. Chinese modesty and humility contrast sharply with Anglo-Americans' effusively laudatory remarks, as interviews with 40 Chinese immigrants to the United States reveal.

When complimented, the immigrants note, the Chinese normally reject the praise by issuing a denial: "Oh, no, no!" They are unlikely to respond with an expression of gratitude or other acknowledgement of its validity as an Anglo-American would.

The Chinese immigrants indicate that when they do compliment, they do so for some significant or outstanding act such as the attractiveness of another person or a student or an employee's superior effort. An Anglo-American, in contrast, offers praise on a wide range from insignificant matters to significant ones, from items of dress to outstanding acts of service.

When the Chinese do compliment, their felicitations carry few adjectives extolling the virtuosity of the deeds. Theirs are "barebones" expressions of congratulations. Anglo-Americans, on the other hand, attach various positive attributes to their compliments, making their remarks flattering in comparison to Chinese compliments.

The Chinese immigrants acknowledge that they rarely compliment to build rapport and support, nor would they compliment someone who did not do well, for the purpose of encouraging them to do better next time. Anglo-Americans generously compliment those who fail to accomplish their purpose, whether it be in a sports activity, in school, or wherever. They give those compliments to stimulate greater effort in future activities.

The Chinese immigrants appreciate most the compliments they receive when they come through a go-between, a person who transmits the compliment on behalf of the individual who does the complimenting. Anglo-Americans prefer that their compliments come directly from the person making the compliment.

If an Anglo-American compliments a Chinese for a laudatory accomplishment, the Chinese do respond as an Anglo-American might, not because the Chinese is acting impolitely or rudely, but rather because that its the cultural way to respond.

Dr. Fong received the Ph.D. from the University of Washington and teaches in the Department of Communication Studies at California State University, San Bernardino. She is active in the Asia/Pacific American Caucus and has been published in *Intercultural Communication: A Reader*, 8th edition, by L A. Samovar and R.E. Porter, (Belmont, CA: Wadsworth, 1997) *Our Voices, Essays in Culture, Ethnicity, and Communication*, 3d edition, by A. Gonzales, M. Houston, and V. Chen (Los Angeles: Roxbury, 2000).

Relationships Around the World: Russia

Russians expect to form deep bonds with others and to assume the obligation of almost constant companionship. They reject reticence or secretiveness among those in close relationship. Russians embrace the whole person in a relationship, not restricting friendships on the basis of interests. Their relationships are intense, demanding, enduring, and rewarding, and they are devoid of competitiveness.

Source: From *Nyet to Da: Understanding the Russians*, by Yale Richmond (Yarmouth, ME: Intercultural Press, 1992).

unlikely to acquire unless the speaker personally discloses it. The discloser unmasks the self as the discloser perceives the self, and the disclosure increases with increased intimacy in the relationship and when disclosure is rewarded. It increases also when there is a need to reduce uncertainty in a relationship.

Although self-disclosure is a universal phenomenon, it differs from culture to culture in perceived intent, amount, depth, positiveness, and honesty. EuroAmericans disclose about a wider range of topics than do the Japanese. Ghanaians readily disclose about family matters, whereas Americans disclose more about career concerns. EuroAmericans disclose more than African-Americans, Mexican-Americans, British, French, Germans, Puerto Ricans, and Japanese.

Far East Asians differ from Americans in what they think should be revealed and what should be kept private. The Americans are more inclined to self-disclose to a wider group of people than Japanese and Koreans, and the Koreans are more willing to self-disclose to more people than the Japanese.

Adaptive Communicative Behavior

A characteristic of competent communicators is their ability to adapt to the specific situation in which they are communicating and to adapt to the people with whom they are speaking. This ability calls for attentiveness and perceptiveness. *Attentiveness* is the extent to which communicators are aware of the special demands of the speaking situation and adjust to them. If the speaking environment is unusually noisy, the attentive communicator will adjust to the noise, speaking as loud as necessary.

Perceptiveness implies that communicators are aware of how the others perceive them, observing how others respond to them and being sensitive to the subtle or hidden meanings in the speech and behavior of the other communicators. If they are not being understood, for example, they will realize this and clarify what they are saying.

Communicators' attentiveness and perceptiveness suggest the degree of their involvement in the communicative interaction. Those who are highly involved see themselves as attentive and perceptive and those with a low degree of involvement do not.

In comparing American, Japanese, and Korean populations on attentiveness and perceptiveness, the results indicated that the three populations were only moderately involved, falling between high and low involvement. They were average, tending to view themselves as socially able, popular with other communicators, and liked by them. They were not outstandingly competent communicators, nor were they failures. They adapted ably to the communication situation and to their fellow communicators.

Relational Communicative Behavior[21]

Communicative behavior that touches upon aspects of intercultural relationships include self-monitoring, orientations to tasks in group relationships, topical matter in interpersonal interactions, and loneliness.

Self-Monitoring

Similar to adaptive behavior, self monitoring relates to communicators' sensitivity to the communicative situation. It reflects the communicators' ability to observe and regulate their expressive behavior and self-presentation. Some monitor a communicative environment skillfully, homing in on cues that tell them what communicative behavior is appropriate in a given environment. *High self-monitors,* they are attentive, other-oriented, and adaptable to diverse communication situations.

Low self-monitors pay less attention to situational cues and have little concern for the appropriateness of their communicative behavior. They attend less to others' expressions and monitor the situation poorly. They are less expressive than high self-monitors, less skilled at employing strategies of social influence, and more internally guided in their behavior.

Culturally based propensities toward self-monitoring would seem natural, especially between Eastern and Western cultures representing

Relationships Around the World: The United States

Interpersonal relationships among people in the United States are numerous and marked by friendliness and informality. Americans, however, rarely form deep and lasting friendships. Relationships change easily as they shift status or locale, and the relationships tend to lack permanence and depth. Americans avoid personal commitments to others and do not like to get involved with people in obligatory ways--for example, having to repay a gift with one in turn.

Americans contrast a "fair-weather friend" with a "friend in need (who) is a friend indeed." Americans prize a mobile, independent existence; therefore, their relationships usually do not involve the deep set of rights and duties characteristic of relationships in more communal societies. Relationships tend to be compartmentalized, revolving around an activity, an event, or a shared history.

An American, thus, can have a friend to play bridge with, another to discuss politics with, and a third to socialize with. In that manner, Americans tend to fragment their personality to some extent and view the other person as a composite of distinct accomplishments and interests. Even though many disagreements can arise in American relationships, these often are not taken seriously and loyalty is not a consideration.

Americans form relationships with people with whom they work, parents of the children with whom their offspring play, people who share political opinions, and people they meet in charitable activities, in playing games, and at occasions for sharing food. Because they are formed around activities, American friendships are not as deep as friendships in other cultures, and a competitive element runs through these friendships.

Because the United States is a pluralistic society, it is dangerous to generalize, as we have just done. Many different cultures make up the country, so these characteristics do not fit everyone. Nevertheless, they do offer a generalized image of Americans of European ancestry.

Sources: *American Culture Patterns: A Cross-Cultural Perspective*, by E.C. Stewart (Washington DC: Society for Intercultural Education, 1972); and *American Ways: A Guide for Foreigners in the United States*, by Gary Althen (Yarmouth, ME: Intercultural Press, 1988).

high-context and low-context dimensions. The members of high-context cultures, with their ability to interpret nonverbal behavior, should be high self-monitors and the members of low-context cultures should be the opposite, insensitive to situational cues.

Studies comparing Japanese and Korean communicators with Americans found no significant difference between these groups. The high-context Japanese and Koreans perceived themselves as similar to the low-context Americans on self-monitoring abilities. All three groups expressed moderate levels of self-monitoring aptitude.

Group Task Orientations

Group task orientations in relational communication relate to roles, an aspect of social structure discussed previously, specifically roles that people play in small-group relationships. Three classes of roles are found in groups engaged in working on some sort of job: task, maintenance, and self-oriented roles.

1. *Task roles* concern completing the job the group has, whatever it may be.

2. *Maintenance roles* deal with the socio-emotional issues that arise in relational situations and relate to helping to promote harmony and cooperation among the group members while creating and maintaining cohesiveness.

3. *Self-orientation roles* are those the members play to satisfy personal needs irrelevant to the job at hand.

In measuring these roles across cultures, the assumption could be that there would be culturally based preferences toward one set of roles or another. The collectivistic cultures, with their stress on harmonious relations, may be maintenance-directed, and the individualistic cultures, with their stress on self-reliance and autonomy, may be self- or task-oriented.

Research measuring the roles in Australia, Japan, Korea, Micronesia, and the United States did not support the assumption. The highest percentage of those sampled among the Americans

---

Relationships Around the World: Philippines

In the Philippines, harmony is the ultimate ideal in creating and maintaining secure and sustaining relationships. Underlying the achievement of harmony are three important values: pakikisama, hiya, and utang na loob.

Pakikisama, getting along or maintaining smooth interpersonal relations, is pursued by a variety of means: being conscious of it as a value and goal, being aware of and respectful of age and authority, being thoughtful about how one speaks and acts, showing sensitivity to hiya and utang na loob.

Hiya connotes propriety, shame, and face — how one appears in the eyes of others. Fear of embarrassment, of losing face, is strong. To be insulted or to lose one's self-respect is intolerable; thus, to behave in a way that ensures no one's "face" is threatened is vital.

Utang na loob, a consciousness of indebtedness, requires the balancing of obligations or debts in relationships. Keeping the scale of obligation in balance is essential and binds the persons more closely in a relationship.

Source: *Considering Filipinos*, by Theodore Gochenour (Yarmouth, ME: Intercultural Press, 1990).

and Australians appeared in the maintenance-role set, and those two groups, along with the Micronesians, had the lowest percentage in the task-role set.

Topics in Conversations

Conversation, the informal exchange of feelings, observations, opinions, and ideas, serves the vital function of establishing and maintaining relations among people. Because it is a widespread communicative activity, conversation is a frequently studied aspect of human communication. One subject area not researched, however, is what people talk about. What do people talk about and with whom?

In an attempt to discover what topics are of interest to conversationalists in different cultures, topics of conversation were analyzed along with the kinds of people engaged most in conversational situations across three cultures: Japan, Korea and the United States.

The results are conclusive. Conversationalists in Japan, Korea, and the United States cover a variety of topic material. Fifteen broad and all-inclusive topics, ranging from personal matters such as a person's face and body, diseases and injuries, personality, sexual relations, and financial problems, to more public issues, such as politics, abortion, and pornography, make up the bulk of their conversational experiences. Not every topic is discussed with each conversational partner.

The majority of the sampled populations in the three cultures did not talk about their sexual relationships with everyone, only to same-sex friends. Too, of the three groups, only the Americans are prone to converse much with relatives, slight acquaintances, and strangers. The others are less willing to converse with these people. But the Americans restrict their talk to less personal matters, avoiding highly personal topics. Even with the friends other than their very closest friends, Japanese and Koreans are circumspect about what they say.

The Japanese and Koreans do not discuss with their parents and siblings topics such as sex relations, abortion, and pornography. Fathers are left out of conversations involving personal matters such as sex, abortion, pornography, and friends of the other sex.

Americans are more willing to talk with almost anyone than are the people from the other two cultures. The Japanese are the least willing, possibly because they are more apprehensive in communication situations.

Loneliness

Loneliness is defined as *a discrepancy between desired and actual relationships*. It correlates with anxiety, depression, self-derogation, feelings of hopelessness, shyness, low self-esteem,

Alone with her flock of sheep all day, this Greek shepherdess may experience signs of loneliness — shyness, depression, low self-esteem — and could be bored and restless with her lot in life.

and feelings of alienation. Lonely people tend to be bored, restless, unhappy, and dissatisfied with their social relationships.

Associated with a small relationship network of friends and acquaintances, loneliness is common and found everywhere. In the United States, 26 percent of the people feel lonely at some time during their life. Those who are chronically lonely may become so because they are ineffective or apprehensive communicators, emitting signals implying that they are not interested in talking with others.

To confirm the presence of loneliness in Korea, it was compared between Koreans and Americans, and the Koreans proved significantly more lonely than the Americans. Growing up in a collectivistic culture, Koreans maintain a close family relationship. In the comparison reported here, the Koreans were university students living away from home. Being away from their family, the Koreans probably were lonely. The Americans, also university students away from home, have been encouraged to be independent and live their own life, so loneliness may not be as influential in their lives as for the Koreans.

Chapter Review

Intercultural relationships bring together people with different conceptions about the duties and responsibilities involved in relationships.

A relationship is the state of being mutually or reciprocally interested. People enter into relationships for companionship or practical gain.

When people first meet, reducing uncertainty is foremost and intercultural situations tend to accentuate it. Reducing uncertainty entails a three-step process: precontact, initial contact and impression, and closure.

Five components of social structure have a bearing on intercultural relationships: self, roles, status, power, and social stratification.

Americans tend to be caught up in the self, whereas other cultures are more interested in the groups (the big "I" versus the all important "we").

Roles are sets of behaviors associated with a position a person holds at a certain time.

Status — the standing or ranking of a person in the hierarchy of a group's structure — is a power-oriented dimension. Those with high status tend to be in control. Status, however, is relative to the situation; different situations call for different status levels.

(Continued)

Chapter Review continued

Power is the ability of a person or group to control or influence other people in some way. It is classified as reward, coercive, expert, legitimate, or referent power.

Stratification means that people rank each other according to their place in their culture's hierarchy. The Eastern and Western worlds view stratification differently.

Four aspects of presentational communicative behavior are communication apprehension, verbal behavioral predispositions, communicator style, and self-disclosure.

Adaptive communicative behavior — the way communicators adjust to the people with whom they speak — is marked by attentiveness and perceptiveness.

Aspects of relational communicative behavior are self-monitoring, task orientation, topics of conversation, and loneliness.

Think About This . . .

1 Seeing a foreign student with whom you would like to form a relationship, what would you do? How would you handle the initial contact stage? What would you say? How would you handle the closure for a low-context person? A high-context person?

2 Explain the "I" and "we" concepts of self. Which one best represents you? Typical university students? Why?

3 What is your standing in the stratification relationships in your family? At school? Among your friends? Why do you place yourself as you do?

4 Evaluate your presentational behavior in terms of communication apprehension, verbal predispositions, communicative style, and self-disclosure. Why do you make those choices?

5 How do you rate yourself as a self-monitor? Explain why you make this rating.

PART THREE

TRANSMITTING INTERCULTURAL MESSAGES

9 Language and Its Cultural Implications

The Academy Award winning director Federico Fellini offered an astute observation about language: "A language is not just a dictionary of words, sounds, and syntax. It is a different way of interpreting reality, refined by generations that developed that language." Caribs, Guycurus, and Samoyeds are able to verbalize symbolically among themselves about the reality around them and conceptualize broadly about that reality, its past, and its future. But Caribs, Guycurus, and Samoyeds interpret reality variously. Because they do not share the same language, their perceptions of reality are different, reflecting their cultural dissimilarities. They would have difficulty interacting with each other over normal daily events and concerns.

As the French philosopher Claude Duneton said, language is like a "house" of the people, a spiritual home for them and, for most, their only place of residence. Caribs, Guycurus, and Samoyeds live in different "houses," and they likely will never enter another's "house."

When we engage in intercultural communication, we are figuratively entering the "house" of another and that person into our "house." Because we do not share the same language, our conceptions of the world around us will be dissimilar. The structure of a language affects the way people communicate, and the structure varies from culture to culture, as do the vocabulary and the resources of expression. Being cognizant of the nature of language and of variations in language across cultures should add to our understanding of intercultural communication.

Photo by Debbie Whittig

The Nature of Language

The question "What is language?" has elicited many different answers. Linguists focus on the phonetic aspects of language, defining it as a series of sounds produced by speakers and received by listeners. Semanticists are concerned with meaning, and their study relates to the transfer of meaning verbally and nonverbally. Grammarians see language as a series of grammatical forms, roots, and endings. Anthropologists define language as a system of cultural knowledge used to generate and interpret speech. Novelists believe that language is a series of words arranged to produce a harmonious or logical effect. Lexicographers conceive of language as a list of words with their separate derivations, histories, and meanings. Psychologists think of language as a system of words, word meanings, and rules for combining those words. Sociologists say language is a system of symbols that have specific and arbitrary meanings for a given society. The average person, however, knows that language is used to communicate with other people.

Adding together these definitions, concocted by Mario Pei, the renowned scholar of romance languages, we obtain a sum total that gives us a conception of language greater than any one of them. Language is a series of sounds, and when these sounds are combined as symbols, they acquire meaning. Symbols are things, such as words, that stand for other things. Grammar is needed to combine the lexicographer's words into logical patterns of thought, as the novelist would want them. Last, to fulfill its function, a language must serve as a medium of communication culturally transmitted from generation to generation.[1]

Transmitted Culturally

Through teaching and usage, a language is passed down through generations. Any child,

born anywhere in the world in decent health, of any racial, economic, social, or geographical heritage, is capable of learning any language to which the child is exposed. To learn the language, the child learns its syntax, the rules used to produce and understand an infinite set of possible sentences. The child learns the sounds or phonetics of a language and its sound system or phonology. The child learns the semantics of the language, or the relationships between sounds and their meanings.

This learning usually occurs unconsciously to a large extent, picking it up informally at home until he or she reaches school age, when more formal school-related instruction takes place. The elements are culturally determined, meaning that the culture determines what the child learns.

Language Differences

We cannot speak or understand other languages unless, of course, we make the effort to learn another language. This is because of the diversity of the elements of languages across cultures.

Phonological Systems

The *phoneme* (a class of sounds that are functionally equivalent) is the basic unit of description for the sound system of each language. All spoken languages contain a number of phonemes. Almost a hundred different phonemes exist, although no language is thought to use more than about 80. The English language uses 45 phonemes. When a baby is born into an English-speaking family, he or she will be able to utter phonemes other than those used in English, but the sounds will eventually disappear from the baby's vocal repertoire.

Language differences partially result from the phonemes different cultures use to make up their sound system. English speakers recognize the sound difference between *vile* and *bile*, but the Zapotecs do not. They cannot hear the distinction between *v* and *b* and vary freely between them. English speakers do not recognize or even hear the difference between the *p's* in *pit* and *spit*. The first is said with a puff of air after *it* (aspirated), and the second has no puff (unaspirated). That difference is important in some languages, such as Quechua, heard in Bolivia. Quechua speakers can have two words with different meanings that are spelled identically except that in their pronunciation aloud, the *p* is aspirated in one and unaspirated in the other. Thus, different languages can use different phonemes, though all languages have some of the same sounds and certain sounds are in every language.[2]

A difficulty that adults face in learning another language arises in pronouncing words that contain phonemes that do not belong to their native language. The Japanese, for example, have trouble pronouncing the /l/ sound, which does not exist in their language. Their /r/ sound pronunciation closely resembles the English /l/; *berry* is apt to sound like *belly* when a Japanese says the word in English.

By definition, phonemes are not meaningful. When they are combined, meaning results, the smallest unit of which is the *morpheme*. Morphemes usually are composed of two or more phonemes, with a few exceptions; *a* and *I* are morphemes composed of a single phoneme. *Fly, paper, listen, nation* are morphemes, and, of course, words in the English language. But not all morphemes are words. The *lis* in listen is an example.

Flypaper has two morphemes — *fly* and *paper*. *Bookkeeeping* is also composed of more than one morpheme — *book, keep, and ing*. The first two are words and *ing* is an inflection, a special type of morpheme applied to the beginning or end of a word, as a prefix or suffix. German, for example, utilizes many inflections.

Morphemes are the units from which words are constructed. English has about 50,000 morphemes. Words make up phrases, and phrases make up sentences, the building blocks of language.[3]

Syntactic Rules

Words can be arranged in sentences in a variety of ways. Subject (S), verb (V), and object (O) can be combined in six possible ways. English follows a predominantly subject verb-object (SVO) order, as do other languages such as French and Spanish. Other languages, such as Japanese and Korean, have the preferred order SOV. Classical Hebrew and Welsh are examples of VSO languages. Malagasy is one of the VOS languages. No languages apparently are OSV or OVS. The object never comes first.

The way questions are formed provides another example of how syntactic rules vary across cultures. In many languages, changes in pitch indicate that a question is being asked. A question comes with a rising pitch as the statement ends. A declarative sentence, in contrast, ends with a falling pitch when uttered aloud.

Some languages form questions in other ways. Thai adds an interrogative particle to the end of what otherwise would be a declarative sentence. To make a sentence interrogative, Zapotec adds a participle at the beginning or one at the beginning and end.

Other syntactic variations are used in the languages of the world. With 239 languages spoken by at least one million persons each and untold numbers of others spoken by lesser numbers, a variety of rules obviously exist and syntactic differences are to be expected.[4]

Semantics

Meaning is a correlation between language and experience. Thus, meanings are attached to words because of the experiences people have while learning them.[5] The study of meaning, semantics, takes into account the different types of meaning words can acquire — denotative, connotative, contextual, and figurative.

Denotative meaning is the relationship between the word symbol and the object or action referred to. Relatively fixed and stable, this type of meaning gets set in our minds with the recurring association of the word with the thing or action referred to. The words and things or actions they symbolize acquire an organic relationship and become properties of each other.

Connotative meanings are the feelings the hearer of the words calls up. Words have an evaluative, emotional, or affective meaning for us that comes from the way the denotative meaning was learned. Denotatively, *bicycle* denotes the object, the light, two-wheeled vehicle, one wheel behind the other. Connotatively, the experiences the user had in learning how to ride the bicycle attach meaning to the word. The feelings may be ones of pleasure, derived from joyful experiences, or, perhaps painful ones, from unhappy, personal experiences. Connotative meanings tend to be stronger than denotative meanings. Emotionally related meanings generate highly intense feelings.

Contextual meanings are derived from the context in which they are used. They are of two types: linguistic and nonlinguistic. The linguistic context deals with the grammatical order to which words belong. In writing, this refers to words, sentences, chapters, and paragraphs, which usually are easily comprehended. Words interact with each other until a understandable meaning comes forth.

The nonlinguistic context refers to vocal inflections, emotional intensity, rate, and speaker credibility, all conditions of utterance that may influence the meaning intended. We can give the sentence "I love you" three different meanings by stressing the three different words. "*I* love you" carries a different meaning than "I *love* you" or "I love *you*."

Figurative meanings are attached to words that are used in an unusual or a nonliterative sense to give beauty or clarity to what is said. In "The machine gun spits bullets," "spits" is used figuratively. Machine guns shoot bullets, but "spits" makes the sentence more dramatic. Idiom — an accepted phrase, construction, or expression holding a meaning different from the literal — is a form of figurative language. For non-English speakers, it can cause many problems.

Foreigners who do not know better are likely to translate literally every word that English-speaking acquaintances utter. One foreigner became totally confused as he tried to translate idioms such as the time-honored *killing two birds with one stone, letting the cat out of the bag, beating a dead horse,* and *kicking the bucket.*

A transnational company warns its overseas executives to avoid American idioms. Foreign business people can become quite bewildered if they interpret literally everything Americans say. Phrases such as *the buck stops here, a dog-and-pony show,* and *it's raining cats and dogs* can confound those who are unfamiliar with their meanings.

Translators have trouble translating idioms properly. In Tagalog, *hipongtulog* literally means *fish sleeping.* Filipinos following the current trend use it idiomatically to mean *indecisive, following the current trend of thought,* or *conforming.* Not knowing the idiom, a translator probably would end up with a hilarious translation.

Interpreting Meaning

A prevailing delusion about language — any language — is that all people speaking the language use words the same way. The words we choose to utter, however, come from a vocabulary that is the product of our special interests and experiences, and the meaning of words reflects our interests and experiences. Our words are received by listeners whose vocabulary represents the product of their interests and experiences, and these are not going to be identical to ours. Their meanings are more than likely to be different than our meanings for the same words. Thus, meanings are in us, not in words. Meanings are contained in the user of words, not in the words themselves.

Intercultural communicators should realize that foreign listeners may not interpret words as the communicators meant them. Hence, intercultural communicators have to be listener-centered. They need to ask themselves, "This is what the words mean to me; will they mean the same to my listeners? They should assume that the words will not mean the same and then should check with the listeners to see if they are understanding the messages the communicators transmit. Foreign listeners have a similar obligation; they should check with the speakers to see if they are interpreting the messages accurately.

I Beg Your Pardon — In Australian Lingo

Australians generally have no difficulty with English usage in the United States. They have spent a great deal of time watching American TV and movies. Unexpected collocations in everyday situations, however, can be confusing.

Australians who believe they may have offended another person say, "Pardon me!" If they do not quite hear (or understand) what is said, they say, "I beg your pardon." Americans reverse this usage. An American who says "Pardon me" wants you to repeat what you said. In my first week in the United States, I took part in the following exchange:

> Me (in Wal-Mart): Thanks very much.
> Clerk: You bet!
> Me (puzzled): I beg your pardon?
> Clerk (confused): How's that?
> Me: I didn't understand you.
> Clerk: Oh! I beg your pardon.
> Me: Oh! (retreating): Thanks very much.
> Clerk: You're welcome, I'm sure. Sir! Sir! You've left your parcel.

I repeated this dialogue all the way back to my apartment so I could relate it to my wife!

—William Crocker, Lecturer Emeritus
Armidale College of Advanced Education
Armidale, Australia

 # Language Across Cultures

A university's curriculum committee abolished the 2-year language requirement for all graduates and instead decided to require a year of foreign language and two courses in the culture of the language, provided that the students had met their high school's language mandate. The committee's members reasoned that people cannot communicate adequately only by knowing the language. They must understand the culture as well. Culture and language are inextricably bound. Language usage is a function of the cultural context. Studying both the language and culture, students should improve their communicating abilities.

Not only are culture and language inseparable, but language also shapes perception. We perceive the world in the way our language allows. The theory of linguistic relativity endorses this position. Another theory, the Bernstein hypothesis, ties oral communication to the cultural context in which the speaking takes place.

The Linguistic Relativity Theory

The theory of linguistic relativity, known as the Sapir-Whorf hypothesis, states that a culture's language determines the behavior and the habits of thinking in that culture.[6] The theory stems from the work of Edward Sapir and his student,

Benjamin Lee Whorf, both influenced by the earlier work of Frank Boas.

Linguistic relativity contends that all people are not guided by the same physical evidence to the same picture of the universe, unless they have similar linguistic backgrounds or can be standardized in some manner.[7] We do not live in the objective world alone, nor in the world of social activity. Instead, we are at the mercy of our culture. We see and hear largely as we do because the language of our culture limits our choice of interpretation. Our language shapes our perceptions of reality. Language is not a reporting device for experience but, rather, a defining framework for it.

We dissect nature along lines our language lays down. The world around us is presented in a constantly changing group of impressions that have to be categorized in our mind through our system of language. We slice up what we see, organize it into concepts, and ascribe significance to it largely because we agree with the members of our language community to do it this way. The agreement is unstated, but its terms are obligatory.[8]

Glance out the nearest window and you will likely see a kaleidoscope of interesting objects — plants, animals, clouds, birds, and buildings, among other things. All of these objects carry names, ones your language assigns to identify them. If you know the names, you can call each by name and tell others what you see, provided that they are members of your culture. If they are not, and use a different language, they will see the scene you see, but they will categorize and name what they see differently than you. Their language will dictate what to say and how to say it. If you see a blooming lilac bush and the word "lilac" is not a part of their language, their description will not match yours even though their retina takes in the same sight as yours.

Languages differ markedly from one another. Because they do, we can anticipate differences in perception as well. These differences can be a formidable barrier in intercultural communication.

The Bernstein Hypothesis

Basil Bernstein hypothesized that social structure mediates between the language at our command and what we actually say. What we pull out of our reservoir of words to say is conditioned by our context at the moment of utterance.

Meeting a friend on campus, our speech probably will consist of slang, colloquialisms, witticisms, and other informal expressions known to us. Our talk is a sort of oral shorthand as we utter words and phrases that are familiar to us. Those who are eavesdropping on our conversation may not completely comprehend what we are saying, but the message is clear to us.

When meeting the instructor on campus, our speech again fits the situation. We speak politely, more formally, and less brusquely, respecting the person we address. In church, we speak quietly and reverently. In a gymnasium, we can yell and scream if we wish. We adapt our speech to our surroundings at a given moment.

Our speech, thus, is constrained by the circumstances of the moment, by the dictates of the social situation. What we say and how we say it come from the cultural climate in which we find ourselves at the time.

Bernstein differentiated two speech codes that we use in various circumstances: restricted and elaborated. We use *restricted code* in personal and intimate contexts such as the home. In this code, words and sentences collapse and are shortened, becoming like a shorthand. With a close friend, we do not always have to say a lot. A brief reference is sufficient to call forth many details we both know.

With the restricted code, not only are the words and sentences shortened, but also the individual sounds begin to merge, as does the vocabulary. The nonverbal aspects begin to carry more of the message, as the communication is played out against a background of assumptions common to the speakers, who share interests, identifications, and expectations. The hidden, implicit cues of the of the social context define the speech pattern.

We practice restricted codes in a variety of settings and always where we know each other well. We mentioned the intimate setting of the home. The workplace could be another social context where communicators use the restricted code, especially when the employees have worked together for years and understand each other and their jobs well. A closed community such as a prison is a possible place for a restricted code, as are military units, gangs, clubs, and friendships.

The *elaborated code* is useful in the classroom, in law, or in diplomacy, as examples. Verbal amplification is necessary in such situations, and details and elaboration are in order. The listeners cannot be expected to guess at what the speaker is driving at. The speaker has to give the facts, express his or her feelings, and verbalize his or her intentions. No mutually shared assumptions or identifications are present in these situations to help carry the meaning. The message has to be explicit. Nonverbal communication will not suffice.[9]

The elaborative and restricted codes can be characterized in this summary fashion:[10]

1. *Elaborative code:* Messages are direct with verbal elaboration and focus on verbal aspects of the message; the code has no expectations that communicators will share meanings or have similar intentions when speaking; messages are oriented toward the individual and are planned.

2. *Restricted code:* Messages are indirect with no verbal elaboration; the focus is on the nonverbal aspects of the message; expectations are that meanings will be shared between communicators and the intentions of others are taken for granted; messages are oriented toward the group and are rarely planned.

Across cultures we see differences in verbal behaviors. Some are more restrictive than others. Japan, for example, observes a restrictive communication code in most communicative transactions. More elaborated communication is *mittomonai* — indecent and even shameful except when used by actors, singers, and politicians.

The collectivistic cultures are more prone to be restrictive in their talk while the individualistic cultures are more elaborative. Social class, however, plays an important role. Upper-class people are apt to be more elaborative and lower-class people more restrictive.[11]

Language Styles

According to Aristotle, style consists of two ingredients — language and diction — both concerned with how to say something.[12] Diction is more properly dealt with in nonverbal communication. Language style, or "a meta message that conceptualizes how individuals should accept and interpret a verbal message,"[13] is a way of organizing alternative ways of presenting a message and the rules for selecting the alternative that best fits the communication situation.

Here are some examples.[14] Fiji Indians employ *sweet talk* when being indirect in religious and political speeches and *jungle talk* when in direct, combative situations. The Ilongot distinguish between acts deemed *crooked* and those seen as *straight*. The Cibecue Apache use *ordinary talk, prayer, and stories* as language styles. The Malagasy resort to *kibary* when they are speaking simply and in an everyday style and *rasaka* when speaking ceremonially. Each term signifies speech at a different level, with a different set of acts and events.

Verbal Communication Styles

Four verbal communication styles can be derived from an analysis of style across cultures.[15]

Direct Versus Indirect Style. The direct versus indirect style alludes to the extent to which communicators expressly state their motives for speaking. In the direct style, the communicator states the message as clearly and logically as possible. All the necessary information is in the message. This is a style typical of low-context cultures such as Western countries. Clarity, specificity, and precision are valued. Nonverbal cues and the context surrounding the verbal message usually do not receive a reaction. Members of Western cultures talk more and are attracted to those who verbalize a lot.

Members of high-context cultures are more apt to employ the indirect style, in which the message depends on the context or is internalized in the communicators and depends less on the words uttered. The meaning comes from where and when the message is said as well as to whom it is said by whom. Users of the indirect style think that those who employ the direct style talk too much, and the direct-style users think the indirect-style speakers do not talk enough or say what they mean.

Elaborate Versus Succinct Style. The quantity of talk is the issue in the elaborate versus succinct style. Rich and expressive language characterizes the everyday talk of the elaborate style, whereas the succinct style favors understatement, pauses, and silence. Arabs exemplify the elaborate style, with much exaggeration, assertion, idioms, and proverbs. Likewise, Mexicans find this style to their liking. In contrast, the Japanese are succinct, sprinkling their conversations with silence, circumlocution, and indirectness, and this is typical of other Asian countries as well.

Personal Versus Contextual Style. The verbal personal language style is individual-centered, stressing the "I" identity or personhood. Verbal contextual language emphasizes the prescribed role relationships, such as father, mother, boss, professor, and other titles that define their place in the hierarchy. Americans prefer to interact with others on a first-name basis and shun titles, formal codes of conduct, and honorifics. The Chinese, in contrast are more formal and use the contextual style as they communicate with others.

Instrumental Versus Affective Style. The instrumental verbal style is sender-oriented and goal-oriented to reach its aims. The affective style is receiver- and process-oriented. Being instrumentally oriented, North Americans follow a step-by-step process in trying to persuade others, whether the listeners do or do not accept them as persons. They are goal-oriented and concerned primarily with their personal success.

Koreans and Japanese are affective in the sense that they do not continue to converse with those whose attitude or way of thinking and feeling is contrary to their own. The Western cultures tend to use an instrumental style, and Arab, Asian, and Latin American cultures adhere to a more affective style.

High-Context and Low-Context Cultures

In high-context cultures the members' messages are implicit and the bulk of the message either resides in the physical context or is internalized in the communicators. Low-context cultures are the opposite. The message is in the words uttered, and it usually comes in elaborate detail, clearly communicated.

Members of high-context cultures read nonverbal cues skillfully and are capable of understanding facial and bodily movements, subtle gestures, and environmental signs more meaningfully than low-context persons do. The coded, explicit, transmitted parts of a message contain little information. Much information comes nonverbally.

Because members of low-context cultures are not as skilled in comprehending nonverbal cues, the bulk of their messages is explicit. Consequently, the people are talkative and often redundant, causing low-context people think they talk too much.

Americans live in a low-context culture, interacting in ways that follow logically from the centrality of the individual. They are direct, informal, and believe in the virtues of frankness and sincerity. They tell it like it is. Americans are impatient with detours and indirectness, wanting to get to the point without "beating around the bush." They place high value on objectivity, innovation, and practicality.

A clear contrast to the American's low-context ways is the high-context Filipino culture. From early childhood, Filipinos learn the importance of groups or contexts in which they live. They are defined by, and linked to, the identity of the groups of which they are members. They are loyal and supportive of family, friends, and associates in their groups. As a result, they become highly sensitive to the communicative interaction.

Figure 9.1 offers some examples of high- and low-context cultures. It also summarizes the characteristics of each.

Types of Languages

Languages have been classified in various ways. The most common is by *kinship*. Languages that are related by their etymology and syntactical nature belong to special family groups. With thousands of languages, kinship listings consume

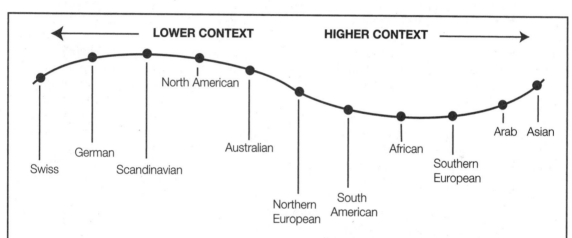

LOWER CONTEXT ← → **HIGHER CONTEXT**

North American

German
Swiss
Scandinavian
Australian

Northern European
South American
African
Southern European
Arab   Asian

LOW-CONTEXT CULTURES

(Information must be provided explicitly, usually in words.)

◆ Are less aware of nonverbal cues, environment, and situation
◆ Lack well-developed networks
◆ Need detailed background information
◆ Tend to segment and compartmentalize information
◆ Control information on a "need-to-know" basis
◆ Prefer explicit and careful directions from someone who "knows"

HIGH-CONTEXT CULTURES

(Much information is drawn from surroundings. Little must be transferred explicitly.)

◆ Favor nonverbal communication
◆ Relate information freely
◆ Use physical context for information
◆ Take into account environment, situation, gestures, and mood
◆ Maintain extensive information networks
◆ Are accustomed to interruptions

Source: *Meeting News*, June 1993.

FIGURE 9.1   Where Different Cultures Fall on the Context Scale

pages of space. Only a few of the major ones are mentioned here.

One large family group evolved from a single ancient language spoken approximately 8,000 years ago. Today that group is called Indo-European, but no one knows by what name, if any, the early speakers called it. The main family members include the Germanic (English, German, and Yiddish, among them), Italic-Latin (French, Italian, Portuguese, and Spanish, among them), Celtic (Irish, Scot, Welsh, and Breton), Hellenic (Greek), Balto-Slavic (Russian, Bulgarian, Czech, and Polish, among them), Indo-Iranian (Hindi, Persian, Albanian, Bengali), and Armenian

In addition to the Indo-European grouping, another 21 families are listed. Among them are the Finno-Ugric (Finnish, Estonian, Hungarian, and Lapp), Altaic (Turkic, Tungus, Mongolian, and possibly Korean), Sino-Tibetan, Austronesian, Niger-Congo, Afro-Asiatic, Eskimo, and Mayan.

If an intercultural communicator were to speak Mandarin, Hindi, Spanish, and English — the top four languages in number of speakers worldwide — he or she could talk meaningfully with roughly 1,850,000,000 people. Even so, that communicator would be unable to converse with monolingual speakers of Arabic, Bengali, Portuguese, Russian, and Japanese, another 9 billion people; or talk with the Beti, Bhili, Bikol, Brahul, and Bugis, Buyi, and millions of other people who speak one of the thousand languages in the world.

Language Variations in the United States

Most English speaking Americans can converse with each other in a comprehensible fashion. They can develop relationships, maintain friendships, conduct conversations, and transact business with few problems. Nonetheless, differences are apparent, especially in microcultural

communication patterns. Gender distinctions can cause miscommunication. Spoken English can vary from one geographical region to another. Elderly people frequently fail to connect with the young; both groups use slightly different language. Blacks can speak a language incomprehensible to whites.

A problem bigger than microculture miscommunication results from the migration of non-English speaking people to the United States. About 14 million foreign-born American residents have reported limited or no English-language proficiency. English is not an easy language. Most foreign-born adults require 5 to 7 years of instruction to understand and speak English well. Serious communication problems are common for the foreign-born and the English-speaking Americans who talk with them.[16]

Not all Americans speak English, and not all English-speaking Americans speak the same English. Traveling around the country, the truth of that statement becomes noticeable.

In a Tucson restaurant famed for its Mexican cuisine, a note on the menu says, "The manager has personally passed all the water served here." Shopping in Pittsburgh, customers encountering a recently hired clerk from Australia are greeted with, "Are you all right?" — the Australian way of asking, "May I help you?" Their reply, "Yes, I'm fine, thank you," probably lost a lot of customers for the clerk. A Los Angeles Parisian-style women's shop displays a sign in broken English: "Dresses for street walking."

Gender Differences

Culture plays a dominant role in male and female communicative behaviors, so much so that talk between males and females can be classed as intercultural. The experience of growing up as a male or a female in any society probably differs, as it certainly does in the United States.

Gender-related communication is similar to intercultural communication in that the differences that being male or female create in communication and behavior are potential barriers to effective communication. Unlike biological sex, gender-related communication behaviors are neither inherited nor caused by chromosome composition. They are acquired. Our genetic determination has nothing to do with the language distinction between sexes or the diversity in subject matter between the sexes. Both represent learned behavior, behavior that either sex can master, but each does in a distinctive way. [17]

Verbal communication patterns of males and females have so many variations that many complete books chronicle these differences. We only sample the variations here, and we do so in three areas: self-disclosure, language used, and subject matter discussed.

Self-Disclosure

Generally, females disclose more information about themselves than males do. Included in that information are intimate matters when talking to other females. Females are less guarded and more honest about disclosing negative details about themselves than are males. Males usually do not disclose negative information about

Communication behaviors are gender-related and are acquired. This Mongolian daughter will learn to communicate largely from her mother and will learn a pattern distinctive from the male members of her family.

themselves to either gender, yet are more apt to reveal intimate matters about themselves to females than to males. [18]

Females use personal talk to create and sustain closeness, learning to disclose personal thoughts and feelings as a primary way of enhancing intimacy, a mode called "closeness in dialogue." Men, in contrast, place less stress on personal talk, believing intimate conversation and self-disclosure is not a path to closeness. They learn to bond with others by doing things together, a mode termed "closeness in the doing." Yet closeness in doing has been found to be less gender-bound than closeness in dialogue. Both men and women do things for people they care about. [19]

Language Used

Pronounced differences have been discovered in the use of language between males and females. Female language is characterized by the use of more adjectives or adverbs such as *sweet, dreadful, precious, darling, lovely,* and *adorable.* Their language includes more intensifiers such as *enormous* (as opposed to *large* or *big*) *so, terribly, awfully, quite* and *just.* Males as a whole use stronger expletives, exclamations, and expressive words than females do. Females are less inclined to show temper, and males swear more freely in the American culture.

Females tend to be more precise in discriminating colors, and name shades more readily than males do. They refer to colors such as *mauve, aqua, and taupe* more readily than males do.

Females use more "tag questions" than males do. A tag question is a statement with a question added: "I got an 'A,' didn't I? . . . You went to the movies, didn't you? . . . That's a good album, isn't it?" Females use more softening, mitigating, and qualifying words or phrases: "Well, let's see. . . . I think so. . . . Perhaps. . . . Maybe so. . . . Seems to me. . . ." They also employ more-disclaimers: "I may be wrong but. . . . You probably won't like this, but. . . ."

Subject Differences

As we have noted, males and females differ in the types of information they disclose to others. They also differ in the types of subjects they introduce into conversations. In same-sex conversations, females talk about men, clothing, and other women. Males talk more about business, money, sports, and other amusements. In opposite-sex conversations, females talk with males about other males or women, and males talk about sports or other amusements in their conversations with females.

Male talk is more thing-centered and is more likely to involve factual information. Female talk is more person-centered and relates more to interpersonal matters. Thus, males are more empirical and females are more emotional in subject-related matters.[20]

At this point, we should interject that gender differences are not limited to the United States. Similar differences are found in Japan,[21] the Philippines,[22] Brazil,[23] Iran, Latin America, Puerto Rico, Saudi Arabia,[24] and Finland,[25] to name a few.

Black English

Black English is a distinctive form of language with a unique and logical syntax, semantic system, and grammar, characteristic of the black ethnic culture. It carries a stigma, however, of being a nonstandard, lower-prestige language by the macroculture, whose members perceive black English as deviant and incorrect speech. Many blacks react to this stigma by code or style-switching, using black English or mainstream American English on a selective basis, switching as the situation warrants.[26]

Blacks value verbal skills, particularly those encouraging interaction among communicators.

The minister's role, for instance, is to involve members of the congregation emotionally, verbally, and nonverbally, enlisting their participation during sermons through their feedback to the minister's message.

The classroom teacher also encourages interaction with spontaneous, participatory, interactive classroom sessions. This interconnectedness is reflected in the call-and-response speaking pattern. It involves a call (speech, sermon) by a speaker (teacher, preacher, politician) and responses by listeners (students, congregation, audience).[27]

Lexicon

The vocabulary unique to or originating in black speech communities ranges from transitory vernacular words to the more enduring words that are part of the black English idiom and a part also of mainstream American English (MAE).

Examples of words that are not MAE are *August ham* (watermelon), *buckra* (a white person), *eel* (a pretty girl), and *woofing* (casual gossip). *Cool* is common to both black English and MAE, but it carries different meanings in the two groups. Among blacks, *cool* is the ability to act on symbolic incidents and subtle varieties of cultural practice with eloquence, skill, wit, patience, and precise timing. In MAE, *cool* is equivalent to savvy, neat, fashionable, and even-tempered. *Ballin* in black English means playing basketball superbly, not a man having sex with a woman, as in MAE. *Cakes* are a sweet confection to MAE users, but to blacks the word may refer to the vagina, cocaine, crack, or heroin. *Heads* in black English refer to a person's children or blacks in general, not the leaders of organizations as in the MAE lexicon.[28]

Both the black English and MAE vocabularies contain approximately 4,000 words showing evidence of African language origins. Almost 2,000 are traceable to the Bantu language. Among the Bantu words with black English and MAE crossovers are common terms such as *ballyhoo* (balapu in Bantu), *jazz* (jaja), *booboo* (mbubu), *goober* (nguba), *yam* (nyambi), *tote* (tota), and *jiffy* (tshipi).[29]

Styles of Discourse

Black discourse follows distinctive verbal styles generally unknown outside of the black community. These have been capsulized into seven communicative forms.[30]

1. *The black sermon.* Best known of the styles, the oratory of the Rev. Martin Luther King, Jr. and the speaking of Rev. Jesse Jackson exemplify the black sermon style. Based on West African panegyric poetry, the prototypical sermon moves through three stages: (a) an invocation or introductory stage featuring dialogue-like interchanges; (b) a more intense delivery and an increase in audience call-responses; and (c) the climax, with physical animation on the speaker's part and a powerful, shouting chant repetition to draw audience responses.

2. *Tonal semantics.* The use of voice rhythm and vocal inflection to carry meaning is another black English style. Pitch, stress, intonation, volume, cadence, and rate are used to alter the meaning of the words. This mode of discourse apparently has its genesis in African languages in which changing pitch, rate, and so on convey totally different meanings.

3. *Narrative story style.* Often called narrative sequencing or narrative form, this style relies on the use of stories that create scenarios with characters, drama, narrative development, and physical animation in response to ordinary inquiries. Explaining a point in the classroom, a teacher might use a story to illustrate the point being discussed. Answering a question through the narrative story style, the respondent would answer with stories from which lessons could be drawn.

4. *Signifying and the dozens.* The verbal put-down is featured in signifying and the dozens. *Signifying* means speaking indirectly rather than directly to criticize another. It is criticism in a roundabout fashion that avoids bluntly challenging another's worth, motives, or behaviors. Instead of complaining about a person being late for a meeting, one could signify by saying something like, "I'm going to buy you a watch," indirectly reprimanding the other for being late.

In the *dozens* (or capping, sounding), the object of the put-down is either the mother or another female relative of the addressee. "Doing the dozens" is an aggressive verbal action, and with obscenities added or sexually explicit talk, the mode is called the "dirty dozens." The name is thought to have come from an original set of verses involving 12 sex acts, each phrased in a way that rhymes with the numbers 1–12.

5. *Rap.* For whites, rap means to talk freely and frankly. In black English, rap holds a much more subtle meaning: It is inventive, fast-paced, and highly connotative with conversational exchanges even amid long personal statements.

Originally, rap referred to a romantic conversation in which a black man tried to win a woman's affection and sexual consent. That meaning has been lost over time.

6. *Emphatic language routines.* Black English achieves emphasis through boasting and bragging, dissing, reading, and talking trash. Mohammed Ali used the *boasting* verbal style when he proclaimed "I'm the greatest" on television and radio. But he was not bragging in the manner of a white person. Instead, he was engaged in braggadocio (or woofin) — outrageous boasting to demonstrate humor and verbal artistry about himself, and not to be taken at face value. Boasting is an acceptable form of discourse in black English.

Bragging about one's abilities is also acceptable and may be a desirable way of reflecting positively on one's accomplishments. Bragging about what one owns or one's social status, however, is not socially suitable.

Dissing (or *to diss*) means to treat a person with disrespect. It is believed to have been clipped from disrespect, although some insist it is short for dismiss. The term can be either a sincere expression of disrespect or less serious if it is part of verbal play.

Reading encompasses "diss" and directly denigrates another person. Reading usually occurs in face to-face situations in front of witnesses for inappropriate or offensive statements or false representations of beliefs and personal values.

Talking trash is another term for dissing. It generally means the art of using strong, rhythmic, clever talk to project an image of badness, to promote oneself, or to promote leadership.

7. *Women's discourse.* Black women are said to use language in ways different from black men or white women. *Smart talk* is a term that refers to black women's outspoken verbal style, to combine various modes of communication, to express strong negative feelings in a humorous way.

Unlike white women, black women are at communicative parity with men to a greater degree. Black women around whites, however, are quiet and suppress their style.

Asian American Variations

Roughly 7 million U.S. residents with Asian roots make up the Asian American population. They represent more than 16 different Asian countries, with the Chinese, Filipino, and Japanese in the largest numbers. Asian Indians, Koreans, Vietnamese, Laotians, Cambodians, Thai, and Hmong are other languages counted among the Asian groups with large numbers. We can conclude that the ancestral and national histories of these people are many and their experiences are varied, with many different languages involved. In an introductory textbook such as this one, covering the nuances typical of each Asian group is not possible. What is offered is a general outline of the practical aspects of Asian American discourse. The analysis should not be considered definitive or universal, merely an understanding of the broad pragmatic facets of Asian American discourse.[31]

Confucian Influences. Confucianism has a major impact on the speaking of Asian Americans as the religious teachings include instruction about words and speaking. Four principal briefings are counted:

1. Words are to define and reflect moral development.

2. Words of embellishment lacking substance are to be avoided.

3. Actions speak louder than words.

4. Appropriate speaking relies on rules of social correctness. Excesses in language are not valued and the eloquence and flowery speaking typical of some cultures is not condoned.

Confucianists would support the notion that language is only *a* means to express oneself. Whether it is or is not ornate is unimportant as long as the words used clearly express the speaker's thoughts.

Politeness and Smooth Process. Generally, Asian Americans exhibit good manners in conversing with others. They are courteous and respectful in social relational situations, trying to maintain the rules of hierarchy when speaking with those of higher social status. They are concerned more with the smooth process of communication than with the outcome. They are oriented to accommodation rather than confrontation, not wanting to disrupt the harmony of the group. Typical Americans are preoccupied with speaking their mind, making their point, arguing forcefully and logically, and being assertive — all antithetical to the Asian way.

Silence and Indirection. In most American communication situations, silence is not golden. Speech classes stress the importance of speaking up and voicing one's viewpoints regardless of the situation. Asian Americans prefer silence in situations in which personal disagreement or conflict is expected, believing that silence is better than disharmony. To maintain social relationships and to save face of others, Asian Americans are apt to use indirect measures. Non-Asian Americans would be more direct and assertive in those situations. To avoid conflict, intermediaries are often called upon in Asian American situations; therefore, the parties involved would not have to address each other and cause disharmony.

Emotional Restraint. Self-control and restraint in emotional expression characterize Asian American cultures. They are likely to hold

Confucianism and Communication

June Ock Yum

June Ock Yum

When I began to research the impact of Confucianism on communication patterns in East Asia, I had no idea that the topic would engender the positive response that it did. My book chapters and articles stirred up considerable curiosity in the subject, indicating the great interest in understanding East Asian communication patterns and their sources of difference with our own. A library search yielded more than 300 books on Confucianism, the majority written by scholars in religion and philosophy, and others by people in business arenas. But virtually nothing had been written about the impact of Confucianism on East Asian communication styles.

One principal difference that caught my attention was the matter of particularistic and universalistic communication styles. East Asian communication influenced Confucianism in this regard. The particularistic style typical of East Asians expects East Asians to differentially grade and regulate relationships and the communication patterns involved according to their level of intimacy, the status of the communicators, and the context in which the communicative action takes place. Thus, Koreans, Chinese, Malaysians, and other East Asians focus on the nature of the situation in which the communication will occur.

In the universalistic style typical of Americans, Canadians, Australians, and Swiss, among other Western groups, each person is treated as a separate individual and the same general and objective rules and process apply to all. Different rules are not applied to different people or different contexts.

The difference is seen in the approach to a business session. Particularistic-type business people spend time getting to know the people they deal with and to understand the context of the communicative interaction before undertaking their business dealings. Universalistic-type business people tend to jump into the business at hand as quickly as possible without devoting much time to knowing their clients.

Western communication specialists are beginning to recognize the differences between the two styles and realize that the universalistic and particularistic approaches constitute a fundamental difference between the East and the West.

Dr. June Ock Yum is an associate professor, Department of Mass Communication and Communication Studies, Towson University, Towson, Maryland. Her research on East Asian communication is widely recognized.

emotional problems within themselves. If they communicate emotional problems at all, they are expressed within the family environment. Some Asians believe that the open verbalizing of emotions is rude and uncultured.

Restraint in expressing emotions earns the respect of most non-Hispanic whites, who tend to view Asian Americans as the model minority. They do not campaign for equal rights, create public disturbances when suffering an injustice, or otherwise display their displeasure with governmental bodies. Yet the Asian American population has achieved success academically and in the world of work. But the highly educated Asian Americans earn less than their white counterparts and are subjected to racial epithets and behaviors. Also, many suffer poverty.

Hispanic Variations

The Hispanic experience mixes and draws from differing cultural systems and, languagewise, four major varieties of Spanish: Mexican, Puerto Rican, Cuban, and European. The term *Hispanic* generalizes across a broad range of cultural meanings and practices, and because it is such a broad term, more culturally meaningful labels are attached to particular peoples, as in Latino/Latina for those who identify with the Latin American culture; Chicano/Chicana for both Hispanic and Mexican-American culture; Cuban-Americans; and Puerto Rican Americans.[32]

The U.S. Bureau of Census shows that approximately 30 million Hispanics live in the United States, more than half of whom are Mexican-Americans (64%). Because of the sheer numbers of Mexican-Americans, their verbal style is examined in depth next. California has the most Hispanic residents, followed by Texas, New York, and Florida. Of the total Hispanic population, roughly 8 million are limited in English proficiency.

Spanish usage flourishes in the United States and is likely to be the second national language for various reasons. The geographical proximity to ancestral homelands fosters native language use and, for that matter, other cultural ties. Then, loyalty to and love for Spanish, in spite of the presence of the dominant English language, will continue. Also, Hispanics have strong extended family ties, which motivates them to cultivate their Spanish proficiency so they can talk with older family members and relatives from abroad. Many Hispanics live in segregated communities where Spanish is spoken almost exclusively. Finally, Spanish entertainment resources are growing and people can enjoy all Spanish programs on TV and radio and in films.

Mexican American

More people cross the 1,500-mile border between Mexico and the United States, going in or out, than any other international border. Depending upon where we live, we may interact frequently with those from across the border who are visiting or emigrating. Or, much more likely, we will interact with Mexican Americans who were born in the United States or are naturalized citizens. In either case, the Mexican language will be a factor as we communicate with them.

To characterize the Mexican verbal style, we will examine it from a broad perspective, one that looks at Mexicans in general wherever they live, Mexico or the United States. Then we turn to perhaps the most important social institution in Mexican life, the family, and its impact on the Mexican way of speaking.

Mexican Verbal Style. From the American perspective, the Mexican language style seems emotional and dramatic. The Mexican speaker is apt to rise above fact, embellishing and creating a flowery sort of rhetoric with a thin or nonexistent line between fact and fantasy. Details are not important. Strong, bold outlines of general principles are preferred. Eloquence and the grand style are prized qualities.

Mexicans delight in verbal play, inserting turns of phrases into otherwise ordinary conversation. To a foreigner, their speech may lack seriousness of purpose. Yet their aim is to be gracious and friendly.

They like to use diminutives, making the world smaller, more intimate, and manageable. They do this by adding suffixes to words and verbally shrinking a problem in the process. In contrast, Americans like to augment, making everything seem bigger than it is. For example: "Hawaii has the greatest mix of ethnics in the world, the best climate of any place, the most cars per capita, and the finest private school system." We think we are being descriptive as we augment. Other cultures think we do a lot of boasting.

In conversations, people come away feeling that typical Mexicans are not always truthful. They may be told one thing only to discover that it had no resemblance to the facts. The rationale offered for this seeming lack of veracity revolves around two sorts of reality: an objective reality and an interpersonal reality.

Some cultures, such as that of the United States, treat everything in terms of an *objective reality*, favoring the George Washington philosophy of "I cannot tell a lie." The Mexican culture and some others view things from an *interpersonal reality*. Because Mexicans want to keep visitors happy, when asked for information or directions, Mexicans don't mind making up the responses if they do not know the correct answer. Stretching the truth a bit will lead to a few pleasant moments together, and a contented visitor, if only for a little while.[33]

Mexican Family Style. Mexicans use distinctive verbal devices to show family affiliation, and these are enactments of values informed by Mexican heritage. Five such devices are the following.[34]

1. *Harmony/Silence.* A main feature of Mexican American discourse is that of maintaining harmonious relationships. Mexican Americans value relationships and work hard to get along with others, especially family members.

They avoid putting others in compromising situations and abstain from activities that will bring shame to the family. Conflict has no social value for typical Mexican Americans, and they engage in antagonistic acts only when all else has failed. To attain harmony, they rely on silence in confrontive situations or attempt to compromise.

2. *Rationality/Emotionalism.* Mexican Americans tend to be emotionally expressive in contrast to Euro-Americans, who emphasize reason over emotion. The themes of emotionalism are courage, self-defense, honor, defense of the family, and defense of women's honor. Emotional expressions are controlled when an opponent could view them as weaknesses. Otherwise, the men in particular see no problem in reciting poetry, serenading their girlfriends, and crying among family and friends.

3. *Personhood.* To Mexican Americans, the person has a soul or spirit, and is superior to lower animals. In addition, a person has life, dignity, and a heart that is considered sacred. No one has a right to use other persons or mistreat them. All exist in the image of God.

4. *Status/Age/Gender.* People with status within the family are treated with deference. Status comes with age and gender, the eldest being respected and treated with special thoughtfulness and women treated as important because they are women. Women in the Mexican American culture are not considered inferior but, rather, as vital to the sustenance of relationships within the family.

5. *Solidarity and Sense of Community.* Mexican Americans value solidarity in family relationships and a sense of community with the other families living in the immediate neighborhood. Solidarity stems from sacrifice. Family members are expected to give up their personal rights, interests, and desires for the family's welfare. Yet, love and caring are part and parcel of solidarity. Moreover, the family is expected to maintain relationships with neighboring families, wishing to make urban survival much easier for all concerned.[35]

Regional Variations

Dialect — a local form of speech confined to a geographical area — reflects unique features of pronunciation, vocabulary, and grammar. These features differentiate it from other regional variations, and none is nationally recognized as an ideal speech pattern.

Regional variations are found in most countries of the world. In the British Isles, the major ones are those of the Scots, Welsh, and Irish, plus dialects typical of the north and south in England. Dialectical differences are present in each part of Japan. The Philippines not only has several dissimilar language groups (Tagalog, Ilocano, and Visayan) but also has dialects of each. Numerous dialects are present in Germany, as in just about every large cultural group in the world.

The United States has well-defined dialectical areas including those of eastern New England, New York City, middle Atlantic, western Pennsylvania, southern mountain, southern, and general American. Each area has differences in pronunciation, vocabulary, and grammar. Even though these dialects do differ significantly in terms of pronunciation, the variations are not so great as to hinder communication for people traveling from one area to another.

Major forces are at work in the country, promoting uniformity in spoken language and thereby reducing regional dialects. Radio and television bring the general American standard to all parts of the country. Ease of travel is making the nation more cosmopolitan and tending to merge the United States into a single large linguistic community.

Although differences are being minimized, pockets of regional dialect are still noticeable. Appalachian people living deep in mountain coves and hollows are isolated to a considerable extent from outside influences. Their manner of speech still carries expressions from earlier times. Examples are:

a-fixin', meaning getting ready (We're a-fixin' to go to the store,)

lollygag, to loaf or loiter (Why's Clem always lollygagin' aroun?)

crick, or stiffness (Mary has a crick in the neck)

red, to clean up (Red up your room before ya fetch gran'ma)

holler, a small valley (Chas comes from over in the holler).

The dialect in Hawaii reflects the population mix. It combines the intonation and simplified structure of the Hawaiian language with phrases from Japanese, Portuguese, Filipino, Samoan, and Tongan, spiced with standard English and teen slang. Hawaiian has no "to be" verb, nor does the dialect. Tenses are simplified: "I wen" (for the past), "I stay" (for the present), and "I go" (for the future). Emphasis differs from standard English; the main point often comes at the beginning of a sentence: "good the cake," You know Kallua High where it is?" "Da best Punahou School." The word "a" is usually changed to "one," and "the" or "this" to "da" or "dees."

Negatives and double negatives abound, as does hyperbole. "Da kine," an all-purpose phrase, substitutes for a word that cannot be remembered at the moment or for "y'know" or "whatchamacallit" — expressions used elsewhere. Other illustrations are: "Eh, bra, howzit? Woddascoops? You wan' pass da tes'? Mo bettah you study. Good dees kin' course, ya? Ass foah me, I stay or I no stay. I like one 'A'. I stay."

A person's dialect influences the perceptions and attitudes that other people will have of him or her. Dialectical differences produce stereotypic reactions as the listeners judge speakers by associating the dialect with the preconceived notions they have of the people who speak the dialect.

Research into the significance of dialect has been extensive. The following generalizations reveal some of the findings.[36] In terms of social status, a person's standing can be determined by the way he or she speaks. Speakers of high-status use fewer "dees" and "dems" than

American Students In Germany

Lothar W. Berger

Lothar W. Berger

Many American students who learned how to speak German in the United States can't understand the people on the streets. The reason is the dialect or slang. It's easy to explain if you take a look at the history of language. For more than 1,000 years variations of language have been spoken in different geographical areas of Germany. Those modifications differ from each other a lot, and they have barely changed.

One reason is the political history. Back in the 19th century, more than 200 independent powers existed in an area that was just about as large as Minnesota. Whoever wanted to go to another area or city needed permission. Even today, some families have been running their farms for 300 years. Since 1901, we have had a standardized orthography, but we still speak a lot of dialects. People from the northwestern part of Germany understand the Dutch better than Bavarians in Munich.

American students often don't know when they should use "you" and "they" to talk to people. "They" (in German, "sie") is like the third plural but is pragmatically used when talking to somebody in the second person. Students call each other "you" and by the first name. But in public life it would be impolite to call somebody "you."

For Germans there is a big difference between their circle of friends and acquaintances. Once again, the old hierarchical structure shows up. "Mister" ("Herr") would be like "Sir."

It's the same thing with titles. When somebody has a Ph.D., he is called Herr Doctor Berger. In companies that have to deal with Americans, people don't worry about it any more. Apart from that, a director is still called Mr. Director, and sometimes even his wife is "Mrs. Director." Don't forget that women didn't have a right to vote until the end of World War II in 1918 (and in Switzerland until 1971). Women were socially represented by their husbands.

German students rent their own apartments in the city and live together privately. Foreign students often live on campus. They usually get rooms separated from each other and keep the door shut. It's the same thing at a university. People have to knock on the professor's door, which is locked, just as it is in public buildings and companies.

On the other hand, German people are more liberal-minded. Men and women are not segregated on campus. Alcohol is not prohibited on campus. Nobody checks or controls their room. In bars, they are allowed to drink alcohol when they are 18. If they want to sit down, they usually ask first and then take a seat wherever there is one left. Still, in Germany many things are more or less dictated by traditions.

Dr. Lothar W. Berger is a professor at the University of Marburg, Marburg, Germany, where he teaches argumentation and ancient rhetoric.

lower-status speakers. As identified by their speech, higher-status speakers are perceived as more credible than lower-status speakers.

Southerners and New Englanders are more readily identified because of their dialects. They are stereotyped regarding their social status and social roles. General American speakers tend to rank higher on sociointellectual qualities, dynamism, grammar, pronunciation, and pleasing to hear. In Canada, English-Canadians are considered more competent than French-Canadians, whose dialect makes them sound poor and ignorant.

Dialect users are rated as less confident and more reticent in the classroom. Employers prefer to hire people who sound intelligent and competent, and pay them more than users of dialect.

 Non-English Speakers

Table 9.1 gives a breakdown of the types and numbers of people speaking a language other than English at home. Accounts abound of fouled-up fast-food orders, taxi drivers who misunderstand directions, health-care professionals who can't communicate with patients, and store clerks who don't understand their customers. These examples underscore a language gap with far-reaching implications as the 25 million foreign-born residents in the USA become a greater portion of the workforce.

The issue of English-language proficiency in the workplace is complicated by civil rights

TABLE 9.1 Persons Speaking a Language Other than English at Home

Language	Persons 5 years old and over who speak language	Language	Persons 5 years old and over who speak language	Language	Persons 5 years old and over who speak language
Speak only English	198,601,000	Portuguese	430,000	Armenian	150,000
Spanish	17,339,000	Japanese	428,000	Navajo	149,000
French	1,702,000	Greek	388,000	Hungarian	148,000
German	1,547,000	Arabic	355,000	Hebrew	144,000
Italian	1,309,000	Hindi(Urdu)	331,000	Dutch	143,000
Chinese	1,249,000	Russian	242,000	Mon-Khmer	127,000
Tagalog	843,000	Yiddish	213,000	(Cambodian)	
Polish	723,000	Thai (Laotian)	206,000	Gujarathi	102,000
Korean	626,000	Persian	202,000		
Vietnamese	507,000	French Creole	188,000		

Source: U.S. Census Bureau, 1990 Census of Population and Housing Data Paper Listing (CPH-L-133).

complaints and discrimination lawsuits brought by foreign-language speakers. Language discrimination is illegal, and employers who hire only English speakers are violating the Civil Rights Act. Yet, by definition, service entails communication, and if workers cannot communicate, the losses in productivity can be enormous. State and federal governmental bodies are scrutinizing English-only legislation to combat the problems of foreign-language speakers in the workplace. Language training is an answer. The demand, however, exceeds the supply of teachers and classes in schools, colleges, and other organizations.

Chapter Review

Language is a series of sounds that acquire meaning when combined as words to which grammar is added to establish logical patterns of thought.

Within a culture, a language is passed down through generations by teaching and usage.

Languages other than our own learned language are difficult to master because of differences in syntax, phonetics, phonology, and semantics.

The phoneme is a class of functionally equivalent sounds. Languages do not use all of or the same phonemes, of which there are about a hundred in all.

The morpheme is the smallest unit of meaning. Morphemes are made up of two or more phonemes, with a few exceptions that have only one.

Words can be arranged in sentences in a variety of ways — SVO, SOV, VSO, and VOS. Beginning a sentence with an object is absent in known languages.

Semantics is the study of meaning. Meaning is the association we put together with a given behavior. Types of meaning are denotative, connotative, contextual, and figurative.

Words don't mean; people mean. This truth about language is a source of misunderstanding.

The Sapir-Whorf hypothesis (the theory of linguistic relativity) holds that a culture's language determines the behavior and habits of thinking in the culture. The Bernstein hypothesis states that a social structure mediates between the language at our command and what we actually say. The hypothesis further describes the restricted code and the elaborated code.

(Continued)

Chapter Review continued

Four verbal communication styles have been identified as representative of various cultures: The direct versus indirect style is concerned with how speakers express themselves. The elaborate versus succinct style relates to the amount of talk in which speakers engage. The personal versus the contextual style addresses whether the message is I-centered or role-directed. Instrumental versus affective style is about sender- and goal-oriented speech or receiver- and process-oriented talk.

Languages can be classified by kinship. About 22 language families are identifiable, the Indo-European being the largest.

Differences among microcultures in verbal communication precipitate miscommunication. Gender, age, geographical, ethnic, occupational, and religious differences can lead to communication problems.

Gender dissimilarities appear in self-disclosure, vocabulary, and subject matter.

Black English has a vocabulary ranging from transitory vernacular words to the more enduring words that are part of the black idiom and mainstream American English.

Black English styles of discourse follow distinctive verbal styles, particularly found in the black sermon, tonal semantics, narrative story style, signification, the dozens, rap, emphatic language (boasting, bragging, dissing, reading, talking trash), and women's discourse.

Asian Americans follow four general discourse influences: Confucian influence, politeness and smooth process, silence and indirection, and emotional restraint.

Hispanic languages flourish in the United States because of the geographical proximity of Mexicans to their ancestral homelands, loyalty to and love of the Spanish, the need to talk to Hispanic-speaking elders, segregated communal living, and the availability of Spanish-language entertainment.

Mexican verbalization differs from English in many ways, five of which affect family life: harmony/silence, rationality/emotionalism, personhood, status/age/gender, and solidarity/sense of community.

Dialect is a form of verbalizing confined to regions of a country. It is significant because people with strong dialects could be considered less than credible speakers, thereby affecting their schoolwork and occupation negatively.

(Continued)

Chapter Review continued

Non-English speakers pose a dilemma in the U.S. workplace at times, especially when the requirements for productivity and competence require good communication skills. This need has to be balanced, by law, with civil rights.

Think About This...

1 If you have studied another language, did you find some sounds hard to make? Why were they difficult to say? Can you remember slang or idiomatic expressions in that language? Give examples. What syntactical pattern did the language follow — SVO, SOV, VOS, VSO?

2 When listening to people speak, what dialects do you hear? What identifies them as dialects?

3 An educator said, "There is no such thing linguistically as a good language or a bad one, a superior language or an inferior one. Each is appropriate for its time, place, and circumstances." What does this statement mean to you?

4 Bilingual education means using two languages as the media of instruction. Many American schools have non-English-speaking pupils. Should schools have bilingual classes to accommodate them? Why or why not?

5 Are these statements true in your estimation? In same-sex conversations, women talk about men, clothing, and other women; men talk about business, money, and sports. Do you agree? Disagree? Why?

10 Communicating Nonverbally Interculturally

Looking for intercultural trouble? What we *say*, we have found out, can invite grief. How we *act* can have a similar effect. Our bodily movements can embroil us in difficulty just as easily as our language can.

When checking-in a line of foreign guests, the desk clerk at London's finest intercontinental hotel discovers the hazards of body language. When an Italian in line asks her a question, she tugs her itching ear. This gesture has no special meaning in England, but the Italian is insulted and says so. In Italy, tugging the earlobe implies effeminacy. The Spaniard in line thinks the desk clerk is calling the Italian a sponger. The Maltese person reads her action to mean, "You're a spy." The Greek considers it a threat. Only the Portuguese individual is pleased; in Portugal the movement signifies something good.

Later a Sardinian woman asks the clerk to call a taxi, and the clerk responds with a thumbs up. The Sardinian slaps the unfortunate clerk's face for making such a devastatingly obscene gesture. In the lobby, a Japanese businessman asks an American what the hotel is like. The American replies with the well-known "A-OK" ring gesture. To the Japanese, this means "money," and he concludes that the hotel is expensive. The Tunisian onlooker thinks the American is telling the Japanese man that he is a worthless rogue and is going to kill him. But the Frenchman, overhearing the question, thinks the hotel is cheap because the ring gesture in France means "zero."

Each culture has its own body language. Because these languages of gesture usually are mutually incomprehensible, an innocent movement in response to a simple question may be an unwitting insult.

183

The Nature of Nonverbal Communication

Nonverbal communication refers to communicative behaviors and events that do not involve spoken or written language. Whereas verbal communication uses words in either oral or written form to carry messages, nonverbal communication relies on nonlinguistic means to transmit messages. Nonverbal communication refers to the information transmitted from speakers to listeners when the dominant meaning is not conveyed by words.[1] Nonverbal communication is a multichanneled process that usually is performed spontaneously, typically involving a subtle set of nonlinguistic behaviors that often are enacted subconsciously.[2]

Though nonverbal and verbal communication systems are treated as independent entities, this is not necessarily so. Actually, they are intertwined, and they should be studied together.

Few verbal messages are transmitted without some sort of nonverbal message involved. We manage conversations through eye movement and contact. Speaking to a group, our nonverbal body movements, facial expressions, posture, speaking time, vocal volume, and quality are carrying meaning also to our listeners. Listening to a person speak, our nonverbal actions transmit messages, perhaps messages of belief or disbelief of the speaker's thoughts.[3] Both verbal and nonverbal behaviors assume roles in an act of communication.

Types of Nonverbal Communication

Nonverbal communication encompasses the following eight distinctive sets of behavior:

1. Bodily or kinesic behavior: gestures, body movements, facial expressions, eye behavior, and posture

2. Physical qualities: body shape, general attractiveness, breath or body odors, height, weight, hair, and skin color or tone

3. Touching behavior: stroking, hitting, holding, and guiding, among others

4. Paralanguage: vocal volume, quality, and vocalizations

5. Proxemics: space, territory, seating arrangements, conversational distance, and architectural influences

6. Artifacts: objects such as perfume, clothes, lipstick, eyeglasses, wigs, jewelry, and beauty aids

7. Environmental factors: furniture, interior decorating, lighting, color, temperature, noise, and music

8. Time: meeting time, arrival and departure time, waiting time, and speaking time.

Characteristics of Nonverbal Communication

Nonverbal communication is a commonplace act of behavior, culturally acquired, and not pancultural, but an essential part of social interaction.

Commonplace

Many people are ignorant about body language and its role in the communication process, intraculturally and interculturally. Our lack of knowledge most likely stems from the fact that we were taught that words are the raw materials of speech. We failed to learn that a smile, a frown, a nod, a bow, and a clenched fist are among the many nonverbal acts that serve as powerful communicators, each without words. Surrounding us are dozens of similar nonverbal communicators, ways of communicating that do not employ oral or written language to carry their meanings. Clothes, bells, horns, traffic lights, photographs, paintings, and musical sounds — all communicate without words. Even silence is an important form of communication.

Nonverbal communication is not unusual; it is common.

Not Pancultural

Nonverbal communication is not pancultural. This means that nonverbal communicative behaviors do not carry the same meanings across cultures. Only a few have universal significance. Most nonverbal signs and symbols are interpreted differently from culture to culture. If we believe the meanings are the same, we only sow confusion and misunderstandings in the foreign people we meet.

A crosscultural survey involving 20 countries revealed that 50 nonverbal behaviors, including forms of facial expressions, body movements, and hand gestures, did not carry the same meaning.[4] Americans were asked to identify the nonverbal messages they received when they saw 20 well-known Japanese gestures. Only a few respondents interpreted the meaning of two gestures accurately. The Japanese meanings attached to the other gestures were inaccurately identified.[5]

Although the signs and symbols themselves are shared universally, the meanings vary from culture to culture. Some aspects of nonverbal coding are universal, yet cultures choose to express emotions and territoriality in different ways, leading them to conclude that most forms of nonverbal communication can be interpreted only within the framework of the culture in which they occur. They describe three ways by which cultures vary.[6]

1. Cultures differ in the regularly used behaviors portrayed. Specific to a given culture are body movements, gestures, postures, vocal inflections, and spatial requirements, amony others.

2. Cultures have display rules that determine when and under what circumstances various nonverbal expressions are permitted, required, prohibited, or preferred. The norms for these rules vary greatly across cultures.

3. The interpretation or meanings attributed to particular nonverbal behaviors vary from culture to culture. Three possible interpretations could be given a specific behavior: It is random, idiosyncratic, or shared. *Random behaviors* have no single meaning for anyone. *Idiosyncratic behaviors* are unique to special individuals or special relationships, and thus have particular meanings only for those people. *Shared behaviors* are meanings a group of people jointly give to a specific nonverbal act.[7]

Culturally Acquired

Our culture tends to determine the meanings we share with other group members. We learn these meanings, unconsciously for the most part, through observation and personal experience. People from other cultures learn as we do as to how, when, and where to use these nonverbal behaviors. Unfortunately, when we meet someone from a foreign culture, we are apt to interpret their nonverbal acts as we would our own. Misunderstandings result.

Socially Important

Nonverbal communication constitutes an important part of our everyday social interaction. The amount of meaning transmitted through facial expressions and paralanguage was compared to actual words. Figure 10.1 presents the results: 55 percent is attributed to facial expressions and other body movements, 38 percent to paralanguage (voice), and 7 percent to the words themselves.[8]

Others believe the relative importance of nonverbal communication varies with the communication situation. When presenting a highly technical report, the verbal communication will carry the bulk of the meaning. In intimate situations, job interviews, and therapy, nonverbal communication may be especially significant. Nonverbal communication is of special importance in intercultural communication situations.[9]

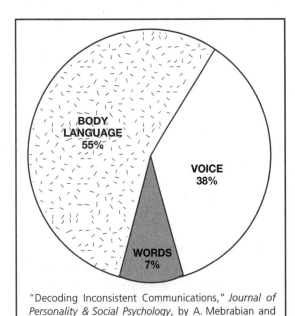

"Decoding Inconsistent Communications," *Journal of Personality & Social Psychology*, by A. Mebrabian and M. Wilner (1967), 6, 109–114.

FIGURE 10.1 Words as Minor Contributors to Transmitting Meanings

Functions of Nonverbal Behavior

Nonverbal communication functions in three important ways: It supports verbal communication, conveys emotions, and suggests immediacy.

Supports Verbal Communication

Nonverbal behavior supports verbal communication in at least five ways.

1. Nonverbal communication can simply *repeat* what we say orally. For example, if we tell a friend that she has a spot on her coat and then point to it, the act of pointing is the nonverbal act of repeating. The same message is carried both verbally and nonverbally.

2. A nonverbal message can *substitute* for a verbal message. If a person merely points to the spot on the friend's coat instead of telling her, the pointing is a substitute for the verbal message.

3. Nonverbal communication can *emphasize* verbal messages. If someone grabs you by the shirt, scowls, and says, "Don't fool with me," the grip on the shirt and the scowl emphasize the point and stress the importance of what is being said.

4. Nonverbal communication can *contradict* verbal messages. If someone says, "Don't fool with me" while smiling and giving a friendly pat on the back, the nonverbal and verbal messages are contradicting each other. The nonverbal behavior suggests, "I'm just kidding; don't take me seriously."

5. Nonverbal messages can *regulate* verbal messages. An eye movement, a shift in position, or a head nod can tell the other person to continue talking, or these movements can say, "Stop — it's someone else's turn to speak." In this instance, the nonverbal message acts as a traffic cop and regulates the flow of speaking.

Conveys Emotions

Nonverbal communication conveys emotions. We can obtain a reading of how people feel by observing their nonverbal behavior. Facial and bodily expressions are more important than vocal expressions in terms of their contribution to the total message, and vocal expressions contribute more than words, particularly when the tone of voice is perceived as spontaneous and believable.

When compared to North Americans, Europeans, and Asians, Iranians are seen as highly emotionally demonstrative.[10] Iranians illustrate the use of nonverbal behavior to transmit their feelings. Iranians use all of their senses and communicate with their whole bodies. Their faces and gestures are expressive and reflect the intensity of their involvement with one another. They speak louder and even shout in a conversation when discussing important or interesting points.

They might cry in the course of a conversation when the situation is emotional. Many hand and arm movements, head nodding and shaking, and leaning toward the speaker typify Iranian conversations. When meeting or parting from friends, Iranians shake hands, embrace, and sometimes kiss each other.

Suggests Immediacy

Certain nonverbal behaviors create positive feelings, called "immediacy" behaviors. They communicate four simultaneous complementary messages that are positive in nature:

1. *Approach messages,* rather than avoidance messages. Immediacy behaviors suggest, "You can talk with me." A wave of the hand, a pat on the back, and a smile indicate that the person can be approached.

2. *Availability for talking.* Moving close to another, facing the person, and establishing eye contact are immediacy behaviors indicating that positive communication is possible.

3. *Increased sensory stimulation.* Behaviors such as eye contact, touching, and close proximity arouse physiological and psychological processes that stimulate interaction.

4. *Personal closeness and warmth.* Immediacy behaviors suggest a willingness to listen and a desire to understand.

In relational situations these immediacy behaviors play significant roles. As immediacy increases in interpersonal encounters, so does liking.[11]

The United States, Finland, and Japan differ significantly in nonverbal immediacy, according to a study sampling the construct in three countries.[12] The Americans and Finns are more immediate than the Japanese are. The Finns are more immediate than the Americans, but not significantly so. The study also revealed that the women in the three countries are more immediate than the men are. The women are able to read nonverbal immediacy cues more accurately in interpersonal encounters.

 # Body Movement

Suppose a strange man were to walk into a bathroom where a young lady was bathing. How would the young lady react? Women from various cultures were asked this question to get their reactions. The answers vividly describe how dissimilar cultures respond with varying gestures. A Mohammedan lady would cover her face. A Loatian would cover her breasts. A pre-Revolution Chinese would hide her feet. A woman from Sumatra would cover her knees. A Samoan would hide her navel. A Western woman would cover her breasts with one hand and her genitalia with the other. The Mohammedan's gesture seems most sensible. How would the stranger be able to identify her later?[13]

Different movements can convey the same message — modesty, in the case of the female bathers. More often, however, the same movements carry different messages, depending upon the part of the world in which they are seen. As we have read, people from various cultures interpret the "A-OK" sign differently — "okay" in America, "money" in Japan, "worthless rogue" in Tunisia, and "zero" in France.

In addition, body movements transmit a variety of messages. Some movements convey emotions; others carry information about personality traits and attitudes. Giving someone a "single-digit salute" (the finger) expresses the saluter's attitude rather clearly. Some movements are quite explicit; others are less clear.

Classes of Movements

To make sense out of the plurality of meanings, a system was devised, classifying body movements into five groups: emblems, illustrators, affect displays, regulators, and adaptors.[14]

Emblems are movements that bring words and phrases to the observer's mind and are directly translatable into specific words. In Bulgaria a nod means "no" and a side-to-side shake of the head means "yes." Most Bulgarians instantly and unconsciously attach those meanings to the sign when they see it. Elsewhere, the nod means "yes" and the shaking head, "no."

Illustrators, directly linked to verbal messages, clarify or explain what is said orally. They accent or emphasize a word or phrase, point to objects, and picture spatial relationships, but they do not stand for words and phrases as emblems do.

A common illustrator in the United States is the outline of a girlish figure that men draw in the air when describing a certain female to their buddies. Men in different countries would use dissimilar illustrators to express the same thought. To describe a pretty woman, an Italian may use the *cheek screw* as if he were creating a dimple. A Greek strokes his cheek because in olden times egg-shaped faces were considered beautiful. A Frenchman kisses his fingers, a special Gallic gesture of praise for a pretty woman.

Affect displays reflect the intensity of emotions and feelings. A person's joy or anger is observable in his or her face and actions. An angry person, face contorted in rage, arms flailing in the air, stomping around in a frenzy, obviously is upset.

Kissing is the strongest lip-mouth display of affection of all time. To the French, the kiss is a serious matter. A 294-page book is available on the subject, and Rodin's "The Kiss" is a famous worldwide sculpture. Hollywood popularized the kiss in the United States, but in countries like Somali, Cewa, Lepcha, and Siriono, the kiss is considered disgusting.

Regulators are the body movements that control the back-and-forth nature of speaking. Head nods, posture shifts, and eye movements can demonstrate whether the speaker intends to continue, repeat, elaborate, speed up, or stop and let the other person speak. At our disposal are regulators such as decreasing loudness, decreasing or terminating the number of hand gestures, relaxing the posture, and slowing the speaking tempo — all signs indicating that the listener should get ready to speak.

Adaptors are unintentional body movements in reaction to boredom or stress. They include things such as rubbing, squeezing, scratching, picking at, and pinching oneself. Tension can be displayed by twirling a pen or pencil, playing with an object, restlessly moving the hands and feet, or fingering one's clothes.

Social taboos are associated with some adaptors. Picking one's nose or teeth is not socially acceptable in public. Scratching body parts in public is forbidden even though baseball players seem to scratch their private parts frequently. Television cameras at baseball games seem to zero-in on the crotch grab.[15]

Varied Meanings

A survey of 1,200 people in 25 European countries attempted to map the geographical distribution of 20 gestures. The researchers' study confirmed what they already knew: The meaning of gestures varies from culture to culture.[16]

The famous "V" for victory sign that Winston Churchill popularized during World War II is interpreted variously throughout Europe. The most common is victory, but it means "two" in Greece and Turkey. When the sign is made palm-forward, it is an obscenity for most of the people of Great Britain. For the world's wags, the sign means that Julius Caesar is ordering five beers.

The vertical horn-sign is used in the United States to mean "two" — two outs, second down, two strikes. In Southern Europe, almost everyone perceives it as "cuckold" — your wife is unfaithful. The fingers-crossed sign means protection in Europe, copulation in Japan, and friendship in the United States.

In Hawaii, the popular "shaka" sign is made with the thumb and little finger extended and the other three fingers folded down. When giving the sign, the hand normally is shaken back and forth, although sometimes the hand is

Meanings Vary Across Cultures

EAR TOUCH

- effeminate
- warning
- good
- informer
- protection
- disbelief
- no meaning at all

THUMBS UP

- okay
- one
- sexual insult
- hitchhike
- direction
- patron
- boss
- husband

VERTICAL HORN-SIGN

- two
- cuckold
- general insult
- protection
- curse

V-SIGN

- horns
- victory
- two
- sexual insult
- Julius Caesar ordering five beers

FINGERS CROSSED

- protection
- friendship
- copulation
- go to bathroom

SHAKA BRA!

jerked down once or twice at the wrist. The gesture means "hang loose," "stay cool," "right on," or "relax." Occasionally a verbalized "shaka bra" accompanies the sign — "bra" meaning brother.

Like all gestures, variations in meaning in the shaka sign occur throughout the world. In Mexico, with the knuckles pointed down, it is an invitation to drink. In Japan, when the fingers are positioned in this way, it means "six"; the thumb is five and the little finger added in equals six.[17]

Eye Contact

Normally we think of eyes as the receivers of information. We use our eyes to see what is happening around us. But eyes also are important transmitters of signals that play a role in everyday social interaction. When conversing with others, how we look them in the eyes and look away can make the difference between a successful encounter and an embarrassing one. Gazing lovingly at someone or staring in a hostile manner may be an unconscious action on our part.

We rarely are aware of what messages our eyes send.

Culture influences how people look. Latin America, the Arab states, and southern Europe exchange much more eye contact when they are having conversations than do North Americans and northern Europeans. North Americans look more at strangers than Europeans do. While speaking, black Americans look more than North Americans, and while listening, they look less. When a black American is speaking, the greater eye contact may be interpreted as intensity, hostility, or power.

These national and ethnic differences may make for awkwardness, and there are more extreme eye-contact customs. For example, the Lua tribe of Kenya forbids the son-in-law from looking directly at the mother-in-law. In certain parts of Nigeria, inferiors do not look at superiors. Members of some South American Indian tribes do not look at each other at all when they are speaking.

 ## Physical Appearance and Clothing

Many nonverbal signs and symbols do not involve movements, yet they carry meaning and have an impact on communicative effectiveness with and across cultures. These cues are associated with physical appearance and the clothing we wear.

Bodily Attractiveness

Television commercials, newspaper ads, and charm courses suggest that physically attractive people are much more socially desirable than unattractive ones. What is attractive to one group of people, however, may not be to another. Voltaire supposedly said, "To a toad, what is beauty? A female with pop-eyes, a wide mouth, yellow belly, and spotted back."

Nevertheless, success, popularity, sociability, and even happiness seem to come easier to more attractive people than to the less attractive. Plainness apparently is a handicap. Attractive people are more persuasive and wield more influence than less attractive people do. In communication situations, we respond more favorably at first to good-looking people than to those who are not as attractive. But beauty is in the eye of the beholder.

Physical attractiveness plays a vital role in human communication. What is it about the body that people respond to? What do people consider in deciding who is attractive? Some characteristics that call attention to individuals are body shape, skin color and quality, body scent, hairstyles, facial hair, and body decoration..

Body Shape

Body shape forms the basis for some people's judgment about others. Fat people are presumed to be jolly, skinny people cold and meticulous, and muscular people energetic. To confirm these perceptions, Sheldon's well-known classifications are based on the relationship of certain body types to specific temperaments.[18] Although his research has been criticized for methodological faults, his conclusions do offer some clues. Sheldon divided body shapes into three classes:

1. *Endomorph*: oval-shaped body, plump, and heavy, with a large abdomen; the endomorph is *viscerotonic* — slow, sociable, emotional, forgiving, and relaxed.

2. *Mesomorph*: triangular-shaped body, bulk at the top, athletic, muscular, firm, upright; the mesomorph is *somatotonic* — confident, energetic, dominant, enterprising, and hot-tempered.

3. *Ectomorph*: fragile physique with a flat chest and skinny limbs; the ectomorph is *cerebrotonic* — tense, awkward, meticulous, tactful, and detached.

The fat endomorph, therefore, is supposed to be jolly, sociable, slow, and relaxed. The muscular, well-shaped mesomorph should be full of energy, self-confident, and a go-getter. The skinny ectomorph is expected to be tense, nervous, and careful.

The more plausible explanation for people's perceptions is based on stereotyping. People expect a fat person to be jolly, a skinny person to be tense and nervous, and a muscular person to be full of vigor, and people treat them accordingly.[19]

Not all people are happy about their body shape. A fitness craze continues to engulf the civilized world, and in the United States tremendous numbers of people are trying to lose weight if they are too fat or to gain weight if they are too slim. People walk, run, and exercise, to become physically fit. But they will run several miles a day, then ride their car a mile to work or school. They will lift weights every day and then take the car to the store a block away.

Further, a lot of short people are eager to be tall. Men buy elevator shoes with built-in supports to add to their height. Women wear high-heeled shoes and bouffant hairdos for the same purpose. Men and women alike admire tall people, although women who are too tall are apt to be considered awkward. Overall, though, tall people are seen as possessing high status, which gives them an advantage in communication situations.

Skin and Its Color

Skin color is a potent nonverbal cue. People make judgments about others on the basis of skin color. If the color is not acceptable, discrimination may be the result. In almost every society, people whose skin color differs from the rest are likely to be treated as inferior and sometimes are denied their rights as human beings. "They can't escape their skin," writes Villanueva about African Americans. "No one will let them."[20]

Skin color has other effects too. In certain societies a tan is popular, a sign of beauty and wealth. A wind-burned and ruddy complexion suggests a field laborer or menial worker. To avoid the leathery skin of an outdoor worker, Japanese women working in the rice fields cover their head and face from the sun and wind. A pale complexion is prized because it is the symbol of a white-collar worker.

In some African cultures women enhance their image with tattoos or by scarring their face and other parts of their body. Men have tattoos because they are a sign of masculinity.

Body Scent

In most cultures people make an effort to smell good. Soaps, sprays, perfumes, mouthwashes, and lotions are among the purchases that people make to exude the proper smell. Odor communicates. Arabs are said to breathe on people when they talk because, to them, good smells are pleasing and a way of being involved with others. Koreans like the smell of kimchee on their breath. Filipinos are meticulous about being clean and are sensitive to the odors of others, especially Americans, whom Filipinos think do not bathe enough.

Not knowing a culture's reaction to body odor can cause uncertainty and ill-feeling. Samovar, Porter, and Stefani warn us to pay attention to the scents around us and the way they influence communication as we move from country to country.[21]

Body Hair

Hair matters. Various male tonsorial styles are on display today, from the long hair of baby boomers, sometimes expressed in the few strands of remaining gray hair gathered into a straggly ponytail, to either a full-bald pate or a buzz cut so short that most armies would consider it subversive.[22] If women's hair is a stage production, men's is only a sort of *tableau vivant*, a living picture.

Hair talks. For men it sends a contradictory message. The current bald-head rage suggests an exaggerated masculinity that, when worn by skinheads, gangster rappers, and bodyguards, expresses menace. Or it might bring to mind a war camp inmate, chain gang, or chemotherapy patient. It also could suggest wisdom and asceticism.

Hairstyles

Hairstyles have much to do with our perceptions of attractiveness and social competence. The style gives us cues about the social norms in another culture and the changing times in any culture.

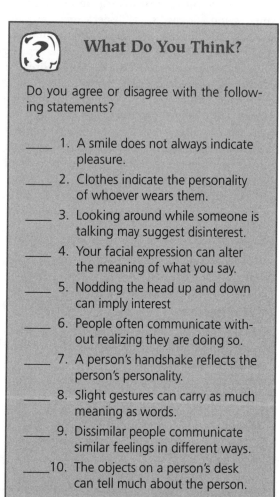

Women's hair has varied over time from punk rock haircuts, to short-cropped hair, salt-and-pepper colored hair, ponytails, hair stacked high on the head and sprayed, to long, loose curls. When the style calls for a part in the hair, curiously, women tend to part theirs on the right and men part on the left. Dying the hair in a multicolored display is another means of self-expression among women, although it is losing its appeal. Although hair is largely a superficial remnant of our evolutionary past and has little practical use, the more hair a woman has, the more sensuality she transmits.

Body Decoration

Every known culture has adorned and decorated the body for all of recorded history. European Neolithic cultures used elaborate spiral skin decorations. Ancient Egyptians painted their faces, using substances and colors common to the times. Ancient Britons dabbed woad on their faces and hair.

Today, body decoration is big business. People spend billions of dollars on cosmetics as a temporary way of changing their appearance. More permanent ways include tattooing and piercing, scarring and mutilation. In tribal cultures, young men and women find identities by cutting or pricking their skin, and reshaping body parts such as the lips or ears. All cultures decorate the eyes. Yanomani women decorate their bodies and faces for ritual occasions.

Clothing

Clothing transmits messages. People see a person's clothes before they hear his or her voice, so clothing makes the first impression we communicate to others. We communicate our identity through our total appearance. The clothes we wear define, sustain, and modify our social identity positively or negatively.

Clothes have two basic functions.[23]

1. They protect us from extremes of temperature, rain, and wind.

2. They satisfy a desire for modesty by masking sexual signals.

The *baju kurung,* a simple knee-length blouse worn over a long skirt pleated at the side, fulfills those two functions for women in Malaysia. The kurung is breezy and well-suited to the country's tropical climate, and it is almost totally shapeless. The kurung does not reveal the body and, therefore, is appropriate for Muslim women, hiding what they have and what they have not.

More important, however, is the way clothing transmits messages about the wearer's personality, attitudes, social status, behavior, and group allegiances. Clothing reflects a culture's value orientation.[24] Muslim women wear headscarves, as modesty is highly prized among Arabs.

Filipinos dress to uphold values relating to status and authority.[25] In England a conservative style of clothing wins influence through its association with social status. The somber colors reveal ambition. English barristers wear wigs as part of their courtroom dress to display their status.[26] In China the tendency is strong to conform to a modest style of dress, so men and women alike dress in nonostentatious Mao jackets and trousers in the winter months.[27] Upperclass Arabs are careful about their dress and appearance in public because the way a person dresses indicates wealth and social standing. Looking their best and dressing well are essential to their self-respect.[28] In African villages, the chief comes to a meeting in his best clothes. Office dress tends to be more formal for men and women, and when in doubt, conservative is better than casual.[29]

With regard to clothing across cultures, we need to learn to be tolerant of external differences so we do not let them interfere with communication. What might be garish or excessively formal probably is a reflection of a culture's set of values.[30] Whatever the attire, there is wisdom in Charles Churchill's, "Keep up appearances; there lies the test; the world will give thee credit for the rest."

 ## Physical Touch

Those who have acquaintances who are blind know that physical touch is a vital form of human communication. For blind and deaf people alike, touch is the principal means of communication. Even the average person without these disabilities relies heavily on touch to communicate. We understand the nonverbal messages of hot and cold, a pinprick, a warm embrace, the dentist's drill, and the helping hand. A slap on the back can mean a touch of friendship or a sign of encouragement. Stroking a dog or cat conveys affection.

In the most basic or primitive form of communication, humans first experience touch from the doctor's hands. As newborn babies, the touching continues with diaper-changing, feeding, bathing, rocking, and comforting — the earliest manifestations of affection and tenderness. Touch remains a crucial aspect of human relations throughout our lives.

Functions of Touch

Touch communicates various messages. One system classifies touching into five categories:[31]

1. *Functional/professional.* Practiced exclusively as part of a job, service, or task, this form of touch is the most impersonal. The physician touches the patient to diagnose illnesses. Barbers, masseurs, hairstylists, dentists, chiropractors, nurses, and tailors touch as part of their work. They touch their patients or clients as though they were objects or nonpersons, thereby preventing feelings about invasion of privacy.

2. *Social/polite.* This type of touch affirms the existence of another person. It suggests a bond between people, like a handshake between two people.

3. *Friendship/warmth*. Reserved for people we respect and hold in esteem, a pat on the back, an embrace or a hug, lets them know we are fond of them.

4. *Love/intimacy*. People we deeply care about receive this form of touch — a kiss, a full embrace, or an affectionate cuddle.

5. *Sexual arousal*. The most personal form, sexual touch is a natural outgrowth of the love/intimacy touch. It also denotes physical attraction only, the sort of stimulation a prostitute might evoke.

Meanings of Touch

Physical touch communicates messages, especially emotional ones. Greetings and departures between friends and loved ones often involve touch — a hug, a kiss, a fond embrace. Touch communicates interpersonal attitudes such as interest and status. It can function to regulate the flow of conversation, and it usually transmits positive feelings. Avoidance of touch can convey derision, disrespect, and refusal. Patterns of touching vary widely from culture to culture, though. What one culture permits, another may not.

Cultural Differences

Edward T. Hall theorized that, with regard to touch, two general classes exist among the

---

Types of Touch

In the Western world, the types of touch (and the body areas involved) are:

patting:	head and back
slapping:	face, head, bottom
punching:	face and chest
pinching:	cheek
stroking:	hair, face, upper body, knee
shaking:	hands
kissing:	mouth, cheek, breast, hand, foot
licking:	face
holding:	hand, arm, knee
guiding:	hand and arm
embracing:	shoulder and upper body
linking:	arms
laying-on:	hands
kicking:	legs and bottom
grooming:	hair and face
tickling:	almost anywhere

Tabu or Not Tabu

A lecture tour took the professor to Khartoum. There, a Sudanese colleague showed him the city. As they walked through the crowded streets, the colleague reached over and took the professor's hand in his. As the two continued walking, hand-in-hand, the professor felt that some sort of communication was being sent, but he didn't have the slightest idea what it was. Too stunned to pull his hand away, the professor and his colleague finished the tour holding hands.

Check the alternative that fits the circumstances:

____ 1. In Sudan, taking the professor's hand was a sign of friendship.

____ 2. Something strange was going on.

____ 3. The Sudanese man wanted to protect the professor from the crowds on the street.

____ 4. The Sudanese man was getting ready to steal the professor's money.

Answers on page 244.

cultures of the world. *Contact cultures* allow much contact, and *noncontact cultures* permit little contact between culture members.[32] Marsh calls the noncontact cultures *cold* cultures.[33]

People in contact cultures communicate in closer proximity to each other. They touch more, face one another more directly, and utilize more eye contact than those in noncontact cultures. Arab cultures represent contact cultures, and Arabs tend to touch other people of the same sex more than people in noncontact cultures do. Seeing Arab men or women holding hands while walking down a street is common. Kissing on both cheeks is a usual form of greeting with members of the same sex, as is embracing. Arabs touch frequently in conversations.[34]

Africans in general are contact people, tending to touch members of the same sex frequently when communicating in public. But whom one can touch varies from country to country. Cross-gender touching in public is not common, yet African men commonly hold hands when walking in public and women walk arm-in-arm.[35] In another contact culture, Spain, greetings often include hugs and kisses in addition to the obligatory handshake at the beginning and end of every conversation. Walking through a crowd touching people is to be expected.[36]

Contact cultures include most Arab countries, Mediterranean and Jewish people, Eastern Europeans, Russians, Hispanics, and Indonesians. Noncontact cultures typically are found in northern Europe, Japan, China, Korea, and other Far Eastern countries.[37] Figure 10.2 presents a continuum of touching versus nontouching cultures.

The United States usually is classed as a noncontact culture, primarily because of its original European settlers. Touching behavior, however, varies among the ethnic groups that make up the country. Blacks and Italian-Americans, to offer two examples, use touch widely to communicate closeness and affection. Anglo-Americans normally are restrained in touching others.

Other variations across cultures are observable. The Japanese, a noncontact people, have considerable bodily contact with their infants. The mother often straps the baby to her back as

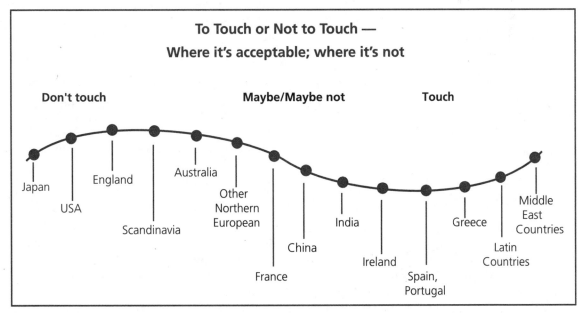

FIGURE 10.2 Touching and Nontouching Nations

she goes about her daily chores — that is, if she is not a working mother as many contemporary Japanese women are. If she does work, the mother's mother or the mother-in-law may look after the child and follow the old custom. Mother, father, and child may share the sleeping space at night, all sleeping together.

Touch Avoidance

Touch-avoidant people have been identified in the United States. These individuals feel uncomfortable in situations requiring touch, and they have negative feelings toward touching and being touched. High touch avoiders feel tension, dislike, and resentment when they are touched and are less likely to reciprocate touch. They remain aloof and can be found in both contact and noncontact American groups.[38]

An American scholar, Beth Casteel, studied touch avoidance across cultures. She compared touch-avoidance differences in gender among respondents in the United States, Puerto Rico, Korea, and Japan. She found no significant differences in same-sex interactions for the Americans and Japanese sampled, but both groups were significantly more touch-avoidant than the same-sex Koreans and Puerto Ricans. In opposite-sex interactions, the four cultures were significantly different from each other. The Japanese and Koreans showed the highest level of avoidance and the Americans and Puerto Ricans had the lowest.

Casteel's findings suggest that the Japanese and the Americans allow women to touch other women but men cannot touch other men. The Koreans and the Puerto Ricans allow men to touch men. In Korea this is a normal practice. Men can be seen sauntering down the streets holding hands with other men or walking hip-to-hip, demonstrating friendship, not sexual interest. Women also can touch same-sex people in Korea and Puerto Rico, as in Japan and the United States. Puerto Ricans and Americans can touch opposite-sex people, but in Japan and Korea this sort of touching is forbidden.[39]

Paralanguage

Nonverbal vocal sounds are important in communicating the speaker's emotional state and personality. Nonverbal vocal sounds communicate *how* something is said rather than *what* is said. Three kinds of vocalizations are

1. Vocal characterizers (laughing, crying, yelling, yawning, sighing, moaning, groaning)

2. Vocal qualifiers (pitch, volume, rate, tone, resonance)

3. Vocal segregates (uh, uh-huh, ooh, umm, hmmm).

Each of these has cultural differences. For example, in terms of volume, Greeks are loud and every conversation seems to be an argument, intense and combative.[40] Arabs shout when they are excited and are troubled if someone speaks quietly.[41] Spaniards also are loud.[42] The Thai and Japanese speak softly; to them, this is a sign of good manners and education.[43]

Laughter is one of the vocal characterizers that reveals a person's emotional state. But laughter does not always express lively amusement, and it carries various meanings across culture. In addition to its comic interpretation, laughter to Africans in a conversation could mean that they are unsure of themselves or are nervous.[44] The Japanese could laugh for joy but also to mask anger, sorrow, displeasure, embarrassment, confusion, and shock.[45] The Chinese laugh when they are nervous or are experiencing social discomfort.[46]

To emphasize their message, ministers in the black community use elongated articulation, lengthy pauses, and interjections of vocal segregates such as *aha* and *uh huh*. These are all attempts to involve the members of the congregation emotionally and nonverbally.[47]

 # Space

The study of how human beings use space to communicate is called *proxemics*, a term Edward T. Hall coined to suggest proximity, the state of being near. The way people use space is determined by their age, sex, status, and cultural orientation. The use of space differs across cultures.[48]

The distance we keep in social interactions affects the impressions others develop about us and affects our ease in communicating with them. Changing distance can express a desire for intimacy or a desire for noninvolment, thereby heightening or reducing one's influence over another. Distance determines how we use eye contact, touch, and vocal volume, and it tells us about relationships between people. If they stay too far away, they may appear unfriendly, cold, or perhaps anxious. If they are too close, they may make us uncomfortable and appear pushy or insensitive.

Each of us carries around a personal space, a movable, portable "invisible bubble" that becomes larger or smaller depending upon the person with whom we are speaking. We include in our bubble our friends and people we like, and we exclude those we do not like.

Latin Americans, Italians, and Puerto Ricans tend to stand closer when talking. Germans, Chinese, Japanese, and Anglo-Americans require more distance. Blacks stand closer to each other than do Anglo-Americans. High-status people stand closer to people of low-status, but low-status people keep their distance from those with high status. Sex differences influence the use of space as well. Women generally prefer to be closer to other women than do men to other men, at least among Anglo-Americans and Northern Europeans.[49]

On elevators, Americans prefer to stand apart. Arabs stand close even if only one other person is aboard. On a bus or a park bench, an Arab will sit close to someone rather than sit alone and leave a space in between. Arabs are not uncomfortable when they are close to or touching strangers.[50]

In Germany, space is sacred and privacy is prized. Germans are apt to be upset when their private space is violated. They have a strong need for space and go to almost any length to preserve it. In German houses with balconies, the balconies are constructed for visual privacy. Yards are well-fenced and are considered sacred. Germans do not like their chairs to be moved or other pieces of furniture placed differently than they were originally. When standing in line, they object to anyone who tries to crash the queue. In German business, each official has a private office, one with a door that always is closed. Open doors are considered sloppy and disorderly. Closed doors protect the room's integrity and provide a protective boundary between people.

By contrast, in a French company, officials share space in a large open area. The boss sits in the center of the room, unless he has a private office — but he will sit in the center there, too, with the rest of the staff members radiating out and the newest hire sitting at the periphery. At home, conditions are likely to be crowded, so the French entertain at restaurants and cafes. Socializing is done outside the home.

The English are brought up to share space with their brothers and sisters. The eldest child gets any available private bedroom. Lacking privacy, the English develop internal barriers within themselves, to shut out interactions with others, which those people are supposed to recognize and honor. Resenting the intrusion of the telephone, they prefer to write notes or letters. Mail service is excellent. Using the telephone is considered too pushy and is reserved for emergencies. The English modulate their voices so only the person being addressed can hear. Others are careful not to intrude on a conversation.[51] Figure 10.3 illustrates the distances in the predominant American culture.

 # Time

Perhaps the most critical dimension in culture is the use of time. Each culture has its own concept of time. In Germanic cultures punctuality is a sign of respect and politeness; being late is rude. Germans believe that people should be exactly on time, neither too early nor too late. To Indonesians, time is an endless pool. Why be pressured or hurry? Business people in India and China respect punctuality, and so do the Taiwanese, Turks, Singaporeans, Scandinavians, and people in many other cultures.

To Saudi Arabians, Allah is the one who controls time; punctuality is unimportant. Nigerians

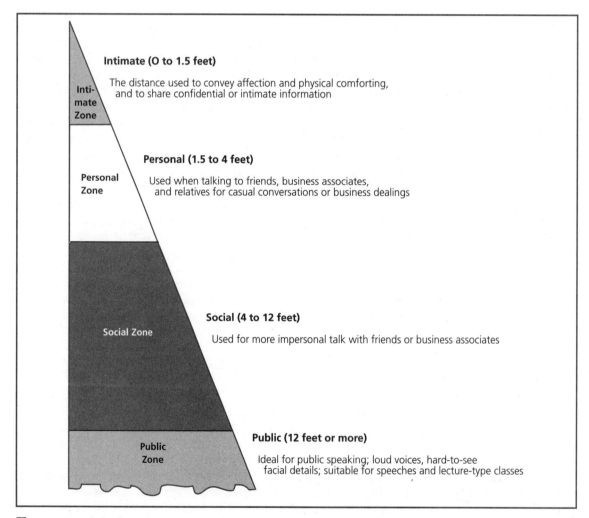

Intimate (0 to 1.5 feet)
The distance used to convey affection and physical comforting, and to share confidential or intimate information

Inti-mate Zone

Personal (1.5 to 4 feet)
Used when talking to friends, business associates, and relatives for casual conversations or business dealings

Personal Zone

Social (4 to 12 feet)
Used for more impersonal talk with friends or business associates

Social Zone

Public (12 feet or more)
Ideal for public speaking; loud voices, hard-to-see facial details; suitable for speeches and lecture-type classes

Public Zone

FIGURE 10.3   Distances in Typical American Communication

believe that what cannot be done today can be done tomorrow; time is flexible. Belarussians believe in punctuality for visitors, but high-ranking Belarussians may be late for business appointments.

All cultures take their own time system for granted and believe others operate within the same time frame. Thus, misunderstandings are inevitable. To function in a foreign country, we must be acquainted with the time system there.

In the American culture, time "talks," and penalties can be imposed for being late or not completing a task on time. In the United States, being late for class in elementary and secondary schools may lead to suspension if it become habitual. Late papers in college may result in a reduced grade or failure. But the Black American culture condones being late for scheduled occasions, especially social ones.[52]

To Edward Hall, the principal difference between cultures is how they handle time, which he divides into monochronic and polychronic cultures.[53] In *monochronic* cultures (for instance, the United States and Northern European)

people do things in order, following schedules. To them, time can be wasted, squandered, or saved. Promptness is essential, and people who are late have committed a grave offense.

In *polychronic* cultures, such as those in southern Europe, Latin America, and the Middle East, people do many things at once, and relationships come before schedules. A business appointment may be delayed for hours while the latecomer deals with a family matter or a personal crisis. Table 10.1 compares monochronic and polychronic people.

Low-context groups are likely to be monochronic; they prefer to do one thing at a time. High-context groups tend to be polychronic; they feel comfortable doing many things at once and are accustomed to interruptions. Scandinavians, who are monochronic, probably would be offended if they were interrupted during a meeting, whereas Arabs, who are polychronic, welcome interruptions as a helpful exchange of ideas.

Monochronic and polychronic time systems do not mix, and they do not change readily. Monochronic cultures take time commitments

TABLE 10.1 Monochronic Versus Polychronic People

Monochronic People	Polychronic People
• Do one thing at a time	• Do many things at once
• Concentrate on the job	• Are highly distractible and subject to interruptions
• Take time commitments (deadlines, schedules) seriously	• Consider time commitments as an objective to be achieved, if possible
• Are low-context and need information	• Are high-context and have information already
• Adhere tightly to plans	
• Are concerned about not disturbing conversations	• Are committed to people and human relationships
• Emphasize promptness	• Change plans often and easily

Source: *Understanding Cultural Differences,* by Edward T. Hall and Mildred Reed Hall (Yarmouth, ME: Intercultural Press, 1989). List derived from materials prepared by Margaret D. Pusch.

seriously; deadlines and schedules are observed. Polychronic cultures take time commitments lightly; people are frequently late.[54]

Western cultures think of time in linear-spatial terms, specifically past, present, and future. To Westerners, time is something to be manipulated, made up, saved, spent, and wasted. Time is an aspect of history rather than a part of an immediate experience. The present is a way-station between the past and the future.

Some other cultures think differently, and the present is most important. In Zen, time is a limitless pool. Events occur, they cause ripples, and the ripples subside. What is significant is the event in the absolute present, not the simple past or unknown future. North American Navajo Indians perceive time as only the reality of the immediate because thoughts about what may happen in the future are not of much use. The Sioux do not have words for time, late, or waiting.[55]

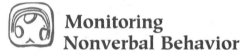

Monitoring Nonverbal Behavior

As we become more sensitive to the role that nonverbal behavior plays in intercultural communication, we must be careful not to make erroneous judgments about the behavior we observe. We should remind ourselves that nonverbal behaviors occur in contexts and the meanings the behaviors signify are always related to those situations and circumstances.

Serving as a teacher in Senegal, the American became upset when speaking face-to-face with students because they never looked directly at him. He would admonish them to look at him when he spoke to them. In response, they would briefly glance at him and then look down again.

Making eye contact when communicating with an elder or a person of higher status is disrespectful or even aggressive in many parts of Africa. Respect is shown by lowering the eyes.

In the United States, glancing away when the teacher personally talks to a student is taken as a sign that the student has something to hide. The teacher in Senegal failed to consider the context as he admonished the Senegalese.

Nonverbal behavior cannot be viewed in isolation, though. Rather, it must be observed as part of a person's total behavior at the time of observation. The Senegal student's lack of eye contact probably was not the sole indicator of his feelings. It must be considered in combination with his other behaviors. If the student was standing alertly before the teacher and otherwise paying attention, the teacher would have other cues as to the student's feelings. The combined behavior must be considered.

Finally, our conclusions about what we observe should remain tentative. The possibility always exists that what we think an action represents is not that at all. Meaning is in us, not in the actions we observe. We give meaning to what we sense, and our meaning may be completely different from what we intended. This final point is particularly significant in intercultural communication situations in which we may have little knowledge about a culture's nonverbal interaction. Unless we are experts in the nonverbal communication practices of a culture, we are on safer ground being hesitant before jumping to conclusions. In the Senegal classroom, the teacher would have been better served by not judging the student's behavior until he questioned someone who was knowledgeable about eye contact in that culture, such as a Senegalese teacher.

Chapter Review

Nonverbal behavior refers to communication and events that do not involve spoken or written language.

Each culture has its own body language. We learn our nonverbal skills within the framework of our own culture.

Nonverbal behavior includes body or kinesic behavior, qualities of physical appearance, touching behavior, paralanguage, spatial relations, and time.

Nonverbal behavior supports speech by repeating, substituting, emphasizing, contradicting, and regulating verbal behavior. It conveys emotions and suggests immediacy.

Body movements are classified into five groups: emblems, illustrators, affect displays, regulators, and adaptors.

Physical appearance involves bodily attractiveness, body shape, skin and its color, hair, clothing, and odor.

Physical touch, the most basic form of nonverbal behavior, communicates a variety of messages depending upon its function. Touching can be categorized as functional/professional; social/ polite; friendship/warmth; love/intimacy; and sexual arousal.

Paralanguage consists of voice qualifiers, vocal characterizers, and vocal segregates.

Space can be thought of as intimate, personal, social, and public.

Two cultural variations in time are monochronic and polychronic.

When monitoring nonverbal behavior, we should take into account the context in which it occurs, be wary of judging it in isolation, and remain tentative about what we see.

Think About This...

1   Explain how nonverbal behavior conveys emotions — for example, love, hate, horror, interest, dominance, sorrow, joy.

2   Distinguish between emblems, illustrators, affect displays, regulators, and adaptors.

3   Listen to your friends talk. Can you identify their speech through their use of paralanguage cues? If so, which ones stand out?

4   Describe the differences between contact and noncontact cultures. Which one do you belong to? Why?

5   Compare monochronic time and polychronic time. To which time group do you belong? Why?

PART FOUR

ACHIEVING COMPETENCE IN INTERCULTURAL COMMUNICATION

11 Adapting to Diversity

mericans overseas often function under demanding conditions. They suffer the hardship of giving up ice-cubed cocktails for warm beer as a way to integrate into the British society. If their reason for visiting Japan is more serious than just having fun, they have to keep their minds on business during the rounds of Geisha houses as a prelude to concluding their deals. When in Spain, they must brace themselves for the rigors of late-evening dinners and talk continuing into the wee hours of the morning. Traveling through Thailand, they can anticipate airport strip-searches for contraband materials. If apprehended with outlawed medications in many countries, the American consulate can do little to reduce jail terms.

In an age of intercultural testiness, Americans venturing overseas soon experience their share. Anthropologists call the series of jolts awaiting even the wariest Americans "culture shock" when they encounter the wide variety of customs, values, attitudes, and beliefs at variance with their own. If Americans experience cultural shock when they visit strange cultures, the tremors that visitors to the United States feel must be twice as confusing and distressing, especially if the visitors are refugees or immigrants expecting to make America their home.

The tremors and jolts we might face when visiting another culture often are attributable to the assumptions we make about the process of perceiving, judging, thinking, and reasoning of the people in the unfamiliar culture. We make these assumptions unconsciously, without realizing we are making them. When the assumptions are correct, ease of communication results. When they are incorrect, misunderstandings and miscommunications are often the consequence.

The most common assumption we make is called *projective cognitive similarity*.[1] We assume that those with whom we are speaking perceive, judge, think, and reason the same way we do. From reading the previous chapters, we know this assumption is fallacious. We understand that people who belong to our culture but are different in age, education, background, and experience frequently encounter difficulty when talking with each other. We also know that people from different cultures have even more difficulty when conversing with us. From the previous chapters, we realize that the effects of our cultural conditioning are so pervasive that we will have problems communicating with people from other cultures. We know we will have little in common with a Cuna Indian woman as she prepares the evening meal.

Culture shock is a given for Americans traveling abroad and for foreigners coming to the United States as sojourning business people, students, tourists, refugees, and immigrants. In this chapter we examine culture shock and the process of becoming acculturated into a new society.

 ## Culture Shock

A colleague reported on what apparently was an emotional shock for a graduate student landing in Honolulu from a small upstate New York town. He picked up the young man and his newly wedded wife and drove them to their campus faculty living quarters, an old army barracks converted into small apartments.

After dropping off their bags, the colleague took them to a local supermarket to buy essential food and other supplies. In the market, they encountered foodstuffs completely alien to them: bamboo shoots, Chinese cabbage, okra, soybeans, taro, avocado, kumquat, litchi, mango, papaya, passion fruit, pomegranate, sushi,

teriyaki meats, sashimi, mahimahi, eel, piles of rice in 50-pound bags — strange food for people from a rural area and a cool climate. They decided to wait until later to buy, so they were driven back to their decrepit housing.

The following Monday, faculty members were looking for the new graduate student. He had failed to attend class. His apartment was bare; the suitcases and people were gone. They had disappeared. No one heard from them again. Presumably they experienced culture shock. The transition was too much.

The trauma of transition faces all who leave home. When we leave the familiar for the unfamiliar, basic changes in our thinking, habits, relationships, and sources of satisfaction are necessary. If we want to survive, adjustments are in order. The graduate student chose to flee rather than try to adjust. In a strange place, where the traditions and customs are unexpected, we may lose our balance and become unsure of ourselves. Our sense of self can be threatened.

Culture shock often occurs during a major transitional period, moving from the known to the unknown. Almost every one who moves suffers from it. It is so pandemic that books have been written about it.

The Nature of Culture Shock

What is culture shock? The phrase was coined by Cora DuBois in 1951 and first used in the crosscultural literature by anthropologist Kalvero Oberg to describe problems of acculturation and adjustment among Americans who were working on a health project in Brazil. He viewed it as an occupational disease of people transported abroad. Because they were forced to cope with a vast array of untried cultural cues and expectations, shock sets in as they discover that their old ways of coping do not work.[2]

Culture shock is precipitated by the anxiety that results from losing the signs and symbols familiar to us in social intercourse. Oberg viewed culture shock as a specific ailment with its own symptoms and cures. Since he first used the phrase, it has become part of the sojourner's jargon, and now it commonly refers to almost any physical or emotional discomfort that those adjusting to a new environment experience. "Homesickness," "uprooting," "travel fatigue," and "jet lag" are among the terms used to describe the culture shock symptoms, although these terms fail to zero-in on the cultural factors responsible for the shock.

The signs and cues we look for include the many ways we habituate ourselves to our daily routines. Among these are cues such as when to shake hands and what to say to people, how to make purchases, when and how to tip, when and how to accept invitations — the ordinary forms of communicative exchange we use every day in our own culture with little problem.

In a strange place, these familiar cues are absent. Barnlund equates the situation to hostile leprechauns getting into the works and rewiring the connections that hold our world together.[3] The actions of others do not make sense, and we have difficulty clearly expressing our own intentions. Our "yes" may be interpreted as "no." Our hand signal for "come" may be translated as "go." Arriving early or late embarrasses or impresses. If we fail to stand or sit at the proper moment, we may insult. A smile may convey disappointment rather than joy. All the cues we use as we go about our daily business may be misinterpreted in a different culture. Going abroad, the props we rely on in our own culture are apt to be knocked out from under us. We get frustrated, and we have to figure out new strategies to get around.

The experience of culture shock is so common and widespread that internationally prominent authors have written about it. In 1862, Leo Tolstoy wrote in *The Cossacks* about the impact of culture shock. More recently, considerable study has produced a body of research about the

problem. Jack London was among the early authors who wrote about the experience of being "foreign." In his 1900 story, "In a Far Country," he wrote:

He must be prepared to forget many of the things he learned, and to acquire such customs as are inherent with existence in the new land; he must abandon the old ideals and the old gods, and oftentimes he must reverse the very code by which his conduct has hitherto been shaped.[4]

London knew of what he wrote. At age 17 he shipped as a seaman to Japan and the Bering Sea. He pirated oysters, sought Alaska gold, wrote for the press about the Russo-Japanese and Mexican wars, traveled throughout the world earning his way by writing. He encouraged travelers to find pleasure in unfamiliar places. For those who can't, he cautioned:

The pressure of the altered environment is unbearable, and they chafe in body and spirit under the new restrictions which they do not understand. This chafing is bound to act and react, producing diverse evils and leading to various misfortunes.[5]

London recommended that people who cannot fit into the new environment return home; otherwise, he concluded, they surely will die.

Symptoms of Culture Shock

The diverse evils and various misfortunes that London alludes to include physical and psychological ailments. Among them are concerns over cleanliness and health; feelings of helplessness, which result in withdrawal; irritability; fear of being cheated or robbed; fear of injury; desire for home and friends; stress, anxiety, loneliness, frustration, paranoia, disorientation, and defensiveness. Fears that the water is impure, that the food, dishes, and bedding are dirty, and that the shopkeepers and food handlers are disease-carriers frequently arise. Minor pains become major concerns.[6]

London warned people going abroad to escape problems at home that going abroad will only exacerbate the problems, so the problems should be resolved at home. Running away will not help.

Culture shock is neither good nor bad, necessary or unnecessary. It comes from lack of knowledge, limited travel experience, and personal resistance to change.

Problems unrelated to culture shock, of course, occur in foreign lands. A person may contract intestinal disorders and exotic diseases. Power shortages can happen. Drinking water may be in limited supply. Tribal wars, ethnic feuds, social disruptions, and political skirmishes make living in parts of the world difficult. Once the problems are overcome, however, the intercultural experience can be satisfying.[7]

Causes of Culture Shock

Studying the research on culture shock, three basic causes stand out:[8]

1.   The loss of usual signs and signals.
2.   The collapse of normal interpersonal interaction.
3.   A danger to our personal unity.

The three causes can be expected in any situation requiring adjustment to new circumstances. And in the intercultural situation, they intensify because of cultural differences. The three causes are not mutually exclusive and no single one adequately explains culture shock. They overlap.

Loss of Familiar Signs. We are surrounded by signs and signals that have been present in our lives since birth and hence are taken for granted until they no longer are present. These signs are physical or social cues that provide order in our social relationships. They are signposts that guide us in our daily

interactions and are consistent with our total social environment.

These signposts could be words, gestures, facial expressions, postures, or customs that help us make sense out of our surrounding social world. They tell us what to do and how to do it, when to be serious, when to be humorous, when to tip, what to say to whom and when, how to eat, when and how to shake hands. They add to our social comfort; they seem automatic and natural. A friend reports:

Entering a Honolulu barber shop for the first time, I saw all of the barbers were women. I didn't know what to do. Did I want a lady cutting my hair? Would they cut it or give me a "wave" instead? What do I say? "Trim around the ears; shorten the top?" Would they understand? They'd have to touch me. Do I want that? All of the familiar things from barber shops back home were missing. I was at a loss.

The signs and signals normal to our environment serve as reinforcers of our behavior because they tell us if we are behaving appropriately. In a new environment, our behavior is no longer clearly right or wrong. Instead, it becomes ambiguous.

In a totally foreign culture, for example, a non-Western, high-context culture with implicit rules of behavior, an American would find few rules to guide his or her actions. In an alien culture, our messages of greeting or our simple attempts to interact with others would no longer get the responses we get at home. Our reactions are likely to be ones of frustration or anger, which we irrationally place on the foreigners with whom we are trying to interact.

When we enter a foreign environment, we feel out of harmony nonverbally. We learned in Chapter 10 that our nonverbal behaviors are culture-bound. In another culture our nonverbal messages do not carry the same meaning they do at home and we feel unsure of ourselves, not knowing what reactions our nonverbal messages are receiving. Helplessness results, with disorientation and panic as possibilities.

Communication Breakdowns. In another culture our inability to communicate in the manner we do in our own culture can lead to the collapse of normal interpersonal interactions. For example, we have learned that we send messages, not meanings. If our receivers come from cultures different than ours, our messages may elicit meanings completely different than we intended. A breakdown is probable. Our nonverbal messages can be completely misunderstood, and, again, a breakdown is inevitable.

Feedback in many non-Western cultures can be circuitous and subtle, and we prefer direct and unambiguous feedback. We would like a clear "yes" or "no," but we are apt to get "if it is the will of God," "maybe," "it is difficult," or a similar ambiguous response. Communication breaks down at this point; we are not sure of what to expect.

Communication breakdowns bring on frustration, hopelessness, a loss of control because we have not developed coping strategies to deal with the ambiguity we confront elsewhere. Culture shock ensues.

Personal Crisis. Entering another culture, our personal process of interacting with others, a process that has served us well in our own culture, no longer is adequate. Our means of selective perception and interpretation no longer works well under the bombardment of millions of new stimuli in the new culture. We no longer have a clear hold on what we should be attending to and what we should be ignoring. Our well-established ways of viewing the world are not as helpful in the new environment, an environment that makes new demands on us. We cannot cope, and severe adjustment problems confront us. The experience can be self-destructive. Fortunately, most people handle and finally overcome the frustration, bringing on greater personal growth. They conquer the culture shock they experience.

Stages in Culture Shock

The experience of being foreign follows a temporal pattern. In adjusting to alien surroundings, the sojourner passes through five phases or stages. When they return home, they go through a sixth stage.

Preliminary Stage

During the preliminary stage, the sojourner is still at home, making plans to leave.

In Julio Ramon Ribeyro's story "Alienation," a mulatto named Lopez prepared for work in New York. To be accepted in the States, Lopez believed a transformation was required, including eliminating every trace of his Peruvian background. He bleached his hair with peroxide and had it straightened. As for his dark skin, he mixed starch, rice powder, and talcum until he found the ideal combination to lighten it. So he would be properly attired, he bought bluejeans and colorful shirts from North Americans living in Peru.

To learn English, he copied words from an English dictionary. That was too hard, so he went to the movies and took in English-language detective stories and westerns. He learned to parrot English well enough to work in a bar popularized by North Americans. Finally fluent in English, and with the money he saved, he went to New York.

Lopez went to extremes to ready himself. His preparation exemplifies the need to get ready. In the process, sojourners build excitement in themselves as they anticipate what lies ahead. They get keyed up, with tension and anxiety developing.

Many college students preparing to leave home for study at a distant school experience a preliminary stage similar to that of Lopez. Transportation arrangements will have to be made. Registration fees have to be paid, and a place to live has to be arranged. Clothes and books have to be packed and shipped. The family might have farewell parties, and friends might do the same. As the days pass, a sense of anticipation will increase, tempered by regret at leaving.

Spectator Stage

Arrival in the new culture marks the onset of this stage, accompanied by a rising tide of emotions. The sojourner sees many strange sights, has many new experiences, and meets new people. Taking in all of this sometimes is hard to comprehend, and it turns into a blur of events.

Upon arrival, most newcomers stay in hotels and associate with nationals who speak their language and are polite and gracious to foreigners. This honeymoon stage may last a few days or up to 6 months, depending upon the circumstances. If an individual is considered important, he or she will be shown the sights, pampered and catered to, and hear glowing talk about goodwill and friendship.[9]

Lopez had that problem upon his arrival in New York. He discovered a conglomerate of people, all wanting to live like a Yankee — Asians, Arabs, Aztecs, Africans, Iberians, Mayans, Chibchas, Sicilians, Caribbeans, Mussulmans, Quechuas, Polynesians, Eskimos, representatives of every language, origin, race, and pigmentation. He was a spectator, watching a melting pot of humanity.

Arriving on campus for the first time, the university student will have to secure dormitory or housing accommodations, meet roommates, locate the dining hall or places to eat, arrange banking, register, buy books, and generally settle in to the new life. Locating classrooms and checking out the social opportunities will keep the new student busy until classes begin.

Participant Stage

The honeymoon is over when the sojourner has to fend for himself or herself. The sightseeing ends and the sojourner has to

A Shocking Experience

After 25 years of Midwestern USA life, William decided to attend the university in Hawaii. Stepping off the plane, he was met by a former colleague from the Milwaukee YMCA where both had worked. Ensconced in the Honolulu YMCA, William was touring Oahu the next day with another YMCA worker. A day later, William accepted a part-time job at the Armed Services YMCA to help pay his way through school.

On campus to register, he passed through a line of upper-division students intent upon harassing the freshmen without incident. He looked too old to be a "green" frosh. His only setback was at the bookstore, where the manager got his kicks ridiculing students — torment William refused to accept.

During his first week at work, the fleet was in and sailors flooded the "Y," so he was busy. After a few weeks, he noticed that his seatmates in his classes avoided him or were absent. His attempts at establishing contact with local girls failed. Food was expensive. Everything had a spurious kind of tax to help pay for a bloated state bureaucracy. Buses to campus were infrequent and costly. He became depressed and anxious. His thoughts turned to home. What was his problem?

_____ 1. Like many Caucasians in tropical climates, William needed to bathe more so as not to turn people away.

_____ 2. Paradise is costly, and William needed a higher-paying part-time job.

_____ 3. William was suffering from culture shock.

_____ 4. He needed to register to vote and help cast out free-spending legislators.

cope alone, looking after the most basic aspects of everyday living.

The newly arrived student will attend classes for the first time and learn about course requirements. He or she will have to arrange a daily schedule to fit class hours, study periods, dining hours, library timetables, and develop social plans, an organizing task that is apt to be formidable for the beginner, yet challenging even for upper-class students.

Lopez encountered problems in this third stage. The money he expected to last 3 months ran out in a month, forcing him to move from his cheap hotel to a church refugee center to a park bench. Snow fell. His Peruvian values clashed with New York values. The girls he met led him on, spending his money until it was gone. He had to adjust; the natives weren't going to adjust to him.

Were he better prepared, Lopez might have avoided a few of the roller-coaster highs and lows as he dealt with differences in perceptions and values. For any sojourner, crossing from the old to the new is like walking a tightrope. Any minute the fall might come.

Shock Stage

After the sojourner has been in the new land a while, culture shock commences. After the person has begun the adjustment process, problems surface, which are difficult to handle. Shock sets in, usually unrecognized by the sojourner, who feels depressed and lethargic for no apparent reason.

Other symptoms appear. The food may be distasteful. Irritability surfaces at the slightest provocation. The hosts' suggestions are viewed as criticisms. Work declines in quality. Loneliness sets in. The sojourner has difficulty communicating his or her feelings to others.

Confronting the abyss between the home culture and the new, the sojourner somehow has to cross it to adjust meaningfully to the new. It helps to think and speak like the natives and to identify with their strange cultural ways.

The school environment can prompt culture shock for students attending class for the first time. University campuses breed culture shock among incoming frosh and transfer students. The first-year students, moving from the rigid high school environment, find themselves in a

Culture shock is common on university campuses. Housing problems, transportation concerns, and questions regarding food make campus life confusing for newcomers. Developing new friendships helps, but that takes time.

strange land on the university campus. Freedom abounds, and they can do what they like — attend classes or not. Living in a dormitory or rooming someplace in the college town, first-year students experience the hazards of making do on their own. Mother and father are not immediately available to assist. Transfer students face their frosh year all over again, looking for a place to live, signing up for classes, getting used to a totally new situation.

The disorientation that older students feel also affects children going to school for the first time. They move from their immediate, known, comfortable surroundings to a substantially different environment, especially if the home functions with a different set of rules. Some children, for example, grow up in home surroundings that demand that the children listen to and do not question the authority of the father with regard to social issues. Teachers, however, expect their students to discuss issues openly with other students and adults. Incongruencies such as these can be shocking. Then, too, educational institutions are highly resistant to change and inflexible in their approach to differences. Cultural shock seems inevitable.

This stage is characterized by the newcomer's hostile and aggressive behavior toward the host country, growing out of the difficulty in adjusting. There are housing problems, transportation troubles, shopping troubles, and the fact that people in the host country are largely indifferent to those troubles. They help, but they do not understand the newcomer's great concern. The entering college student, not prepared by his or her high school training for studying and test-taking, complains that no one really helps, just gives "lip service." "Study," my teacher says, but how, what, when?"

Adaptation Stage

If the sojourner reaches the fifth stage, identification with the new land has progressed satisfactorily. In-group relationships develop with the locals, and the sojourner feels a sense of belonging and being accepted. The sojourner feels at home.

Lopez finally overcame his culture shock, and he adapted. He learned to speak like a native and to dress in the native style. His adaptation speeded up when he enlisted in the army. The army gave him something worthwhile to do, fed him well, and provided him a comfortable place to sleep.

Immigrants by the millions went through processes akin to the one just described. They experienced culture shock on the way to becoming acculturated and finally assimilated into the American culture. Many thousands more are having similar experiences daily, not only in the United States but in many places in the world. Some fall by the wayside, but most succeed.

Many nations provide assistance to the newcomers, the immigrants. Colleges and universities throughout the world help incoming foreign students to adjust. Individuals who intend to leave home to study, work, or live abroad can prepare for the emotional low points and reduce the effects of cultural shock.

The fifth stage ends the transition period for immigrants and others who intend to stay in the new land.

Re-entry Stage

For people returning from an overseas sojourn, intercultural re-entry constitutes a sixth stage in the culture shock process. Students, corporate employees, military personnel, technical-assistance workers, government employees, and missionaries are among the returning sojourners. The re-entry stage is compulsory for them. They will encounter culture shock in reverse.

In *Alienation*, the hero, Lopez, had no reason to think about returning home to Peru. Re-entry was not part of his life. Lopez entered the American army during the Korean War and was decapitated in battle.

W-Curve Theory. Those who do return undergo a phenomenon of adaptation and readaptation known as the *W-curve*. This is one of several theories explaining the re-entry phase.[10] According to the W-curve theory, depicted in Figure 11.1, the sojourner's visit overseas occurs in a predictable fashion. It begins to follow a U-curve pattern. Immediately upon entry into the new land, the visitor has feelings of euphoria. Those feelings change to culture shock and discomfort as the reality of the new life sinks in. Once the adjustment to the new culture begins, a gradual feeling of fit and comfort replaces the shock. The sojourner starts out on a high, sinks to a low, then experiences a high once again — like the shape of a "U."

Upon re-entry to the home culture, the U-curve is repeated. There is the high, the shock, the readjustment — a second U-curve. Combining the two curves, we make a "W" — hence the reference to the W-curve of adaptation and readaptation. The re-entry, however, often is as intense and perhaps more challenging than the overseas adjustment. Moreover, it is apt to be totally unexpected and most sojourners are unprepared for the disorientation and confusion that re-entry brings upon their return home.

Two classes of returnees — students sojourners and professional sojourners — have been studied extensively.[11] We share a few of the problems they face during re-entry.

Student Sojourners. The reasons for students' going abroad are various. Some want to pursue a degree in a foreign institution because

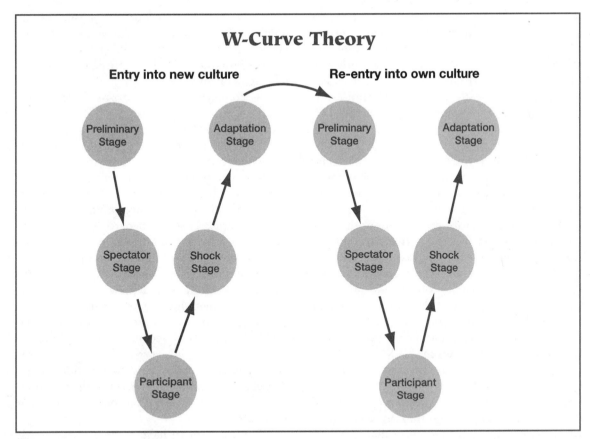

FIGURE 11.1 Stages of culture shock for people leaving home culture for a foreign one, then returning.

the degree is more prestigious or is unavailable at home. Some go overseas to study a selected language. Universities conduct semester-long study tours to places such as Spain to learn Spanish. Some students want to further their understanding of a specific subject area — for example, studying archaeology at a dig site. Other students participate in exchange programs. Some just want to travel and take leave from school to do so. Others have a father or mother who accepts an overseas assignment and the student goes along and continues his or her schooling in a foreign land.

In addition to the challenge of readjusting to home life upon their return from abroad, students can encounter totally unexpected problems. A major vexation stems from the courses of study in another culture. Often, credits earned overseas do not transfer to the home school, extending the desired date of graduation. Once back home, students realize that their social network has changed. Former friends have moved, married, or gone to work, with subsequent alterations in their lifestyle. The sojourner is not included in the new network.

Various ethnic groups have specific problems. Blacks may travel to Jamaica or some other country with a predominant black population. While there, they enjoy the status of a majority culture member only to return home and have to resume minority status without the support they received overseas. Nigerian students studying in the United States forget the reality of life in their homeland. Their education and lifestyle in the USA takes on fantasy-land proportions compared to their underdeveloped economy back home. Returning home, they have to resume living in an underdeveloped system and culture shock sets in.

Japanese students may travel with their parents to another culture, a country to which the father was transferred for work reasons. Attending school in the new land, they are confronted with an educational system unlike that they had known. Upon their return, they confront serious readjustment problems. Their foreign training

has given them different skills and areas of knowledge, and they have to scramble to readjust to the school system.

The research indicates that students have a much more difficult time readjusting than adults do. Apparently their overseas experience causes many more changes in their life than in the lives of adults. Re-entry culture shock creates considerable disorientation and confusion.

Professional Sojourners. Upon returning to the home-country workplace, many issues confront professional sojourners. For corporate employees, the most profound of these are role or status reversal issues. They return to discover that they are persona non grata — unacceptable persons. After several years working for their company abroad, their work responsibilities at home have diminished. They have less decision-making power — in the number of employees working for them, in their office space, and in their assignments. While living abroad, professionals commonly receive cost-of-living adjustments — more pay, housing allowances, cars and drivers, tuition for the children's schooling, and travel expenses. Losing these perks can cause financial problems upon return.

Many employees accept overseas positions because of the expectation that their sojourn will qualify them for a promotion or an upgrade in their status. These predeparture expectations frequently do not become reality. Home management changes and new supervisors are not aware of previous commitments, and the returnees are faced with a new set of circumstances for which they are unprepared.

Further, the corporate culture may have been altered. New technology brings about changes in workplace procedures, and the returnees have to learn how to function in the changed environment. The skills they learned overseas have no bearing on the new corporate culture.

Women seem to have more difficulty with re-entry than men do, particularly those who sojourn in countries where they experience more liberal gender roles than in their own country. After years of instructing in American schools, Yoko returned to Japan to teach. She found herself a minority of one in her Japan university. Her ideas to revitalize the curriculum in her department, to evaluate student performance, and to conduct faculty research fell upon deaf ears. Back "home," she soon found herself isolated and lonely.

Inventory of Re-entry Problems. The American intercultural expert Nobleza Asuncion-Lande inventoried the re-entry problems returnees are likely to face. These encompass six general adjustment areas.[12]

1. *Cultural* — adjustment to daily personal and work routines; personal identity problems

2. *Social* — feelings of social alienation, superiority; frustration caused by conflicting attitudes

3. *Linguistic* — practicing speech mannerisms learned abroad that are misinterpreted at home

4. *National and political* — changes in political conditions at home calling for new political views

5. *Educational* — lack of professional educational programs and support groups found overseas

6. *Professional* — resistance to change by colleagues; inability to communicate what was learned abroad

Asuncion-Lande's list does not include financial problems, the sorts of problems we mentioned: loss of cost-of-living allowances, travel expenses, relocation costs. These matters add to the disorientation that returnees have to deal with and exacerbate the culture shock of the re-entry stage.

On Re-entering One's Culture

Nobleza C. Asuncion-Lande

Nobleza C. Asuncion-Lande

Thinking back over the comments of people I've met who have studied overseas, this seems to be typical — the first month after returning home was hell. I was depressed and didn't feel at home any more. For a long time, I didn't want to let go of the new life I had learned.

The above quote is a typical observation of individuals returning from a memorable overseas experience as they begin to readjust to their home culture. In many ways, the challenge of readjustment is similar to experiences upon entering a new culture. The return experience is known as *reverse culture shock* or *re-entry shock*.

Re-entry shock is precipitated by the anxiety one feels when attempting to reestablish oneself in one's home culture after a prolonged absence. It is aggravated by a feeling of anger or alienation at the discovery that one has become a stranger to one's home culture.

The research literature indicates varying degrees of re-entry shock from temporary disorientation to full-blown mental breakdown. Individuals who have been successful in adjusting to a new culture seem to have great difficulty in readapting to their home culture. One reason is that their self-confidence in being able to adapt to a new culture has been severely tested. They recognize

(Continued)

On Re-entering One's Culture (continued)

that they have changed as a result of having lived in a different culture, but the consequences of that change in their home environment are unexpected or even unrecognized.

Among the physical and psychological manifestations of re-entry shock are being "under the weather," over-all weakness, fatigue, migraine headaches, loss of identity, questioning one's decision to return home, alienation from family and friends, and nostalgia for the host country. The period of recovery normally takes from 6 weeks to 3 months. In rare cases, it lasts longer or the person returns to the host culture.

Re-entry shock seems to follow four distinctive patterns of response. The first is the initial excitement of return. The returnee is much feted by family and friends, and is the object of admiration and envy. The person is happy to be back among familiar places, objects, and relationships.

The second stage is *questioning*. In beginning the process of reestablishing oneself in the home environment, questions about the wisdom of returning home emerge. Observed changes in the home culture are viewed as threats rather than as challenges. The person begins to take defensive measures, and these are accompanied by feelings of frustration and irritation.

The third stage is an emerging *sense of control*. The perceived threat to one's self esteem may evoke conscious or unconscious attempts to change one's surroundings to reduce feelings of dissonance and helplessness. One way is to take a detached view of the life one had in the host culture as a period of growth, as a tool for discovery about oneself or as an exciting excursion in a journey through life. Sometimes it is not possible to make many of these changes. A lot depends on the stability of one's support system in the form of family and friends.

The final stage is *re-adaptation*. The person comes to a realization that he or she may not be able to change his or her surroundings. This is the learning phase of the re-entry experience. It is also the stage at which intercultural communication skills play a vital role.

A returnee who has had a significant experience in another culture is likely to realize that aspects of one's own communication behavior have changed. Awareness of the potential reactions to these changes may considerably ease his or her readjustment. This phenomenon of awareness is not, however, as easy as one might think. Most individuals assume that they already know all there is to know about the culture in which they were born and bred. Thus, they do not expect to face difficulties when re-entering their old culture. They fail to realize that their outlook on life may have changed by their intercultural experience, or that their old environment has changed as they have changed themselves. Unanticipated changes can exert a strong influence on individual reactions upon one's return. They often arise at the level of "out of awareness," contributing to the difficulty of determining the underlying cause of frustration or conflict during the re-entry period.

Some evidence, however, suggests that the problems of re-entry can be minimized or controlled through proper preparation. Thinking about a potentially stressful event may force one to analyze it and to prepare for its effects. It is important that returnees be aware of the potential psychological and social problems they must face upon return. Problems may be associated with self or cultural identity, interpersonal relationships, role changes, professional and societal expectations. In addition, the returnee must realize that readjustment, though relatively painful, may lead to a new self-understanding and cultural sensitivity.

Nobleza Asuncion-Lande is a professor in the Department of Communication Studies, University of Kansas, Lawrence. She is president of the Pacific and Asian Communication Association and has held office in other communication associations as well. She writes extensively on intercultural communication topics.

Acculturation

Beyond culture shock lies *acculturation,* the process alluded to in the adaptation stage of culture shock. This process of learning and adjusting to a new set of behaviors affects immigrants, students studying abroad or even going to school at home, professional sojourners and even people just changing jobs at home. Like overseas visitors, these people have to adapt to new surroundings.[13] The adaptation is psychological, calling for a different set of behaviors that will fit the new circumstances.

Acculturated?

You are walking to a Filipino village when you come upon a couple going your way. The peasant woman is loaded down with baskets tied to her back, but the man walking with her is carrying nothing.

____ a. You walk up to the couple and offer to carry some of the load. The man vigorously shakes his head and motions for you to leave, which you do.

____ b You go up to the man and yell at him, bawling him out for treating his woman like a pack horse.

____ c. Although you feel sorry for the woman, you assume that this is the custom. You greet the couple and walk on, figuring it's not your place to interfere.

Answers on page 244.

The Nature of Acculturation

Anthropologists, for whom acculturation is a concept of considerable interest, have defined it as *culture change that results from continuous, firsthand contact between two distinct cultures.*[14] One is the culture left behind (the home culture) and the other is the new one (the host culture), the culture being joined.

The changes can be physical, biological, cultural, social, and psychological.[15] Among the *physical* concerns of everyday living acculturation are finding a new place to live, locating places to shop, figuring out transportation to and from school or work, selecting schools for the children, and deciding on a bank. The *biological* changes encountered include new and different foods and beverages, possible new bacteria and viruses, new plant and animal life, and perhaps a new climate, among others.

Cultural changes are at the heart of acculturation. The familiar institutions of the previous culture are altered or new ones take their place. Values, beliefs, and attitudes undergo change, and a new set of motivating forces may be needed. *Social* changes are necessary — new friendships, in-group and out-group patterns, and new people with whom to interact, such as doctors, dentists, grocers, auto mechanics, and hair stylists. *Psychological* changes can bring on alterations in behavior, as we noted, that could affect mental health.

Personal Developments

Acculturation involves four developments that affect behavior: adjustment, identification, competence, and role enculturation.

1. *Cultural adjustment* refers to a person's feelings of comfort in the host society. He or she seeks to feel at home and not a total outsider. For example, if the person has a strong need for inclusion, opportunities ideally are present to meet and interact with other people. Cultural

adjustment refers also to judgments by hosts that the newcomer is aware of the appropriate behaviors, is able to maintain cordial relations with local people, and, in general, is able to behave like a member of the culture.

2. *Identification* means that the individual attains a sense of belonging to the host culture. He or she can demonstrate this sense in a number of ways. The individual can apply for citizenship — although this is difficult and time-consuming in a few countries. If the new culture is a democracy, the person can identify with it by voting or accepting positions of leadership in the society. Buying a house is an indicator that the person wants to stay in the culture. Becoming involved in the society's group activities — clubs, associations, churches — is also an indicator.

3. *Cultural competence* requires a willingness to learn the language and increase one's own knowledge base about the adopted culture. Indicators of competence are positive attitudes about the culture and feelings of self-confidence. People who have a favorable attitude learn the culture's language faster than those who have unfavorable attitudes. People with personal confidence can meet their everyday needs through interactions with their hosts in a variety of situations.

4. *Role enculturation* means that the newcomer adopts the set of behaviors associated with the various positions he or she holds in the host culture. For example, if newcomers are students at a university, they will follow the behaviors that students practice in the new culture. Coming from Israel, where the classrooms are noisy and exhibit much spontaneous interaction, a student would be role-enculturated in an American university by behaving quietly, listening, and asking questions when given the opportunity. A homemaker newly arrived in Japan would be role-enculturated by limiting her activities to caring for the children, keeping house, cooking,

and looking after her husband's needs because societal norms in Japan dictate that these are the acceptable roles for women.

Communication and Acculturation

Underlying acculturation is communication. Newcomers must learn the appropriate behaviors in the new culture, and they learn these through communication. By talking with others, newcomers pick up the communicative skills needed to cope with the new environment.

> *An American teacher of English at a Tokyo university said that he never really felt a part of the school or the community until after years of struggle, he finally learned the Japanese language and its cultural rudiments. Then, he stated, everything fell together for him. He could talk intelligently with people, he made many friends, and he ended up getting married. Through his communicative capability, he acquired the cognitive skills of the new culture, learned the affective patterns, and then was able to play his proper role in society. Now his job, food, language, friends, leisure-time activities, and kinship ties are all found in the Japanese culture, and someday he may become totally assimilated.*

Colleen Kelley and Judith Meyers created an inventory for measuring the skills useful in enhancing intercultural communication effectiveness.[16] The inventory helps people determine whether they are interculturally adaptable along four dimensions: emotional resilience, flexibility/openness, perceptual acuity, and personal autonomy.

1. *Emotional resilience.* Being among people from another culture can be frustrating, confusing, and lonely. What is needed is an ability to maintain a positive, buoyant, and exuberant

state of mind. Being adaptable requires a person to tolerate strong emotions and cope with ambiguity and stress. Qualities worth having include keeping one's self-confidence and self-esteem in the face of the unfamiliar while maintaining positive feelings toward new experiences.

2. *Flexibility/openness.* To become acculturated, a person has to adapt to different ways of thinking and acting. Flexibility and openness are helpful in developing and maintaining relationships with people from another culture. To be flexible and open, a person needs to be tolerant of others, liking and finding comfort with all kinds of people.

3. *Perceptual acuity.* Because a new culture probably will bring with it an unfamiliar language and nonverbal characteristics, sensitivity to verbal and nonverbal behaviors, as well as to interpersonal relationships, will speed up acculturation. Perceptual acuity means the ability to read people's emotions, the context, and the meanings that messages convey. Understanding one's own impact on others also sharpens one's perception of others.

4. *Personal autonomy.* The main characteristic associated with personal autonomy is a strong sense of identity. It means the ability to maintain one's own values and beliefs and to assume responsibility for one's actions. Respect for self and others is part of personal autonomy. Individuals with high personal autonomy know how to act on their own decisions while respecting other's decisions.

The Kelley and Meyers inventory suggests areas of adaptability that will accelerate the acculturation process and make life in the new culture much more pleasant. Culture shock, they emphasize, is inherent in moving into a new culture and generally has some negative effects. Being able to deal with these will make for a more fruitful experience.

 # Adapting on a Short-Term Basis

Our concentration to this point has been on becoming acculturated on a permanent or long-term basis — the sort of adjustment required of immigrants and refugees. But tourists, students, and business persons typically are temporary guests. Their stay is limited to a specific period — the tourist maybe a week or two, the student a semester or school term, and the business person a few days or a week. Some short-term strategies are useful for those who do not intend to make the host culture a permanent living place: nonacceptance, substitution, addition, synthesis, and resynthesis.[17]

1. *Nonacceptance* is the coping mechanism that tourists practice most commonly. The sojourner (or temporary resident) behaves as he or she would at home. The tourist does not take the time and effort to learn the norms of the country visited. Actually, if the tourist's travel covers several countries in a matter of days, there is little point in becoming educated about the countries visited. Reading travel guidebooks about each should be sufficient.

Some people who intend to spend a longer time in a country also follow this practice. A business person, for example, spending a month or two conducting commercial ventures in another culture may be aware of business peculiarities in the host country but refuses to engage in them. Many countries, for example, consider kickbacks and bribes as acceptable ways of doing business. The business person who refuses to conduct business in that fashion is practicing nonacceptance.

2. *Substitution* means that sojourners learn the responses most appropriate in the host country and behave accordingly. They use the communicative tactics that find favor with the hosts, substituting them for their own style of

communicating. If the Thais greet each other using the *wai*, an American sojourner would substitute the *wai* for the handshake normally used for greetings in America. In Singapore, where littering in public is forbidden, an American who litters at home would substitute the Singapore behavior for his or her own — or in Singapore go to jail!

3. *Addition* requires more selective application of knowledge. Sojourners make judgments about what behavior is appropriate in a given situation and then behave according to the host culture's rules while in the presence of members of the host culture. When alone, they revert to their normal behavior. While in the host country, therefore, they are adding a set of behaviors.

We can imagine a group of foreign students using addition as they learn at an American university. In the presence of members of the host culture, they behave as the hosts would. Among themselves, they behave according to home-country rules.

4. *Synthesis* is a coping mechanism that integrates home and host cultural patterns. Samoan and Tonga men walking on Los Angeles streets may combine the *lava-lava* (a printed calico waist cloth or kilt worn around the loins) with a Western-style shirt, tie, shoes, and socks. They are synthesizing the Samoan or Tonga style with Western-style attire. A Hawaiian luau may consist of typical Hawaiian foods (imua-baked pig, poi, lomi-lomi, and so on), as well as typical Western dishes (ice cream, cake, coffee, rolls and butter, and salad). The food represents a synthesis of several cultures. So, too, sojourners can integrate the behaviors of several cultures, mixing them up as they conduct their daily business.

5. *Resynthesis* refers to the practice of some sojourners, who remove themselves from the home and host culture and set out to observe a set of behaviors in certain situations that are alien to both cultures. They become, in effect,

> ## Understanding Another Person
>
> *In his classic novel,* The Razor's Edge, W. *Somerset Maugham acknowledged how difficult it is to know people. Men and women, he wrote, are not only themselves. They are also the region in which they were born, the city dwelling, the farm, in which they learned to walk. They are the games they played as children and the old wives' tales they overheard.*
>
> *They are the food they eat and the schools they attend. They are the sports they follow and the poetry they read. They are the God they believe in. You can know them only if you are them.*

members of a new culture — their own — in selected circumstances, coping with the new and unusual by doing something new and unusual of their own, being nonethnocentric.

For example, an American residing in London for a short period may find London food too bland for his or her taste but does not want to return home saying that he or she sought out American food to eat. In a resynthesis, the person eats Chinese or Japanese food, creating a different set of behaviors. In Thailand, the resynthesizing American would not shake hands or employ the *wai* to greet someone but would bow instead.

 ## Assimilation and Pluralism

At least two perspectives on adapting to the American culture have been advanced: assimilation and cultural pluralism.

Assimilation

Assimilation is *the process by which subordinate groups or cultures adopt the characteristics of the dominant culture.*[18] The possibilities are several. In one, the cultural patterns of the subordinate culture disappear as the members adopt the cultural patterns of the dominant group. A second possibility is demonstrated when the distinctive patterns of the subordinate culture become part of the dominant culture. They blend into one. Finally, some patterns of the subordinate culture disappear and some become part of the dominant culture. In any case, if assimilation is effective, the subordinate group loses the characteristics that set it apart from the dominant one.

Two positions on assimilation have been advanced in the United States, each with strong supporters.[19] The *Anglo-conformity* position expects immigrants to renounce their ancestral culture in favor of that of the Anglo-Saxon core group or macroculture, to maintain the English language and English-oriented cultural patterns as standards of American life.

The *melting pot* position advocates the amalgamation of all cultures in the United States into a new and unique American culture. All cultures would blend into one, divesting themselves of age-old animosities brought from their homelands and become fused into one cohesive group. Intermarriage between whites, blacks, and Asian Americans would assist in accomplishing the amalgamation. This process has been slow, however, and miscegenation laws in several states prevented the melt until these laws were repealed.

Cultural Pluralism

Cultural pluralism calls for cultural groups to maintain separate and distinct ethnic entities.[20] Many immigrants and minority groups do maintain ethnic communities and enclaves — Chinatown, Harlem, and Korea Town among them. Milwaukee, for example, had its Little Italy, Polish Heaven, Little Germany, and its own Harlem. Now pockets of Vietnamese, Koreans, Filipinos, and other groups are found in the city, in neighborhoods primarily European in background.

The cultural pluralism theorists want to maintain enough subsocietal separation to guarantee continuance of the ethnic cultural tradition without its interfering with the group's responsibilities to overall American civic life. Cultural pluralism, however, does not engender broad social support and a majority of Americans apparently do not subscribe to the values that undergird cultural pluralism. Nevertheless, cultural pluralism exists in the sense that ethnic and cultural diversity is a characteristic of American life and Americans do have the right to maintain their ethnic identity while sharing a common culture with other Americans.

Chapter Review

A common characteristic of intercultural communication is to assume that the people with whom we are speaking perceive, think, judge, and reason the way we do. This assumption is called *projective cognitive similarity*.

Culture shock is the generalized trauma affecting individuals in a new and different culture. It is precipitated by the anxiety that results from losing familiar signs and symbols for social intercourse.

Six stages accompany culture shock. In the preliminary stage, we are getting ready to leave for the new culture and the tension and anxiety associated with preparing to leave key us up.

After we arrive in the new land, we enter the spectator stage. We tend to be treated well as we experience the new place.

The participant stage arrives when we have to fend for ourselves — find a place to live, a job, places to shop — and live on our own.

Then the shock stage sets in and we experience physical symptoms and mental anguish that are difficult to handle on our own.

If we survive the shock stage and remain in the new culture, we enter the adaptation process, making the behavioral adjustments necessary to fit in.

If we return home after our sojourn, we encounter another stage — re-entry. The W-curve theory hypothesizes that sojourners re-entering their home culture pass through the five stages all over again as they readapt to their previous surroundings.

Returning sojourners are likely to face adjustment in one or several areas: cultural, social, national/political, educational, professional, and financial.

Acculturation is the culture change that results from continuous, firsthand contact between two different cultures. The changes are physical, biological, cultural, social, and psychological. These involve four developments: cultural adjustment, identification, cultural competence, and role enculturation.

An inventory developed to measure our adaptability to a new culture checks our ability to adapt in four areas: emotional resilience (Are we stable enough to stand up to new experiences?), flexibility/openness (Are we open to new ideas? Can

(Continued)

Chapter Review <small>continued</small>

we change our own behavior?), perceptual acuity (Can we read the verbal and nonverbal meanings of another culture's members?), and personal autonomy (Are we strong enough to maintain our own beliefs?).

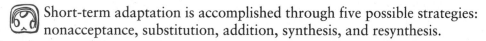 Short-term adaptation is accomplished through five possible strategies: nonacceptance, substitution, addition, synthesis, and resynthesis.

Assimilation is the process by which subordinate groups or cultures adopt the characteristics of the dominant culture The Anglo-conformity and melting pot positions are two of those advocated as means of assimilation in the United States.

Cultural pluralism calls for ethnic groups to maintain separate and distinct cultural identities while fulfilling the broad, civic responsibilities of living in the United States.

Think About This...

1   As a freshman, did you experience culture shock during your first weeks on campus? If you did, what were your symptoms? Recall your experiences during the five stages in the entry process. What happened? Returning home after the first semester, describe your re-entry to your home life.

2   What do you think caused the culture shock you experienced? Discuss your experiences in terms of three explanations given in this chapter.

3   Describe the nature of acculturation. Explain cultural adaptability.

4   Distinguish between the ways of short-term adaptation.

5   What is assimilation? Pluralism? Which one do you favor? Why?

12 Coping With Cultural Diversity

I ntercultural communication specialist Guo-Ming Chen reminds us of what we should know: Cultural diversity has become the norm rather than the exception in the United States because of the shifts in population. The changing cultural character of neighborhoods, schools, and the workplace calls for us to adjust to the unfamiliar and to learn to work and live together without being adversely influenced by the differences that people may bring to a communication encounter.

Diversity in our population demands the ability to understand people from dissimilar cultural backgrounds. To interact competently with people from abroad beginning to populate the United States, we will benefit from a larger repertoire of knowledge and skills than most of us now possess.

 ## Communication Competence

Intercultural communication entails competence in three areas: cognition, affect, and behavior.

1. Cognitively, we are knowledgeable when we grasp how our culture, needs, values, beliefs, attitudes, verbal and nonverbal behavior, social institutions, and relationships influence our interactions with people from other cultures. This information is culture-general, applicable across cultures. With a specific culture in mind — for example, if we plan to attend school in France for a year — we should become familiar with that country's culture as well.

2. Affectively, we are sensitive to our own emotional reactions in unfamiliar situations and also attuned to the emotions of those with whom we speak.

3. Behaviorally, our skillful use of communication behaviors promotes appropriate and effective interaction with people from other cultures as well as our own.

To communicate competently, therefore, we must bring awareness, sensitivity, and skill to intercultural encounters. We must understand our culture and our place in it, be sensitive to our feelings and those of the people with whom we communicate, and use appropriate communication skills to enable effective communication.

 ## Criteria of Intercultural Competence

What knowledge, emotions, and behaviors promote our conception of competence? What can we do to enhance our communication with people from other cultures? From the literature, we have gleaned criteria that represent significant predictors of competence in intercultural communication. These criteria also can serve to measure our success as communicators within our own culture. They are listed in no special order.

- *Display of respect*: expressing acceptance of and positive high regard for people of other cultures.
- *Nonprejudicial*: responding to the ideas of others in a nonjudgmental, descriptive manner.
- *Personalization of knowledge*: recognizing that what we know of the world is individual in nature; it represents our understanding based on our experience and training and may not represent the thinking of other people.
- *Empathy*: projecting oneself into another person's point of view so as to think

momentarily the same thoughts and feel the same emotions as the other person.

- *Regulation of interaction*: moderating the flow of communication by turn-taking, initiating interaction and terminating it, based on the knowledge of the needs and desires of the other communicators.
- *Tolerating ambiguity*: adjusting to new and often equivocal situations with a minimum of personal discomfort.
- *Role-playing*: performing both the task roles related to the purpose of the intercultural interaction and the maintenance roles related to the promotion of harmony and cooperation among the communicators.
- *Self-orientation*: avoiding communication that calls attention to oneself, bragging, showing disinterest in the contributions of others.
- *Ethnocentric behavior*: understanding that one culture is not "better" or "worse" than another, just different from one another.
- *Open-minded*: receiving others' ideas with an impartial and impersonal frame of mind; receptive to the ideas and arguments that others advance.
- *Cognitive perception*: receiving and comprehending a wide range of communicative behaviors and comprehending them.
- *Self-esteem*: respecting oneself as a person of value and worth.
- *Risk-taking*: attempting new ways of behaving, such as eating different foods, visiting new places, meeting people of different races, religions, and nationalities.
- *Sensitivity to cultural variations*: discerning distinctions between cultures, such as differences in family relationships, governance, religious practices, education, and economics.
- *Listening ability*: actively listening to others and fostering an encouraging atmosphere.

The criteria are culture-general. They pertain to communicative behaviors that people use universally to evaluate effectiveness of communicators. Each culture undoubtedly displays these behaviors in its own distinctive ways. Within cultures, we will discover communication practices and styles of speaking unique to the culture.

 ## Achieving Competence

Previous chapters covered many of these criteria. The following pages provide additional information about becoming competent intercultural communicators. This chapter covers five areas: listening, language, nonverbal behavior, intercultural relationships, and personal orientation matters.

Listening

Listening involves more than staying awake, paying attention, and being courteous to the speaker. It also requires active, empathic, and supportive behaviors. These behaviors inform the speaker, "I understand; please continue."

The listener tries to create an encouraging atmosphere, permitting the speaker to express himself or herself. The listener feeds back to the speaker neutral summaries of what he or she heard. The speaker then will know that the listener has understood and the speaking can continue.

Defensive Behavior

A speaker's defensive behavior can obstruct listening. Defensiveness can be aroused through expression, manner of speaking, and the content of the speaker's messages.

Defensiveness can be decreased by creating an open and trusting atmosphere, one that is supportive. This climate can be fostered through descriptive talk that is problem-centered, yet tentative or provisional.

Descriptive talk. Descriptive talk contrasts with evaluative talk — talk that seems to be judging the listener. Speech acts that seem to be genuine requests for information or as material with neutral loadings is descriptive. Specifically, presentations of feelings, events, perceptions, or processes that do not imply that the listener has to change a behavior or an attitude are minimally defense-producing.

A favorite strategy of Americans is to blame others for one's mistakes.[1] Mexicans are blamed, for example, for the influx of drugs into the United States. This judgmental attitude creates defensiveness in Mexicans; they have to prove that the inflow is not their fault but, rather, results from the American demand for drugs. Their defensive posture leads to misunderstandings, complicating relations between the two countries. Instead, the Americans could be descriptive and set forth the reasons for the high drug consumption without placing blame.

Interestingly, Mexicans and Latin Americans have been described as guarding against offending others, avoiding direct questioning of another's beliefs or actions, and directly criticizing another's behavior. They place more emphasis on manners and courtesy in interpersonal relations, striving for harmony and positive interactions. They try to abstain from criticizing, insulting, or offending.[2]

Problem-oriented talk. Communication used to control listeners evokes resistance. A great deal of our social intercourse is developed along lines of someone trying to do something to someone else. Our attempts to change attitudes, influence others, or restrict activity produce defensiveness. Implicit in these attempts is the assumption that the listeners are ignorant, unable to make decisions, unwise, possessed with wrong or inadequate attitudes, or uninformed.

To counter the defensiveness generated by attempts to control, we can communicate the desire to collaborate in defining a mutual problem and seeking a solution. Through problem-oriented talk, the speaker implies that he or she has no predetermined solution, that the speaker and listeners should work together to uncover one. The speaker makes no attempt to persuade the listeners to accept a solution the speaker has conceived already. If the Americans suggest that they and the Mexicans work together to find common solutions to the drug problem, the Americans are problem-oriented, decreasing defensiveness in the process.

Equality in Speaking. Speaking as equals, the speaker implies that he or she is much like the listeners, even though they may have differences in talent, ability, power, status, or appearance. Speaker and listeners are on an equal plane and little significance is attached to any differences that might be present. Defenses thereby are reduced, and the communicators can enter into participative planning with mutual trust.

The Americans discussing the drug influx from Mexico could say, "Do it our way or we'll cut off our financial aid to Mexico." This message would precipitate defensiveness. If the Americans instead were to say something less defense-arousing and more sharing, the results would be more satisfactory: "Each of us has ways of doing things that are best for us. We're not sure what works for you, but you know. You're probably not aware of our needs. So we're in this together. Let's try to work out the best way to cut down or eliminate the flow of drugs and meet both of our needs."

We should interject a caution at this point regarding the example of Mexican behaviors in intercultural encounters. Like most Latin Americans and Hispanics, Mexicans give high marks to treating others as equals. This attitude, however, is likely only in horizontal relationships and not among superiors or subordinates. If the American negotiators in our example are equal to the Mexicans, equal treatment can be expected. If the Americans are subordinate or superior, equality will be absent.[3]

Tentative Talk. Dogmatic people seem to know the answers to problems, to require no additional data, and to regard themselves as instructors. They put others on guard. They need to be right, to want to win arguments rather than solve problems, and to see their ideas as truths to be defended.

We reduce listeners' defensiveness when we communicate that we are willing to be provisional, ready to investigate issues rather than take sides. When we convey the feeling that we are ready to solve problems instead of debate, listeners begin to feel that they have some control over the shared problem. As tentative communicators, we are less certain, more provisional, and willing to look into common concerns with the listeners.

Negotiating dogmatically with the Mexicans, the Americans could say, "This is the way to eliminate the flow of drugs. Stop your people from using your country as a conduit. Stop making drugs in Mexico."

Being tentative, the Americans could say, "We've found that prison terms for drug smugglers cut down their desire to bring in drugs. We're not sure what will help in Mexico. Why don't we sit down and try to decide what will work best for both of us."

Being Open-minded

Close-minded people shut off their minds to new information and are unwilling to listen to views that do not agree with their own. In adopting this attitude, they learn little and find fault with a lot.

Open-mindedness, in contrast, calls for us to be receptive to others' ideas to the extent that we fully understand what they are saying. We may not agree with what they say or accept it, but we should understand it. We should give the speaker a full hearing. We are tolerant of the speaker's viewpoint, recognizing that views contrary to our own may have merit. When listening to a foreigner, we listen to understand.

Being open to new and different ideas is essential to learning, and by shedding the erroneous belief that we can know all there is to know about something, our learnability increases. We can become teachable by developing a sincere humility that we can never know or say everything about anything, by remembering that whatever we know, there is always more.

Evaluating What Is Said

Once we understand what a speaker is saying, we can evaluate the message. Understanding precedes evaluation. Too often, when we listen, we evaluate what we are hearing, and, then, if what we judge what we hear as unacceptable, we reject the message. A better way is to understand first what is being said and then evaluate what we heard. By first understanding the speaker's message, we are less likely to judge it negatively.

To judge what someone has said, we need several skills. We should be able to discern fact from fiction or the speaker's opinions. We should be capable of determining whether the speaker is logical or emotional. And we should maintain an objective attitude — that is, be open-minded.

In judging a speaker's message, we must be wary of being taken in by glibness or charm in delivery, which could be covering up an unsound message. Often we fail to listen critically to those who outrank us. We automatically assume they are right. We are in awe of what they say because they have higher status than we do.

We should be careful also of being taken in by subject matter beyond our comprehension. We accept what we hear because we do not know better. Abroad, poorly prepared tour guides are notorious for glibly spewing forth questionable information about the sights being seen and the people being met. Tourists figure the guides should know; they are the hired experts.

I arrived in Hawaii on Wednesday. The next day I got a job at the YMCA. Saturday and Sunday I was taking a YMCA busload of people around the island of Oahu, acting as their tour guide. I hadn't been there long enough to tour the island myself. I acted knowledgeable. I read the signs that pointed out the attractions and recited what I read. The bus driver would clue me quietly about important sights coming up. As the tour ended, people complimented me on my excellent commentary. After a few weeks of guiding, I did begin to learn superficially about the main tourist attractions.

To be effective critics, we must verify our understanding of what was said by questioning the speaker until the message is clear in our minds. Then we can criticize, expressing our positive reactions to the message or reacting negatively to what we heard.

Evaluation is aided by asking ourselves simple questions about what was said. Does the speaker have a personal motive for saying what was said? Is the message factually based or based on personal feelings? Am I prejudiced toward new ideas, toward the speaker?

Being Empathetic

Reducing defensiveness, being open-minded, and listening critically are steps toward achieving empathy. Empathetic listeners project their own personality into the personality of the speaker so they can understand the speaker better. Empathetic listeners share in the speaker's emotions and feelings, reaching beyond the words uttered to find the real emotions and feelings that the words are attempting to transmit.

Listening empathetically, we listen more to the meanings than the words, reaching behind the words or seeing through them to find the person being revealed. We can do this in four ways.

1. *Paraphrasing* is rewording the thought or meaning in a speaker's message. The listener concisely states in his or her own words what the speaker said.

The 90-year-old convention attendee would have enjoyed his trip a bit more if he would have paraphrased. Twenty years prior to this meeting, while attending a series of meetings in Seoul, he had arranged a night in a bawdy house for two of his friends, both considerably younger than he was.

Twenty years later, the two friends, realizing the old gentleman was at the convention, reciprocated. They hired the most beautiful girl they could find and sent her to his room. When he opened the door to her knock, she quietly stated, "Super sex." The old man replied, "I'll have the soup."

If he would have paraphrased what the girl said, the man may have understood the message and had the super sex.

2. *Reflecting feelings* means giving back to the speaker, in a concise manner, the feelings the speaker is communicating. Encountering the 90-year-old, the two friends asked, "Did you have super sex?" Reflecting the friends' feelings, the man responded, "You're disappointed because I chose the soup."

Reflecting feelings encourages disclosure of emotions, which suggests that the listener can share with the speaker the events described. The listener empathizes in this fashion.

3. *Reflecting meanings* is a third way of achieving empathy Taking his girlfriend for a ride in his new car, the driver was in awe of the many dashboard gadgets. Seeing one, he muttered, "Low fuel." If the girl had reflected meanings and been empathetic, she would not have puzzled her friend, by her reply, "I love you too."

4. *Summarizing* means briefly restating the principal themes and feelings a speaker expresses over a long period of talk. The listener can help the speaker sort out what the speaker said with the recapitulation and, at the same time, show the speaker that the listener was attending to the speaker's message — in other words, displaying empathy.

Language

You do not have to be a watchmaker to tell time, nor do you have to be a linguist to spend a week or two in a foreign country — although it would be helpful. You cannot understand what is happening in an alien culture unless you can understand what things people think and talk about and how they think and talk about these things. To gain that understanding, knowledge of the language is necessary. So the advice given to people who intend to conduct business in a foreign land or who expect to live there for a while is to learn the language along with its culture.

Whether we learn the language, use interpreters, or muddle along on our own, we need to keep in mind that *people mean, not words*. Words can have four different kinds of meaning: denotative, connotative, contextual, and figurative. We have no reason to believe that our fellow communicators, here or abroad, are using words to mean the same thing that we think the words mean. Asking for clarification is good counsel in any language.

Languages present other sorts of barriers of which we should be cognizant. We describe fact/inference confusion, indiscrimination, and allness, three of many barriers in language.

Fact/Inference Confusion

In normal conversation, we can make two kinds of statements about what we perceive. *Statements of fact* are ones that can be confirmed by observation to determine whether they are true or false. *Inferences* are statements about unknown events based on other events that are known. Inferences are guesses, deductions, judgments about what occurred or what may occur.

Statements of fact or inference are difficult to differentiate. Like many languages, our language is devoid of clues to help us make the distinction. As a result, we often confuse fact and inference and behave at though the inferences we make are facts. Misunderstandings are the consequence.

We can look at a man we knew 20 years ago when he was known to us to be 70, and we can say, "That man is 90 years old." The statement is factual; it corresponds directly to what we know as a fact. We also might say, "That man needs super sex." Unless we actually know he does, the statement would be an inference. We inferred about his needs. We made a judgment about what we think he needs.

If we had jumped to the conclusion about his needs, we would be guessing. As we discovered, the man really needed food, and we confused fact and inference, a process coming about in this fashion:

1. We perceive something happening.

2. We can make a factual or an inferential statement about what we perceive.

3. We infer but fail to realize we did so.

4. We act on the inference as though it were a fact.

5. We end up taking a calculated risk, one that is embarrassing, costly, or fatal.

Occasionally we cannot avoid inferring. We assume that the food we eat in a foreign land will not poison us, even though it looks strange. We assume that we will be safe in our hotel room, that the tour guide will not get us lost in an insecure place, that our plane will not explode en route. Without making some assumptions, we would have a difficult time living a normal life. But when we are dealing with people, we will be better off checking our statements and theirs to make sure we are not confusing fact and inference.

Indiscrimination

Another language barrier that creates havoc in intercultural communication is indiscrimination, neglecting differences while overemphasizing similarities — a problem we discussed previously under the term *stereotyping*. This barrier stems from our human tendency to group like things together and attach the same label to them.

Everyone is unique. Everyone is unlike everyone else. An archbishop put it this way:

In my travels over two-thirds of the world in my 55-plus years, the one thing that impresses me is that no other person looks like me. I do not need to get tired of myself, because every time I see someone else, I see someone different.

When we fail to discriminate, our language often is the cause. It leads us to focus on similarities. Certain nouns make it easy for us to group people: French, Germans, Koreans, English, Anglo-Americans, Black Americans, Filipinos. These nouns make classification easy, and our tendency is to classify someone the first time we meet him or her. We are apt to be uneasy until we do so. Who is this person? A Jew? Gentile? Buddhist? We want to pigeonhole the person, and our language helps us do this.

Although pigeonholing people is not undesirable in itself, we are forced to do so to deal with the complexities around us. We order our world by classifying. When we attach an evaluative label to the people we classify, though, that label becomes the basis for judging each member of the class, overlooking the unique values of each person. If we think of Africans as cannibals, that label will come to mind every time we see an African person.

Allness

When we talk about something, we abstract. We focus on some of the details of the thing we are talking about and neglect others. In ordinary conversation we cannot cover all the details; we cannot possibly say all there is to say about something. We are forced to be selective and to speak about some aspects and forego consideration of others. We have to abstract. It is a necessary part of communication.

The barrier in communication arises when we are unaware that we are abstracting and assume that what we know or what we say is all we really need to know or say. We behave on the basis of the few details we know. We judge the whole by the parts we perceive, and we become intolerant of those who disagree with our judgments. Our talk takes on a note of assurance that implies we know all there is to know on the subject. We are guilty of *allness*, a language barrier that presumes that anyone can know all there is to know about a subject.

The allness barrier is hard to overcome. When we believe we know everything about something, we fail to realize the details we omitted. We think that there is nothing more worthwhile to say on the subject. We said it all. But there always is more.

We can deal with our tendency toward allness by reminding ourselves that we never can finish saying all there is to say. In our mind, we should add an *etcetera* to what was said. The *etcetera* says, "There is more. I may not know what it is, but unquestionably there is more."

One college graduate stated the point this way:

> When I got my bachelor's degree, I knew all about my major. Nobody could tell me differently. I was encouraged to go on to my master's. I didn't see what more I could learn, but I went on.
>
> After I got that degree, I had absolutely no reservations. I knew everything about my major. A professor thought I had potential, so he encouraged me to earn a doctorate. Again, I didn't see why; I now knew it all.

> I got the doctorate. Now I know I know hardly anything about my major, and in my lifetime, I'll never learn it all.

Indirectness

Our attention should be drawn to another language matter important in intercultural communication — *indirectness*. In the United States we can say what we think, within the bounds of good taste. We usually do not beat around the bush but come right out and say what is on our mind. In some other cultures, directness is frowned upon, especially when talking about people. Hall illustrates the point with the Japanese, a people who practice the art of indirection:

> Negotiations in Japan are like a minuet. One step forward, one step to the side, one step back. The more important the communication from a Japanese, the more indirect it will be.[4]

Likewise, the Japanese do not say *no* to a request; saying *no* is impolite. Then, too, *yes* does not necessarily mean *yes*. More likely, a Japanese will mean, "Yes, I hear you" or, "Yes, I understand," but not "Yes, I will" or "Yes, I agree."

Of course, the Japanese are not the only people who are politely indirect in their use of language. The Chinese, Indonesians, Filipinos, Taiwanese, Singaporeans, and Malaysians are among others who consider a "no" as impolite and a "yes" to mean many things other than, "Yes, I agree."

Restricted Codes

Highly influential in intercultural communication are two concepts described previously: the elaborated/restricted code and the concept of high/low context. Some cultures communicate in great detail. Members of those cultures use the elaborated code, explaining at length about the subjects of their messages. They represent low-context cultures. In contrast, we find people of other cultures who say little. They rely on the context and their nonverbal behavior to carry the bulk of the message. They employ a restricted code and are members of high-context cultures.

When we converse with people using a restricted code, we should ask for clarification if we do not understand their messages. By restating and amplifying their remarks, we can obtain a clearer understanding of their meaning. If they do not understand us, we can reciprocate. We can clarify what we mean, elaborating until we achieve mutual understanding.

Latin American cultures are classified as high-context. Members of those cultures are not as explicit as Northern Europeans or North Americans. Latin Americans rarely are explicit when asking a favor or saying no. The meanings

---

Cultural Awareness

In developing an intercultural perspective, people go through four stages:

1. *Unconscious incompetence* — The communicator is not aware that cultural differences exist between people; hence, the person is unaware that he or she may be making crucial mistakes. Instead, the person trusts his or her intuition.

2. *Conscious incompetence* — The communicator is aware that differences exist but he or she does not understand what they are or how involved they may be. The communicator knows a problem exists.

3. *Conscious competence* — The communicator knows that differences exist, knows what some are, and tries to modify his or her behavior to be sensitive to them, but hasn't completely replaced old behaviors with new ones.

4. *Unconscious competence* — The communicator's culturally appropriate behavior now comes naturally to him or her.

This exercise calls for you to assign the stage of awareness you think the person is in who made the statement. Write the stage's number (1,2,3,4) in the blank before each statement.

____ 1. The people from the other culture really aren't much different from me.

____ 2. I'll never understand people from the other culture.

____ 3. They have no problem understanding me.

____ 4. I wonder what they think of me.

____ 5. Working with people from this culture requires extreme care.

____ 6. They seem to behave in a logical fashion.

____ 7. I'm able to relax around these people.

____ 8. I'll never figure out these people.

Answers on page 244.

Based on *Figuring Foreigners Out,* by Craig Storti (Yarmouth, ME: Intercultural Press, 1999), pp. 157–160.

of their messages often are conveyed by gestures and other nonverbal signs. Or the rank and position of the speakers transmit their meaning, forcing subordinates to read between the lines. People from low-context cultures have difficulty dealing with Latin Americans because the former are not used to paying a great deal of attention to context factors to decipher what is being said.

Mexican Americans often use elaborate and indirect expressions in an effort to maintain harmonious social relations. This can cause misinterpretation by listeners who do not understand the pattern. North Americans could believe that Mexican Americans are not forthcoming or are trying to hide something. Mexican Americans in communication with Anglo-Americans perceive the Anglos as being too direct and too plain. They are blunt in comparison to the Mexicans, who use language expressively and associatively.[5]

Nonverbal Behavior

From our review in Chapter 10, we are aware of the ubiquitous nature of nonverbal behavior. We know that in different places, the same nonverbal sign or signal may carry a meaning different from the one we give to it. We cannot rely on a nonverbal message's transmitting the same meaning from culture to culture. Yet it would be impossible to learn the meanings of the same gestures, postures, and signs in different cultures.

What to do? We can observe and ask. We can watch how people in another culture treat space, time, and eye contact, among like behaviors, and adjust our responses accordingly. When a certain gesture seems to carry a meaning contrary to the one we give it, we can ask what the gesture means. By watching and asking, we learn.

Then, too, we can turn to books about the cultures in which we are interested and pick up information on their nonverbal uses. For example, among books available on Latinos and Latin American, many contain details of their unspoken communication patterns. Glancing through these books, we learn that Latin Americans use gestures much more frequently than North Americans do, and these gestures convey various meanings. Latin Americans gesture to express feelings, answer questions, call people or send them away, greet people, and so on.

We learn, too, that Latin Americans stand and sit at closer distances that North Americans find uncomfortable. Latin American children lower their eyes when being addressed by an older person such as a teacher, to show their respect for the person. North Americans look the person in the eye to convey the same meaning. Latin Americans touch more frequently than do North Americans and are less likely to plan activities ahead of time. They are more present-oriented than North Americans. Latin Americans express their emotions more openly than North Americans, whether the emotions are of pleasure, pain, joy or grief.[6]

 A Nonverbal Sign

You are visiting a Chinese holy temple and notice shoes lined up outside the door.

_____ a. You walk into the temple with your shoes on because it seems silly to you to take them off.

_____ b. You take off your shoes as you've seen others do and walk into the temple.

_____ c. You hesitate as you are about to enter, then decide not to go in because you don't want to take off your shoes.

Answers on page 244.

Based on *Figuring Foreigners Out*, by Craig Storti (Yarmouth, ME: Intercultural Press, 1999), pp. 157–160.

As we become sensitive to and judge the nonverbal behaviors of people from other cultures, we must keep in mind three points:

1. Nonverbal behavior always occurs in a context, and the behavior should be assessed in terms of that context.

2. Nonverbal cues cannot be viewed as isolated parts of a person's behavior but, instead, the person's total behavior must be considered when making judgments.

3. Our conclusions about what we perceive must be kept tentative, recognizing that what we may see as a form of nonverbal behavior may not be that at all in the culture whose people we are judging.

Intercultural Relationships

We already have learned how to develop and maintain relationships with people from other cultures. To achieve competence in those relationships, we highlight certain aspects here — of which reducing uncertainty is primary.

Managing uncertainty and anxiety is necessary for effective intercultural communication and adjustment.[7] In beginning a relationship

Relationships often begin with a handshake. We introduce ourselves, ask the other people where they are from, what they do, and where they live.

with a person from another culture, a first step is to reduce uncertainty. Our first impressions come during the initial moments of talk. We look for similarities in background and interests, and we ask questions to draw those out.

In low-context cultures such as the Northern Europeans, we can speed up the development of a relationship by self-disclosing — sharing ourself with the others. Being open, relaxed, friendly, attentive, and animated are qualities of communication that enhance relationships in any culture. Our ability to observe and regulate our expressive behavior and self-presentation helps us determine what communicative behavior is appropriate in a given circumstance. If we are shy and apprehensive in communication situations, we will not interrelate well.

Self/Group Orientations

Because most of us grew up in the United States, a basically individualistic culture, we tend to be self-oriented. When abroad, we may come into contact with people from collectivistic cultures who are more group-oriented. In developing and maintaining relationships with people from collectivistic cultures, we want to foster harmonious relations and to support their group's activities.

This type of relationship is important for those who are preparing to interact with Latin Americans, for example. As North Americans, our usual pattern is to think first and foremost of our own wishes, needs, and interests. Latin Americans express what is good for the other. Latin Americans may interpret our individualistic behavior as selfish and egotistical.

Collectivists make greater distinctions than individualists between members of the in-group, normally members of the extended family, and outsiders, those who do not belong to the family. In Latin America no institution is more important than the family. Among North Americans, the family is important, but not to the same extent as among Latin Americans.[8]

Status

Because inequality in social standing is prevalent in many cultures, care must be taken to address people of higher status properly in those cultures and observe formalities in speech. We can eliminate some misunderstandings by becoming acquainted with status differences in the countries we visit.

A friend says:

When I travel abroad, I note subtle deference to persons of high status by persons of lower status. My Korean friend, a multimillionaire who in my view as an American shouldn't defer to anyone, is bowing and scraping forever to persons who by some act of good fortune hold a higher status in life. My Korean friend can buy and sell a hundred times over the people he defers to, and he's downright servile in the process.

My friend, who is a university professor sort of as a sideline to his money-making enterprises, gets upset when I don't knuckle under to the people he kowtows to. I'm chastised because I don't worship his department chairman, a person half as good as my friend. Why should I? I was a chair myself, and chairs aren't better than anybody else. But that's the Korean way — different than the American.

Personal Orientation

Previously we provided guidance on how to recognize and deal with needs, values, beliefs, and attitudes — the essentials of our personal orientation system. Those elements of the system differ across cultures and, because they do, we need to be cognizant of them. Our self-identity or sense of personhood is anchored in this system, which we acquired through our socialization and upbringing. The system represents reality and truth and dictates the way we think and behave. It defines us as members of our culture and serves as a powerful motivating force in our life.

Whenever we interact with people from other cultures, we must be careful not to tread on those vital elements of their personal way of behaving. We have to observe their ways of doing things and, if they seem strange to us, we can ask about them. To truly achieve competence, however, we need to do more than inquire.

In our shrinking, highly interdependent world, training to be interculturally competent is not a luxury reserved for an elite group of statesmen or visiting dignitaries. Training is a necessity we all must undergo if we plan to live and work abroad. More important, learning to live with people who are strangers in our land is essential, and our educational system should provide us with that training.

 # Competence Training For Work Abroad

Training in intercultural communication is especially crucial to people expecting to work abroad, whether they be governmental workers, business personnel, members of the military, missionaries, or media personnel. Problems associated with sending these people overseas are well-documented and include the following:

- Only about 20 percent of government personnel working on developmental projects perform effectively overseas.

- A board of inquiry found that Canadian peacekeeping forces involved in the death of Somali civilians were unable to understand the Somali way of doing things.

- American business personnel working overseas fail at their jobs 15 percent to 40 percent of the time; less than 50 percent perform adequately.

- Poor adaptation of spouse and family is a main reason for early return from overseas assignments.
- American firms lose $2 billion per year in direct costs because of the premature return of workers.[9]

Apparently some individuals are marked by a striking incapacity for intercultural communication, regardless of circumstances. Looking closely at these problem situations, we can conclude also that some people are marked by a strikingly effective capacity for intercultural communication, regardless of circumstances.

Achieving Success

What makes for work success overseas? Daniel Kealey reviewed the literature on overseas adjustment and summarized the current state of knowledge.[10] Table 12.1 offers a profile of skills based on his review. The skills listed represent the core nontechnical requirements for screening and selecting overseas workers. Nontechnical skills are those related to becoming personally adjusted to living in the new culture. They have no relationship to the technical skills needed to do one's job competently.

TABLE 12.1 Nontechnical Skills for Overseas Life

A. Adaptive Skills
   1. Possessing positive attitudes about working abroad; desiring to go abroad to work.
   2. Being flexible and receptive to new ways of doing things.
   3. Coping with the stresses of transition from home to abroad.
   4. Being calm and steadfast despite difficulties in adjusting.
   5. Having a stable and well-adjusted family.
   6. Being stable and emotionally well-balanced.
   7. Accepting oneself.

B. Crosscultural Skills
   1. Viewing the constraints on family and self realistically.
   2. Tolerating the conditions that overseas life brings.
   3. Becoming involved in the local culture.
   4. Accurately perceiving fellow workers and bosses to minimize friction.
   5. Being sensitive to local cultures.

C. Partnership Skills
   1. Being capable of establishing a working relationship with fellow workers from overseas.
   2. Being open to others' ideas and behaviors.
   3. Having a strong commitment to the overseas assignment.
   4. Confronting obstacles and being able to overcome them.
   5. Building strong interpersonal relationships.
   6. Being self-confident.
   7. Analyzing situations and recommending solutions.

Based on "The Challenge of Interpersonal Selection," by Daniel J. Kealey, in *Handbook of Intercultural Training,* 2d ed. edited by D. Landis & R.S. Bhagat (Thousand Oaks, CA: Sage, 1996), pp. 86–87.

The skills directly concern the three major challenges encountered on an overseas assignment:

1. Adjusting calmly and competently to the emotional upheavals experienced by the worker and his or her family — *adjustment skills.*

2. Understanding the new environment, which calls for *communication skills* to function effectively in the new culture.

3. Interacting successfully with fellow workers from the new culture while on the job — *partnership skills.*

Training Content

Table 12.2 presents content that should be included in intercultural training.[11] This subject matter can be incorporated into learning activities appropriate to the cognitive, affective, and behavioral domains of intercultural communication

TABLE 12.2 The Content of Intercultural Training

A. Intercultural communication
  1. Culture and communication
  2. Language and communication
  3. Nonverbal behavior and communication
  4. Role of needs, values, beliefs, attitudes in communication
  5. Cognitive differentiation: perception
  6. Communication styles
  7. Cultural adjustment to shock

B. The intercultural communication process
  1. Learning alternative responses to cultural differences
  2. Developing intercultural sensitivity
  3. Describing, interpreting, evaluating intercultural events

C. Intercultural relations and cultural differences
  1. Similarities and differences in relational patterns across cultures

  2. Differences in needs, values, beliefs, and attitudes
  3. Differences in gender, religion, status, socioeconomics, race

D. Factors that inhibit or promote communication
  1. Openness, flexibility, emotional resilience
  2. Status equality, shared goals, cooperation
  3. Language differences

E. Area studies
  1. History, political and economic systems
  2. Religions
  3. School systems
  4. Family and social relations
  5. Fine arts, sports
  6. Medicine, science

Based on "Ethics in Intercultural Training," by R. Michael Page & Judith N. Martin, in *Handbook of Intercultural Training*, 2d ed., edited by Dan Landis & R.S. Bhagat (Thousand Oaks, CA: Sage, 1996), p. 54.

competency. Those activities can be arranged in a sequential order that allows learners time to become acquainted with each other and to adjust to the psychological stresses the learners encounter.

Passive activities, such as listening to lectures, are followed by low-risk but active lessons involving group discussion. Problem-solving experiences come next, as they are medium-risk activities familiar to most learners. Case studies or critical incidents also are medium-risk activities, and they follow the problem-solving discussions. Role-playing, a high-risk activity, is next in the sequence. Simulations, another high-risk activity, conclude the training.

The lectures, discussions, and group problem-solving activities tend toward a cognitive emphasis. The remaining activities are affective or behavioral. [The *Workbook* accompanying this text supplies examples of all but the lecture forms of these activities.]

An important adjunct to the training sequence is a set of briefings on the geographical areas in which trainees may be working. These could be included as part of the lecture material or as outside reading assignments. In whatever way the material is presented, it should include factual information about the specific countries to which trainees are being assigned, information about the people's needs, values, beliefs, and attitudes, and details about problems that trainees will face in the country of their choice. The factual information should encompass the country's history, family, social structure, religion, philosophy, education, fine arts, economics, industry, government, medicine, science, and sports.

Problems that trainees may confront in the new land might relate to matters such as how foreigners are received, cleanliness and sanitation and health concerns, lack of privacy, transportation, financial matters, and ethical concerns (bribery, theft, dishonesty), among others. [The *Workbook* for this text provides an exercise, "The Cultural Resume," which requires learners to prepare a geographical-area briefing.]

 # Morals in Intercultural Encounters

My Japanese friend and I have engaged in many dealings with Japanese entrepreneurs of various types. Being conversant in Japanese, he did the negotiating, and I listened. Because I could understand most of the interaction, I got the drift of what was being negotiated. I was frequently surprised. My friend made claims and promises that I thought were distortions of the truth. He would tell me one thing and the Japanese entrepreneur something entirely different.

After a few years of witnessing this sort of negotiation, I began to realize that my friend and I were operating according to different ethical systems. What I considered immoral had no moral significance to him, or perhaps was positively moral. I learned about ethical absolutism and ethical relativism the hard way — from encounters we had with our business associates in Japan.

Morals, or its etymologically related term, *ethics*, are accepted rules and standards of human behavior that distinguish between right and wrong, goodness or badness of human behavior. What is good or bad is basically what our culture decides it is. Ethical standards are products of specific cultures, so one way of behaving may have a high moral value in one culture but no ethical significance in another, or may even be considered ethically wrong. My Japanese friend's behavior may have been ethically sound in his culture, or perhaps of no ethical significance. To me, the behavior was immoral.

In intercultural encounters, depending upon with whom we interact, we could approach ethical standards from an *absolutist* set of principles or a *relativistic* set.

Ethical Absolutism

Ethical absolutism emphasizes what is right or wrong in accordance with a set of universally fixed standards regardless of cultural differences, minimizing the significance of cultural context.[12] The good and bad behavior is fixed in a set of standards that should be applied to all cultures.

In the United States, the macroculture, the dominant culture, defines what is right and wrong and establishes the criteria by which ethical behavior is evaluated. For example, the dominant culture decides that each citizen must pay taxes on a certain percentage of the citizen's income. Other, nondominant groups may believe that U.S. citizens should pay no taxes on income but, rather, on items they purchase, or that each citizen should pay the same amount regardless of income. The views of these nondominant groups, however, are generally ignored.

What is right is what the dominant group believes is right. One set of standards is applied to evaluate a range of practices. Thus, cross-situational consistency is preserved. At the same time, a set of standards is being imposed that some people may not consider appropriate under the circumstances. To be culturally absolutist, using the tax example, all cultures should rightfully impose taxes on a percentage of each citizen's income.

Ethical Relativism

Ethical relativism emphasizes the principles of right and wrong in terms of the values and goals of a specific cultural group. Each cultural group has its own set of moral principles, which may or may not be similar to those of another culture. Standards of moral behavior are tied to each cultural context, which is likely to change from culture to culture, from time to time. Using income taxes as an example — the United States may determine that its system is ethically sound; Canada, with a different method of paying for government expenditures, may use a different method of collecting fees; China might have a third way; and so on from culture to culture.

An alternative for guiding our actions in our diversified world is *contextual relativism*, a way of evaluating a moral standard from its context.[13] This alternative means that each application of ethics would have to be made on a case-by-case and a context-by-context basis. I would have to judge how ethical my friend's negotiation techniques were on the basis of the Japanese standards as they applied in the circumstance under question. Not only would I have to know Japan's ethical standard, the language, and the culture, but I also would have to know much about the specific situation in which the negotiations took place.

Admittedly, my judgment of my friend's behavior would be sounder than if the judgment were a relativistic or an absolutist one. It would require a thorough knowledge of the Japanese culture — more, perhaps, than I possibly could acquire without extensive study, and probably much more than absolutely necessary. Some believe that ethics has a tyrannical hold on human behavior as we obey our moral laws even in the absence of a parent or other judge.[14]

Chapter Review

To communicate competently interculturally, we must be prepared in three areas: cognition, affect, and behavior. The cognitive area relates to knowledge about ourselves and the people from other cultures with whom we plan to interact. The area of affect is concerned with sensitivity to our emotions and those with whom we will interact. The behavioral area concerns the effective use of the communication skills needed in interaction situations.

Fifteen criteria for measuring intercultural communication competence range from displaying respect to showing empathy to risk-taking and listening effectively.

Competence can be heightened by listening skillfully, recognizing language barriers, understanding nonverbal behavior, relating interpersonally, and understanding personal needs, values, beliefs, and attitudes.

Listening can be improved by reducing defensive behaviors, speaking descriptively, being problem-centered, speaking as equals, being tentative, being open-minded, understanding, then evaluating, and being empathetic.

When communicating interculturally, we have to remember that people mean, not words. Fact/inference confusion, allness, and indiscrimination present language barriers to effective communication.

Some cultures rely on indirection to uphold harmony in interpersonal relationships. Some apply restrictive codes, and others elaborated codes as communicative devices. Some are low-context and some are high-context cultures.

Few cultures practice identical nonverbal behaviors. These behaviors are not universal but carry different meanings in different cultures.

Individualism and collectivism play roles in communication across cultures. Individualistic cultures are apt to be more self-oriented and collectivistic culture more group-oriented.

Status has a bearing on interaction. Many cultures defer to high-status people. A few treat people more or less equally.

If we plan to work or live abroad beyond a few weeks of touring, training is necessary.

The training should center on preparing sojourners to adjust to the new environment, to communicate effectively in it, and to interact successfully with fellow workers or students.

(Continued)

Chapter Review continued

The subject areas of training essentially equate the content of this text, beginning with knowledge of the communication practices at home and abroad, culture, perception, personal orientation systems, social institutions, interpersonal behavior, language, nonverbal behavior, and cultural adaptation processes.

Morals (ethics) are accepted rules and standards of human behavior that distinguish between right and wrong, goodness and badness. What is good or bad is determined by culture, and variations will appear across cultures.

Absolutist ethical standards emphasize what is right or wrong in accordance with a set of universally fixed standards regardless of culture.

Ethical relativism emphasizes what is right or wrong in terms of the values and goals of given cultural groups. Each culture has its own set, which may or may not be similar to those in other cultures.

Answer Key

Chapter 1 What Would You Do?

As noted in the Preface, it's "early times," and perhaps you aren't sensitive yet to possible cultural differences, so if your choice isn't the following, don't be dismayed.

a. Incorrect; there's something amiss and you're missing it.

b. Correct; the old man doesn't want you to take the photo — without paying the child. At several locations in Hong Kong, children and ancient-looking old timers pose for tourists who frequent those areas — for pay. You didn't know about this custom, so you correctly put away your camera.

c. Incorrect; you'll probably get the picture and learn a few words of Hong Kong slang from the child in the process.

Chapter 2 Behavior: Universal, Cultural, Personal

It's still "early times," but sensitivity isn't required here, just a bit of thought, and text reading, especially lists.

1. Personal
2. Universal
3. Universal
4. Universal
5. Cultural
6. Personal
7. Personal
8. Universal
9. Cultural
10. Personal

Chapter 3 A Greek Puzzle

Still early, but time is passing quickly. Check the ( ), for therein lies a clue.

a. Incorrect; you've not made a friend.

b. Incorrect; this could be a possibility, one that often works at home but you're not home.

c. Correct; he or she will tell you that jerking one's head up and down isn't a universal gesture for "yes;" in this case, it's a Greek gesture for "no," meaning "I don't change American money."

Chapter 4 Nancy is Attacked

Attribution is at work here, and in new and strange cultures, we are apt to seek causes for people's behavior. Possible causes are noted here.

1. Incorrect; nothing in the story suggests that this occurred.

2. Correct; at the time of the incident, a woman wearing shorts while alone on the street is unacceptable and a sign of immorality; Nancy's behavior was uncharacteristic of a morally proper woman, so he concluded that she was a prostitute.

3. Incorrect; a possibility but nothing suggests it.

4. Incorrect; yet it can be construed as a correct answer because a woman walking alone on Iranian streets is not appropriate behavior for a lady.

Chapter 5 Individualism — Collectivism

Thought is required here. If you've read the descriptions of these two values, you should score well — with thought.

1. I	4. C	7. I	10. I
2. C	5. C	8. C	
3. I	6. C	9. I	

Chapter 10 Tabu or Not Tabu

It's way past "early times." You're in the twilight zone, and you should know the correct answer for this one without even guessing.

1. Correct; in a contact culture, male friends often hold hands.

2. Incorrect; dictionaries list many meanings for "strange," but none applies here.

3. Incorrect; a possibility is that the streets were crowded, but the first answer is more appropriate.

4. Incorrect; do you know a professor anywhere who would steal another person's money? More important, do professors have money to steal?

Chapter 11 A Shocking Experience

1. Incorrect; people living in warm climates should bathe more, unquestionably, but the absence of seatmates was more of a question of a boring set of lectures.

2. Incorrect; tropical isles tend to be costly, mostly because of high shipping costs, and the prohibitive costs probably contributed to his anxiety, but there's a better answer.

3. Correct; this is the better answer. After going through the preliminary stages, shock finally set in, especially when local girls turned him off, a typical response to newcomers, particularly aggressive ones.

4. Incorrect; his vote would fulfill his responsibilities as an American citizen, but it isn't likely to throw out of office a 50,000-person bureaucracy.

Chapter 11 Acculturated

Are you acculturated? No more "early times." This answer you should easily get correct. If not, s-t-u-d-y and think a bit, too.

a. Incorrect; at least you left, but the old man probably told you in Tagalog to mind your own business — which is good advice.

b. Incorrect; if your message was in Tagalog, he likely caught on, but you're battling age-old customs.

c. Correct; you assumed correctly.

Chapter 12 Cultural Awareness

A good British detective would be in the solving stage if he were dealing with a crime. This exercise, however, has several possible answers for each statement so it shouldn't be easy. If you answer all of them correctly, you've reached the Sherlock Holmes stage of detecting.

1. Stage 1; the phrase "really aren't much different than me" rules out the other possibilities; the person making the statement is truly not aware.

2. Stage 2; the speaker is aware he's got a problem but doesn't know what it is.

3. Stage 1; a competent intercultural communicator would not assume that his messages were being understood; he'd check.

4. Stage 2 (possibly 3); in stage 2 the speaker is aware of possible incompetence; in stage 3, the speaker knows but is still struggling to find the best way.

5. Stage 2; the speaker is aware of his incompetence.

6. Stage 3; the speaker knows, but has to be more confident.

7. Stage 1 (or possibly 4); the speaker is ignorant, or, if 4, extremely confident.

8. Stage 2; this statement suggests that the speaker is beginning to be conscious of existing differences.

Chapter 12 A Nonverbal Sign

The early times are long past. If you pass this one, you're ready — ready at least to enter Chinese temples.

a. Incorrect; start reading the text all over again.

b. Correct; you'll pass!

c. Incorrect; always wear slip-on shoes while touring in the Far East.

Notes

Preface

1. *Public Speaking in a Diverse Society*, by Pat Kearney & Tim Plax (Mountain View, CA: Mayfield, 1996).

Chapter 1

1. *USA Today*, Sept. 7, 1999, 1A, 13A.
2. *Multicultural Education in a Pluralistic Society*, 3d ed., by D. M. Gollnick & P. C. Chinn (New York: Merrill, 1990), p. 225.
3. *USA Today*, Sept. 7, 1999, p. 13A.
4. *Newsweek*, May 5, 1997, p. 59.
5. *Communicating with the Japanese,* by J. V. Neustupny (Tokyo: Japan Times, 1987), pp. 31–32.
6. *Honolulu Advertiser*, Dec. 8, 1997, p. A5.
7. *USA Today*, Sept. 7, 1999, p. 11A
8. *International and Intercultural Communication*, by H. D. Fischer & J. C. Merrill (New York: Hastings House, 1976), p. 17.
9. Ibid.
10. *Time*, Fall 1993, p. 3.
11. *Public Speaking in a Diverse Society,* by P. Kearney & T. G. Plax (Mountain View, CA: Mayfield, 1976), pp. 14–15.
12. U.S. Department of Justice, Immigration and Naturalization Service, *Annual Report*, May 1999.
13. *Intercultural Communication: A Reader*, 8th ed., by L. A. Samovar & R. E. Porter (Belmont, CA: Wadsworth, 1997), p. 5.
14. "College Hate Speech Codes: A Personal View from an Absolute Perspective," by L. M. Collier, "*Howard Journal of Communications*, 1995, 5:4, 269.
15. *International Herald Tribune*, Nov. 16, 1999, p. 10.
16. *International Herald Tribune,* Jan. 3, 2000, p. 5.
17. *Japan Almanac.* (Tokyo: Asahi Shimbun, 1999), p. 72.
18. *International Herald Tribune*, Jan. 3, 2000, p. 7.
19. *Culture, Communication and Conflict: Readings in Intercultural Relations*, 2d ed., by G. R. Weaver (Needham, MA: Simon & Schuster, 1998), pp. 267–268.
20. *Culture, Communication and Conflict,* Weaver, p. 273.
21. Development of a Measure of Interpersonal Communication Competence," *Communication Research Reports*, by R. B. Rubin & M. M. Martin, *11* (1994), 111–125.
22. "Teaching the Intercultural Communication Course," by D. W. Klopf & R. Kuramoto, *Human Communication*, 2 (1999), 11–12.
23. "Teaching the Intercultural Communication Course," 12–20.

Chapter 2

1. *The Silent Language*, by E. T. Hall (Greenwich, CT: Fawcett, 1959), p. 10.
2. *Communication and Culture,* by A. G. Smith (New York: Holt, Rinehart & Winston, 1966), pp. 1–10.
3. *Intercultural Communication*, by E. M. Rogers & T. M Steinfatt (Prospect Heights, IL: Waveland, 1999), pp. 62–63.
4. *The Ugly American*, by W. J. Lederer & E. Burton (New York: Norton, 1958), p. 268.
5. *Speaking Culturally: Language Diversity in the United States*, by F. L. Johnson (Thousand Oaks, CA: Sage, 2000), p. 45.
6. *Anthropology: The Cultural Perspective*, 2d. ed., by J. P. Spradley & D. W. McCurdy (Prospect Heights, IL: Waveland, 1989), pp. 30–31.
7. *Communication Between Cultures,* 2d ed., by L. A. Samovar & R. E. Porter

(Belmont, CA: Wadsworth, 1995),
pp. 46–47.

8. "Culture: A Critical Review of Concepts and Definitions," by A. L. Kroeber & C. Kluckhohn in *Paper of the Peabody Museum,* 1952, p. 47.

9. *Public Speaking in a Diverse Society,* by P. Kearney & T. G. Plax (Mountain View, CA: Mayfield, 1996), p. 11.

10. *Public Speaking in a Diverse Society,* p. 11.

11. *Intercultural Interactions: A Practical Guide,* 2d ed., by K. Cushner & R. W. Brislin (Thousand Oaks, CA: Sage, 1996), p. 10.

12. *Anthropology,* p. 21.

13. "Culture and Basic Psychological Principles," by H. R. Markus, S. Kitayama, & R. J. Heiman, in *Social Psychology: Handbook of Basic Principles,* edited by E. T. Higgins & A. W. Kruglanski (New York: Guilford Press, 1996), p. 864.

14. *Multicultural Education in a Pluralistic Society,* by D. M. Gollnick & P. C. Chinn, 3d ed. (New York: Merrill, 1990), p. 5.

15. *Intercultural Communication in Contexts,* by J. J. Martin & T. K. Nakayama (Mountain View, CA: Mayfield, 1997), pp. 46–47.

16. Ibid.

17. *Honolulu Advertiser,* Feb. 22, 2000, A1, A8.

18. *Multicultural Education,* p. 10.

19. "Contrasting and Comparing Cultures," by G. R. Weaver in *Culture, Communication and Conflict: Readings in Intercultural Relations,* edited by G. R. Weaver (Needham, MA: Simon & Schuster, 1998), pp. 72–76.

20. In *Beyond Culture* (Garden City, NJ: Doubleday, 1976), p. 11.

21. "The Common Denominators of Culture," in *The Science of Man in World Crisis,* edited by R. Linton (New York: Columbia University Press, 1945), p. 78.

Chapter 3

1. *Multicultural Education in a Pluralistic Society,* by D. M. Gollnick & P. C. Chinn, 3d ed. (New York: Merrill, 1990), p. 12.

2. *Public Speaking in a Diverse Society,* by P. Kearney & T. G. Plax (Mountain View, CA: Mayfield, 1990), p. 11.

3. *Communication Between Cultures,* 2d ed., by L. E. Samovar & R. E. Porter (Belmont, CA: Wadsworth, 1995), pp. 60–61.

4. *Intercultural Communication: An Introduction,* 2d ed., by F. E. Jandt (Thousand Oaks, CA: Sage, 1998), p. 10.

5. *Multicultural Education,* Gollnick & Chinn, pp. 12–13.

6. Ibid, p. 13.

7. In "Living In/Between," by R. Morris, in *Our Voices,* 2d ed., edited by A. Gonzales, M. Houston & V. Chen, (Los Angeles: Roxbury, 1997), p. 170.

8. *Multicultural Education,* pp. 13–14.

9. Ibid, p. 14.

10. "Communicating in a Multicultural Society," by S. Ishii & D. W. Klopf, *Dokkyo International Journal,* 13 (2000) pp. 191–204.

11. *Communicating Today,* 2d ed., by R. Zeuschner (Boston: Allyn & Bacon, 1997), pp. 397–398.

12. *Interpersonal Communication: Everyday Encounters,* 2d ed., by J. T. Wood (Belmont, CA: Wadsworth, 1999), p. 92.

13. *Interpersonal Communication: Relating to Others,* 2d ed., by S. A. Beebe, S. J. Beebe, & M. V. Redmond (Boston: Allyn & Bacon, 1999), pp. 386–387.

14. *Intercultural Interactions: A Practical Guide,* 2d ed., by K. Cushner & R. W. Brislin (Thousand Oaks, CA: Sage, 1996), pp. 297–298.

15. *Interpersonal Communication,* Beebe, Beebe, & Redmond, p. 105.

16. *Multicultural Education,* Gollnick & Chinn, p. 114.

17. *You Just Don't Understand: Women and Men in Conversation,* by D. Tannen (New York: Wm. Morrow, 1990) p. 43.

18. *The Power to Communicate,* 3d ed., by D. Borisoff & L. Merrill (Prospect Heights, IL: Waveland, 1998), pp. 43–44.

19. *Interpersonal Communication,* Beebe, Beebe, & Redmond, p. 105.

20. *Multicultural Education,* Gollnick & Chinn, p. 78.

21. *The Multiracial Experience: Racial Borders as the New Frontier,* edited by M. P. P. Root (Thousand Oaks, CA: Sage, 1996), p. x.

22. "Being Hapa: A Choice for Cultural Empowerment," by D. Kimoto, in *Our Voices: Essays In Culture, Ethnicity and Communication* edited by A. Gonzales, M. Houston, & V. Chen (Los Angeles: Roxbury, 1997), p. 157.

23. *The Multiracial Experience,* p. xiv.

24. "A Review of the Concept of Intercultural Sensitivity," by G-M Chen & W. J. Starosta, *Human Communication,* 1:1(1997), 2.

25. *Sociology*, 4th ed., by N.J. Smelser (Englewood Cliffs, NJ: Prentice Hall, 1991), p. 164.

26. *Multicultural Education*, Gollnick & Chinn, pp. 48–58.

27. *Intercultural Communication*, by E.M. Rogers & T. M Steinfatt (Prospect Heights, IL: Waveland, 1999), p. 238.

28. "Beyond Cultural Identity: Reflections on Multiculturalism," by P. J. Adler, in *Basic Concepts of Intercultural Communication: Selected Readings*, edited by M. J. Bennett (Yarmouth, ME: Intercultural Press, 1998), p. 226.

29. Executive Committee: Association of College Unions-International, July 1987. Quoted in *Intercultural Communication*, by Jandt, p. 425.

30. "Multiculturalism and the Normal Human Experience," by W. Goodenough in *Applied Anthropology in America*, 2d ed., edited by E. M. Eddy & W. L. Partridge (New York: Columbia University Press, 1987), p. 214.

31. Association of College Unions, see note 29.

32. "Sapphire and Sappho: Allies in Authenticity," by B. J. Allen, *Our Voices*, 1997, p. 144.

33. "Intercultural Communication," by T. Steinfatt & D. M. Christophel, in *An Integrated Approach to Communication Theory*, edited by M. B. Salwen & D. W. Stacks (Mahwah, NJ: Erlbaum and Associates, 1996), p. 330.

34. "Intercultural Communication," by E. Glenn & E. Stewart, *Communication*, 3, 1974, p. 26.

35. *"Intercultural Communication,"* by Steinfatt & Christophel, p. 319.

36. *Dynamics of Intercultural Communication*, 3d ed., by C. Dodd (Dubuque, IA: Wm. C. Brown, 1991), pp. 22–27.

37. *Communication Across Cultures*, by S. Ting-Toomey (New York: Guilford, 1991), p. 16.

38. *Strategies for Marketing to Japanese Visitors*, by K. Nishiyama (Needham Heights, MA: Ginn, 1989), p. 109.

39. *A Further Analysis of Communication Style Among Japanese and American Communicators*, by S. Ishii, C. Thomas, & D. Klopf, paper presented at Tokyo convention of the Communication Association of Japan, 1994.

40. *Understanding Japanese Communicators*, by A. Sato (Tokyo: *Japan Times*, 1992), pp. 77–89.

41. *Communicating in Personal Relationships Across Cultures*, by W.B. Gudykunst, S. Ting-Toomey, & T. Nishida (Thousand Oaks, CA: Sage, 1996), p. 37.

42. "Intercultural Communication," Steinfatt & Christophel, pp. 323–324.

43. *Preventing Prejudice: A Guide for Counselors and Educators*, by J. G. Ponterotto & P. B. Pedersen (Newbury Park, CA: Sage, 1993), pp. 5–6.

44. *Intercultural Communication*, by E. M. Rogers & T. M. Steinfatt (Prospect Heights, IL: Waveland, 1999), p. 56.

Chapter 4

1. *Human Behavior: An Inventory of Scientific Findings*, by B. Berelson & G. A. Steiner (New York: Harcourt Brace & World, 1964), p. 88.

2. *Perception*, by J. E. Hochberg (Englewood Cliffs, NJ: Prentice Hall, 1978), p. 9.

3. "The Role of Culture and Perception in Communication," by M. R. Singer in *Culture, Communication and Conflict: Readings in Intercultural Relations*, 2d ed., edited by G. R. Weaver (Needham Heights, MA: Simon and Schuster, 1998), pp. 36–37.

4. *Intercultural Interactions: A Practical Guide*, 2d ed., by K. Cushner & R. W. Brislin (Thousand Oaks, CA: Sage, 1996), p. 14.

5. *Human Motivation*, by R. Geen, W. Beatty, & R. Arkin (Boston: Allyn & Bacon, 1984), p. 25.

6. *Cross-Cultural Communication*, by D. Klopf & M-S Park (Seoul, Korea: Han Shin, 1992), p. 33.

7. *Interpersonal Communication: A Question of Needs*, by M. Scott & W. Powers (Boston: Houghton Mifflin, 1978), p. 25.

8. *Intercultural Communication*, by L. Harms (New York: Harper and Row, 1973), p. 20.

9. "Toward a Sociological Theory of Motivation," by J. H. Turner, quoted in *Bridging Differences: Effective Inter-group Communication*, by W. Gudykunst (Newbury Park, CA: Sage, 1991), p. 106.

10. "A Theory of Human Motivation," by A. Maslow, *Psychological Review*, 50 (1943) 295.

11. *Psychology*, by C. Wade & C. Tavris (New York: Harper and Row, 1987), p. 380.

12. "The Cultural Relativity of the Quality of Life Concept," by G. Hofstede, in *Culture, Communication and Conflict*, edited by G. R. Weaver (Needham, MA: Simon and Schuster, 1998), pp. 148–158.

13. *The FIRO Scales*, by W. Schutz (Palo Alto, CA: Consulting Psychologists Press 1967), p. 25.

14. *Korean Communicative Behaviors: Recent Research Findings*, by D. W. Klopf & M-S Park (Seoul, Korea: Communication Association of Korea Press, 1994), pp. 17–21.

Chapter 5

1. "Culture and Business: Interacting Effectively to Achieve Mutual Goals," by Mu Dan Ping in *Culture, Communication and Conflict*, 2d ed., edited by G. R. Weaver (Needham, MA: Simon and Schuster, 1998), p. 531.

2. "Cultural Influences on Identity and Behavior: India and Britain," by P. Laungani in *Personality and Person Perception Across Cultures*, edited by Y-T Lee, C. R. McCauley, & J. G. Draguns (Mahwah, NJ: Lawrence Erlbaum, 1999), p. 191.

3. "Cultural Influences," by Laungani.

4. *Social Psychology Across Cultures: Analysis and Perspectives,* by P. B. Smith & M. H. Bond (Hemel Hempstead, England: Harvester Wheatshaft, 1993), p. 22.

5. *Intercultural Interactions: A Practical Guide*, 2d ed., by K. Cushner & R. W. Brislin (Thousand Oaks, CA: Sage, 1996), p. 319.

6. *Communication Between Cultures*, 3d ed., by L. Samovar, R. E. Porter, & L. A. Stefani (Belmont, CA: Wadsworth, 1998), p. 60.

7. *Communicating Across Cultures*, by S. Ting-Toomey (New York: Guilford, 1999), pp. 57–58.

8. *Communication Between Cultures*, p. 62.

9. *Communicating with Americans*, by D. W. Klopf & M-S Park (Seoul, Korea: Han Shin, 1994), pp. 14–21.

10. "Value Priorities and Social Desirability: Much Substance, Some Style," by S. H. Schwartz, M. Verkasalo, A. Antonovsky, & L. Sagiv, *British Journal of Social Psychology*, 36 (1997), p. 7.

11. *Communication Between Cultures*, p. 73.

12. *Communicating Effectively with the Chinese*, by G. Gao and S. Ting-Toomey (Thousand Oaks, CA: Sage, 1998), p. 9.

13. "The Cultural Relativity of the Quality of Life Concept," by G. Hofstede, in *Culture, Communication and Conflict*, pp. 149–150.

14. *Communication Between Cultures*, p. 70.

15. "The Cultural Relativity," by G. Hofstede, in *Culture, Communication and Conflict*, pp. 149–50.

16. Ibid., p. 149.

17. Ibid., p. 150.

18. *Understanding Vietnam*, by N. L. Jamieson (Berkeley: University of California Press, 1995), p. 312.

19. *Intercultural Competence: Interpersonal Communication Across Cultures* by J. W. Lustig & J. Koester (New York: Longman, 1999), p. 87.

20. *Intercultural Communication in Contexts* by J. N. Martin, & T. K. Nakayama (Mountain View, CA: Mayfield, 1997), p. 53.

21. "A Multidimensional Measure of Cultural Identity for Latino and Latina Adolescents," by Felix-Ortiz de la Garza, M. D. Newcomb, & H. F. Myers in *Hispanic Psychology: Critical Issues in Theory and Research*, edited by A. M. Padilla (Thousand Oaks, CA: Sage, 1995), p. 38.

22. *Variations in Value Orientations*, by F. Kluckhohn & F. Strodtbeck (Chicago: Row, Peterson, 1961), p. 11.

23. *Managing Cultural Differences*, 3d ed., by P. R. Harris & R. T. Moran (Houston: Gulf, 1991), pp. 265–266.

24. Ibid, pp. 265–267.

25. *Intercultural Competence*, p. 80.

26. *Communication Between Cultures*, pp. 58–59.

27. *Managing Cultural Differences*, p. 41.

28. R. B. Kaplan, quoted in "The Role of Culture and Perception in Communication," by M. R. Singer, in *Culture, Communication and Conflict*, p. 47.

29. "The Role of Culture and Perception in Communication," by M. R. Singer, in *Culture, Communication and Conflict*, Singer, p. 47.

30. "Dominant Cultural-Patterns of Hindus in India," by N. Jain & E. D. Kussmanin in *Intercultural Communication: A Reader*, 8th ed., edited by L. A. Samovar & R. E. Porter (Belmont, CA: Wadsworth, 1997), pp. 89–97.

31. "Differences in World View Among Japanese, Puerto Rican, and American College Students," by S. Ishii, P. Cooke, D. Klopf, & J. Fayer, *Otsuma Women's University Annual Report*, 25, (1993), 96.

32. *The Relationship Between Culture and World View: A Cross-Cultural Comparison of Japan, Korea, Puerto Rico and the United States.* Unpublished master's thesis by P. Cooke, West Virginia University, 1992.

33. *The Social Psychology of Interpersonal Discrimination*, by B. Lott & D. Maluso (New York: Guilford, 1995), p. 23.

34. *Intercultural Communication*, by E. M. Rogers & T. M Steinfatt (Prospect Heights, IL: Waveland, 1999), p. 81.

35. "The Role of Culture and Perception in Communication," by M. R. Singer, in *Culture, Communication and Conflict*, p. 41.

36. *Introduction to Social Psychology*, by D. J. Schneider (San Diego: Harcourt Brace Jovanovich, 1988), pp. 180–181.

37. Ibid.

Chapter 6

1. "Asian Indian Americans," by M. Sheth, in *Asian Americans: Contemporary Trends and Issues*, edited by P. O. Min (Thousand Oaks, CA: Sage, 1995), pp. 182–183.

2. *Folkways*, by W. Summer (New York: New American Library, 1906), pp. 28–29.

3. *Folkways*, pp. 27–28.

4. *Public Speaking in a Diverse Society*, by P. Kearney & T. G. Plax (Mountain View, CA: Mayfield, 1996), p. 19.

5. *Public Speaking*, p. 27.

6. "Domestic Multiculturalism: Cross-Cultural Management in the Public Sector," by N. J. Adler in *Culture, Communication and Conflict: Readings in Intercultural Relations,* edited by G. R. Weaver (Needham, MA: Simon & Schuster, 1998), p. 124.

7. "Social Psychological Foundations of Stereotype Formation," by D. Mackie, D. Hamilton, J. Susskind, & F. Rosselli, in *Stereotypes and Stereotyping*, edited by C. N. Macrae, C. Stagnor, & M. Hewstone (New York: Guilford, 1996), p. 41.

8. *Elite Discourse and Racism*, by T. A. van Dijk (Newbury Park, CA: Sage, 1993), pp 202–209.

9. "Social Psychological Foundations," p. 42.

10. Ibid., pp. 42–43.

11. *The Social Psychology of Interpersonal Discrimination*, by B. Lott & D. Maluso (New York: Guilford, 1995), p. 80–180.

12. "A Chinese Stereotype Image of Japan and Its People," by T. Yoshitake, *Communication*, 6 (1977), 23.

13. Published by Addison-Wesley, Cambridge, MA, 1954, (p. xiii).

14. *Communicating Prejudice,* by M. L. Hecht (Thousand Oaks, CA: Sage, 1998), p. 4.

15. Ibid., p. 4.

16. Ibid.

17. "Stereotyping, Prejudice, and Discrimination: Another Look," by J. Dovidio, J. C. Brigham, B. T. Johnson, & S. L. Gardner, in *Stereotypes and Stereotyping*, p. 278.

18. *The Nature of Prejudice*, by G. W. Allport, p. 9 (Note 13).

19. *Preventing Prejudice*, by J. G. Ponterotto & P. B. Pedersen (Newbury Park, CA: Sage, 1993), pp. 10–11.

20. *Elite Discourse and Racism*, pp. 39–44.

21. Ibid., p. 59.

22. "Tolerance/Intolerance: A Multidisciplinary View of Prejudice," by J. R. Baldwin, in *Communicating Prejudice*, pp. 24–56.

23. *Preventing Prejudice*, pp. 34–35.

24. "The Use of Hate as a Stratagem for Achieving Political and Social Goals," by R. K. Whillock, in *Hate Speech*, edited by R. K. Whillock & D. Slayden (Thousand Oaks, CA: Sage, 1995), p. 32.

25. "Twins Separated at Birth: The Strange Case of Michael Levin and Leonard Jeffries," by J. Dee, in *Howard Journal of Communication, 5 (1995)*, 290.

26. "Hate Speech—The Egalitarian/Libertarian Dilemma," by J. J. Hemmer, Jr., *Howard Journal* (1995), 307.

27. "There's Such a Thing as Free Speech and It's a Good Thing, Too," by S. A. Smith, in "*Hate Speech,*" by Hemmer, pp. 248–49.

28. *Intercultural Communication: An Introduction,* by F. Jandt (Thousand Oaks, CA: Sage, 1995), 63.

29. *Preventing Prejudice,* by Ponterotto & Pedersen, pp. 34–35.

30. "Civil Rights Issues Facing Asian Americans in the 1990s," by K-T Chun & N. Zalokar (Washington DC: U.S. Commission on Civil Rights, 1992), pp. 130–131.

31. "Ageism in Interpersonal Settings," by M. Pasupathi, L. L. Carstensen, & J. L. Tsai in *The Social Psychology of Interpersonal Discrimination*, Lott & Maluso, pp. 160–161.

32. "Ageism," pp. 177–179.

33. "Distancing from Women: Interpersonal Sexist Discrimination," by B. Lott, in *The Social Psychology*, pp. 13–14.

34. "Communication of Sexism," by L. Rakow & L. Wackwitz, in *Communicating Prejudice,*" pp. 100–102.

35. Ibid., pp. 106–108.

36. "Civil Rights Issues," pp. 153–155.

37. "Class Acts: Middle-Class Responses to the Poor," by H. D. Bullock, in *The Social Psychology,* Lott and Maluso, pp. 135–140.

38. "Communication of Classism," by D. Moon & G. L. Rolison, in *The Social Psychology*, p. 132.

39. Ibid., p. 133.

40. "Interpersonal Heterosexism," by J. Fernald, in *The Social Psychology*, p. 80.

41. Ibid., pp. 92–110.

42. "Shaking Hands with a Clenched Fist: Interpersonal Racism," by D. Maluso, in *The Social Psychology*, p. 51.

43. *Intercultural Communication*, by E. M. Rogers & T. M. Steinfatt (Prospect Heights, IL: Waveland, 1999), p. 56.

44. *The Nature of Prejudice*, pp. 57–59.

45. "Bigotry and Bias Are Alive and Well," by M. Robinson, in *International Herald Tribune*, March 23, 2000.

46. Ibid.

Chapter 7

1. Compiled from *Sociology*, 4th ed., by N. J. Smelser (Englewood Cliffs, NJ: Prentice Hall, 1991), pp. 244–264; *Culturgrams: The Nations Around Us*, by David M. Kennedy, Center for International Studies (Provo, UT: Kennedy Center, 1985–86); *Intercultural Competence*, 3d ed. by M. Lustig & J. Koester (New York: Longman, 1999), pp. 267–269; *Communication Between Cultures*, 3d ed., by L. A. Samovar, R. E. Porter, & L. A. Stefani (Belmont, CA: Wadsworth, 1998), pp. 105–111.

2. *Anthropology: The Biocultural View*, by F. Johnston & H. Shelby (Dubuque, IA: Wm. C. Brown, 1978), pp. 410–419.

3. *Communication Between Cultures*, 2d ed., by L. A. Samovar & R. E. Porter (Belmont, CA: Wadsworth 1995), pp. 242–245.

4. *Human Behavior in a Global Perspective,* edited by M. Segall, P. Dasen, J. Berry & Y. Poortinga (New York: Pergamon, 1990), pp. 124–125.

5. "Intercultural Communication and the Classroom," by J. Andersen & R. Powell, in *Intercultural Communication: A Reader,* 6th ed., edited by L. Samovar & R. E. Porter (Belmont, CA: Wadsworth, 1991), pp. 209–221.

6. "Cross-Cultural Psychology and the Formal Classroom," by K. Cushner, in *Applied Cross-Cultural Psychology* edited by R. Brislin (Newbury Park, CA: Sage), 103.

7. "Intercultural Communication and the Classroom."

8. "Approaches to Learning of Asian Students: A Multiple Paradox," by J. Briggs, in *Asian Contributions to Cross-Cultural Psychology,* edited by J. Pandey, D. Sinha & D. P. S. Bhawuk (New Delhi: Sage, 1996), pp. 180–199.

9. "Cross-Cultural Psychology," pp. 98–99.

10. *Sociology,* p. 289.

11. *Anthropology: The Cultural Perspective*, 2d ed., by J. Spradley & D. McCurdy (Prospect Heights, IL: Waveland, 1989), 385.

12. *The Elementary Forms of Religious Life,* by E. Durkheim (Glencoe, IL: Free Press, 1966), p. 62.

13. *Sociology*, pp. 288–309.

14. *Nana I Ke Kuma,* by M. Pukui, E. Haertig, & C. Lee (Honolulu: Queen Liliuokalani Children's Center, 1972), p. 23.

15. Ibid.

16. "Religious-caused Complications in Intercultural Communication," by R. Smart, in *Intercultural Communication: A Reader,* 5th ed., edited by L. Samovar & R. Porter (Belmont, CA: Wadsworth, 1988), pp. 63–75.

17. The statistics and general data about the major religions noted in this chapter are from *Time Almanac 2000 with Information Please,* 1999, pp. 404–410.

18. *Anthropology*, p. 206.

19. "What is an Economy For?" by James Fellows, *Atlantic Monthly*, January 1994, pp. 55–70.

20. Ibid.

Chapter 8

1. *Honolulu Advertiser*, January 26, 1997, E1–E10.

2. *Exploring the Greek Mosaic*, by B. J. Broome (Yarmouth, ME: Intercultural Press, 1996), p. 138.

3. *Update: Federal Republic of Germany,* by N. P. Loewenthal (Yarmouth, ME: Intercultural Press, 1990), pp. 41–45.

4. *Personal and Public Speaking*, 5th ed., by D. Klopf & R. Cambra (Englewood, CO: Morton, 1996), p. 146.

5. *Fundamentals of Human Communication*, by J. C. McCroskey & V. P. Richmond (Prospect Heights, IL: Waveland, 1996), pp. 223–224.

6. *Welcoming the Japanese Visitor*, by K. Nishiyama (Honolulu: University of Hawaii Press, 1996), p. 157.

7. *Dynamics of Intercultural Communication*, by C. Dodd, 3d ed. (Dubuque, IA: Wm. C. Brown, 1991), p. 32.

8. *Welcoming the Japanese Visitor*, pp. 160–161.

9. "Cultural Assumptions and Values," by E. C. Stewart, J. Danielian, & R. J. Foster, in *Basic Concepts of Intercultural Communication*, edited by M. J. Bennett (Yarmouth, ME: Intercultural Press, 1998), p. 163.

10. Ibid., pp. 163–171.

11. *Into Africa: Intercultural Insights,* by Y. Richmond & P. Gestrin (Yarmouth, ME: Intercultural Press, 1998), p. 60.

12. *Interpersonal Communication: Relating to Others,* 2d ed., by S. A. Beebe, S. J. Beebe, & M. V. Redmond (Boston: Allyn & Bacon, 1999), pp. 300–301.

13. *Exploring the Greek Mosaic,* p. 71.

14. *Communicating Effectively with the Chinese,* by G. Gao & S. Ting-Toomey (Thousand Oaks, CA: Sage, 1998), p. 37.

15. *A Fair Go for All: Australian/American Interactions,* by G. Renwick (Yarmouth, ME: Intercultural Press, 1991), pp. 28–29.

16. *Avoiding Communication: Shyness, Reticence, and Communication Apprehension,* 2d ed., by J. Daly, J. C. McCroskey, J. Ayres, T. Hopf, & D. Ayres (Cresskill, NJ: Hampton, 1997), pp. 3–4.

17. "Correlates and Consequences of Social-Communicative Anxiety," by J. Daly, J. P. Couglin, & L. Stafford in *Avoiding Communication,* pp. 21–44.

18. "Cross-Cultural Apprehension Research: Procedures and Comparisons," in *Avoiding Communication,* pp. 269–281.

19. "The Measurement of Verbal Predispositions Scale: Development and Application," by C. Mortensen, P. Arnston, & M. Lustig, in *Human Communication Research,* 3 (1997), 146–158.

20. The cross-cultural comparisons in this section and the next are drawn from *Korean Communicative Behavior* by D. W. Klopf & M-S Park (Seoul: Communication Association of Korea, 1994), a compilation of results from a decade-old series of research projects involving researchers and subjects in Pacific-area countries, partially funded by the Communication Association of Korea.

21. The cross-cultural comparisons in this section are drawn from Japanese *Communicative Behavior: Recent Research Findings,* by D. W. Klopf, S. Ishii, & R. Cambra (Tokyo: Pacific and Asian Press, 1994), a compilation of results from a series of research projects involving researchers and subjects in Pacific area, USA, and European countries, partially funded by the Pacific and Asian Communication Association.

Chapter 9

1. *The Story of Language,* by M. Pei (New York: New American Library, 1965), pp. 107–108.

2. *An Introduction to Language,* by V. Fromkin & R. Rodman (New York: Holt, Rinehart & Winston, 1974), pp. 70–78.

3. *Psychology,* by L. Benjamin, Jr., L. J. Hopkins, & J. Nation (New York: Macmillan, 1987), p. 231.

4. *An Introduction to Language,* pp. 224–236.

5. *Theories of Human Communication,* 6th ed., by S. Littlejohn (Belmont, CA: Wadsworth, 1999), pp. 155–156.

6. *Theories of Human Communication,* p. 192.

7. *Speaking Culturally: Language Diversity in the United States,* by F. L. Johnson (Thousand Oaks, CA: Sage, 2000) p. 51.

8. Ibid.

9. *Theories of Human Communication,* pp. 193–196.

10. *Intercultural Communication: Roots and Routes,* by C. Calloway-Thomas, P. J. Cooper, & C. Blake (Boston: Allyn & Bacon, 1999), pp. 148–149.

11. *Theories of Human Communication,* pp. 193–196.

12. *The Rhetoric of Aristotle,* by L. Cooper (New York: Appleton-Century-Crofts, 1932), pp. 181–182.

13. *Culture and Interpersonal Communication,* by W. Gudykunst & S. Ting-Toomey (Newbury Park, CA: Sage, 1988), p. 100.

14. "Fifty Terms for Talk: A Cross-Cultural Study," by D. Carbaugh, in *Language, Communication, and Culture: Current Directions,* edited by S. Ting-Toomey & F. Korzenny (Newbury Park, CA: Sage, 1989), p. 100.

15. *Culture and Interpersonal Communication,* pp. 100–105.

16. *USA Today,* Feb. 28–March 2, 1997, IA, 8–9A.

17. *Communicating Today,* 2d ed., by R. Zeuschner (Needham, MA: Allyn & Bacon, 1997), pp. 393–394.

18. *Fundamentals of Human Communication,* by J. C. McCroskey & V. Richmond (Prospect Heights, IL: Waveland, 1996), pp. 301–302.

19. *Interpersonal Communication: Everyday Encounters,* 2d ed., by J. T. Wood (Belmont, CA: Wadsworth, 1999), p. 251.

20. *Fundamentals of Human Communication,* p. 303.

21. *Communicating with the Japanese,* by J. V. Neustupny (Tokyo: Japan Times, 1987), pp. 30, 75.

22. *An Exploratory Study of Perceived Values Among Filipinos in Hawaii,* by A. Golis, (unpublished manuscript, University of Hawaii, 1978).

23. *Behaving Brazilian: A Comparison of Brazilian and North American Social Behavior,* by P. Harrison (Cambridge, MA: Newbury House, 1983), pp. 24–31.

24. *Managing Cultural Differences*, 3d ed. by P. Harris & R. Moran (Houston: Gulf, 1991), pp. 382–386, 500–507.

25. "Social Styles of Finns and Americans," by C. Sallinen-Kuparinen, C. Thompson, & D. Klopf, *Psychological Reports, 68* (1991), 193–194.

26. *African American Communication: Ethnic and Cultural Interpretation*, by M. Hecht, M. J. Collier, & S. Ribeau (Newbury Park, CA: Sage, 1993), 19, 89.

27. *But I Thought You Meant . . . Misunderstandings in Human Communication*, by J. T. Wood (Mountain View, CA: Mayfield, 1998), p. 163.

28. *Speaking Culturally*, pp. 133–136.

29. Ibid., p. 137.

30. Ibid., pp. 150–156.

31. Ibid., pp. 238–241.

32. Ibid., pp. 161–162.

33. *Good Neighbors: Communicating with the Mexicans*, by J. C. Condon (Yarmouth, ME: Intercultural Press, 1985), pp. 41–46.

34. "The Rhetoric of *La Familia* Among Mexican Americans," by M. Gangotena, in *Our Voices: Essays In Culture, Ethnicity and Communication*, edited by A. Gonzales, M. Houston, & V. Chen (Los Angeles: Roxbury, 1997), pp. 75–81.

35. Ibid.

36. *Dynamics of Intercultural Communication*, 3d ed., by C. A. Dodd (Dubuque, IA: Wm. Brown, 1991), pp. 127–142.

Chapter 10

1. *Communicating Today*, by R. Zeuschner, 2d ed. (Boston: Allyn & Bacon, 1997), p. 80.

2. *Intercultural Competence. Interpersonal Communication Across Cultures*, 3d ed., by M. W. Lustig & J. Koester (New York: Longman 1999), p. 205.

3. Ibid, p. 206.

4. "Sekai 20-kakoku Nonbabaru Jiten," by N. Kanayama in *Japanese Communicative Behavior: Recent Research Findings*, edited by D. W. Klopf, S. Ishii, & R. E. Cambra (Tokyo: Pacific & Asian Press 1997), p. 68.

5. "Japanese Nonverbal Communicative Signs: A Cross-Cultural Survey," by S. Ishii in *Japanese Communicative Behavior*, p. 69.

6. *Intercultural Competence*, p. 208.

7. Ibid., pp. 208–211.

8. "Decoding Inconsistent Communications," by A. Mehrabian & M. Wiener, *Journal of Personality and Social Psychology*, 6 (1967), pp. 109–114.

9. *Intercultural Communication*, by E. M. Rogers & T. M. Steinfatt (Prospect Heights, IL: Waveland, 1999), pp. 162–165.

10. "Communication in Personal Relationships in Iran: A Comparative Analysis," by F. Zandpour & G. Sadri, in *Communication in Personal Relationships Across Cultures*, edited by W. B. Gudykunst, S. Ting-Toomey, & T. Nishida (Thousand Oaks, CA: Sage 1996), pp. 192–193.

11. "An Intercultural Comparison of Immediacy Among Japanese and Americans," by L. Boyer, C. Thompson, D. Klopf, & S. Ishii, *Perceptual and Motor Skills*, 73 (1990), pp. 65–66.

12. "Nonverbal Immediacy Differences Among Japanese, Finnish and American University Students," by D. Klopf, C. Thompson, S. Ishii, & A. Salinen-Kuparinen, *Perceptual and Motor Skills*, 73 (1991), pp. 209–210.

13. *Gestures: The Do's and Taboos of Body Language Around the World*, by R. Axtell (New York: John Wiley, 1991), p. 14.

14. "The Repertoire of Nonverbal Behavior: Categories, Origins, Usage, and Coding," by P. Ekman & W. Friesen, *Semiotica*, 1 (1969), p. 25.

15. Ibid.

16. *Gestures*, by D. Morris, P. Collett, P. Marsh, & M. O'Shaughnessy (New York: Stein & Day, 1979), p. vii.

17. Ibid., p. 51.

18. *Atlas of Man: A Guide for Somatyping the Adult Male of All Ages*, by W. Sheldon (New York: Harper & Row, 1954), p. 108.

19. *Nonverbal Communication in Human Interaction*, 3d ed., by N. Knapp & J. R. Hall (New York: Holt, Rinehart and Winston, 1992), pp. 13–16.

20. "Scenes from an Individual of Color: On Individuals and Individualism," by V. Villanueva, Jr., in *Communicating Prejudice*, edited by M. L. Hecht (Thousand Oaks, CA: Sage, 1998), p. 237.

21. *Communicating Between Cultures*, 3d ed., by L. Samovar, R. Porter, & L. Stefani (Belmont, CA: Wadsworth, 1998), p. 162.

22. "Hair: Taking It All Off the Top," by K. Knorr, *International Herald Tribune*, March 1, 2000, p. 21.

23. *Eye to Eye: How People Interact*, by P. Marsh (Oxford, England: Andromeda Oxford, 1988), p. 63.

24. Ibid.

25. *Considering Filipinos*, by T. Gochenour (Yarmouth, ME: Intercultural Press, 1990), p. 59.

26. *Eye to Eye*, pp. 62–64.

27. *Encountering the Chinese: A Guide for Americans*, by W. Hu & C. L. Grove (Yarmouth, ME: Intercultural Press, 1991).

28. *Understanding Arabs: A Guide for Westerners*, by M. K. Nydell (Yarmouth, ME: Intercultural Press, 1987), p. 71.

29. *Into Africa: Intercultural Insights*, by Y. Richmond & P. Gestrin (Yarmouth, ME: Intercultural Press, 1998), pp. 132–133.

30. *Communicating Between Cultures*, p. 154.

31. *Fundamentals of Human Communication: An Interpersonal Perspective*, by J. C. McCroskey & V. P. Richmond (Prospect Heights, IL: Waveland, 1996), p. 189.

32. *The Hidden Dimension*, by E. T. Hall (Garden City, NY: Doubleday, 1996), pp. 13, 57–58.

33. *Eye to Eye*, p. 90.

34. *Understanding Arabs*, pp. 44–45.

35. *Into Africa*, p. 95.

36. *Spain Is Different*, by H. W. Ames (Yarmouth, ME: Intercultural Press, 1992), pp. 66–67.

37. "Explaining Intercultural Differences in Nonverbal Communication," by P. Andersen, in *Intercultural Communication: A Reader*, edited by L. Samovar & R. Porter (Belmont, CA: Wadsworth, 1990), p. 289.

38. *A Cross-Cultural Study of Touch Avoidance*, by B. Casteel (Master's thesis, West Virginia University, Morgantown, 1992).

39. Ibid.

40. *Exploring the Greek Mosaic: A Guide to Intercultural Communication in Greece*, by B. J. Broome (Yarmouth, ME: Intercultural Press, 1996), p. 71.

41. *Understanding Arabs*, p. 104.

42. *Spain Is Different*, p. 69.

43. *Intercultural Communication: Roots and Routes*, by C. Calloway-Thomas, P. J. Cooper, & C. Blake (Boston: Allyn & Bacon, 1999), p. 167.

44. *Into Africa*, p. 88.

45. *Kiss, Bow, or Shake Hands*, by T. Morrison, W. A. Conaway, & G. A. Borden (Holbrook, MA: Bob Adams, 1994), p. 208.

46. *Encountering the Chinese*, p. 27.

47. *African American Communication: Ethnic Identity and Cultural Interpretation*, by M. L. Hecht, M. J. Collier, & S. A. Ribeau (Newbury Park, CA: Sage, 1993), p. 93.

48. *The Hidden Dimension*, Hall, p. 1.

49. *Eye to Eye*, p. 42.

50. *Understanding Arabs*, pp. 44–45.

51. *Understanding Cultural Differences: Germans, French and Americans*, by E. Hall & M. Hall (Yarmouth, ME: Intercultural Press, 1990), pp. 13–15.

52. *African American Communication*, p. 112.

53. *Understanding Cultural Differences*.

54. Ibid., pp. 173–174.

55. Ibid., pp. 13–15.

Chapter 11

1. *Managing Cultural Differences*, 3d ed., by P. Harris & R. Moran (Houston: Gulf, 1992), p. 59.

2. "Understanding and Coping with Cross-Cultural Adjustment Stress," by G.R. Weaver, in *Culture, Communication and Conflict: Readings in Intercultural Relations*, 2d ed., edited by G. R. Weaver (Needham, MA: Simon and Schuster, 1998), p. 187. For additional writings on adaptation, what it entails, how it occurs, and the factors involved, see Y.Y. Kim, *Becoming Intercultural* (Thousand Oaks: Sage, 2001).

3. "Communication in a Global Village," by D. Barnlund, in *Intercultural Communication: A Reader*, 8th ed., edited by L. Samovar and R. Porter (Belmont, CA: Wadsworth, 1997), p. 34.

4. *On Being Foreign: Culture Shock in Short Fiction*, edited by T. Lewis & R. Jungman (Yarmouth, ME: Intercultural Press, 1986), p. xvii.

5. Ibid, p. xviii.

6. *Dynamics of Intercultural Communication*, 3d ed., by C. Dodd (Dubuque, IA: Wm. C. Brown, 1991), p. 305.

7. *Managing Cultural Differences*, p. 225.

8. "Understanding and Coping with Cross-Cultural Adjustment Stress."

9. "Culture Shock and the Problem of Adjustment in New Cultural Environments," in *Culture, Communication and Conflict* (1998), p. 185–186.

10. "Reentry Training for Intercultural Sojourners," by J. N. Martin, & T. Harrell, in *Handbook of Intercultural Training*, 2d ed., edited by D. Landis and R. S. Bhagat (Thousand Oaks, CA: Sage, 1996), p. 310.

11. Ibid., pp. 310–314.

12. "Reentry Training for Intercultural Sojourners," p. 314; for a summary of the entry-re-entry research literature, see "Crossing Cultures: The Relationship between Psychological and Socio-cultural Dimensions of Cross-Cultural Adjustment," by C. A. Ward & A. Kennedy, in *Asian Contributions to Cross-Cultural Psychology*, edited by Janak Pandey, D. Sinha & D. P. S. Bhawuk (New Delhi, India: Sage, 1996), pp. 289–306.

13. *Dynamics of Intercultural Communication*, p. 310.

14. "Counseling the Hispanic Client: A Theoretical and Applied Perspective," by J. M. Casas & M. J. T. Vasquez in *Counseling Across Cultures*, 3d ed., edited by P. B. Pedersen, J. G. Draguns, W. J. Lonner, & J. E. Trimble (Honolulu: University of Hawaii Press, 1989), p. 164.

15. "Psychology of Acculturation: Understanding Individuals Moving Between Cultures," by J. W. Berry, in *Applied Cross-Cultural Psychology*, edited by R. W. Brislin (Newbury Park, CA: Sage, 1990), pp. 232–253.

16. *The Cross-Cultural Adaptation Inventory* (Yarmouth, ME: Intercultural Press, 1992).

17. *Applied Cross-Cultural Psychology*, Brislin.

18. *Multicultural Education in a Pluralistic Society,* 3d edition, by D. Gollnick & P. Chinn (New York: Merrill, 1990), p. 18.

19. Ibid, pp. 19–20.

20. Ibid, pp. 2–21.

Chapter 12

1. "How to Succeed in Business Abroad," by C. Tavris, in *Signature*, Jan., 1987 p. 25.

2. "A Framework and Model for Understanding Latin American and Latin/Hispanic Cultural Patterns," by R. D. Albert, in *Handbook of Intercultural Training*, 2d ed., edited by D. Landis and R.S. Bhagat (Thousand Oaks, CA: Sage, 1996), p. 334.

3. "A Framework," p. 333.

4. "How to Succeed," p. 26.

5. "A Framework," p. 342–343.

6. "A Framework," p. 341–343.

7. "Designing Intercultural Training," by W. B. Gudykunst, R. M. Guzley, & M. R. Hammer, in *Handbook of Intercultural Training*, p. 73.

8. "A Framework," p. 333–338.

9. "The Challenge of International Personnel Selection," by D. J. Kealey, in *Handbook*, p. 83.

10. Ibid., p. 84.

11. "Ethics in Intercultural Training," by R. M. Paige & J. N. Martin, in *Handbook*, p. 54.

12. *Communicating Across Cultures*, by S. Ting-Toomey (New York: Guilford, 1999), p. 271–275.

13. Ibid.

14. *Intercultural Communication: Roots and Routes,* by C. Calloway-Thomas, P. J. Cooper, & C. Blake (Boston: Allyn & Bacon, 1999), p. 115.

Web Sites

Africa Online

http://www.africaonline.com

A resource for information on Africa, including Namibia, Kenya, Tanzania, Swaziland.

Asia Source

http://www.asiasource

A resource for obtaining information on the Asia Society, including information on the arts, culture, business, economics, government, society, and history.

Center for Disease Control and Prevention, Travelers' Health

http://www.cdc.gov/travel/index.htm

Provides health information for traveling to other countries, plus helpful related links to other sites on world health.

Crosscultural Communications (Chinese)

http://mimsmedia.utdallas.edu/ crosscultcomm/Default.htm

Describes implications and considerations arising in communicating between Chinese cultures and U. S. cultures.

Currency Converter

http://www.xe.net/ucc

Allows you to perform interactive foreign exchange rate conversion on the Internet.

Electronic Embassy

http://www.embassy.org

A resource providing information on all of the foreign embassies of Washington DC.

Foreign Languages for Travelers

http://www.travlang.com/languages

Audio and text instruction on learning a foreign language via the web.

Governments on the WWW

http://www.gksoft.com/govt

Database of governmental institutions: parliaments, ministries, offices, law courts, embassies, city councils, public broadcasting corporations, central banks, and multi-governmental institutions.

Immigration and Naturalization Service (INS)

http://www.ins.usdoj.gov

Up-to-date information about the agency and the services the INS provides.

International Constitutional Law

http://www.uni-wuerzburg.de/law/index. html

The constitutions of more than 130 countries of the world, information about their laws on freedom, rights, plus some history and news of the country.

Intercultural Relations

http://kumo.swcp.com/biz/theedge

Articles on intercultural relations from 1997 through 1999.

Japan Information Network

http://jin.jcic.or.jp

In-depth information on the Japanese culture.

Korea on the Internet

http://www2.hawaii.edu/korea/ koreaotherlinks.htm

Links to Korea, Korean Studies, and the Korean-American community.

Latin America and Caribbean Countries

http://lanic.utexas.edu/subject/countries.html

A listing of Latin American and Caribbean countries, detailing information on each country's academia, art and culture, economy, general information, government, human rights, newsgroups, and travel and tourism.

Library of Congress Country Studies

http://lcweb2.loc.gov/frd/cs

A handbook program that describes and analyzes the historical setting, social, economic, political, national security systems and institutions of countries throughout the world. Also examines the interrelationships of those systems and the ways they are shaped by cultural factors.

National Association for Ethnic Studies

http://www.ksu.edu/ameth/naes

A forum for scholars and activists concerned with the national and international dimensions of ethnicity. Click on the "Ethnic Web Sites Other Resources" for an expansive list of website links.

One World

http://www.fiu.edu/~escotet/index1.html

A source for linking to international and intercultural development; links to live radio and television, statistics on countries, and much more.

(Online) Dictionaries

http://www.yourdictionary.com
http://www.elite.net/~runner/jennifers/language.htm

Indexes online dictionaries, thesauruses, and other resources containing words and phrases by languages throughout the world.

Orient Encyclopedia

http://i-cias.com/i-e.o/2b.htm

An encyclopedia covering all countries and cultures between Mauritania in the West and Iran in the East, Turkey in the North and Sudan in the South.

Russian and East European Network Information Center

http://reenic.utexas.edu/reenic.html

Collection of links with information about East and Central Europe, Russia, and independent countries of the former Soviet Union.

United Nations

http://www.un.org

Offers educational resources on countries around the world. Check "Cyber School Bus" under site index.

U.S. Census Bureau

http://www.censuls.gov

Disseminates data about the people and economy of the United States.

U.S. State Department Background Notes

http://www.state.gov/www/background notes/index.html

Provides information on the geography, people, government, economy, history, political conditions, transportation and communication, defense, foreign relations, and travel and business information of foreign countries.

University Currency Converter

http://www.xe.net/~ucc

Performs interactive foreign exchange rate conversion.

Web of Culture

http://www.webofculture.com

Commercial site offering languages information, translating dictionaries, gestures, and many references to culture.

Western Connecticut State University World Area Studies

http://www.wcsu.ctstateu.edu/socialsci/area.html

An extensive list of worldwide links, developed by the university's Department of Social Sciences.

World Encyclopedia

http://www.emulateme.com

An encyclopedia with national anthems, flags, maps, weather, and news; simplified version of the CIA World Factbook.

The World Factbook

http://www.odci.gov/cia/publications/factbook/index.html

A Central Intelligence Agency (CIA) site providing maps, geography, government, economy, and other information about countries throughout the world.

Index